Two Houses Half-Buried in Sand

Two Houses Half-Buried in Sand

Oral Traditions of the Hul'q'umi'num' Coast Salish
of Kuper Island and Vancouver Island

Beryl Mildred Cryer

Compiled and edited by Chris Arnett

Talonbooks

Talonbooks
P.O. Box 2076, Vancouver, British Columbia, Canada, v6B 3s3
www.talonbooks.com

Typeset in Perpetua and Scala Sans. Printed and bound in Canada.
Printed on 100% post-consumer recycled paper.

First printing: December 2007

The publisher gratefully acknowledges the financial support of the Canada Council for the
Arts; the Government of Canada through the Book Publishing Industry Development
Program; and the Province of British Columbia through the British Columbia Arts Council and
the Book Publishing Tax Credit for our publishing activities.

LIBRARY AND ARCHIVES CANADA CATALOGUING IN PUBLICATION

Cryer, Beryl Mildred, 1887–1980
    Two houses half-buried in sand : oral traditions of the Hul'q'umi'num' Coast Salish of Kuper
Island and Vancouver Island / Beryl Mildred Cryer ; edited and compiled by Chris Arnett.

Includes bibliographical references.
ISBN 978-0-88922-555-8
    1. Hul'qumi'num Indians—History. I. Arnett, Chris II. Title.

E99.S21C79 2007   971.1'20049794   C2007-901089-X

To the ancestors and their descendants:

Ehara taku toa i te toa takitahi
Engari takimano, no aku tupuna.

My strength comes not from one source
But from thousands, from my ancestors

Hul'q'umi'num'-speaking people from Vancouver Island, Saltspring Island and Kuper Island in Yakima, Washington, picking hops in the 1930s. Included in this group are Joe Wyse (front row, centre), Jennie Wyse (front row, left) and Tommy Pielle (second row, centre), all of whom contributed stories to Beryl Cryer. Courtesy Snuneymuxw Archives.

About the Title

The title for this collection of Beryl Cryer's writing, *Two Houses Half-Buried in Sand*, was chosen to reflect several things.

Most of the stories Cryer collected were obtained from people with family connections to the ancient village of Puneluxutth' on Kuper Island. The word Puneluxutth' describes how the old-style longhouses that once stood on the sandy gravel spit at the north end of the island had the appearance of being half-buried in sand. There is also an allusion in this phrase to the origin story of the Puneluxutth' people, whose ancestors, a tiny man and woman, emerged from half-buried logs and sand; it is time that their stories emerge once more, after being "half-buried" for decades in the official British Columbia Archives.

The expression "two houses" also refers to the notion of multiple families. A village such as Puneluxutth' is made up of many families with connections to other families on Vancouver Island and the British Columbia mainland. Thus Beryl Cryer recorded stories not only from Kuper Island, but also from Nanaimo, Chemainus, Cowichan, Nanoose, Comox, Musqueam and Squamish.

Finally, "two houses" is a metaphor for two peoples: the predominantly white and British Hwunitum' newcomers,[1] and the indigenous populations who found their lands and resources quickly overrun and dispossessed by them. By the time these stories were recorded and written in English on Depression-era Vancouver Island, there had already been a century—over three generations—of contact between local Hul'q'umi'num'-speaking people and the industrialized West. Oral histories, though detailed, were now conveyed in English: it is evident that in the 1930s, ancient native culture continued, as these accounts demonstrate, though half-buried by an onslaught of Hwunitum' culture and language.

Beryl Cryer, a descendant of the House of Halhed, driven by ethnographic interest and a desire for excellence, gained the trust of noted elders in this region of British Columbia and recorded what they had to say. Although she didn't fully comprehend everything she was told, she was an outsider the elders trusted to help the newcomers emerge from a colonial mindset, half-buried by ignorance.

Table of Contents

Acknowledgements

This book would not have been possible without the support of many friends and colleagues. I would like to thank the Hul'q'umi'num'-speaking people who have encouraged and guided me through the complexity of their culture. Dr. Ellen White, Florence James, Arvid Charlie, Bob Rice and the late Ernie Rice shared valuable information on cultural practices, language and orthography. It was an honour and privilege to work with these cultural experts. Huy tseep q'u, ah siem. Thanks to Eric McLay, archaeologist for the Hul'qumi'num Treaty Group, for his cheerful encouragement and assistance in locating some of Beryl Cryer's articles.

I would also like to thank the staff of the British Columbia Archives and Records Service and the Royal British Columbia Museum, particularly Dan Savard and Grant Keddie, who were always willing to answer questions and provide access to the archival collections. Loraine Littlefield, researcher for the Snuneymuxw First Nation, generously shared her knowledge and photographs concerning Beryl Cryer. Thanks, as well, to Basil Halhed, who shared valuable family information. Fellow Salt Spring Islanders Frank and Gail Neumann also deserve special mention for their many hours of hospitality and patient counsel regarding computer-related matters.

I also thank the staff at Talonbooks for once again taking on an unwieldy project and supporting it throughout, with good humour, advice and style. Special thanks to Karl Siegler and Gregory Gibson for their astute editing skills. Our national institution for the Arts, the Canada Council, provided a generous grant in 2005 to facilitate completion of the manuscript. Finally, I would like to thank my loving family: my dear sweetie, Barb, and my cool guys, John and Carl, for putting up with Dad's chaotic, sometimes obsessive, research and writing.

—*Chris Arnett,* SALT SPRING ISLAND, SEPTEMBER 11, 2007

A Note on Orthography

When Beryl Cryer recorded and published these stories in the early 1930s, she included Hul'q'umi'num' names for people, places and things. At the time, there was no standardized writing system for the language, so she developed her own method of writing Hul'q'umi'num' words. Basically, she wrote down how the word sounded to her, breaking it down into hyphenated syllables. Thus the name Qleysuluq was written as "Cly-sack," Xalputstun was rendered as "Chul-Ped-Sun," Chuhaasteenxun became "Chuhas-Tane-Hun," and so on. Cryer was not, however, consistent in accurately replicating all Hul'q'umi'num' phonemes.

Although contemporary speakers have little trouble recognizing some of the names—in cases when they can deduce the sounds Cryer was attempting to convey—other transcriptions are more problematic, and Hul'q'umi'num' speakers must rely on their knowledge for certain words to "make sense." To provide current students with greater access to the language, I have replaced most of Beryl Cryer's transcriptions of native words with the writing system developed and used today by Hul'q'umi'num'-speaking cultural experts to standardize spellings and make the written language "keyboard friendly."[2] Where Cryer's orthography could not be interpreted with reasonable certainty, her original transcription remains.

I have also consulted the current writing system for anglicized Hul'q'umi'num' words such as Penelakut (Puneluxutth'), Lamalcha (Hwlumelhtsu), Musqueam (Hwmuthkwi'um) etc. One notable exception is the word Cowichan, which Cryer used in a generic sense throughout her work to refer to a people and a place—the Hul'q'umi'num'-speaking settlements under the gaze of Shquw'utsun, known to the settlers as Mount Tzouhalem, but named for a giant frog who lay on his side basking in the warm sun.

Introduction

Stories are teacher. Stories telling you something. You learn when you get old; you'll be happy that you have listened because someday you gonna use those.   —*Mary Rice, Tommy Pielle*[3]

... I don't know what else to do with the collection: so am packing up my loose leaf folders—such as they are and making a gift of them to you to do as you like with them. They may be of some interest to students. They were considered authentic by several Anthropologists when I was writing them, and kept me interested besides bringing in a few necessary dollars.

I loved my old Indians and they came from miles around or sent word to me, that they might tell me something of their old days.
                                                                —*Beryl Mildred Cryer*[4]

The Hul'q'umi'num' Central Coast Salish oral traditions brought together in this book were published during the Great Depression in the *Daily Colonist*, a newspaper in Victoria, British Columbia. In late 1931, Beryl Mildred Cryer, a forty-five year-old housewife, mother and part-time journalist from the small town of Chemainus was invited by the newspaper's managing editor and amateur historian, Bruce McKelvie, to submit accounts of native histories and mythologies for the newspaper's popular *Sunday Magazine*. Over the next three years, Beryl Cryer contributed sixty articles based on narratives by distinguished native elders, male and female, from Vancouver Island and Kuper Island, all of whom were fully aware of her intentions to publish their information. Although there was some financial incentive, certainly for Cryer, and she always "paid a little something" for the informants' time, the elders seized the opportunity more so to share their knowledge with an outsider whom they trusted to convey their message. Although framed by a style of writing intended for a 1930s audience, the narratives recorded by Beryl Cryer preserve detailed accounts of nineteenth- and early-twentieth-century Central Coast Salish history and culture from recognized cultural authorities. The elders entrusted their histories to Cryer, who endeavoured to maintain the accuracy of their words. As a result, the stories in this book, when sifted from the sand of 1930s popular discourse, reveal some of the best accounts of Central Coast Salish mythology and oral history available.

Given her lack of training as an anthropologist, and with a production schedule in mind, Beryl Cryer used a simple methodology to acquire stories from her storytellers. She would show up at their homes, rarely with appointments, or the elder(s) would seek her out, and they would talk. Sometimes Cryer had a specific question or topic in mind, but more often it was the elder who directed the course and content of the interview. Cryer never separated the story from the storyteller, and it is this simultaneous documentation of source and subject that makes her work particularly valuable. Cryer employed a writing strategy, borrowed from the work of Mohawk writer Pauline Johnson, of visiting an elder's home and recording the elder's narrative as it unfolded in the course of their conversation. However, unlike Pauline Johnson, who often used a sermonizing tone throughout her work, sometimes radically altering the original story, Cryer minimized her own textual authority, allowing her informants to "speak for themselves." She paid particular attention to the physical environment in which the stories were told to her, and included such details as the furnishings inside the home, or the elder's clothing. Because of the descriptive interview format of her writing, and her attention to the setting, the stories convey, in contrast to more formal ethnographies, the sense of being in someone's living room or kitchen, listening to a conversation filled with unexpected twists and turns as new subjects come up.[5]

Most of Beryl Cryer's work for the *Daily Colonist* was produced between January 1932 and March 1935 when she visited elders, often within walking distance of her home in Chemainus (although she occasionally had access to a vehicle). She worked primarily with a well known Puneluxutth' cultural authority, Mary Rice, who directed her to other knowledgeable persons within the Puneluxutth' community at Hwts'usi' (Bonsall's Creek) and to Snuneymuxw cultural authorities related to her through marriage. There is a strong sense of contemporaneity between the publication of the articles and the time they were written. A few stories were written over the course of months, and at least one took several years, but, by and large, the stories were produced and published as Cryer collected them. This is evident in the stories themselves when a specific month is mentioned, the passing of an elder, or recent seasonal food gathering, all which suggest most of the interviews and subsequent stories were written fairly close to the time they appeared in the *Daily Colonist*. By examining the order in which the stories were published, one can trace her movements through the native communities in search of knowledgeable elders to provide stories. After soliciting seventeen stories from her at her cabin in Chemainus over the spring and summer of 1932, Cryer questions Mary Rice about a specific story. The elder, not knowing the details, sends her to someone else, Ts'umsitun, at Hwts'usi'. Later, in the first months of 1933, Mary Rice introduces her to other authorities, such as Joe and Jennie Wyse of Nanaimo, the parents of her eldest daughter's husband, and so Cryer moves through an ever-expanding network of informants.

In her travels, Beryl Cryer's reputation often preceded her. When, for example, she appeared at an elder's home in Hwts'usi' in late 1932 or early 1933:

he seemed rather doubtful as to the advisability of letting me in, but when I introduced myself, he recognized my name and, taking me by the hand, threw his door open wide. 'Iichnawmukw', I want some stories about the old days,' I told him. 'I know, my boy has told me! ... Ankuty (old) stories, eh? And for newspaper?' he was greatly impressed ...[6]

Or so she thought. She was then forced "to listen to a long and only partially understood tirade against the fishing laws," which, to her credit, she faithfully recorded in full. Loraine Littlefield cites this account as evidence that Cryer "was sympathetic to the injustices and included the discussion in such a way so as not to offend the readership as it was not fashionable or legal in the 1930s to show too much support for native people."[7] As her work progressed, Beryl Cryer gained recognition among the elders as an "honest person" who faithfully communicated what she was told, even if, as she often admitted, she did not always fully understand.

The narratives of the women Beryl Cryer worked with are particularly valuable given the overwhelming lack of female ethnographic texts from this period. The women elders' familiarity with the English language, and the camaraderie of gender, allowed topics that would not be readily discussed with Hwunitum' men. Stories from and about women, their spiritual training, naming ceremonies, work and many other aspects of their daily lives from the 1860s to the 1930s are presented in Beryl Cryer's writing in wonderful detail. Her writing gives insight into the agency of native women on Vancouver Island in the 1930s, at a time when the culture was under incredible pressure from all directions, and declining native populations had not yet began to recover. With the onset of the Depression, many women became the economic mainstay of the family, often relying heavily once again on traditional food gathering. Cryer portrays her storytellers as powerful influences in their families, commanding authority and respect, and always contributing to the family income. Because the majority of Beryl Cryer's inform- ants were women, her work is an important addition to the male-oriented ethnographies of the late-nineteenth and early-twentieth centuries, and challenges the misconception that "native women of the past left no written record of their culture, history and personal experiences."[8]

This careful attention to authenticity and detail in her work, however, is not to ignore the native stereotypes that Cryer, herself, occasionally invoked in her writing, a stylistic anomaly that has obscured the value of her work. Unflattering descriptions of elders' physical appearances and clothing appear occasionally and, though thankfully brief, are a jarring reminder of prevalent social attitudes so ingrained that any writing on indigenous people, to be acceptable to the popular audience, tended to be couched in contemporary racial stereotypes. At best, Beryl Cryer preserves a vivid visual image at the person's expense, but her caricatures never fall to the depths of overt racism evident in other stories published by the same newspaper. Beryl Cryer's occasional lapses into the colonial mainstream are overwhelmingly compensated, I hope the reader will discover, by her dedication to communicating faithfully, and accurately, the words of the elders with whom she collaborated.

There was urgency and purpose in the narratives given to Beryl Cryer by the elders from Vancouver Island and Kuper Island. Their stories are part of a five-thousand-year-old cultural tradition in a region of the Northwest Coast that felt the cutting edge of European colonialism, which began with a catastrophic small-pox epidemic in 1785, followed by years of warfare as musket-armed northerners swept down in search of loot and slaves. The balance of power was re-established in the 1840s by marriage alliances and through the rise of able Central Coast Salish war leaders. After the discovery of coal at Nanaimo in 1849, there was a succession of military confrontations with colonial forces, which culminated in 1863 with the deaths and executions of native resistance leaders and the destruction of one major village, Hwlumelhtsu, on Kuper Island. The ensuing years saw an influx of Hwunitum' (white) settlers, the destruction of natural resources and shifting jurisdictions of successive colonial governments which undermined and diminished native authorities. In 1891, native people comprised one third of the population of British Columbia; by 1931, they represented little over three percent.[9]

Native people did not react passively to the massive changes that confronted them. After Bill 13, the British Columbia Indian Lands Settlement Act, removed valuable reserve land, political and hereditary leaders realized the only viable means to obtain recognition of their rights under the British legal system was to appeal to the Judicial Committee of the Privy Council in London, England. In an earlier case arising in Southern Nigeria, the Privy Council affirmed that aboriginal title was a pre-existing right that "must be presumed to have continued unless the contrary is established by the context or the circumstances."[10] The executive of the Allied Tribes of British Columbia, an uneasy alliance of Coast and Interior peoples, approved a petition to the Canadian Parliament requesting the establishment of a select committee that could be part of the necessary first step in accessing the Privy Council. Paul Tennant has documented how the special joint committee of Canadian politicians had a covert intention "to keep the British Columbia land claim from getting to court and so to the Judicial Committee in London."[11] The end result of this political agenda was that in 1927 the Canadian government reacted to the petition by the Allied Tribes, making it illegal to fund or research land claims.[12] Native histories were effectively denied entry into the records of the colonial judicial system for over two decades thereafter.

In the absence of a legal forum to hear their arguments, Beryl Cryer's connection to the largest newspaper on Vancouver Island became an avenue for native elders to reach a white audience with respect to their land claims issues. The elders interviewed by Cryer between 1932 and 1935 seized the opportunity to provide her with information that would prove without question, they believed, their ancestral rights to the land. They knew that what they said would be faithfully recorded by a white woman and placed in the public record—the newspaper. "Soon the names of those villages will be forgotten like the people who lived there," her main informant, Mary Rice, told her. "That is why me and my brother want you to write about them, so that some people will 'member when the Cowichan Indians had many villages and were a great tribe."[13] When Beryl Cryer visited Joe and Jennie Wyse in their home in Nanaimo, Joe Wyse welcomed her with a formal speech in his language which his wife translated: "He thanks you, white lady, for coming to hear his stories. Always he has wanted to tell what he knows to the white people, but nobody has time to listen. If you will write it for him, he will tell you … "[14] The subject matter of the stories Beryl Cryer recorded, particularly those concerning place-names, family histories and Origin Stories, were more than just "yarns," as she affectionately called them, but sxwi'em, mythologies set in the ancient past, and syuth, "true histories," personal reminiscences and the stories of immediate ancestors, told not only for enjoyment, but to transmit cultural teachings and to document history.

Beryl Cryer's preservation of both authorship and context underscores the collaborative nature of her work, and is probably her most significant contribution to Central Coast Salish oral literature. Additional value comes from the descriptions of her storytellers, which capture some aspects of their individual personalities, something rarely documented in more formal studies. Regarding the Northwest Coast oral traditions collected by Franz Boas in the 1880s, Randy Bouchard and Dorothy Kennedy observe that, although the texts collected by him are valuable for the field of ethnography, there is little in them that "might reflect the original narrative form or personal style of the storyteller."[15] This is certainly not the case with Cryer's work, in which the storytellers are living, breathing collaborators, keen on having their stories accurately recorded.

Beryl Cryer paid little attention to the prevailing Boasian orientation of "salvage ethnography" which sought to isolate pure pre-contact elements of native culture from post-contact influence.[16] The people Cryer worked with in the 1930s inhabited both worlds and she recognized the strength and continuity of their culture despite the outer trappings of Western culture. On one occasion, following a visit a family at Hwt'susi', she notes the modern appearance of the home and its furnishings, and the contemporary fashions of the young women who engage in an animated discussion of xwult'up, a powerful winter spirit:

> I looked at the family sitting round on their beds, with their marcelled heads and silk dresses, educated from earliest childhood in the local Industrial School, two generations of them, and a third playing outside the

door. Yet deep in their hearts the old superstitions persist, never to be eradicated.[17]

Newspaper articles about indigenous peoples written by non-professionals for a popular audience, consisting primarily of one cultural group, generally lack credibility among scholars as valid ethnography.[18] A survey of most British Columbian newspapers and magazines over the last century-and-a-half reveals "popular ethnographies" filled with racial stereotypes and misinformation for the sake of "good stories."[19] By the 1930s, this type of writing, particularly when it described indigenous cultures in British Columbia, often reflected popular assumptions about native people rooted in racist ideologies from the late-nineteenth century; these assumptions were widespread among all levels of colonial Canadian society. Native points of view were rarely considered. As Maori scholar Linda Tuhiwai-Smith writes, "the negation of indigenous views of history was a critical part of asserting colonial ideology, partly because such views were regarded as clearly 'primitive' and 'incorrect' and mostly because they challenged and resisted the mission of colonization."[20] As a consequence, there is a tendency in academic anthropology to either ignore "popular ethnographies" altogether or, at best, regard them as the product of enthusiastic, if untrained, amateurs.

However, the same review of British Columbia print media will also reveal texts with ethnographic data that are quite valuable, once accommodations have been made through critical contextual analysis. For example, once allowances are made for Cryer's authorial voice, the narratives of the elders she worked with emerge largely authentic and intact, the way she heard them. Clearly, when dealing with "popular ethnographies," caution must be exercised, but we should be equally careful not to "throw the baby out with the bathwater."[21]

Assessing the accuracy of Beryl Cryer's "popular ethnography" and accepting it as authentic would be difficult without access to a wide range of information about, and experience with, Central Coast Salish culture. Equally important is an understanding of Beryl Cryer, the woman, within her own cultural context. It has been suggested that because her original notebooks have not been located, we can not be sure if the stories that appeared in the *Daily Colonist* are as the elders told them, and whether details have been left out or meaning misconstrued.[22] Fortunately we have several, indirect sources with which to judge the accuracy of her work.

First and foremost, she can be judged by the company she kept. Beryl Cryer's mentor and main informant, indeed the true author of over half of the accounts in this book, was Mary Rice, a well known Puneluxutth' cultural authority and storyteller from Kuper Island whom Beryl Cryer knew from a young age. Through her close association with Mary Rice, Cryer was introduced to other knowledge-able men and women elders, including Mary Rice's brother Tommy Pielle, as well as Ts'umsitun and Latits'iiya of Hwts'usi', Joe and Jennie Wyse of Xwsol'exwel, Johnny and Rosalie Seletze of Xinupsum, Kathleen Stockl-Whut of Qw'umiyiqun' and others. These elders were all recognized authorities among their own people. They were born in the longhouses of their grandparents and grew up exposed to the cultural teachings and life-ways of their elders, while adapting to the cultural impact of the industrial West. Many of their narratives are unique and can be found nowhere else in the academic literature.

Most of these elders spoke English, which had, well before the 1930s, replaced the trade jargon Chinook as a *lingua franca* among the native populations of British Columbia.[23] The narratives, transmitted by a mutually intelligible language, are therefore less likely to have been misconstrued. Mary Rice, in particular, "spoke excellent English." Like many women their age, they had spent a lifetime in the new western economy and interacted with Hwunitum' and their language through work, church and residential schools. Beryl Cryer, for her part, was also somewhat familiar with the Hul'q'umi'num' language through years of exposure. "I do know a good deal," she once wrote a friend, "but I can't *talk* it."[24] By way of comparison, the anthropologist Franz Boas, who collected oral traditions in the same region some fifty years earlier, was forced to rely almost exclusively on the Chinook trade jargon, which the Hul'q'umi'num'-speaking missionary Thomas Crosby called "a wretched means of communication, poor in expression and almost destitute of grammatical form."[25]

Another important source with which to gauge the accuracy of Beryl Cryer's work are thirty-two letters of private correspondence she wrote to William A. Newcombe, an assistant biologist at the Provincial Museum in Victoria, and son of well known ethnologist and collector, Dr. C.F. Newcombe.[26] In these letters, written between 1928 and 1936, she constantly questions Newcombe, and alludes to conversations they had concerning Coast Salish culture, dates and other corroborations. Her tone is always deferential and self-deprecating to the "expert" Newcombe, though it is quite evident that she knew more than he did about the subject, (which is probably why he encouraged her work). On at least one occasion, she sent Newcombe a typewritten copy of what appear to be notes taken from an interview with Mary Rice in 1932, and she asks him to verify specific points in the story she was working on. Newcombe lent her scholarly books and papers to familiarize her with standard ethnographies. Her attention to scientific accuracy is evident in a letter where, commenting on some material that Newcombe had lent her, she criticized a map in an article by Franz Boas for an inaccurate line of division between the Cowichan and Nanaimo dialects of the Hul'q'umi'num' language.

As a woman, Beryl Cryer was sensitive to potential criticism directed towards her from "experts" in a male-dominated field, so she strived for accuracy and authenticity in the collection of her data. She was also conscious of her Halhed family line, which included the respected Orientalist scholar Nathaniel Brassy Halhed (1751–1830) whose work with the East India Company produced grammars and dictionaries for Persian, Sanskrit and Bengali.[27] Quality was important— her letters to Newcombe document her desire to authenticate the histories she was recording. He was obviously aware of her abilities, as were other male figures in the field, such as George Thornton Emmons, but it was Newcombe who urged her to faithfully record what she was told, for the sake of ethnographic accuracy— and she did.

Beryl Cryer was not, however, infallible. Errors occurred, attributable either to her lack of cultural understanding, or to inexplicable artistic licence. For example, in a story describing the wedding of Mary Rice's eldest daughter, Beryl changed the English names of the bride and groom from Ellen and Jimmy to "Mary" and "Johnny." She also constantly referred to Mary Rice as Siamtunaat ("Tzea-mnte-naht" in Cryer's transcription), a name she erroneously states was originally Mary Rice's mother's name. In fact it is an honorific "young woman's name" given to Mary Rice by her aunt, who was from Burrard Inlet.[28] Fortunately, these errors occur infrequently, and can easily be identified through critical analysis.

Another essential source of comparative material for the work of Beryl Cryer is a well-established and growing body of literature on Coast Salish culture produced over the last century-and-a-half. A review of this literature corroborates many of the details in Beryl Cryer's work, thereby reinforcing its significance. References to some of this material can be found in the annotations and footnotes that accompany the stories in this book. In many instances Beryl Cryer's work augments the often fragmentary nature of oral traditions recorded in, for example, the extensive notes made by anthropologist Diamond Jenness, who worked with other Central Coast Salish elders during the same time period.[29] Because of her regard among the native elders she worked with, Beryl Cryer was able to record detailed accounts of Central Coast mythology either ignored, or only partially documented by transient scholars. Franz Boas' publication of a Snuneymuxw myth, "The Man and the Whale,"[30] which he recorded during his brief visit to Vancouver Island in 1884, is a bare outline of the story. In contrast, the version recorded by Beryl Cryer as narrated by Jennie Wyse, is much longer and contains a wealth of detail, including the names of the protagonists, omitted from the Boas version.

Other Origin Stories have their cognates in the scholarly literature and although details may differ, as Richard Atleo observes in his analysis of Nuu-chah-nulth Origin Stories, "the general verity of these stories cannot be found in word-for-word authenticity but in the commonalty of themes conveyed by the same stories from different families."[31]

In addition to the wealth of mythological data, Cryer's accounts of spiritual training, female naming ceremonies, potlatches, winter dancing, weddings, funerals, shamanic healing, early contact with Europeans, warfare and material culture bear favourable comparison with other published accounts. Not only does Cryer's inclusion of diverse topics of material culture, such as mat weaving or the construction of camas ovens, preserve critical detail missing from academic ethnographies, it demonstrates the continuation of the traditional native economy into the 1930s. Many persons and events recorded by Beryl Cryer cannot be found in any existing ethnographic literature. Among other stories in this collection, the historical accounts of a mid-nineteenth-century Haida raid on Puneluxutth', a retaliatory raid against the Yukw'ulhta'x, a break-out from a Nanaimo jail, a speech giving the history of an exceptional Central Coast Salish house painting, and an eyewitness description of the signing of the last Douglas Treaty in 1854 at Nanaimo, are the the only native accounts of these events available, and stand as significant contributions to British Columbia historiography.

Readers used to more recent stereotypes of native people may be surprised at some of the language used by the storytellers in these accounts. The stories of early-nineteenth-century warfare and certain cultural practices are graphic. Killing and violence are often described in a casual manner, with candour Westerners might find disconcerting. The people narrating these accounts were confident culture-bearers completely at ease with their identities and history. In their world-view, there existed none of the moralizing ideology of the Europeans. Destruction and death comprised simply one aspect of a polarity of existence ranging from the negative, destructive powers of darkness to the positive, creative powers of light.[32]

Ultimately, Cryer's work will be judged by the living culture—by elders who recall these stories and the relationships of the historical personages, and by students of the culture who recognize parallels in other sources, particularly an emerging literature of archival and oral histories. The elders Beryl Cryer interviewed are well remembered and their descendants recognize many of the stories and the Hul'q'umi'num' and Snuneymuxw names. Cryer was always keenly interested in the language, and she developed her own spelling system to write native names and words. Because other stories she recorded from the elders are not as well known today, we have to trust that Cryer delivered them as they were told to her. Her long experience with native people, her friendship with the consummate storyteller Mary Rice, and her recognition of voice—and hence authorship—in all her submissions to the *Daily Colonist*, vouches for the authenticity of the work. The author and elder, Ellen White, Mary Rice's granddaughter, has examined some of the Cryer texts and believes they accurately convey the voice of her grandmother Xalunamut, expert storyteller, historian, mid-wife, weaver, healer and food gatherer. The late Ernie Rice, another grandchild of Mary Rice, also remembered Beryl Cryer's visits to his grandmother's cabin on the shores of Chemainus Harbour. He recalls the high regard Mary Rice had for her as someone who would communicate their stories faithfully because, as he put it, "she was a very honest person."[33]

Another way to evaluate the ethnographic validity of Beryl Cryer's writing is to consider the life and the ethnographic career of this remarkable woman based on her brief autobiography[34] and the letters she wrote to William Newcombe. While a British immigrant woman of privileged upbringing, Beryl Cryer's exposure to an ancient culture, the circumstances of the Great Depression and her writing ability allowed her to preserve a unique perspective on the lives of Hul'q'umi'num'-speaking Central Coast Salish people of the 1930s and the rich heritage they continue to share with all of us.

Beryl Mildred Cryer—A Brief Biography

The Halheds, like all Hwulunitum',[35] appeared suddenly in British Columbia, and constituted a specific class of immigrants typified by Cole Harris:

> In the late-nineteenth century to early-twentieth century emigrations from the British Isles to British Columbia included a good number of educated, upperclass people. There was a fair share of Oxbridge education and venerable family names. Some of these people brought money, but most came with little more than public school education, well-developed imaginations and an educated upper-class English civility.[36]

The Halheds were part of this group and their eldest daughter Beryl, despite the economic realities of life in her adopted country, into her old age, would "carry her class."[37]

She was born Beryl Mildred Halhed on March 9, 1887 on the islands of Aotearoa, in Auckland, New Zealand.[38] Her father, Richmond Beauchamp Halhed (1857–1947), was from Harbledown, near Canterbury, Kent, and came of age at the height of the British Empire in a wealthy family with connections to the East India Company. He and his wife, Gertrude Ellen, née Fielding (1858–1928), like many of their privileged generation, were inspired to relocate to distant outposts in the Empire, like New Zealand and British Columbia, where the familiar institutions of Great Britain were transplanted and maintained.

Sometime prior to 1883, Richmond and Gertrude Halhed immigrated to Auckland, New Zealand where they started a family. Gertrude gave birth to two boys, Frank and Maurice, followed in 1887 with the birth of their first daughter, Beryl. Shortly after she was born word came of the death of Richmond's father in England. Beryl was only a few weeks old when the family returned to England to settle affairs in the family estate. England proved unsuitable to the ambition of the young family, and the following year Richmond Halhed decided that they would immigrate to Canada. He left ahead of the family to find a suitable place to relocate. Within months he had made his way to British Columbia, purchasing land on Vancouver Island at Shawnigan Lake. Soon, Gertrude, his two sons and the infant Beryl, accompanied by their maid, Emily White, joined him in Victoria, the provincial capital.

Family life alternated between a rented house in Victoria and the Shawnigan Lake property, and another girl, Maithal, was born in Victoria, in 1890.[39] A growing family and financial considerations prompted Richmond to accept a constable position with the British Columbia Provincial Police at Chemainus, a small community and shipping port on the east coast of Vancouver Island. The young family arrived in Chemainus in 1898, in the midst of unprecedented industrial activity. Newly opened copper mines created instant townsites on nearby Mount Sicker and down the coast at Crofton, where a smelter was built. Chemainus was the site of one of the earliest sawmills on the east coast of Vancouver Island, and forest resource extraction continued unabated to meet growing domestic and international demand. A logging railway was pushed through the ancient forest of the Chemainus River south of the town, and the Victoria Lumber Company Mill in Chemainus was on its way to becoming one of the largest mills in the British Commonwealth. Within a short time, the Halhed family purchased pioneer settler Matthew Howe's property on the beach at the head of Chemainus Harbour, adding six more rooms to the house and various outdoor amenities, including a long picnic table under the trees and a concrete tennis court.[40]

The Halhed family immediately fell in with the society of other privileged British immigrants who were eager to recreate the institutions of Great Britain in Chemainus. They joined the Anglican Church of St. Michael and All Angels, and became active members of the exclusive tennis club. Richmond Halhed, due to his position as police constable, and the fact that he was a first cousin of Boy Scouts founder, Lord Robert Baden-Powell, was secure in his standing as a leading, influential citizen. His wife Gertrude Halhed took a leading role in community causes, starting with the building of the Chemainus hospital, which she was instrumental in advocating following an outbreak of typhoid within a year of their arrival, in which Frank, Halhed's eldest son, was stricken. She was an active organizer of the annual Hospital Ball, and was always eager to perform "extras" as an accompaniment pianist for the musical performances. A busy social life revolved around the tennis club and its attendant gala balls where the Halhed girls made their appearances decked out in the latest fashions, which were duly noted in the local newspaper. The Halhed home, with its waterfront location at the head of Chemainus Bay, spacious grounds and private tennis court became the scene of numerous social events. A steady stream of important visitors and personalities

The Halhed family and friends with Lord Baden-Powell, at the Halhed home in Chemainus, circa 1910. Beryl Halhed is second from the right. Courtesy Snuneymuxw Archives.

Beryl Cryer with family and friends in Chemainus, 1922. Beryl Cryer is fourth from the left, back row. Courtesy Snuneymuxw Archives.

attended these events, including the Viceroy of India, Lord and Lady Willington, the Lieutenant Governor of British Columbia and, of course, Lord Baden-Powell, Richmond Halhed's famous cousin.[41]

Early on, the Halheds made the acquaintance of local native people who, despite a significant decline in population over the preceding century, were a visible, everyday presence in the town of Chemainus. Interaction between European newcomers and native people varied in degree throughout British Columbia in the 1930s, but it was closest in rural areas, where populous native communities existed alongside growing centres inhabited by immigrants. This was particularly true of Chemainus, which had many ancient native communities and camps, popularly called "reserves," nearby. Located south of the town on the Chemainus River was Xulel-thw (Halalt), recently relocated from its original location on Willy Island at the river's mouth. Further south at Bonsall's Creek was the Puneluxutth' community of Hwts'usi'. To the north across Stuart's Channel were the communities of Thuq'min' (Shell Beach) and Shts'um'inus (Kulleet Bay), where the name Chemainus originated. Northeast, off the coast of Vancouver Island, was Kuper Island, home to three more communities: Hwlumelhtsu at the south end of the island and, to the north, Puneluxutth' and Yuxwula'us, the latter being the site of an infamous Roman Catholic residential school built by the Canadian government in 1890. Native men from these communities worked in the logging and fishing industries, and as longshoremen, while many women worked as domestic servants for households in the town of Chemainus.

Visible reminders of an ancient culture existed closer to home. The Halhed house on Chemainus Harbour was, itself, located on the site of the winter village of Sunuwnets. Two large circular depressions lay between the tennis court and the beach, marking the burial place, Beryl eventually learned, of smallpox victims. Across the bay, easily visible from the house, was the traditional burial site of Sunuwnets, under a wide overhanging rock bluff where, Beryl later wrote, "lay the ancient remains, partially covered with rotted rush mats and pieces of canoes."[42]

The young Beryl was also exposed to native people and culture by her father Richmond Halhed who, in his role as provincial policeman, interacted in various ways with the native community in the course of his law enforcement duties. Halhed relied on native constables as guides or trackers and, apparently, attended native ceremonies. Photographs, apparently taken by him, record native ceremonies at Alert Bay and Kwa'mutsun (Quamichan), although it is unclear why he was in attendance.[43] On at least one occasion Beryl herself attended a potlatch at Kwa'mutsun, likely with her father. She also visited Puneluxutth' on Kuper Island, but was more familiar with the mission of the Company for the Propagation of the Gospel in the New England and Parts Adjacent in America, established in 1880 by the Reverend Robert Roberts on the old village site of Hwlumelhtsu at Lamalchi Bay.[44] Beryl Cryer later recalled "many happy holidays" at Lamalchi Bay in company with the Roberts family where she would have come into contact with Hwlumelhtsu families who lived in the two longhouses adjacent to the Mission Chapel.

In 1904, a visit to Chemainus by the renowned Mohawk writer and platform recitalist Pauline Johnson prompted much interest and excitement in the community. The entire Halhed family attended her reading at the Community Hall, and Beryl later recalled watching Johnson climbing along the piles of driftwood logs along the beach in front of their home while her tour manager watched from one of the family boats. This early exposure to a Canadian literary figure whose work celebrated, if romanticized, aboriginal life-ways, may have sparked a desire in Beryl Cryer to be a writer in a similar vein. Johnson's series, "Legends of the Capilanos" (later renamed "Legends of Vancouver"), which appeared in the pages of the *Daily Province* between April 1910 and January 1911, featured Johnson's literary device of framing stories within the context of conversations between writer and elders. This stylistic model would be used by Cryer years later in her *Daily Colonist* articles.[45]

Pauline Johnson likely had a profound influence on the young Beryl Halhed. Johnson was a public voice for native people, and an advocate for the New Woman, a modernist movement that promoted the aspirations and independence of women in patriarchal society. Authors Veronica Strong-Boag and Carole Gerson observe that Johnson's writing, "while on the surface quite romantic and essentialist, can also be seen as strategically crafted interventions in the ideological battle to legitimatize the claims of First Nations (and also of women) for respect and civil rights."[46]

The writings of Pauline Johnson, and the proximity of native communities and workers, led to an interest in local native culture for the adolescent Beryl Halhed and her younger sister, Maithal. But it was through their contact with a Puneluxutth' woman named Xalunamut, better known to non-natives by her English name, Mary Rice, that the girls found their primary source of information regarding native mythology, traditions and culture. The fact that Mary Rice, despite her apparent poverty, was born of a "noble family" appealed to the British "upper-class" pretensions of the two young women.[47] And she told great stories.

Mary Rice was born at Puneluxutth' on Kuper Island, between 1855 and 1865, in the noble house of her grandfather, a famous warrior who bore the name Xulqalustun.[48] Her maternal grandfather was the equally famous warrior Quyupule'ynuxw of Burrard Inlet and Hwmuthkwi'um. When his daughter Solowtunaht married Mary's father, also called Xulqalustun, she brought the first swayxwi mask to Kuper Island. When she was a young girl, Mary Rice was sent to live with relatives in Saanich, but moved back to Kuper Island at adolescence. She was trained as a thi'tha, a specialist in interactions with the spiritual world. As her granddaughter Ellen White recalls, "She was called thi'tha for her work in the bighouse and all that, and during purification work, and puberty rites, marriage rights and stuff like that, delivering babies and healing. She was also a shne'um, and she'nam was the person who could see things far away, see what's happening and stuff like that."[49] In 1879 Mary Rice married a man named Paris Teeters, variously described as a "tall sturdy Texan" and an "Indian Circus Rider."[50] The couple "lived on Galiano [Island] for a few years" where the Shaws, early settlers at the north end of the island, knew them. In her memoirs, Margaret Walters (née Shaw) described Mary Rice as "most intelligent and very sensible" who "spoke a certain amount of English."[51] Teeters "died very suddenly leaving his affairs unsettled" and Mary "while under no obligation to do so ... sought work elsewhere and finally paid all his debts."[52] In 1888, she married George Rice, of Squinomish and Irish ancestry with whom she had four children: Ellen, Emma, George and Charlie.[53] The family purchased the twenty-seven acre island called Xextl'qun, soon to be known as Rice Island (and now Norway Island), adjacent to the village of Puneluxutth'.[54] In 1895, while the children were quite young, George Rice Sr. had a massive heart attack and died while fishing in Trincomallee Channel.[55] Widowed, with four small children to care for, Mary Rice found life on Rice Island difficult. Because her husband was not recognized as a status Indian, Mary lost her government Indian status, which denied her the right to live on reserves such as Kuper Island where she was born. As a result, she was forced to move to Chemainus with her four small children to find work to support her family. When Beryl Cryer first made her acquaintance, she knew little, if anything, of Mary Rice's cultural background. "When I first knew her," Cryer later recalled:

> she lived with her two girls, in a shack close to the Government wharf, making a scanty living doing housework for women who knew her. Her two boys were getting an education at the Kuper Island Industrial (as we then called it) School, with Father Donkele in charge.[56]

Within the European community of Chemainus, Mary Rice became known as "the village washerwoman," finding steady employment with various Chemainus families and millworkers.[57] Well-to-do households with live-in maids, such as the Halhed's, often sought outside help, generally native or Asian workers, to assist with the heavier household tasks. It was probably through this work that Mary Rice first made the acquaintance of the Halhed household, assisting Emily White, the professional maid who had accompanied the Halhed family from England. As Beryl Cryer later recalled, Mary Rice "helped my mother's maid for years."[58]

In addition to her domestic work, Mary Rice was the local midwife and healer within the colonial Chemainus community. As Ellen White recalls, "Granny worked. She knew how to clean homes, she knew how to cook, she knew how to deliver babies, and she knew how to give the medicines, to rub the people when they were ailing and stuff like that—massaging them to heal them."[59]

In 1920, Mary Rice became the recipient of a Mother's Pension, a monthly allowance created by the Provincial government to aid single mothers.[60] She was recommended for the pension by "friends who admired her courageous struggle to bring up her children," whereupon she moved into a three-room cabin built by her son, Charles, on the beach at the edge of the orchard fence on the Halhed property. There she lived for the next fourteen years and continued to interact with the Halhed family, mostly assisting Gertrude Halhed who, by that time, suffered from an unspecified illness. Ellen White states that today it would be called a nervous breakdown. Mary Rice would kindly "lecture" Gertrude, bathe her in a nearby stream, and administer medicines.[61]

The Halhed girls had, by now, moved away from the family home on Chemainus Harbour to live elsewhere in town. Both had married: Maithal in 1917 to Donald Ross, and Beryl in 1920 to William Claude Cryer, who owned a store in Chemainus.[62] Besides their married life, the women involved themselves in the establishment of the first local Girl Guide troop, an institution created by their father's famous cousin Lord Baden-Powell. The organization was intended to promote British Imperial values and reinforce female support roles in the context of male-oriented military training. Part of the Scout and Guide movement was an interest in natural sciences and "native life-ways." Mary Rice's fireside storytelling on the beach in front of the Halhed family home, as she looked after (and trained) her grandchildren, impressed the Halhed girls, now young married women, and leaders of the local Girl Guide movement. The 1920s were prosperous and, as the Halhed sisters settled into "the good life," they sought other aspirations outside hearth and home and community service.

By 1927, Beryl Cryer and Maithal Ross decided to collaborate in writing down some of the stories Mary Rice had told them, and to try to sell them to news-papers. The *Vancouver Province*, where Pauline Johnson had success with "Legends of the Capilanos," was the obvious choice for their own "Legends of the Cowichans." As Maithal Ross explained in a letter to Newcombe:

> When we first thought of writing out the Legends we submitted two or three to the *Vancouver Province*, having noticed similar articles in the Sunday edition but in returning them, Mr. Lukin Johnstone implied that such material had been overdone: 'each tribe throughout the Dominion has its own legends many of which have been published.'[63]

The sisters next approached Hugh Savage, managing editor of the *Cowichan Leader*, a small newspaper in Duncan, on Vancouver Island, who agreed to publish their work and featured their column on the front page of each scanty issue. Between December 15, 1927 and November 29, 1928, when they penned the last of their collaborative efforts, the Halhed sisters submitted fifteen "Legends of the Cowichans" under the pseudonym "CRYOSS," the combined first and last syllables of their respective married names.[64]

The stories are thematically accurate, recognizable accounts of Central Coast Salish Origin Stories, as related to them by Mary Rice, but, as Cryer and Ross both admitted, were written in a "somewhat flowery style," as the following excerpt from their first column clearly demonstrates:

> In the beginning, when the rule of Sumshalthot (the sun) was undisputed and it was always summer, no frost, snow, or biting winds—but ever, long days filled with golden sunshine and the singing of birds, and the forests were bright with scarlet honeysuckle and waxen petaled dogwood—in those days, Sumshalthot made two women. High up, on a mountain, he made them.[65]

By the summer of 1928, their enthusiasm for continuing the series had waned, primarily due to lack of financial incentive. On September 5, 1928, Beryl Cryer wrote to their friend William "Billy" Newcombe, an assistant biologist at the Provincial Museum, and son of the well known ethnologist collector Dr. C.F. Newcombe:

> ... to ask your advice about the Indian Legends which Maytie and I have been doing for the 'Cowichan Leader.' We have done a good many and Mr. Savage has written for more, but he pays so poorly—admits it himself—that we are getting a bit fed up with the things and are wondering whether we could dispose of those we have done in any manner? Savage suggested they would probably sell well in a small book form but that would necessitate illustrations, also a certain amount of capital, I suppose, and as we are neither of us blessed with a surplus of wealth—that would be out of the question. I wondered whether you could make any suggestions as to their disposal as having done them, we feel we would like to make a bit more out of them if possible?[66]

Newcombe responded favourably, but specifically questioned the sisters about the authenticity and style of the texts. Maithal Ross responded to his concerns:

> We read all the similar stuff we could find, and copied the somewhat flowery style the other writers had adopted, but although we have not used the actual words Mary used in telling the stories, we have been careful to in no way alter the sense of any of them.[67]

Ross' letter continued by offering her and Cryer's thoughts on turning the stories they had written into a children's book complete with illustrations. She noted, "Berrie thinks that a Miss Carr in Victoria specializes in painting Indians, and wondered if you knew anything about her."[68] She also reiterated their main motivation:

> Of course, to be perfectly frank, we only want to publish the legends in the hope of making a penny or two, but whether a publisher would pay for

such material is open to question. Certainly it would not be worthwhile to get the things out ourselves and chance losing everything we had put in. We are horribly ignorant, we do not know if we would have to arrange with an artist for illustrating, and if so, if he would have to be paid by us or by the publisher ... We could of course alter the way they are written if you think that would make them more saleable.[69]

Newcombe encouraged the sisters, and agreed to write an introduction for their collection of Indian Legends to "vouch for their authenticity."

Instead of locating an illustrator, the sisters decided to use "some photos of old Mary arrayed in a blanket woven of the hair of a mountain goats and dogs (or so she says) which has been handed down through several generations. So we thought we would send them in with the stories."[70]

They also decided not to use the title "Legends of the Cowichans" for the stories. There was disagreement over a title suggested by Newcombe "so after much palaver and arguing—we have decided to try 'When the World Was Very Young,'" an appropriate title given the content of Mary Rice's Origin Stories, which made up the bulk of the texts.[71] Newcombe wrote that he did not like the title, and Cryer wrote back to thank him:

especially as you wrote exactly as I had hoped you might! I did not care for the title ... but my good sister is a terror—pigheaded is the only word that describes her. When she read your letter she began to think again and after much talking we arrived at "Tceah's People," she absolutely balked at the word Blue-jay!! So there it is and with that we can use all your nice intro-duction and do you think it will do? Anyways we have sent them off to Dent's representative in Vancouver and he has acknowledged them—that's as far as it's gone. Will let you know when I hear further from Mr. Spencer re. our Legends. Hope they don't pack them back again![72]

The publisher turned down their manuscript and soon Beryl and Maithal were preoccupied with their dying mother, as well as Cryer's young daughter Rosemary who had recurrent health problems. The "Legends of the Cowichans" recast as "Tceah's People" was all but forgotten.

Newcombe, meanwhile, had given copies to Bruce McKelvie, the managing editor of the *Daily Colonist* in Victoria, who had gained local recognition, through his own newspaper articles on British Columbia history, as an "authority." McKelvie was impressed, but not too interested in the Origin Stories and mythology of "Legends of the Cowichans." His life's work as an amateur historian and newspaperman was to promote and popularize the brief period of European history in the province, to instill a national pride and sense of identity within an immigrant population without significant roots. He met Beryl Cryer and offered her a position at the *Daily Colonist* as Chemainus correspondent reporting on the social calendar of the town.

Regarding her interest in native culture, McKelvie steered Beryl Cryer in a different direction from the stylized writing of "Legends of the Cowichans" to more straightforward accounts of native history. McKelvie shared the "salvage" view of professional anthropologists regarding local native cultures and lamented "the fast disappearing few who can recall old stories of Indian Mythology" and that "death and fading memories are making it increasingly difficult to save information of the early Indians for posterity."[73] McKelvie apparently visited the Indian Agent's office in Duncan where he examined a collection of framed photographs, one of which featured a very old, white-haired man wrapped in a blanket with the caption, "Chief Hul-ka-latksun First chief to welcome Roman Catholic Missionaries in the North Pacific." Intrigued, he had a suggestion for Beryl Cryer. As she recalled, many years later, McKelvie "asked me to find out who were the first of our Indians to befriend R.C. missionaries when they landed on the Coast of B.C. If I could write an account he might publish it."[74] Beryl Cryer knew the right person to to ask, and Mary Rice told her. The old man in the photograph was her grandfather.

Once the Halhed family recovered from the death of Gertrude, Beryl Cryer focused on her society column for the *Daily Colonist*. She submitted one final piece for the *Cowichan Leader* in September 1929, almost a year since their last "Legends of the Cowichans" article. Very different in style from the previous submissions, it was titled "Cowichan Indian Legends (As narrated by Mary Rice, granddaughter of Chief Khullkhullestan)."[75] For the first time, Mary Rice was acknowledged as the source of the information and, although the byline credits CRYOSS, comparison with later writing indicates that Beryl Cryer was now the sole author. The "flowery language" of the earlier work was replaced by clear prose, written as a first-person narrative by Mary Rice.

It is very likely that, in addition to her conversations with McKelvie and Newcombe, Beryl Cryer read J.N.J. Brown's critique of Pauline Johnson's "Legends of Vancouver" (formerly "Legends of the Capilanos"), which appeared June 18, 1929 in the *Vancouver Province*, a paper well-read in the Halhed household. Brown, a friend of Pauline Johnson, argued that communication difficulties between Pauline Johnson and her informant Chief Joe Capilano, rendered her stories inauthentic. "The Legends of Vancouver," he wrote, "will live as emollient, romantic stories with beautiful flow of language—but their mythology is not historical, as carved out by the Indians themselves."[76] Beryl Cryer took note of this critique. Her last piece for the *Cowichan Leader* featured a writing style more conducive to accurate communication of Central Coast Salish oral tradition, and established the format for her work with the *Daily Colonist*.

As the Great Depression loomed, and the town of Chemainus began to feel the effects of declining export lumber trade and rising unemployment, the Halhed sisters, hopeful of making some money, tried one last time to publish their "Legends." In October 1929, Beryl Cryer wrote William Newcombe, who had been out of touch for almost a year, and asked him if he could return the manuscript copy they had sent him a year earlier.[77] He did, and offered suggestions for improving it, which the women immediately accepted. In early January 1930, Maithal wrote back, thanking him for his "encouraging letter," adding that "we are at once starting to re-type them in order to submit them to the publishers you suggest. When this is done I wonder if you would add to your kindness by writing a letter, to be enclosed with the legends, vouching for their authenticity? As we both feel your name would carry much weight. How very kind of Mr. McKelvie to allow us to mention his name."[78] Despite the positive support from Newcombe and McKelvie, a worsening economy, and possibly the subject matter of their manuscript, prevented any interest in it on the part of publishers.

Beryl Cryer continued her Chemainus society column until October 1931, when she received a surprising communication from McKelvie "asking me to hand all material to Mrs. Bruce Irving, as my coverage for the last month had not been satisfactory! It was a most abrupt and somewhat insulting letter, and I and everyone else was furious!"[79] What happened next led to her remarkable, though brief, ethnographic career.

Beryl Cryer reacted instantly to the news of her dismissal. It happened that on the very day she received her termination notice, the publisher of the *Daily Colonist*, Mr. Matson, had passed through Chemainus on his way to Nanaimo. Cryer knew this, and the following day she persuaded her brother Frank to drive her to Nanaimo where she caught up with Matson. "I told him my pitiful story," she explained in a letter to Newcombe:

> and he was as nice as could be, promised I should continue and told me not to stop sending in news, until he returned to town … Well, I did as he told me, and he was away nearly a month, then, as you probably know, returned to town one afternoon and died the following morning. Of course I thought that finished my affair and I sent no more news.[80]

Within a short time, however, Cryer received a message from "Mrs. Matson" through her sister Mrs. A. J. Coles, that "it was Mr. Matson's last wish that I should continue with the news." In December, after internal wrangling and politics at the *Daily Colonist*, Beryl Cryer received two more letters. The first was from Matson's son, Jack, who informed her:

> that he found it impossible to go over McKelvie's head and reinstate me but that he had spoken to Mr. McK. And made him understand that he was to

show me 'every consideration possible and to do all he could for me.' My second letter was from Mr. McKelvie himself, a very different letter this, in which he regretted all that had taken place and 'should Mrs. Irving at any time relinquish the position, I would immediately give first refusal to me, in the meantime would I consider writing Feature articles on Historical incidents, connected with the Indians' He mentioned the death of Tzouhalem [a famous nineteenth-century warrior] on Kuper as an instance.

Cryer was very excited by this unexpected turn of events, and immediately began work on a number of stories Mary Rice had told her about her grandfather, Xulqalustun. Fearful that McKelvie might change his mind, she appealed to Newcombe to intercede on her behalf:

> Now this is where you come in: I know that you know Mr. McKelvie (hope you are not a great friend?) Would you, if you ever get a chance tell a few white lies for an old friend, and make him think that in me he has a 'find' that I know all kinds of authentic Legends and stories of early days amongst the Indians? As a matter of fact I do know quite a bit, Old Mary has told me several good yarns, and I am now working some up for the paper, but they are not exactly Historical. However I think they would make quite as good reading as 'Soliloquies in Victoria's Suburbia' or 'Two Rovers!'[81]

She asked Newcombe for any suitable photographs:

> as they want pictures if possible, with the articles? I would awfully like to get some of a Potlatch, and have you one of Penelakhut either the Spit or village, and I am enclosing the photo you once sent me of the Bluffs on Galiano, have you by chance the film of that? As that would do to illustrate that yarn of Mary's about the murderer hiding on Galiano, and being found by her grandfather? If you should know of any thing that would help me would you tell me? As I sadly miss the monthly cheque in these terribly hard times, and must make what I can to help out, now that the mill keeps cutting wages.[82]

By February 4, 1932, Beryl Cryer had written six articles based on Mary Rice's reminiscences of her grandfather, and submitted them to the *Daily Colonist* where they were well-received. She was extremely pleased when McKelvie wrote back "congratulating me and saying they would 'look forward to welcoming a continuation of the series, giving me "all rights reserved"' (My hats will scarcely fit!)"[83] On Wednesday, February 17, 1932 the first installment of her series on Mary Rice's grandfather, a reworking of the 1929 *Cowichan Leader* piece, appeared.

Beryl Cryer's submissions to the *Daily Colonist*, as she informed Newcombe, were "not exactly Historical," in the sense that McKelvie may have wished. She had borrowed a literary device used by Pauline Johnson in her 1910–11 "Legends of the Capilanos" series by embedding the native account in a narrative, where the writer "puts herself in the company of the native storyteller, with herself as listener to a story that spontaneously arises."[84] However, in marked contrast to Johnson's work, where the text "clearly reconfigures native stories to suit a moral and political project, while framing them as 'true stories' in how they represent what was told to her,"[85] Cryer had no such agenda. Where Johnson frequently layered her own interpretations over the stories with "a weighty sermonizing tone" and moral message, Cryer allows the storyteller to "speak for herself," giving the reader a relatively unadulterated perspective on a wide range of subjects and local history, largely hidden from white audiences.[86]

Once the *Daily Colonist* accepted the six "Hu-Ka-Latkstun" stories, Beryl immersed herself in collecting more histories from Mary Rice at her cabin by the Halhed family home. She kept in regular contact with Newcombe, who sent her photographs and tried to answer her inquiries regarding her research. Cryer's thoroughness demonstrates her dedication to acquiring accurate and detailed information, as well as her growing interest in the cultural material she was given. On one occasion, she wrote that:

> Mary has told me of an old man, who used to sit on the bank of the river, shake a rattle and charm the salmon—stop them from going downstream! Could you give me any idea what sort of rattle this would have been— Wood? and carved?[87]

Ever mindful of accuracy, another letter asked:

> whether the people in the Archives look up records etc. for one? I have quite a good yarn that should be verified before publishing and it is so hard for me to get down. I thought I would ask you what you thought before daring to write Mrs. Cree or whoever the proper person would be?[88]

Newcombe replied that he would look up the story, so Cryer sent him a two-page typewritten summary of Mary Rice's account of nineteenth-century feuds between Central Coast Salish and northern peoples.[89] It may be the only record of her notes and, as such, provides valuable insight into her writing process, and to the meticulous attention she paid to recording exactly what Mary Rice told her, without altering the narrative. In the letter Cryer sent with the transcript, she asked:

> Does your kind offer still hold good of looking up my story in the archives? If you really have time here it is—if too busy please don't bother, Mary is usually pretty accurate I find, but in his case I would like to be certain that the man Cly-aack was not caught for thirteen years.[90]

The first five articles appeared on different weekdays through mid-February through April 1932. Beryl Cryer had not heard from McKelvie for a month when he finally contacted her "very apologetically" informing her that, "they want all I can send them—for the *Sunday Magazine* section."[91] Her first regular weekly story in this section—the sixth, and final, installment in the "Hul-Ka-Latkstun" series—appeared on May 22, 1932. At thirteen-and-a-half-cents an inch, four articles a month provided much-needed family income and incentive to keep collecting stories. By September 1932, Beryl Cryer had written seventeen accounts of Puneluxutth' history from Mary Rice, with occasional input from Mary's brother, Tommy Pielle.[92] Soon her circle of informants began to widen.

In the fall of 1932, Beryl Cryer visited Mary Rice about a specific topic and was directed by her to seek out another elder in the Puneluxutth' community of Hwt'susi'. There, Cryer made the acquaintance of Ts'umsitun and his wife, Latits'iiya, who provided information for four articles.

Aside from their stories, Cryer was particularly impressed with the fine sweaters made by Latits'iiya and her daughters, although she disliked the patterns they used, which were taken from old crochet books in order to make the sweaters more saleable. Cryer, always on the lookout for opportunities to make a little extra cash, began to consider having sweaters made with "original Salish designs." Newcombe sent her some "very lovely patterns," and Cryer hoped that her husband Claude would "work on them, enlarging them a bit. I think they will be awfully effective worked into the sweaters."[93] She pursued her idea further, and apparently had Latits'iiya make a few samples. She wrote Newcombe for the address of a Miss Ravenhill who:

> had that little Indian curio store on Gov't Street? I have been wondering
> whether, in the event of my getting the sweaters knitted—with original
> Salish designs—Miss Ravenhill would handle them. What do you think? I
> might write her, regarding the idea, or run down again if necessary as I
> suppose it would be better to have some on view, and then book orders—
> if there were any to book!![94]

Things now went much smoother on the writing front, and Beryl Cryer's contributions to the *Sunday Magazine* were well received by the public. McKelvie informed her that, "he was flooded with letters asking about me and congratulating him on the series."[95] After a meeting with Cryer in his Victoria office in early November 1932, she wrote that "he was terribly eulogistic about my efforts and he is giving me all the assistance he can, re. publishing a book—even to writing himself to the publishers!"[96] McKelvie lent her three academic works: one by Franz Boas, another by James Teit, and the *Thirty-fifth Annual Report of the Bureau of American Ethnology, 1913–14*, "from which he suggested I should take ideas for children's tales ... I guess I've found a soft spot in his heart? He also offered me back the [Chemainus] correspondence as Mrs. Irving is leaving, but I turned it down."[97] Beryl Cryer was, evidently, busy in her new-found career.

Fans of her column sometimes wrote her directly, offering ideas about specific topics and requesting information. Once, she wrote Newcombe telling him that she "had two letters from people asking for stories re. the caves on Thetis Is[land]" but "I can get nothing out of the Indians here about these caves"[98]—an indication that her elders were not necessarily prepared to divulge everything about their cultural practices, especially if it did not relate to land claims issues. One elder, Tatawalyt, when questioned, replied that Newcombe himself might be able to tell her "as she thought, long ago, Robby Roberts, Dr. Newcombe, and you explored them most secretly. She thought the braves used to keep their "Tomanie-wai" [Tamanahous] sticks there. Do tell me how long ago was that dance '*done*' here."[99] Another correspondent questioned, "whether I can tell him of good clam shell banks 'having read my Indian stories!' as he is starting a 'manufactured product' requiring lime and would prefer using shell!!"[100]

In November 1932, the main employer in the town of Chemainus, the Victoria Lumber Company Mill, shut down due to falling demand for export lumber. The effects of the Great Depression continued to ripple through every sector of the provincial economy, including daily newspapers. Beryl Cryer's feature articles in

William Cryer and unidentified woman photographed by Beryl Cryer inside old house at Shts'um'inus (Kulleet Bay), 1930s.   Image PN 5959 courtesy Royal British Columbia Museum.

Chris Arnett

the *Sunday Magazine*, which had appeared every week since May, began to run less frequently, as the *Daily Colonist* struggled with its own financial predicament wrought by dwindling ad revenues. With only two articles published in two months, she wrote to explain the situation to Newcombe:

> Sad to say, Mr. McKelvie has written me that the 'Colonist' is having a hard time to keep going—has cut out most of its correspondents, and I am the only contributor to the Sunday paper (not on the staff) that they are able to keep and can only accept—two (he wrote me) stories a month—as a matter of fact they are only printing one which scarcely makes it worth the trouble and expense of collecting them. He 'hopes to soon be in a position to ask me to increase the number' but I am afraid things don't look any too bright do they? The mill here has been closed since Nov. and there seems no chance of starting up yet—so we are all 'feeling the pinch!' Well, I suppose the experience is good for one, but I hope it doesn't last too long.[101]

The hard times of the Hwunitum' population of Chemainus during the Great Depression were not shared by all native people. Mary Rice and her extended family always earned cash through their hop cultivation in central Washington, and with other work, and they continued to rely on traditional subsistence activities. They also supplied needy Hwunitum', including the elder Halhed and his new wife Emily, the former family maid, with food, and provided Chemainus shopkeepers with much-needed cash. As Ellen White recalls:

> My Dad always said, and Granpa Tommy always said, "Why are they so poor? Even those rich like the Halheds, the Johnsons and all that—Dad would bring them food. What the heck was the name of that owner of that store on the corner? When we were kids we used to go in there and point and he'd say: 'Just one penny.' And we'd put all our pennies on the counter for a soft drink with ice cream in it and he would be so happy. Dad and them fed them because we had a lot of money. We'd go to the States and I'd swear Dad and them always had about three sacks of money.[102]

Undeterred by the gloomy economy, and spurred, it seemed, by her own research interests regarding Coast Salish culture, in particular the "moons" of the Central Coast Salish calendar, Beryl Cryer continued collecting information and writing.

> I have collected my 'Salish moons' with such vigour that I now have 16!" she informed her friend Newcombe. "That won't do. Must try and get to Cowichan Gap [Porlier Pass]. Old John Peters will know them—as he is very ancient and in his youth was a hunter for the tribe.[103]

Beryl Cryer began to travel further afield, at some expense, driving or being driven, as far as Nanaimo, in search of stories. Mary Rice directed her to seek out her "co-parents in law" Joe and Jennie Wyse, knowledgeable Snuneymuxw elders who lived in Nanaimo and whose son Johnny was married to Mary Rice's eldest daughter, Ellen. When she arrived on their doorstep in January or February of 1933, they had been expecting her. Sugnuston (Joe Wyse) greeted Beryl Cryer with a formal speech in their living room, thanking her for listening to what he had to say. His wife, Jennie Wyse translated for him: "Always he has wanted to tell the whiteman what he knows but no one would listen." He continued his speech, translated by his wife, naming the communities that make up the Snuneymuxw, the history of the Hwunitum' discovery of coal at Nanaimo and relating the only eyewitness native account of an 1854 Douglas Treaty.[104] Following this initial meeting she made regular visits to Nanaimo over the next six months to interview either Joe or Jennie Wyse and was introduced to other Snuneymuxw notables, such as the storyteller, carver and former athlete, Wilkes James.

During the spring and summer of 1933, as the Great Depression continued to affect the ability of the newspaper to pay its writers, only one or two articles appeared a month, and none in August or September. In September, Beryl Cryer complained to Newcombe that "McKelvie appears to have stopped using my tales. He has some down there—so have written asking him whether he wants more." She was, however, delighted to inform Newcombe that she had finally collected the names of the thirteen Central Coast Salish months. She had made a special trip to the north end of Galiano Island where she "got them all from old John Peter ... He is a Penelakhut man and as a boy kept neighbour's chickens out of Gov. Douglas' garden for $2.50 a month."[105] She had gathered information on the names of the months from ten different elders but expressed some concern about her data:

> I find it very difficult to decide about these moons. I had 12, then went to John Peter and he gave me 13 but many of them quite different to the ones I already had. I believe O. Smythe in Duncan has 13. I will see whether he will let me compare mine with his ... Is it correct to call them the "Salish Moons" or Coast Salish? And I wonder there are only 12 in those lists you sent to me? as of course they watched the moons and there are 13.[106]

Newcombe had sent her lists of months from published accounts of Clallam and Kwakwa'wakw ethnographies and continued to send material. "Really you are too good!" she wrote him, "Fancy bothering to copy me all those 'Moons'—thank you most awfully. Now I am 'shaking in my shoes' in case I don't do justice to the material you have supplied me with! So please don't judge me too harshly when you see the result."[107]

On October 22, she wrote Newcombe telling him that, "I have sent McKelvie my article on the 'Moons.' If you see him and he mentions them, better tell him they are worthy of a front page at least! If there is not quality, there is, at least, quantity!"[108] She decided not to incorporate Newcombe's information into her article, but included it as an appendix to her original work.

Beryl Cryer's reputation reached beyond Vancouver Island and attracted the attention of other establishment figures such as George Thornton Emmons (1852–1945) who, in his heyday as a collector of ethnological artifacts, amassed large collections of Northwest Coast, primarily Tlingit, art for the American Museum of Natural History, and other American institutions.[109] Now, in his early eighties, his collecting interests had shifted to Central Coast Salish objects, particularly swayxwi masks. In October 1933, Emmons was in Victoria and wrote to Cryer. In his long letter to her, he included photographs of swayxwi mask copies (made by "a whiteman"), and asked for her assistance in acquiring information on authentic masks, and the ceremonies associated with them. As she confided to William Newcombe, she was in a quandary about how to proceed:

> I received the enclosed letter yesterday. What about it? As a matter of fact, I have been trying to collect a bit about the mask myself, also keeping in mind that you once asked me to try and find out what secret ceremony they had in connection with it. It was not until I saw you in Vic. recently that I realized that what I call the "Schoy-Whey" and what you call "Xai-xai" were one in the same thing! I want to ask your advice about his Mr. Emmons. If I give him what little information I have regarding this mask, how shall I do it? And what should I ask for 'PAY'!
>
> If I send him my notes, what is to prevent him from using them, and then saying they are useless to him? (Am I being very distrustful?) At the same time, I can't expect him to pay before examining what information I have?? I believe there is a man at Bonsall's Creek who has a real old mask, but most are new ones … What is also troubling me is, if I give Mr. E. what little I have collected, am I entitled to make use of it for my own articles?… Hope you don't think me an awful nuisance bothering you in this manner, just tell me if I am.[110]

Cryer showed Emmons' photographs to Mary Rice, who immediately recognized the masks were fake. As Beryl informed Newcombe, "I showed Mary (Who may use the mask, through her Mother, (the father could not use it) the pictures enclosed by Mr. Emmons, and she said, 'What's the matter with these things? Where's their feathers, and their whiskers? They look all wrong to me—Too new—I think!'"[111]

Within a few weeks Emmons paid a visit to Cryer's home in Chemainus after which she dutifully informed Newcombe:

> Well, I had a most interesting tea with your old friend. He is certainly very charming but—like most Americans—'I' figured largely in his conversation.

Swayxwi mask "carved by a whiteman."
Photo by George Emmons given to Beryl Cryer.
Image PN 6066 courtesy Royal British Columbia
Museum.

He began asking questions regarding the mask, but then said he would write me a few questions. He has certainly kept his word and has sent me two pages full of questions. I really can't spare time to answer them all, as he wants Legends and Ceremonies etc. etc. It's a case of "I'm not greedy but I like a lot!" with the old man. Wanted to know whether I knew of anyone with Indian curios or any old masks—but my mind was a blank![112]

Cryer made some effort to locate an old swayxwi mask for Newcombe, not Emmons, visiting Hwts'usi' where she was "unlucky to find my man away and ran into Chief Edward (a regular old rotter). He has the 'Schy-Why'—but when I asked him a few questions, told me that if I would pay him $20.00 he would tell me all about it! So I left him."[113] Hulbertsun did tell her that his uncle Jimmy Johnny of Nanaimo had an old mask "too rotten to use" which he might part with and Mary Rice also gave her "the name of another old man at Nanaimo who, she thinks, has an old mask, but not as old as Jimmy Johnny's. She seemed to think this was the original from Musqueam."[114]

Beryl Cryer decided to learn more about the swayxwi mask for her own information and informed Newcombe of her decision to study the Hul'q'umi'num' language in more detail. "Mary can sing all the different songs connected with the 'Schy-Why' ceremonies," she wrote:

I thought I would really try and learn the language and then I could get these songs. They would be rather interesting. Would you tell me which you

Chris Arnett

consider the best book for me to get in order to study the language? I do know a good deal but can't *talk* it—Mary is going to teach me.[115]

In December 1933, Newcombe sent her a Coast Salish "alphabet" from an unknown source and a copy of Franz Boas' "Notes on the Snanaimuq" and she wrote back thanking him "for all your trouble in looking up these things up for me."[116] But she had some questions reading Boas' work: "Why does Boas make no mention of the Cowichans? he speaks as though—at that time—all the territory now called 'Cowichan' was 'Snanaimuq'?" She also wrote that she had "not even tried to answer Mr. Emmons' questions! Has he left town yet, I wonder?"[117]

Her enthusiasm to take her research further, by learning Hul'q'umi'num', coincided with fewer of her articles appearing in the pages of the *Sunday Magazine*, as the newspaper struggled to stay afloat through ongoing difficult times. "Old McKelvie isn't doing much with my yarns nowadays—is he?" she complained to the always-sympathetic Newcombe. "Only one a month. I shall have to stop collecting if he doesn't buck up."[118] Her *magnum opus*, "Moons of the Cowichans" finally appeared on December 17, 1933, almost sixty days after she submitted it, and no articles would appear for three more months.

A letter written to Newcombe in the depths of a harsh winter on January 31, 1934, communicated a growing disillusionment stemming from the lack of published articles, financial constraints at home, such as the lack of a vehicle, "fearful weather" and obligations to help out her husband, William, in his Chemainus store—all of which denied her the luxury of visiting elders and studying Hul'q'umi'num'.

> It is most interesting—but I fear I shall never get far with the Salish language—have so little chance to get in touch with the people. You ask 'What has happened!' re. my Articles—I ask that question also. They have one down there—but since the 'Moons' there has been nothing and I cannot spare the cash to collect stories if they are not going to print them—as it is—they are taking so few—only one and possibly two if short— a month—and that barely covers expenses, getting to the Indians and paying them a little for their stories … Only wish some other paper would take them. Savage of the 'Cowichan Leader' would like them—but he pays far less than the Colonist and they are only 13½ cents an inch.
>
> It has been such fearful weather, have not been again to Bonsall's Creek or Nanaimo—will try to get there as soon as possible as soon as things clear a bit—if only we had a car! or a fortune![119]

She confided to Newcombe that, desperate to make some extra money, she had collected all her *Daily Colonist* articles published to date and had shipped them off to "MacMillans," a London publishing house, "but fear they will not accept them—times are not good enough yet for the publication of such a book."[120]

She suspected some prejudice against her and her articles among certain staff at the *Daily Colonist*:

> Do you know MacCallum who edits the 'Sunday Magazine' section of the 'Colonist?' I always feel that he does not want my articles? Probably am quite wrong—but I have written to him at different times and he has never troubled to answer whereas McKelvie answers at once and has always been so nice about them. Here's hoping they take some more soon.[121]

In March 1934, Beryl Cryer's articles appeared once more on the pages of the *Sunday Magazine*, but publication was now sporadic, with only five articles making it to press over the following year. These articles were among her best due to the extra time she had at her disposal for composition. In the spring of 1934, she was introduced to Johnny and Rosalie Seletze of Xinupsun who gifted her with two very important accounts, which were made all the more significant by the Seletzes' deaths only a few months later. Also, during that summer, an event occurred which, more than anything, had a major effect on Beryl Cryer's career as a writer. Her old friend, mentor and liaison to the native community, Mary Rice, finally moved from her small, three-room cabin at the edge of the Halhed property on Chemainus Harbour to Rice Island, to be with her son, Charles, and his family.

Beryl Cryer continued her research and writing, but now without the guidance of her teacher Mary Rice, who had always been ready to provide her with counsel and direction. In the winter of 1934–35, curious to learn of the smilhu, the winter spirit dance, Cryer attended a gathering at Xulel-thw, and subsequently published an article about her experiences there. As a result of doing so, Cryer may have violated protocols regarding the use of recording equipment— namely her pencil and her notebook.[122] Following the publication of "The Smilhu" on March 3, 1935, her articles continued to appear in the *Sunday Magazine*, but all of them were based on earlier research and many were reprints of "The Legends of the Cowichans" written collaboratively with her sister years before. Something had changed in the native community regarding Cryer's work, and her access to informed authorities abruptly ceased. In January 1936, she became ill, followed by a debilitating arthritic condition. Things improved by August of that year but, as she informed her friend Newcombe, "I can use my hands for everything except writing."[123]

In 1938, William Claude Cryer sold the family business in Chemainus and he, Beryl and their daughter, Rosemary, moved to Victoria. She gave up writing as a career, but maintained her interest in native culture. She joined the British Columbia Indian Arts and Welfare Society, a group comprised primarily of white women who advocated for the "preservation" of indigenous art and culture.

Mary Rice passed away in 1949, and it may be no coincidence that Beryl Cryer, in that same year, finally published a book of her stories.[124] Entitled *The Flying*

Canoe: Legends of the Cowichans, the forty-one page book, which featured line illustrations by Betty Newton, included six stories, two from the "Legends of the Cowichans" series, co-written with her sister Maithal, and originally published in the *Cowichan Leader* some twenty years earlier, and four rewritten versions of stories first published in the *Daily Colonist*.[125] In the foreword he wrote for the book, Bruce McKelvie praised Beryl Cryer for "doing a real service to British Columbia":

> It was my privilege, a few years ago, to offer some encouragement to Mrs. Cryer, in the collecting of Indian Legends. In this work she achieved great success when the stories were published in the Victoria 'Daily Colonist.' They were not only true to native tradition, but were presented with real sympathy and understanding.
>
> I am pleased indeed, that Mrs. Cryer has decided to publish a few of these most excellent legends.
>
> It is with the utmost pleasure that I commend 'The Flying Canoe' to every lover of aboriginal lore.[126]

Clearly intended for a young, non-native audience, the book included a short introduction by Beryl Cryer. Still mindful of the ethnocentric expectations of her audience, which she did little to dissuade, Beryl Cryer introduced the reader to the true author of the book in a vignette that evoked the setting in which she first experienced Central Coast Salish oral traditions:

> I know a lovely, sandy beach, with tall Fir trees growing at one end, and at the other, a little green clearing with one old Maple tree in the middle.
>
> Under this tree there is a tumbledown little house, and in the house there lives—who do you think?
>
> A PRINCESS! Not the kind of princess you think about and picture to yourself, but an Indian Princess.
>
> She is not a bit like a princess, for she is very, very fat, and very, very old, and I'm afraid, quite poor.
>
> Long ago, her father was a great Chief of the Cowichan Tribe, and Tzlah-Mia,[127] (for that is her name) was their princess, but now her father is dead, and she lives all alone in her tiny house under the Maple tree.
>
> She is never lonely, for she has lots of grandchildren. There are always fat, brown babies playing under her tree, or splashing in the water in front of her house.
>
> In the evening, if it is warm, Tzlah-Mia builds a fire of drift-wood, on the beach. There she sits making rush mats, or spinning soft, white wool for her knitting, while she tells stories to her grandchildren.
>
> One evening I went to the beach to see Tzlah-Mia and to hear some of her Indian stories.

Her fire was blazing gaily, and two of her grandchildren were piling logs upon it, making the sparks fly up, up, until they seemed to join the stars in the sky.

It was very quiet on the beach, only the soft lap, lap of the water as the tide came over the stones.

Then, far back in the woods a little Owl called, and was answered by his mate.

'Ha—a, Haa aaaaaaa.' Soft and clear it came, over and over again. *Tzlah-Mia held up one wrinkled brown finger.*

'Hear that?' she asked. 'Those two talk to each other. I can't tell what they say now.' She shook her head sadly. 'Long ago my people knew, because in those days, all the birds, and animals, and fish, could take off their coats of feathers and fur, just as we take off our clothes, and they would walk and talk just like men and women!'

'Tonight I will tell you some stories about those long-ago days, when only Indians lived in this land, and all the people, and birds, and animals lived like good friends.'

Tzlah-Mia's fingers were busy amongst her clams which she had dug that morning. She had laid them on hot stones beside the fire, to make them open. Now she was taking them from the shells and was threading them on thin Cedar sticks, which she stuck in the ground before the fire, drying them for the winter.

As she worked, she told us the stories which I have put into this book, hoping that you may enjoy them as much as I did.[128]

As always in Beryl Cryer's writing, knowledge surfaces, like the roots of a cedar tree or the houses along a beach, half-buried in sand.

Sometime after her husband William died in 1957, Beryl Cryer left her beloved West Coast to live with her daughter Rosemary's family in Welland, Ontario, a place she "detested," but in which she was resigned to stay in order to be near her daughter and her three beloved grandchildren. In 1967, at the age of eighty, she wrote to William L. Ireland, Provincial Librarian and Archivist at the Provincial Archives in Victoria, inquiring about the feasibility of having her collection of stories published, and asking if he might be willing "to write me a little Foreword? Don't be afraid of hurting my feelings," she wrote:

> should you feel the material to be not sufficiently interesting to send a Publisher, for of course I quite realize that Indians are not a particularly interesting subject to many people. Still, when I was writing them Mr. McKelvie told me that he was flooded with letters asking about me and congratulating him on the series. Also when Miss Wright read three at one of the B.C. Ind. etc. meetings, Miss Ethel Bruce was kind enough to get up and congratulate me on 'Your style, I could listen to them all night.'[129]

Ireland agreed and wrote in reply that he enjoyed "the samplings you sent along, partially because of the information they contain but mainly because of the difference in style. All too frequently I find collections of Indian legends a little too stilted but when you combine with them the details about your informant my reaction is quite different."[130] He promised to send the stories to Donald Mitchell, an archaeologist teaching in the Anthropology and Sociology Department at the University of Victoria, who also happened to be the son of publisher Howard Mitchell, of Mitchell Press.

Donald Mitchell, too, recognized the value in her work and agreed that "the pieces Mrs. Cryer has produced do seem worth gathering and producing as a single publication. Tales and texts are not particularly plentiful for the Coast Salish groups and hers seem to be quite faithfully reported."[131] It was his opinion, however, that "they would not meet learned standards for anthropological texts or folklore." He made a further observation that, in his opinion, given the political climate of the day regarding academic study of native spirituality, "some pieces ... might not now be politic to include. I have in mind the descriptive one on the winter dance, some portions of which the present Cowichan and Nanaimo would not wish disclosed."[132] Not interested in working on the material, or sending it to his father in its present format, Mitchell offered other suggestions regarding rewrites, footnotes and introductions by authorities on Coast Salish culture—all of which added up to a daunting task for both Ireland and the eighty-year-old Beryl Cryer.

Ireland forwarded Mitchell's pertinent comments to Cryer adding that Mitchell's response "would seem to be rather encouraging but leaves unanswered the question of publication, how to finance and by whom. Whether a Canadian publisher would pick it up would naturally depend on his reaction to a finished manuscript and whether you feel up to taking it this far on speculation I have no way of knowing."[133] He suggested she consider Mitchell's suggestions, but in the meantime send a copy to Victoria for safekeeping.

Beryl Cryer responded immediately to Ireland, thanking him for having:

> taken so much trouble with my Indian stuff, and now I am going to make matters even worse by 'dumping it in your lap'! Oh please don't say what you are thinking, but I don't know what else to do with the collection; so [I] am packing up my loose leaf folders—such as they are and making a gift of them to you to do as you like with them ... I do hope you will take charge of them and should you feel they aren't worth keeping—put them in your incinerator. Preparing the material on the chance that some publisher might accept it, seems such a gamble, and I might consider it if I were younger, but not now; so they are yours to deal with as you see fit.[134]

Following this letter, a large package arrived on Ireland's desk. Inside it were folders containing Cryer's yellowed, undated columns from the *Daily Colonist*, cut and pasted on numbered pages of looseleaf paper, with some handwritten headings and notation—the precursor of the book you have before you. Upon receipt of her material, Ireland wrote back that he was delighted with her decision "for certainly it is worth preserving and otherwise all your work and deep affection for our Indian peoples and their legends could so easily be lost." He added that he had "no inclination, even remotely, to think of an incinerator.[135]

There was no further communication and on February 17, 1980, Beryl Mildred Cryer died at the age of ninety-three in the Welland County General Hospital, a world away from the beloved Chemainus of her youth.

I discovered Cryer's work in the British Columbia Provincial Archives when it was referenced in David Rozen's 1985 Master's thesis, "Place-names of the Island Halkomelem."[136] The Archives still held her three boxes of single, lined pages and the original newspaper columns, the preliminary sources for a book she never finished. As I read the small print, I was at first disconcerted by its journalistic style but as I continued, the stories began to emerge.

Beryl Cryer's work with the Central Coast Salish elders of Vancouver Island and Kuper Island during the Great Depression was born of mutual necessity, yet carried out by Cryer with verve and a dedication to accuracy. Although she was an outsider, ignorant of many things regarding the indigenous peoples of her adopted land, she possessed a genuine affection for the elders she worked with at a time when racism was rampant and the native people of Vancouver Island hovered barely on the cusp of recovery after a half-century of declining populations. She carried their message, even if inadvertently, to the newcomers and earned, for a little while at least, the trust and respect of the people she worked with. She conveyed Hul'qumi'num and Snuneymuxw origin stories and history to the non-native populations of southern Vancouver Island until her 1935 account of the winter dances ended the collaboration with her informants—it had revealed her own deeply acculturated prejudice in the presence of vital, sacred, indigenous ceremony: "Watching and listening," she wrote, in a hitherto uncharacteristic, conscious, philosophical and introspective commentary on what she had witnessed, "one felt how thin was the veneer of civilization! In fact, I began to fear that my own layer was none too thick." Privately, she cared for and respected the people who had contributed their stories to her ethnographic project for all those years. Publically, however, she was finally unable to overcome the Eurocentric, hierarchical worldview still predominant in Canadian society.

Things would change slowly, if at all.

In 1974, the once-dormant Chemainus Valley Historical Society resurrected itself, and organized an oral history project in which the descendants of the "pioneers" were asked to write down their memories of the Chemainus district prior to 1940, and have these accounts eventually published for posterity. The committee in charge of the project quite conveniently "decided that the native Indian history should be left to the many talented native Indian writers and artists because only they could do justice to their story."[137] This apparently "well-meaning" accommodation of native voice, however, resulted in a conspicuous omission from the writing of Chemainus' regional history, and served only to further diminish awareness of an ancient people. There was, however, one notable contribution. As a Halhed, and a member of one of the more prominent, though long-departed families, Beryl Cryer was contacted at her home in Welland, Ontario, and asked to submit a piece, which she did, providing many memories and observations of her family and neighbours in early twentieth-century Chemainus.

She went beyond the committee's mandate, however:

> I feel that I should mention at least one of our native people. After all, this land we call our own, was theirs before they were pushed onto Reservations, with no recompense so far as the province of British Columbia is concerned. For they are not 'Treaty Indians,' with the exception of one band, at the extreme corner of the province.[138]

Cryer concluded her contribution with a tribute to her mentor, Mary Rice, recalling her knowledge of medicinal plants which she had used "to help my people." She mentioned not a word about her brief writing career which so often featured Mary Rice's stories:

> Mary still clung to the old crafts taught her years ago, and each spring she would gather great masses of rushes that grew beside the lagoon, carrying them on her old back and struggling along the beach to her cottage, bent nearly to the ground with her load.
>
> She taught me how to make the rush mats used by her people for generations to line the walls, to sleep on and for coverings. She also taught me to card the sheep's wool, and I watched her spin it and knit the beautiful Cowichan Indian sweaters for which her people are so famous.
>
> When there was an extra work to be done in our home we would ask help from Mary and she would so willingly drop whatever she might be doing and come to our aid.
>
> When I last saw her she was living with a daughter near Yellow Point; she was quite blind, but was sitting out in the sun, with a grandson brushing her hair. She recognized my voice, and taking my hand between both of hers, she held it against her heart, crooning over it—"Ah, Ah, Ah"—and swaying back and forth, in the beautiful old Indian custom with which Indian women greeted their friends, in the old days.[139]

Oral Traditions of the Hul'q'umi'num' Coast Salish of Kuper Island and Vancouver Island

as told to Beryl M. Cryer

Mary Rice (Xalunamut).   Image PN 6455 courtesy Royal British Columbia Museum.

Xulqalustun—A Friend of Governor Douglas, Part I[140]

This article was the first in a six-part series about Mary Rice's grandfather, a famous Puneluxutth' leader who carried the name Xulqalustun (circa 1790–1886). The first installment introduces the reader to Mary Rice and, unfortunately, to Cryer's occasional use of caricature and stereotype. What follow, however, are oral traditions told by Mary Rice in which a female siowa from Shts'um'inus (Kulleet Bay) dreams the arrival of the first Hwulunitum' (Europeans). Xulqalustun has similar dreams that are realized a year later, when he participates in the first meeting between Puneluxutth' people and the crew of an unknown European sailing vessel off present-day Steveston.

SIAMTUNAAT CAME TO SEE ME TODAY, and I guessed at once that she had "membered" another story.

I often think that there must be a touch of Irish in her, for she is a very temperamental old Indian, either in the depths of woe, on account of some misdemeanor on the part of one of her innumerable relations, or else smiling upon all she meets, her little eyes twinkling away as though life were one huge joke. Today I could see that things were going well with her, as she came slowly up the path, leaning on her stick, her face wreathed in smiles as she caught sight of me at the window.

Of all the Indians I know, Siamtunaat is the only one who takes a real pleasure in telling stories of the old days, of her grandfather Xulqalustun, Chief of the Cowichans[141] and "Good friend of Governor Douglas." Of the coming of the white men to these shores, and endless tribal legends, which she sometimes tells to her grandchildren, but—"Ah, these chilrun!" she shakes her head until the long earrings dance madly against her fat brown cheeks, "they laugh at my stories. They don't want them any more."[142]

She speaks excellent English, for although her first husband was an Indian circus rider (she still treasures his beaded suit with the bird embroidered in the front), her second was a white man, and it is by his name, and that given by the priests, that she is best known, but I prefer her Indian name.

As a girl she was named Xalunamut which means "not seen before," and is what she calls her "singing name," on account of the curious singing ceremony which takes place when a maiden comes of marriageable age and is named and presented to the tribe.

Several years ago this name, as the custom is, was passed on to her granddaughter, and she took the name of her mother—Tzea-mntenaht (a great name).[143]

I was quite right. As she plodded up the steps Siamtunaat announced, "I memember another story you never hear." She sat down and I waited. One must give her time. Like all Indians, she cannot be hurried. So we talked about her family and things in general whilst she retied the black silk handkerchief over her white hair, carefully fastened the gay shawl about her ample shoulders, with a large silver brooch, and vigorously mopped her smiling old face with a rather dubious-looking rag.

Now she was ready!

"I think I tell you before," she began, "how my grandfather, Pielle Xulqalustun, Chief of the Cowichans, was a very wise man! He knew many things that would happen, for he had dreams. Well, up at Kulleets Bay (Chemainus Bay)[144] there lived an old, old woman, so old that not even the oldest of our people could tell when she had been young; and this woman had dreams also![145]

"One day she told my grandfather that in her dreams she had seen a great canoe coming to our land. It was tall—tall and longer than two war canoes, and it moved without paddles! It had trees growing on it, and on these trees were wings, white and shining as a sea gull's wings. The men in this canoe were strange, too, for they had black faces, and their hair was so" (here she crooked her gnarled old fingers to indicate curls). My grandfather laughed when he heard this story, but that night he, too, had a dream. He saw the great canoe that the Kulleet woman had seen, but when he looked up, and up to where men were walking, he saw a stranger sight than the woman had told of, for these men had white skins, and fire and smoke were coming from their mouths, and on their bodies were not blankets, but some tight coverings!

"Well, next day he told the Cowichans of this dream, and no one dare say it could not be true, for he was a great and wise man. Nearly a year after this, Xulqalustun and his people left the village of Puneluxutth', on Kuper Island, and paddled to Canoe Pass for the fishing.[146] Every year they fished in that place for sturgeon and in the Fraser River for sockeye salmon, which they caught in small nets made of willow bark that one man could use.

"Very early one morning, they were paddling out to fish when, far, far away, my grandfather saw some funny thing coming over the water. On and on it came and, not knowing what it might be, the Cowichans went back to the shore, painted their faces, put their feathers on their heads, and, taking spears, set out to meet this strange thing.

"As it got closer my grandfather gave a mighty shout. 'Oheeeeee!' he cried, 'it is the canoe I saw in my dreams. See, as I told you, there are tall trees growing upon it, and the wings with which it flies over the water.'

"Nearer and nearer came the canoe, and as it moved over the quiet water the sun came into the sky and shone upon the great wings until they were shining like silver. Then, as the Cowichans watched in wonder, there came a shout, and at the sound the wings folded as a bird folds its wings, and the strange canoe lay still upon the water.

"And now my grandfather and his men did not know what to do, for why had this bird canoe come to their land? So, raising their voices, they chanted the war cry of the tribe, and for two days and two nights those men, with their faces painted for war, paddled round and round that canoe, and not once did they stop for food or drink, and not once did they stop that long, loud cry of our war song. As they paddled they could see the strange men looking down at them, and their faces were white as Xulqalustun had dreamed, and out of their mouths came smoke, so the Cowichans thought they must be eating fire!

"Soon my grandfather saw that they did not want to fight, but came as friends, for they laughed, and waved their hands, so that at the end of two nights, the Cowichans sang no more, but they, too, laughed, and waved to the men.

"Well, my grandfather used to laugh when he told us how those strange men had hard white sticks they were eating, and they broke off pieces of these sticks and threw them down into our canoes and pointing to their mouths, called out 'Bis-kit, Bis-kit!' But the Cowichans thought they were really sticks and threw the pieces into the water.[147]

"Soon the White Chief called to my grandfather and, making signs of friendship, he gave Xulqalustun a charm.

"It was flat, like my hand, one end sharp, and at the other was a hole. Through this, Xulqalustun put a thong of deer skin and hung it about his neck so that it lay upon his breast, and he showed it to all he met, telling them how great a charm the White Chief had given him.

"Long, long after, the big canoe came again and the White Chief showed my grandfather how his people put a stick in the hole of this charm and with it cut trees in the forest.

"After this the canoe came to our land very often and the men brought them presents of beads, bright and shining, blankets, and strange food. In return, the Cowichans gave meat, fish, and skins, and there was great friendship between the White Chief and my grandfather. But one summer a bad thing happened, but this I must tell you in another story, for it is late and I must go home and cook supper. I have relations come to stay, oh! They make lots of work!

Off she went, a picturesque old figure, nearly as broad as she is long, yet with a curious dignity about her, for is she not the granddaughter of that "good friend of Governor Douglas?"

Xulqalustun, Part II[148]

The second installment of the Xulqalustun stories describes Mary Rice's grand-father's participation in the capture of Hwlumelhtsu leaders at Montague Harbour on June 3, 1863.

THE NEXT TIME WE MET I REMINDED SIAMTUNAAT of her promise to tell me of the "bad thing" that happened to the "Great canoe with wings."

"Ah yes," she said, nodding thoughtfully, "I will tell you that. Well, that white chief and his men on the strange canoe were always good friends of Xulqalustun and the Cowichans. But on the other side of Kuper Island there lived a tribe—the Hwlumelhtsu—they were a bad, cruel people and they did not like these white men coming.[149]

"Every Summer the Hwlumelhtsu went to another island to hunt and fish, and always they made their camp on the beach. One year they were in this camp and the white men came along in their great canoe and, seeing the Hwlumelhtsu camp, they landed, bringing with them presents as they had to the Cowichans. The Hwlumelhtsu, with wickedness in their hearts, made friends, and that night they gave a feast for the white chief, and he and his men brought their food and a drink that was hot and strange, for it made the braves feel good and big, and brought great courage to their hearts. Later this courage grew to a madness, until they did not know what things they were doing, and they killed the white chief and his men.

"In the morning they went out to the canoe and brought it ashore, took out all the food and more of that hot drink, and all the bright and shining things that the white men gave to our people for skins; and they took down the wings from the tree, for they thought these things would be good to put on their houses. Then when the canoe was empty they made a great fire and burned it; and as it burned they feasted and danced and sang in their madness.[150]

"Well, some of the Cowichans were out fishing and they saw the sky all red and bright and, not knowing what it could be, they went to look. There on the beach they found the Hwlumelhtsu dancing and making strange noises as though evil spirits were in them. Softly they paddled nearer, and there where the flames leaped high they saw the white men lying dead, and their canoe all broken and burning, with no trees, no white wings, all one big fire.

"When my people saw this they hurried back to Puneluxutth', where they told Xulqalustun their story. 'Let us go and punish these Hwlumelhtsu,' they said, 'for they have killed our good friends and have burned the canoe with wings!'

"But, as I have told you, my grandfather was a wise man. 'No,' he told them, 'keep away from the Hwlumelhtsu, for well I know that there will be trouble for any who have done harm to this white tribe.' And so he left the village, and in a few

Mary Rice and Beryl Cryer

days there came a great war ship—'Man-o'-War' my grandfather called it—with many, many white men, and the white chief came to Xulqalustun and talked to him.

"'Tell me,' he said, 'what do you know of those white men and their boat?' And Xulqalustun told him of his good friends the white men, and he showed the charm which he always wore about his neck to the white chief, telling him it could cut great trees and logs, and he told him that there was great sadness in the village, for the Cowichans had seen the burning of the canoe and the white men lying dead.

"'Well,' the white chief said to my grandfather, 'we have been to the Hwlumelhtsu village, and there we found food (flour) from the canoe, and on top of some of the houses were the wings from the boat. There we took seven men prisoner, but there is one more, and he is the chief of the village; he must be caught and punished with the others. You are chief here, and so you must come with us and help us find this last man; and until you come back no person must leave the village—all must stay here.'

"'I will come with you,' said my grandfather, 'for the Hwlumelhtsu chief is of my house, a man named 'Uxchewun,[151] and I know he is a bad and cruel man.'

"So the white men came off the ship and they carried the Cowichans' canoes far up the beach, and on every canoe they put a mark (number) and on the back of every man, woman and child they made the same marks, so that they could tell if any left the village.

"After this Xulqalustun said 'good-bye' to my grandmother and their two boys and he was taken out to the war ship, and all the tribe, with those strange marks on them, gathered on the beach and watched their great and wise chief go away to help the white men.

Now there were other men on the warship—taken by the white chief until the Hwlumelhtsu chief should be found. These were Chief Sihwoletse' from Valdez Island (who was later named O'Shea!),[152] and Hwulaamthat, and Quola-quoi (who were called Jacob and Joe!), and were from Kuper Island.

"Well, for two months they sailed and sailed all round the islands looking, always looking for that bad man 'Uxchewun. One day they landed at Stockade Bay, on Galiano Island,[153] and as he went along the beach, looking under trees and bushes for some tracks of the man, my grandfather found a canoe far back out of sight!

"Now Xulqalustun was a mighty hunter with eyes like those of an eagle, and very soon he found tracks in a clear place, and they were the tracks of a man, a woman and a child! Ah, how he shouted with joy, for he knew that 'Uxchewun had a wife and child with him. 'Oheeeee!' he shouted, 'Ah! Ah! 'Uxchewun, I will get you! Why have you killed my friends and kept me like a prisoner from my people and my home all these days? Now I have you, ugh! Ughhhh!'

"The white chief heard his shouts and came hurrying up, and, seeing the canoe and the tracks, he said to my grandfather, 'Good, we will get him now,' and he told his men to move out so and so (fan-wise), and in this way to climb up the mountainside. So they followed the tracks. Sometimes they were in soft mud and easy to find, then would come rock and no marks could be found. But my grandfather went first and his quick eyes found tracks now here, now there.

"The white men soon got tired, for they had never climbed in this way before, and they said 'Let us rest for a time and have some food.' But Xulqalustun waved his stick and shouted 'Come! Come! I Xulqalustun go to kill um!' and he would not wait.

"'Listen,' the white chief told him: 'You must not kill this man, the white men will punish him. It is law!'

"On and on they went, and now the men far away came closer, closer, until they had 'Uxchewun and his wife and child amongst them. Ah, but how tired and thin they were. Their hair hung over their faces and it was all hard and dirty, and they could scarcely walk. 'Oh-aaaaa!' shouted Xulqalustun, 'now we will kill you, Oh-eeeeeee!' But 'Uxchewun threw himself on the ground and tears were running down his face.

"'Ah, Xulqalustun,' he cried, 'do not kill me, for remember, I am of your house. Let the white men kill me, for, see, I am nearly dead now, and my child cannot walk for want of food!'

"Again the white chief told my grandfather, 'The man and his family must not be killed. If you kill these people, then you also must be punished; it is the white man's law!' So they turned and went down the mountain, Quola-quoi helping the woman, Hwulaamthat, carrying the child, and 'Uxchewun going with the white men.'[154]

"When they were all back to the ship they did not go to Puneluxutth', but sailed to the white men's village off Fort Victoria. Here they found all the Hwlumelhtsu held prisoner, and here Xulqalustun and those others stayed for many days.

"At last Xulqalustun and the others, with the Hwlumelhtsu tribe, were taken out to where 'Uxchewun stood with seven other Hwlumelhtsu who had killed the white men, and ropes were put about their necks and the white chiefs hanged them.'[155]

When all this was finished Xulqalustun returned to Puneluxutth', and for many days and nights talked to the Cowichans, and he told them that a good and wise man had told him many things, so that now he knew that wherever men who came from the great white chief across the water lived and made laws, there all would be cared for; but that no man must kill another, or, by the white man's laws, he also must die.

"And from that time Governor Douglas was a good friend to my grandfather, Pielle Xulqalustun, and every six months Governor Douglas gave him big presents of food, blankets and clothing for himself and his people."

Mary Rice and Beryl Cryer

Xulqalustun, Part III[156]

Mary Rice tells a story from her grandparents' time about an unsuccessful attack by Haida warriors on the village of Puneluxutth'. Following the smallpox epidemic of 1782 which depleted Central Coast Salish settlements, musket-armed northern people, who were unaffected by the early epidemic, began to raid the south. These raids increased with the establishment of Hwunitum' trading posts at Fort Langley in 1827 and Victoria in 1843. The story focuses on the bravery of Mary Rice's paternal grandmother Tliqwahwu'iit, who goes to extraordinary lengths to save her youngest children.

I HAD BEEN TRYING TO FIND OUT what age Siamtunaat might be; but like all the old Indians she is delightfully vague as to dates.

"Tell me," I asked her, "what can you remember, far—far back?"

"Ah!" She thought awhile, leaning forward, a knotted old hand on either knee. "Far back—far, far back I remember I see heads on sticks at Puneluxutth'." Again she sat thinking, her old eyes looking away back seeing, who knows what pictures passing before her.

I waited in silence, hoping for another of her stories from out of the dim past. At last it came.

"When my grandfather Xulqalustun was chief of the Cowichans—just a young man—there was always fighting, for the Cape Mudge Indians and the Haidas from Queen Charlotte Islands used to come down in their great war canoes and fight our people.

"They would kill our men and take the women and children back to their villages as slaves, and there they had to work very hard, and were treated very badly.

"Well, one day my grandfather and my grandmother—her name was Tliqwahwu'iit; they called her 'Polly' later—and their two little boys went out to Cowichan Gap (Porlier Pass) to fish for salmon and halibut. They had not been fishing very long when a big dogfish cut my grandfather's line, and away to the bottom went his good hook, made of hemlock knot, that he had finished steaming and bending that very morning.

"Ah! But Xulqalustun was mad! 'My good hook has gone,' he said. 'We had better go home; it is no use staying out here if I have nothing to fish with.' So they turned the canoe round and sadly paddled towards their village of Puneluxutth'.

"The sun was high in the sky; it was very hot, and they were paddling slowly, quietly along when—'Stop! Ah! What is that?' They listen, listen—and soon a noise came along the water, very softly—only the Indian's good ears could have heard it.

"My grandfather raised himself in the canoe and he looked far away, as far as the eye could see; and so they waited, listening, looking. Suddenly Xulqalustun pointed. 'Canoes!' he said. 'War canoes—coming swiftly! Paddle quickly, quickly, the Haidas are coming!' Ah! How they paddled! And always they could hear the sound of the fierce Haidas' paddles growing louder and louder as their war canoes swept through the calm water.

"As they got close to the Puneluxutth' beach, Xulqalustun gave a loud cry and all the braves came running down to meet them.

"'The Haidas are here!' he called. 'Many canoes filled with fighting men. Send your women and children into the woods and tell them to stay hidden until we have killed or driven away these men!'

"And now the chief and his men painted their faces and put on their feathers and, taking spears, bows and arrows waited for the coming of the cruel Haidas.

"At the same time the women were hurrying about, gathering dried clams and deer meat into baskets, wrapping their babies in soft cedar bark, and taking skins and blankets to cover their children. Then, when all was ready, slipping away into the dark woods behind the village, so that when the Haidas came to the shore all was quiet; no women or children left.

"My grandmother had four children at that time, three boys and one girl, and these must all be hidden.

"Now Xulqalustun had told her of one good hiding place, so she took cedar bark that she had soaked and beaten until it was soft as cloth, and this she put about the smallest boy and bound him on her back. In with him she put some dried fish and clams; then, carrying her little naked baby girl in her arms, she started off, followed by the two boys, each with a bundle of dried clams in his hands.

"On through the dark woods she hurried until she came to a great big cedar lying on the ground. Very carefully she pushed aside the bushes and there was all one side of the tree hollowed out. In this place she put the two boys, but there was no room there for her and the two little ones; so on she went searching for another hiding place.

She was not far from the beach when, clearly, the wind brought to her the shouts of the Haidas. In her fear she ran—how she ran!—until she came to the water. Not far away was another island (Thetis), and feeling that she would be safe there, she stepped into the water. Then she stopped; for how could she swim with the baby in her arms? There was no time to wait if she would save herself and her babies; so, reaching behind her with one hand, she put the wee boy's arms around her neck and then, taking the baby's little shoulder in her teeth, she started her swim across to the other island.

"I remember my grandmother telling me how the baby on her back (my uncle) laughed when he felt the warm water on his fat legs as she waded out; and my aunt often showed me her shoulder with the marks still on it where my grandmother's teeth went deep into the soft flesh as she carried her.

"It was not far to the island; but it must have seemed miles to that poor woman. At last she dragged herself up on the rocks, where she rested and washed the blood from her baby's shoulder; then off she set to find a hiding place.

"For two days she stayed on that island, feeding the little boy with the clams she had brought, but taking little herself, for she was too full of fear and too sad, wondering what happened to her husband and her two boys to feel the need of food.

"All the first day she heard the shouts and war cries of the Haidas and of her own people; but the second afternoon all was quiet; yet she was afraid to leave her hiding place, and there it was that Xulqalustun found her.

"Oh! But he was glad to see her and their two babies.

"'Come,' he said. 'The Haidas are gone. We have killed their chief and many of the men. Come and see!'

"'Where are our boys?' asked my grandmother. And Xulqalustun told her how he had hunted through the woods when the fighting was finished, calling, calling, and how the little boys had crawled out from their hiding place and had run to him.

"'They are waiting for you,' he said. 'Come.' He put them into his canoe and took them back to the village.

"My grandmother told me that all along the point that is called Puneluxutth' Spit, there were stakes driven into the ground, and on every stake was put the head of a Haida. That is where I, too, saw heads on sticks; but the ones I saw were not so old; they were taken in some later fighting.

"Later on, when Xulqalustun had been to Fort Victoria and had learned white men's laws, and the good priests had talked to him, he would sit and think of all the men he had killed and of all the heads he had cut off and put high on sticks, and he would be sorry, and cry, and cry, and he would talk to the Cowichans, telling them, 'Never, never must we do these things again!' And as he told them so have they remembered, for he was the wisest chief the Cowichans ever had."

Xulqalustun, Part IV[157]

Beryl Cryer probably started work on this article by February 4, 1932. In a letter she wrote to William Newcombe on that date, she describes her recent discovery of a collection of old photographs of native people, and a single framed image of the Roman Catholic Bishop, Modeste Demers, hanging on the wall in the Indian Agent's office in Duncan.[158] At the top of the group was a picture of Mary Rice's grandfather. The photographs belonged to a Mrs. Dwyer, who was the daughter of the local Indian Agent, William Lomas, who served in the area from 1881. Cryer had copies made of the photographs, and gave one depicting Xulqalustun to Mary Rice. When she receives the photograph, Rice tells Cryer how her grandfather died of grief over the death of his daughter.

Unfortunately, at the outset, Cryer makes derogatory remarks about the appearance of the aged Puneluxutth' warrior in the photograph (taken circa 1882), which reminds us of the cultural and racial superiority the majority of Anglo-British Columbians felt over native peoples at this time.

"I HAVE HAD A LUCKY FIND!"

Some time ago I asked Siamtunaat whether she could remember what her grandfather—that old chief of the Cowichans, and hero of many of her tales—looked like.

"Ah, yes," she replied, "I know—long, long ago (must be fifty years, because Xulqalustun died about forty-six years ago), Mr. Lomas, the Indian Agent, took a picture of him; Oh a nice picture!" She clasped her hands as though in ecstasy at the recollection. "He fix his blanket, so, and his legs and arms are all bare. Oh, it is a nice picture!"

"Have you got one?" I asked her. She shook her head. "No, not me; my brother, Tommy Pielle, you know they call him 'Sugar Tommy'? he has one, on Kuper Island." She thought again. 'I know, I think I saw one at Duncan, in the Indian Agent's office. You go there, they will show you." I thanked her and hurried off to get in touch with their office.

Upon making inquiries, I was told that there was a picture of Chief Xulqalustun, but it was in a frame with a number of old-time celebrities, the whole being the property of a daughter of the late Mr. W. Lomas, first Indian Agent at Duncan.

I was most kindly given permission to make use of these photographs, and last week visited the Indian Agent's office and carried off my first "find" in triumph.

Such quaint characters are pictured here, each with a short description under each; but how I wish that there were some dates!

Occupying a place at the top is "Chief Hul-ka-latksun, first chief to entertain Roman Catholic missionaries in the North Pacific." How old was he, I wonder? This pathetic old figure draped in his blanket! It is hard to realize that this is the same

Xulqalustun of Puneluxutth'. Photo by William Lomas, circa 1885.
Image PN 5922 courtesy Royal British Columbia Museum.

mighty warrior who, with face painted and feather headdress, led his band of Cowichans against the ferocious Haidas, taking fierce pride in the number of heads he could obtain to hoist on sticks about his village; and who many years later became that "friend of Governor Douglas" repenting of his evil ways with bitter tears.

Next came "The Right Rev. Bishop Demers, Roman Catholic Bishop of British Columbia."[59]

In the centre is a very ancient withered old couple, brother and sister, sitting before their house of woven rushes, their blankets about them. "Tokw'at and T'ulkun, Somenos Indians." Their faces have looked out from many a picture postcard.

Then comes "Ce-Who-Latza," that Valdez Island chief who sailed with Hul-ka-latksun on the "Man-o'-War" in the search for the Hwlumelhtsu murderer. He is resplendent in naval uniform, possibly a souvenir of his voyage.

"Lohar, chief of the Comeaken band,"[60] also in uniform and "wearing a medal presented by the Governor-General for special services."

A "Group of Indians at a Quamichan Potlatch" (in which every possible style of headgear is depicted), taken many years ago.

"The first Kuper Island Industrial School Band," with the late Rev. Father Donkele, who will live long in the hearts of the Indians."[61]

There is a group of three men, whose names are not recorded. Under this picture is written, "Indian constables, Quamichan Indians."[62] One I know is Constable Tom, who did much good work with the Provincial Police many years ago.[63]

From this paragraph one learns that the truly fashionable wore the top button only of the coat fastened, allowing the garment to hang well open, thus permitting full view of waistcoat and watch chain.

"Micheal Cooper, chief of the Songhee band, Victoria." And another of "Michael Cooper's wife and sister."

Last but by no means least, is a dignified but extremely disagreeable looking old gentleman sitting on a box, resplendent in an ancient pair of trousers, a long coat many times too large for him, a scarf knotted about his neck, tall silk hat, and bare feet. It is Chief Kom-Quil-Ache of Qhwimux.

I have given Siamtunaat a copy of her grandfather's photograph. She was delighted with it.

"Ah, the poor old man," she said. "He was very, very old, but he was strong, stronger than many young men. Would you believe that a man as old as that could live for two months without any food, only a little water to drink?" I admitted that it did not seem possible. She laughed triumphantly. "No? Well Xulqalustun did that thing. He was older than that picture when his daughter, my aunt, died (You know, the one I told you about who was carried in my grandmother's teeth, when she swam away from the Haidas?)

"He liked that daughter very much, and at first no one told him that she was dead; then his son took him to where she lay, and told him that she had been killed.

He looked at her just once, then he went into his house, lay down on his bed, and there he stayed.

"Not once did he eat, only sometimes he would drink a little water, and every day he went down to the sea and washed himself, for he was a very clean man, always washing. Every day he got weaker and weaker, at last he could not walk but had to crawl to the water's edge like a little baby.

"All his people tried to make him eat. 'You will die if you have no food,' they told him.

"'Let me die,' he said, 'It is what I want, now that my daughter is gone,' and he would crawl to his bed, turning his face from all food that was brought him.

"Then one morning he did not wake, and, when they went to look at him, he was dead." For several minutes she rocked her body to and fro, holding the picture in front of her and gazing at it from different angles. "Uh-huh, a very nice picture," I heard her murmur.

"Where did they bury Xulqalustun?" I asked her.

"At Puneluxutth', out past the village," she told me. "He was buried the Indian way—you know, with a little cedar house over him."

"There were others buried in the same place, and long after when white people came and camped on that beach, Father Donkele talked to all the Indians and told us that it would be better if all the graves were moved up the hill. So the people gave money to Father Donkele, and he got some men from Duncan to come and dig graves and to move all the people from the little cedar houses where they had been put many years before. My brother Tommy Pielle and I, we gave fifteen dollars and the day the men moved Xulqalustun's bones we went and watched.[164] Next time I see you I will tell you of something we found buried under the cedar house with my grandfather. I think no other people know of this; but I will tell you for your story. Very carefully she wrapped her precious picture in what I imagine was her handkerchief; then, gathering her shawl about her, got slowly and laboriously to her feet, and with a nod and a smile, went on her way.

Xulqalustun, Part V[165]

Mary Rice tells the story of transferring the grave of her grandfather from its beachside location to the Roman Catholic cemetery on the hill above the village. She describes the remains of a "counting ball" found among the grave offerings.

Yesterday I paid a special visit to Siamtunaat, for I was curious to learn what it could be that was found buried with her grandfather Xulqalustun under "the little house of cedar" at Puneluxutth'.

I found her in her house busily carding wool, for she is an industrious knitter. Siamtunaat lives alone—that is when she is not overrun with relations—on the beach, in a house built for her by her son.[166] The house consists of a kitchen and two bedrooms partly partitioned off. The kitchen walls are neatly papered with newspapers, and it is spotlessly clean, but smells strongly of smoked fish and oil, but I did not care to look in those bedrooms. Where she puts the endless relations when they come to stay I cannot imagine.

It required a good deal of tactful manoeuvring before I managed to lead the conversation into the right channel; for this was one of Siamtunaat's "off" days. She was full of woe. Long rambling stories of the follies and frailties of members of her family (and their name is legion), poured from her, and I had almost given up hope of a "story" when I happened to notice the picture of Xulqalustun, that I had given her, propped up against a cup on the table.

I leaned over and picked it up, and my hostess "bit" immediately.

"Ah!" she sighed deeply, "that nice picture!" "You were going to tell me," I began, when she interrupted, "I know, I nearly forgot. I will tell you how my grandfather made balls—counting balls. But first I must tell you what no one knows! Of the time the Indian graves were moved away from the beach at Puneluxutth'.

"Well, I think I told you before, how Tommy Pielle, my brother, and I, we paid $15 for men to come from Duncan and move our grandfather's bones to the new grave.

"Father Donkele told us that all relations must be there to see the work done. So one day Tommy Pielle and I went over to Puneluxutth' with Father Donkele, and we sat on a log on the beach and watched the men work. First they took away the little cedar house that was over my grandfather, and then they dug a little way.

"Very soon they stopped. 'Come and look!' they called out. 'What's this?' We went up to the grave and looked, and there we saw a funny thing."

She paused, like the true lover of the dramatic that she is.

"Well, all the ground where they had dug was covered with little white balls— so—(measuring half the nail of her little finger)—and some bigger. Ah, so many! Every time the men dug, their shovels had lots and lots more of these white balls.

Mary Rice and Beryl Cryer

"Father Donkele and I picked some up and looked at them. I tried to break one with my nail but it was too hard. 'They look like some kind of bean,' said Father Donkele. 'What can they be?' 'I think they must be beans,' I told him, 'but how did they get here? And so many—there are bags and bags full!'

"Now, Tommy Pielle had not talked much; he was thinking. By and by he began to laugh. 'I know what they are!' he said. 'They are the counting balls. Don't you 'member, when they put our grandfather here they put his balls for counting with him? That's what those things are!' And he sat down on the ground and laughed and laughed.

"When he told me, of course, I 'membered too, and I began to laugh to think that Father Donkele and I had called those things beans!"

"At the recollection of this tremendous joke Siamtunaat forgot the last of her woes, and rocked back and forth, shaking with laughter.

"But what were they?" I asked, "and what were Xulqalustun's counting balls?"

"Ah!" she exclaimed, highly delighted that she had aroused my curiosity. "Now I will tell you.

"Many, many years ago, when Xulqalustun was Chief of the Cowichans but a young man, he was very fierce and a great fighter; he killed lots and lots of people. Well, then, when he sailed to Fort Victoria on the man-o'-war, a good man, the priest, talked to him and told him what a bad man he had been, and that he must not kill any more people. My grandfather liked that priest, and after that all priests were his friends. There was one good man, called Father Rondeau,[167] who used to come to Puneluxutth'. Ah, Xulqalustun did like that man! Often he used to come and talk to the Cowichans. One day he told my grandfather he would teach him to count the days and the weeks and months. Xulqalustun was very pleased, for then he would be able to tell what day his friend Father Rondeau would be coming.

"First the priests told my grandfather to get a lot of pieces of willow bark, and on these he tied knots.

"Sunday came first—that was a big knot, tied about six times over, I think. Then came six little knots, tied three times over, one for each day. Then another Sunday knot. When he had made four Sundays, and the little knots in between, there came a very big knot, for that was a month. Xulqalustun was, oh! so pleased with this, and he never forgot; no matter what he was doing, every night he got his willow bark and tied a knot, and he rolled the bark as I roll my wool for knitting, into a ball. No matter where he went, he took his counting ball; when the ball got so big it was hard to wind, he put it away and made another. I can 'member when my grandmother was an old woman she made counting balls too, and so did my mother, but they used sacks. They would pull the sacks to pieces and tie the pieces of strings, making their balls in that way. Xulqalustun made these balls for many years, until he died, and all those big balls he kept; he would never throw any of them away.

"When he died we thought, 'What can we do with all these balls of willow bark?' We did not like to burn them, so we put them with my grandfather in the little house of cedar. The bark between the knots has broken and gone, but the hard knots that my grandfather tied so long ago in the days when Governor Douglas was at Fort Victoria, they are all there, for all those little white things we thought were beans were the hard knots he tied to count with."[168]

"What did you do with them?" I asked.

Siamtunaat held up her hands and raised her eyes to the ceiling.

"Ah, such a time we had, Tommy Pielle and I! We picked them all out of the earth—every one—and, oh, my back did ache! Then when the men moved my grandfather's bones—just as they were with the crucifix in his hands—we put all those little knots in the new grave with him. We could not throw them away, for he had always said that they must be kept.

"Your grandfather must have been a very old man when Mr. Lomas took his picture," I said. "How old was he, do you think?"

Siamtunaat thought a while, then shook her head.

"I can't say, but I know he was a very, very old man when he died, and I know that my mother was more than one hundred when she died—we live a long time!"

She took the photograph of Xulqalustun from the table and looked at it for some time in silence.

"Ah, such a good man!" she said. "And always such a good friend of Governor Douglas!"

Xulqalustun, Part VI[169]

Mary Rice narrates an account of a Puneluxutth' war expedition to Cape Mudge and tells of the hardship of those Puneluxutth', including her grandfather, who were forced to make a perilous return journey.

I WAS PASSING SIAMTUNAAT'S COTTAGE THIS MORNING, when she called to me from the window.

"My brother Tommy Pielle, is here, and we have 'membered one more story about our grandfather Xulqalustun, that you never heard before." I ought not to have stopped, but could not resist hearing a little more of the old Cowichan Chief of whom she is so proud.

Tommy Pielle opened the door to me and, I was glad to see, left it open, as the stuffiness in the little kitchen was almost unbearable. Siamtunaat dusted off a chair and pushed it towards me, picked up her knitting from the table, drew her chair closer to the stove and, having settled herself comfortably, began the story at once.

Kom-Quil-Ache, the Qhwimux leader who assisted Xulqalustun after the Puneluxutth' attack on the Yukw'ulhta'x. Image PN 5921 courtesy Royal British Columbia Museum.

"You know," she said, "another day I told you how the Haidas came to my grandfather's village of Puneluxutth' to fight? Well, this time I will tell you how the Cowichans went away to fight the Cape Mudge people, and what happened to my grandfather, and why always after that time his foot had a hole in it and he could not walk quite right.

"Now, before this, the Cape Mudge Indians had come to a Cowichan village when the men were away, and had carried off many of the women and children— they were not Puneluxutth', but other Cowichans. Well, the Cowichans said, 'We must fight these people and take their heads.' So one night more than thirty great war canoes filled with the best fighters—twelve men in each canoe—gathered at Puneluxutth'. All the men had on their hats of feathers and paint upon their faces, and in the canoes were spears and bows and arrows. At Puneluxutth' my grandfather, Xulqalustun, was waiting, and that night there was great feasting and the men sung of how brave were the Cowichans, and how many heads they would carry back with them after fighting the Cape Mudge people.

"Next day all the village was awake before night came. The Puneluxutth' painted their faces, and put on feathers like the other Cowichans, all the canoes got together, and as light came into the sky and the ducks flew out from their nesting places to feed, away the Cowichans went, singing the war song of the tribe.

"My grandmother and all the women and children sat on the shore and watched their men leave, not knowing whose places in the canoes might be empty when they came home.

"Well, there they went, their paddles dipping all together, making the great canoes move through the waves, and the wind blowing the feathers on their heads as though they were waving to the women left behind. My grandmother told me that the wives sat there nursing their babies until the last canoe was gone from sight and all that was left them was a little of the war song coming back on the wind—and soon that, too, was gone.

"Oh, it was a big fight! But my grandfather did not see much of the fighting, for, quick, like that (here Siamtunaat blew violently), a wind came, such a wind as you never saw! And it blew the canoes all ways. The canoe with Xulqalustun and eleven other men was blown away from the others and, seeing this, the Cape Mudge canoes started after them. Oh, how they paddled! They could not turn, for the waves were too high, but kept on and on, leaving the other Cowichans far behind, and always following after them were the three canoes, for the men could see a chief's feathers and they wanted Xulqalustun's head badly.

"Now it was night and very dark. The wind blew and rain came, but still the Cowichans kept paddling. They could no longer hear the canoes chasing them. 'Wait a little,' said my grandfather, 'wait and rest,' and as he spoke—ah! Ah! The canoe hit a rock under water and broke in two pieces!

"My, how those men had to swim! Xulqalustun 'membered where the shore would be, and as he swam those high waves he called to his men: 'Keep together and come after me!' And in that way they all got safely to the beach.

"There on the rocks they lay, all wet and cold, and too tired to move. What were they to do? Their canoe and all their fighting things were lost. Only two things were left them. One man had a knife of stone, and another had the Kwatakwata."[170]

"Siamtunaat," I interrupted, "what is the Kwatakwata?" Tommy Pielle, delighted to get a chance to air his knowledge, answered for her. "That's the name of the fire thing!" he said, "the cedar sticks they make fire with. See," he added, "the man holds two sticks in his hands—so—and rubs, rubs them very quickly on the little dish that has cedar bark made very soft and small, and when he rubs, he says 'Kwatakwata!'—till fire comes." He looked to Siamtunaat for approval of his description, but she ignored him, none too pleased, I fancy, at his interruption.

"Now," she said, "the man had his Kwatakwata well wrapped up in cedar bark, and when he took off the bark the cedar sticks were quite dry.

"'We must not make a fire here,' said my grandfather. 'We must get far back in the woods where no man can see us.' So early, early, before light came, they started off, Xulqalustun going first and his men coming behind.

"All that day, they walked, eating a few berries that they found, but not stopping to light a fire until they were far back from those other Indians. Then they made a fire and ate some fern roots which they found. For thirteen days they kept back from the shore, always walking, walking through the thick bush, and oh! they got so hungry and thin for they had no food. My grandfather told me that one man had a shirt made out of the skin of a deer, and he took that off, held it in the flames of the fire to burn the hair off, then cut it in pieces and gave a piece to each man to chew.

"Well, Xulqalustun knew that if they did not get to the beach, where they could find food, they would die, so he led them down and down until they could see the water. Then he told them to gather long pieces of willow bark; 'If we make strong ropes of this bark, we will be able to make a raft with logs which we will find on the shore.' When they got to the beach, the water was far out, and taking sticks, they dug clams. My, how hungry they were! They ate and ate those clams until they could eat no more, and then they lay on the sand, and taking the willow bark, they rubbed and rubbed it and twisted it until they had made a thick, strong rope.

"Now they began putting the logs together. It took a long time, for they were weak and tired, but at last the raft was finished.

"They pushed it out on the water and they all got on it, then taking poles for paddles they started off, when, 'Listen! What was that?' Ah! From far away came shouts and the sound of a war song—the Cape Mudge Indians coming in their canoes!

"Ah, these poor men! All that work for nothing! Back to the shore they went, and back, back into the woods.

"That day they came to a river, and at the edge of the water found burnt sticks and some bits of fish and bones, where Indians had been eating. Ah, they were so hungry; they took those bones and sucked them, and all the little bits of fish they ate.

"Well, on they went, climbing along the bank of the river when suddenly my grandfather gave a great 'Ah! Ah!' and his men saw him fall. Quickly they ran to him and found that he had jumped on a broken branch and the sharp wood had gone right through his foot! Oh, what pain he had when they took his foot off the stick. They helped him to the water, and there he washed the blood away, and taking moss from a maple tree he put it in the hole, put more moss on the foot and tied it up in a piece of soft cedar bark, then, leaning on a thick stick, he started off again.

"'Now,' my grandfather thought, 'it is foolish going further up this river; we must get to the other side.' So they swam across and went on climbing through the bush.

"Poor Xulqalustun's foot was very sore and swollen. 'Go on,' he told the others, 'I will follow slowly,' but not one would leave him. One day they came to a lake,[71] and there, pulled up on the shore, they found a raft! Oh, they were glad to see that raft, but it was too small to hold so many men. Xulqalustun and three men got on it and they paddled to the edge of the lake, and then they waited for the others who walked along the edge. At the end of the lake was a river, and down that they went until they came to the sea again.

"The first thing they saw was a dead seal on the rocks, and quickly a fire was made, and, cutting the seal into pieces, they cooked and ate it. My grandfather washed his foot in the sea water, put new moss in the cut and tied it up again. On they went along the beach, and it was not very long before they came to Qhwimux (Comox). My! The Qhwimux Indians were surprised to see them! Their chief Kom-Quil-Ache, gave them a lot of dog salmon, and a big canoe to go home to Puneluxutth' in. And after resting for a day they paddled away to their home.

"Oh they laughed and sang with joy when they got to the village. But what was wrong? Why did no one come to welcome them when they shouted? With hearts filled with fear they went from one house to another. All was quiet, the houses shut and empty, no one in the village. Xulqalustun and his men stood and looked at each other and they thought, 'Can it be that the Cowichans were beaten? and the Cape Mudge people have carried away all our women and children?' Then Xulqalustun looked at the trees and at the grass, and he began to laugh.

"'I know,' he told the others, 'I forgot we have been away so long. This is the time for the salmon. Everyone has gone to Hwts'usi!'

"You see," Siamtunaat explained, "every year the Puneluxutth' went to Hwts'usi—what you now call Bonsall's Creek—for salmon. All day they would catch them and would dry them before the great fires in the village.

Mary Rice and Beryl Cryer

"Well," she continued, "they got back into the canoe, paddled around Kuper Island, and then over to Hwts'usi'. It was quite dark when they got there, and as Xulqalustun went near one of the houses he heard a woman crying. He looked inside the house but it was dark.

"'Why are you crying?' he called.

"The woman answered, 'I cry because my husband is lost.'

"'What was your husband's name?' asked my grandfather.

"'He was the Chief, and he was called Xulqalustun,' replied the woman, still crying. 'But who are you? You must be a stranger that you ask me these questions?'

"'Come outside and I will show you who I am,' Xulqalustun told her.

"The woman, still nursing her baby and crying hard, went to the door, and, taking her arm, Xulqalustun led her up to the fire.

"'Look at me,' he told her, 'and see who I am!'

"Ah! My poor grandmother! How happy she was when she found it was her own husband beside her! All the camp was wakened, the other men found their families, and all got busy making food ready for those poor men. Then they all had to tell of everything they had done and of all they had seen. 'And did you see the heads we have put up?' Xulqalustun was asked. 'No,' he told them. 'When we found the houses were empty we came quickly to find you. Tell me, how many men have we lost in the fight?' 'Only two,' they told him, 'and they were your brothers; but as you have all come safely home again, maybe those others will come one day!'

"Well!" Siamtunaat leaned forward and spoke in an impressive whisper. "Can you believe it? About New Year's Day the Puneluxutth' had a big dance and that night the moon was round, and bright like day, and the water was far out. Some of the people, looking out from the dance house saw something on the sand, far away.

"'What is that?' asked one.

"'It looks like a man, two men!' said another. 'See, there is a canoe at the edge of the water!'

"So they stood watching, and soon more and more came out from the dance to see what those outside were looking at. Then two men walked up to where the people stood, and the moon shone on their faces, and they were my grandfather's two brothers!

"Well, my grandfather told me how all the Puneluxutth' shouted with joy. The dance stopped, and soon all the people were sitting round the great fires while the two men told their story.

"After the big wind had come a lot of the Cowichans got to land, where there was great fighting. These men were the last to get out of their canoe, and as they stood up ready to leap from the canoe, Cape Mudge Indians hit them on their heads and, thinking they had killed them, left them lying in the canoe, not waiting to take their heads. When the men woke up it was dark and the canoe was far out on the water. Taking their paddles they paddled all that night, not knowing where they were, and in the morning found they were in strange water, with no food and nothing to drink.

"Well, all that day they paddled, and then another great storm came and blew them along until some time in the night they were thrown up on a lot of rocks, where they lay like dead men. In the morning their canoe was gone and there they were—lost!

"For weeks they lived on the beach, hiding, and looking for enemies to come, but in all that time they saw no people. Then they began walking along the beach, on and on, until at last they came to Si'she'lh [Sechelt]. There they hid in the bushes, and watched, trying to think how they could get away from that place.

"One night one man said to the other, 'I know what to do; come with me!' Still keeping in the bushes, they went to the place where the people put their dead in canoes among the bushes. 'We will take one of these canoes,' said the man, and then went about looking at the canoes, trying to find a good one, but they were all badly broken. At last they found one that only had a big crack along one side, and, tipping the dead man and his things out on the ground, they carried the canoe away along the beach until they were far from Si'she'lh.

"Now they got busy. They got a lot of pitch from the trees, and for nine days they worked at the canoe, fixing the place where it was broken. Now it was finished and, taking a lot of clams to eat on the way, they started for Puneluxutth'.

"When the men had finished their story the Puneluxutth' made a great feast and danced and sang all the night; and my grandfather, Xulqalustun, danced, and he made a song which he sang to his people, telling how fine and brave the Cowichans were, but that the Puneluxutth' were the finest and bravest of them all."

Siamtunaat's Recipe[172]

Mary Rice is recovering from food poisoning after eating a large plateful of steamed camus bulbs at a gathering in Esquimalt. The publication of this article, on May 29, 1932, and its reference to a camus feast, matches the timing of the traditional camus harvest when families would locate to their fields in the Gulf Islands and harvest the bulb. Large amounts of the delicacy would be cooked and served at gatherings such as the one Mary Rice attended. A detailed description of traditional camus preparation is discussed (hence the title) followed by Mary Rice's humorous recollection of her first experience with bread and butter, and her mother's introduction to the use of flour by an early female settler on Salt Spring Island.

I HAVE LEARNED A NEW RECIPE and I am going to pass it on for any who wish to use—if they feel equal to it!

I had always imagined that the Indians prepared their food in the easiest and quickest manner possible, but the most intricate recipe in my cook book fades into insignificance when compared with this one told me by Siamtunaat.

But first I must tell you that Siamtunaat has not been well.

"Oh! Such pains!" she groaned, as though still feeling the agony of a week ago. "My son Charlie's wife[173] and their girl, they rubbed me all night. Oh, I was sick!"

I registered sorrow and made groaning sounds on a smaller scale in sympathy. "What was it?" I asked. "Had you caught a bad cold?" "A cold!" Her look of agony changed to one of derision. "No, not that! Worse than a cold. You see, we had all been to a big dance at Esquimalt, and I ate some Indian food. I can't do that anymore. Charlie said to me: 'Mother, why did you eat that stuff? You know Indian food always makes you sick?' I told him, 'Well, they brought me a big pan full and it looked so good I thought I would try a little;' but oh! how bad I was!"

She rocked herself back and forth at the recollection of the pain.

"What Indian food did they give you—fish?" I asked.

"No, not fish; they gave me ly-camas—a big pan full."

"You mean that blue flower that comes in the Spring?—camas?" I asked her. She nodded quickly. "Yes, that flower—some say camas and some ly-camas. The Indians dig up the root and eat it."[174]

"Tell me about it, Siamtunaat," I begged; "is it nice?"

"Ah, yes; it's nice—sweet, very nice and sweet."

"How do you cook it?—do you boil it?" This amused her intensely.

"Boil it? No! I'll tell you how to cook it, then maybe, sometime you can try!" She laughed once more as though at a huge joke.

"Who knows?" I thought. "Ly-camas may prove to be a delicious dish, although it seems a sin to dig up the roots of these beautiful flowers. But I am always keen to learn a new recipe, so I waited patiently whilst Siamtunaat collected the ingredients and arranged them in correct order in her memory.

"Well, now," she commenced. "First you have to dig the ly-camas. I think some time in May is best. The Indians dig lots and lots and put it away to use when, maybe, they have a dance and plenty of people to feed. Now I'll tell you what to do when you want to cook it. First you make a big fire and put lots and lots of smooth stones to get hot in it. Then dig a hole in the ground—very deep—as high as you, I think."

"Now," continued Siamtunaat, in the impressive tones that all good housewives use when giving their favorite recipe: "Now you must get busy. Pick about two sacks full of salal, and two sacks of that nice green fern (sword fern), and a lot of fir boughs. Then you want a bucket of water, a long pole, and the ly-camas you are going to cook. When all these things are ready and the stones are very, very hot, carry some of the stones and put them all over the bottom of the hole."

Siamtunaat was thoroughly interested in her recital now.

"When the stones are in, take the pole and stick it up the middle of the hole, then put in the ly-camas. Now on top of the ly-camas pour in some salal, then some hot stones and more salal. After that put in the ferns with hot stones in the same way, and on top put the fir branches. When all these things are done, you must put lots of earth over everything."

"And now it is left to cook, is it?" I suggested helpfully. Such a look of scorn she gave me.

"No, no! there is more to do before it can cook," she explained. "Now take away the pole, very carefully, so that the earth does not fall down the hole, and pour in the bucket of water; then fill up the hole very tightly with dry moss, so that no steam can come out. Now it's down there cooking, but it takes a long time to cook, and must be kept hot, so get a lot of sticks and logs and make a big, hot fire on top of everything, and that fire must burn for two days and two nights!—and then the ly-camas is ready to eat. But, ah!" She clasped herself and drew in her lips, as though again feeling the spasms of pain racking her body. "Never again can I eat it, never again! Now I can only eat your kind of food—Indian food makes me, oh, so sick!"

"But you haven't always eaten our food, have you?" I asked. She began to chuckle, in a quiet way, to herself.

"I can 'member," she said, "long ago, when I was a little girl, I came with my father, in his canoe, over here to Chemainus. My father had some ducks and deer meat for a white lady living here. Well, we paddles all the way from Kuper Island, and we landed on the beach where the lady lived. My father carried the meat up to the house, and I took the birds. I 'member the lady was very nice to me, and when we left she gave me a big piece of bread. I knew what bread was, for my mother made a kind of bread, and we had some white men's things for food. The priests had given my mother potatoes and some seeds of cabbages, pumpkins, and carrots. But on this slice of bread the lady had put something. I did not know what it was and I didn't like the look of it, so I took a stick and tried to scrape it off. It had gone down into the bread and I couldn't get it all away, so I threw the bread on the beach."

Siamtunaat laughed at the recollection. "And now," she said, "how funny it is. Now I must always have some butter on my bread, and it makes me sick to eat Indian food."

She settled herself more comfortably in her chair, rearranged the handkerchief about her head, and her eyes grew dreamy. I knew that look. She was "going back"—searching the storehouse of her memory for something. Suddenly she laughed, and the large silver brooch fastening her shawl rose and fell tumultuously.

"I know a very funny story about my mother I will tell you," she said. "It's about the time my mother first saw flour."

"One day my father and mother (they were called Solomon and Siamtunaat: my name is same as hers)[175] had been out fishing and had caught a lot of salmon. It was very early, not much sun showing yet, so my father said, 'Let us go to Saltspring Island and trade these salmon for some things. There was a lady on Saltspring Island who used to trade with my people, giving them nice vegetables and clothes for salmon. So off they paddled, my mother taking a load of salmon in a basket up to the house. The lady was very glad to see so many fish, and said to mother: 'I'll trade you some carrots and cabbages and some flour for all these fish.'

"My mother thought that sounded good, so she nodded her head, and while the lady took the salmon into the house, she went to the garden, where they got the vegetables. She walked about looking at everything. There were the cabbages, and the carrots, and some other things, like onions, and pumpkins, that she knew the names of, but there were no strange vegetables there; where was the flour that the lady had said she would trade? She walked all around the garden again, looking, looking, but there was nothing that could be flour, so she walked round to the other side of the house, and there she looked at everything, but not a thing could she find that would be good to eat. Then a thought came to her. 'Perhaps the lady had stored them in the house!' So she went into the kitchen and there she looked in boxes and under the table. She even opened a door into the pantry.

"The lady had been watching her, wondering what she could want. At last she said, 'What are you looking for, Siamtunaat?' 'You trade me flour,' said my mother. The lady nodded her head. 'Yes,' she said; 'I'll trade you vegetables and a little flour.' My mother pointed out the window. 'There cabbage, carrot,' she said, 'but no flour!' Ah! But the lady did laugh! 'You funny girl,' she said; 'did you think flour grew in the garden? Wait, I'll show you.' She went into the pantry and brought out some flour in a spoon. 'See!' she said, 'that's flour!' She held out the spoon, and my mother took it, smelt it, and put some in her mouth!

"Oh, such a time they had! Poor mother, with all that dry flour in her mouth, thought that she would die! She coughed and choked, and then—she couldn't help it—she spat it onto the lady's clean floor. My, how the lady did laugh, and the more she laughed, the worse my mother choked. At last she saw a bucket of water in a corner of the room. She ran and took a big, big drink, and after that she felt better, but she was, oh, so mad with the lady for fooling her like that. She began to pick up the salmon, to leave, when the lady stopped her. 'No, no, Siamtunaat,' she said, 'come with me and I'll show you what to do with flour.' She took my mother by the hand and led her into the pantry. There she opened a box and took out a loaf of bread. She cut off a piece and put into her mouth, and gave a piece to mother. My mother often told me she had never eaten anything so good as that bit of bread. She chewed and chewed it and did not like to swallow it, for it was so good.

"'Now come,' the lady said, 'and I will show you how to make bread.' She showed my mother how she made bread and cooked it, and mother tried to learn, but it seemed very hard to her. She laughed and nodded and said 'Yes, yes,' but I don't think she understood much.

"When she left, the lady gave her a lot of vegetables and about three pounds of flour in trade for twenty salmon. My mother did not use the flour for a long time, she was afraid she would spoil it, so she put it away. Then one day the priest brought her some flour and showed her how to make bread and to cook it in the ashes, and after that she often had bread—not the kind I make, she just mixed her flour with some water and then put it in the hot ashes to cook. When it was done she scraped off the ashes, washed it and dried it, and put it away. I 'member when we were chilrun how good we thought that kind of bread was, but now"—she sighed and shook her head—"now, I s'pose I couldn't eat even that! Never again can I eat Indian food!"

Siamtunaat's Potlatch[176]

A photograph of a stl'un'uq ("potlatch") at Kwa'mutsun inspires recollection of a memorial stl'un'uq held by Mary Rice and her family at Puneluxutth' to repay the men who helped her bury her second husband, George Rice, who died in 1895.

WE HAD BEEN TALKING OF INDIAN CUSTOMS and I had turned out a lot of old photographs to show Siamtunaat. She was very interested, and clucked her tongue and grunted with delight as she examined them.

"Ah, Ah-hhh! That's good," she exclaimed, picking out one of a potlatch. "That's like my potlatch!"

"Your potlatch?" I asked her. "Did you give a potlatch, Siamtunaat?" She nodded and smiled broadly, evidently delighted at being asked.

"Yes, yeeeesss! Long ago I had a fine potlatch. Now the 'Govment' won't let us have potlatches. They tell us we make ourselves too poor. Now we can only have dancing and singing."

"Tell me about your potlatch, Siamtunaat, will you?"

Siamtunaat loves to talk. She is never happier than when she is telling stories of the Indians for, although she often speaks in a condescending manner of "those Indians!"—on the strength of having once been married to a white man—yet I know that at heart she is true Indian, and tremendously proud of the fact that her grandfather was chief of the Puneluxutth', of the Cowichan Tribe.[177]

Mary Rice and Beryl Cryer

A stl'un'uq (potlatch) at Kwa'mutsun, circa 1912. A copy of this photo, in Beryl Cryer's manuscript, is marked "RBH," the initials of her father, Richmond Beauchamp Halhed.

Image PN 1455 courtesy Royal British Columbia Museum.

For some time she sat turning over the pictures, saying nothing, but I could tell that she was thinking, putting her thoughts in order before beginning her story.

"You know," she began, my first husband was an American Indian. He came from Hwmuthkwi'um, and when he died, thirty-five years ago, I had all my little children and not much money. What was I to do?[178] Now you see, when one of our people die, the 'Govment' pays for the funeral. But my husband did not belong to the country, so the 'Govment' said they must send him back to the States—they could not bury him. Well, I felt so bad! I never ate, I never slept; all day I just cried, for what could I do? I did not want him to be sent to the American side.

"Then Tommy Pielle came to me and he told me that some of my good friends were going to bury my husband, so the 'Govment' need not pay, and the 'Govment' said that would be alright. So my brother Tommy Pielle, Reuben Johnstone, Johnny Peters and another man—I forgot his name—they all dug his grave and buried him.

"Now always after that I kept thinking, 'Those men did that for me and they must be paid back,' but I never had enough money to pay them.

"Well, many years after my second husband was dead, and all the children were grown up, I said to my son Charlie, 'Charlie,' I told him, 'Do you know that I never paid any money for your father's funeral?' Charlie said, 'Is that so? What'll you do about it?' and I told him, 'Charlie, we must have a potlatch!'

Siamtunaat drew herself up and made this statement with the air of a dowager duchess announcing that she would hold a reception.

"So we got to work.

"First Tommy Pielle and Charlie called all the people. From Esquimalt, from Saanich, from all the Islands, everywhere, right up to Nanaimo, no one was forgotten; they called them all to our potlatch.

"Oh, such work we had! So much to do! So much to think about! You know Tommy Pielle and me, we have a big house at Puneluxutth', the biggest house over there. More than eight hundred people can go in it. It is the same all ways (square) and it is high, high! with two holes in the roof where the smoke goes away; and all round inside there is a high place (raised platform), where the people put their things and where they sleep.

"Well, in that house we had our potlatch.

"First, Charlie bought a new canoe—he paid twenty-five dollars for it and, oh, it was a nice one. Then I got a big picture made out of my husband's little picture, and I put it in a good frame. I got some cloth to give away, and, well! What do you think?"

She leaned nearer to me and lowered her voice confidentially—

"I went to the store and I got nearly two hundred yards of cloth, and I only paid five cents a yard for it! Me and the girls cut it up into pieces, two and a half yards in each piece, and that took a long time.

"Then we bought cups for the people to use—oh, the cups! (She threw up her hands, and closed her eyes at the thought of those cups.) Tommy Pielle, he bought six hundred and we got more! And pans—oh, so many pans! At another store we bought ten double blankets to give away; and of course we gave lots of money—I forgot how much, but it was a lot. One man at Kwa'mutsun, he had given me five dollars at his potlatch, so I gave him the same money back, and a woman, Michell's wife, she had given me two and a half dollars and a blanket when they had a potlatch, and I gave her the same back—all the people who had given to me at their potlatches, I gave back to them, and so I was square.

Siamtunaat leaned back in her chair with the contented and virtuous manner of one who has paid her debts and owed no man, but, could that be so?

"Now, you see," she continued, "all those people were coming, and we had to give them lots of food."

"How long did a potlatch last?" I asked.

"Well, some longer than others. The people stayed for a week at our potlatch. And my! the food they ate! Tommy Pielle killed three of his heifers, and Charlie got seven hundred ducks—"

"Seven hundred, " I exclaimed. "Siamtunaat, whoever shot them all! and who took all the feathers off and got them ready to eat?"

How she laughed. "Oh!" she chuckled, "those feathers! Me and the girls we pulled and pulled until there were feathers all over the place, but we got them finished and all ready to eat. Lots of the men helped Charlie shoot the ducks. All his friends came and helped.

"And now"—she drew the shawl about her shoulders and settled herself in her chair—"now I must try and 'member some of the things we got from stores. First, bread. There were eleven hundred loaves of bread. Thirty boxes of hard biscuit. Six sacks of sugar. More than seventy pounds of tea (we gave each woman one pound when she came), fifty boxes of apples and fifty boxes of oranges. And potatoes! There were lots more things, but I don't 'member them."

I sat speechless. How much had this entertainment cost them? They must have spent every cent of their small savings and run heavily into debt besides. No wonder the 'Govment' has vetoed a custom by which entire families beggar themselves for years to come.

"I suppose the people brought their own blankets?" I asked her.

"Oh, yes!" she said, "they all brought blankets, but I gave every family a nice new rush mat. It took all my clean mats!"

"Well, we got everything ready at Puneluxutth'. Charlie carried the new canoe into the big house, and he took a blanket, and he made my husband's picture sit on the blanket in the canoe.

"Now all the people began to come—in canoes, in boats, they kept coming all morning. Some had started very early, before it was nearly day, and they were tired and hungry. When they had all come there were more than seven hundred, men, women, and chilrun. Oh, those chilrun! There were chilrun everywhere!

"First they had dinner, and then Charlie held up the picture and told all the people that we were giving the potlatch to pay for his father's funeral. After that Tommy Pielle carried the picture round and showed it to everybody, and told them how my friends had buried my husband because he was an American, and now I was paying them back. Then we gave the money and the blankets."

"How did you give the blankets?" I asked her. "Did Tommy Pielle throw them to the people, as I once saw the Indians at a Kwa'mutsun potlatch—throwing blankets from high platforms?"

Siamtunaat shook her head. "No, we have no high places to throw from at Puneluxutth'," she said. "Charlie and Tommy Pielle carried the blankets outside and threw them at the men we wanted to give them to; and Emma, my girl, took the cloth and gave a piece to every woman.

"When the giving was finished we had dances. Great fires were made—five fires in our one house! and there we danced and sang. Oh! It was a good time! We who danced put paint on our faces, and some had big faces to wear, and hats of feathers, with clothes!—such fine clothes, you should see. Beads and feathers, and shells, all very fine!"

"And did you dance, Siamtunaat?"

"Me? Me dance?" She looked at me incredulously, and I felt that I had indeed made a faux pas as she got laboriously to her feet, then, with hands clenched in front of her, elbows held tightly against her sides, she swayed violently from side to side. "Yes! Yes! I dance!" she exclaimed, as she stamped her old foot on the ground and beat her fists together.

"I put paint on my face—some black and a little red—and I hold the rattle you see in my picture, the rattle that my grandfather made. And then I dance, dance!"

I could picture it all—the huge roughly-built cedar lodge, with the five great log fires blazing down the centre, the flames lighting up the lower portion of the lofty room, with those seven hundred Indians sitting round on their raised plat-form, the reds, blues and many-hued dresses and shawls making bright spots of colour against the rough walls, darkened with age and smoke from countless such fires. In one corner the "musicians"—men sitting alongside a board raised on two logs, on which they kept up a monotonous and regular drumming, whilst up and down and around the fires stamped and swayed a figure, her white hair uncovered and hanging loosely about her shoulders, face painted in curious markings of black and red, and shaking her crude rattle, the prized possession of her family—Siamtunaat, the civilized, once married to a white man, who can no longer eat "Indian food," but who at heart is surely true Indian.

The Wedding of Ellen and Jimmy Joe[179]

Mary Rice had advised Beryl Cryer she would describe Puneluxutth' marriage ceremonies to her, but when Cryer arrives, Rice is away. Instead, she records an account by Tommy Pielle of a conflict between the Roman Catholic missionary priest and two of his uncles over the issue of polygamy. He then describes the 1901 "arranged" marriage between Mary Rice's eldest daughter, Ellen, to Jimmy Joe, son of Joe and Jennie Wyse of Nanaimo. "Upper-class" marriages were arranged between families of similar social standing. As Loraine Littlefield points out, the ceremony documented by Cryer is similar to those described by Franz Boas twenty years earlier, but with the introduction of a second ceremony, a Christian marriage, and with it the opportunity to distribute even more wealth.[180]

WHEN I WENT TO THE BEACH THIS AFTERNOON I found Tommy Pielle building a fire in front of Siamtunaat's house.

"Cleaning up," he explained with a grin. "I'm staying here but Siamtunaat's away today."

"I'm sorry," I said. "I had hoped to hear a story she had promised to tell me."

Tommy Pielle's eyes lighted eagerly. Here was his chance. "Sit down," he invited, pointing to a very damp log, "I can tell you stories just as good as my sister." He piled more wood upon the fire and stood, hands deep in pockets, with his back to the leaping flames.

"See now," he began, "has my sister told you about the time the priest got mad with our uncle because he had so many wives?"

"No," I said, "she was going to tell me about an Indian wedding today."

He laughed happily. "Oh, that! I can tell you just as well, but first I'll tell you about my uncle; it'll make you laugh."

"Now, I had two uncles, there was Swilhultun, and Sts'althun. Swilhultun had five wives but Sts'althun used to change a little: sometimes he had two and sometimes he had four wives. Well, you know, after the priests had come to this land, and had talked to the Indians, they told them all kinds of things, so that all the Indians 'got religion.' They used to sing and pray all the time, but they still kept all their wives. Bye-and-bye, when the priests knew them better, they told the people that it was not right for a man to have more than one wife, and that every man must send away all his wives, keeping only one.

"At first, there was a lot of trouble about it, but my grandfather, who was Chief, was very good friends with the priests, and he told the Puneluxutth' that they had to send away their women, and after a time everyone did this, except my uncle Sts'althun. At that time he had four wives and he would not send any away. One day the priest went to see him and he talked and talked, but it was no good.

"'No!' said my uncle, 'I need all these women. There is lots of work to be done. Go away,' he said, 'I am an Indian and I want my four wives. You are white, and you have not even one.' And he would say no more. 'Some day,' the priest told him, 'you will be sorry. I will wait for that day.'"

Tommy Pielle roared with laughter. "Now, see," he said, "here is where my uncle got fooled! You see, he had three nice young wives and one very old one: he kept her because she did the work that the others left. Well!"—he paused dramatically—"in two months those three young wives got sick and died, and all he had left was the old one! My, he was mad! 'That priest was right,' he said. 'He told me I would be sorry—and I am. If I had known these girls were going to die, I would have sent them all away and taken the most beautiful girl in the village for my wife. Now I am left with this old one, and I have to keep her and not take anymore!' Well, when he saw things like that would happen if he did not do as the priest told him, he 'got religion' too, but he had to keep his old wife until she died. The priests would not let him send her away."

Tommy Pielle shook with laughter and poked the fire vigorously with a long stick.

"Now," he announced, "I will tell you about the time Siamtunaat's eldest girl got married. My! It took a lot of money, but we had a good time. Well, at that time Siamtunaat was working over at Chemainus, but her children lived at Puneluxutth'. There was a Snuneymuxw man living at Puneluxutth' called Jimmy

Joe, and he liked the look of Siamtunaat's girl Ellen. Bye-and-bye he told me he wanted to marry her. Well, after we had talked about it a bit, I sent to Chemainus for my sister, and she paddled over in her little canoe to see about the wedding.[181]

"She talked to Jimmy Joe and he said he was ready to marry, so my sister and I, we called all our relations and some of his to come to the wedding.

"The first day of the wedding Jimmy Joe's father came to Kuper Island, and he brought ten big boxes of biscuits to give away to the relations when they came.

Now, in the middle of our great house is a very big post. Well, Jimmy Joe's father brought an old-fashioned Indian blanket—made of mountain goat hair—and he folded this blanket and put it on the ground against the post.

"At one end of our house we made a big fire where Siamtunaat and I sat down. Well, about five o'clock in the afternoon in came Jimmy Joe and sat down on his father's blanket by the post, and there we were, sitting beside our fire—no one else in all the big house! All night Jimmy Joe sat there saying nothing. In the morning I called to him and he came over and sat at our fire, and I went over and got his blanket, folded it again, and put it in a corner by our fire for him to sit on. There he sat for all that day and all that night. Next morning—it was Easter Sunday—and lots of people were at Puneluxutth', all the friends and relations came into our house and Jimmy Joe took up his blanket and went back to his post.

"Now all this time, Ellen had been in the house with the other children, and had not seen Jimmy Joe. When everyone had come into the big house, Ellen came in. My! she looked nice. She had a fine new dress on, and her hair all washed and hanging loose over her shoulders, and an Indian blanket round her.

"Now I took the things Siamtunaat and I had to give to the Snuneymuxw people. There was one Indian blanket, and twenty double blankets, and I folded them and put them in two piles. Then Ellen came from our fire and she sat on one pile of blankets, and Jimmy Joe came from the post and he sat on the other pile. Now Siamtunaat called out to all her relations, and she said: "Twenty blankets are not enough for Cowichans to give to the Nanaimo people! See, I will give ten dollars!"

"Now," said Tommy Pielle, importantly, "Now I got up and I called out, 'See! More must be given for a Snuneymuxw man. My sister and I will each give ten dollars!' So now all the relations began to give and soon we had $100 to give, and a lot more blankets. And Jimmy Joe's father, he gave $100, too.

"Now they were married, and Ellen went with the women to get ready to go away. Ten women got all her things and packed them; some packed her clothes, some her dishes, and some her blankets and other bedclothes. And all the time there was Ellen sitting and crying, making oh! such a noise! I had killed my fattest cow and all the meat had to be packed, too. They had a big boat full of things to go to Nanaimo.

"Well, that was the Indian wedding, and they went off to Nanaimo to live. When they got there Jimmy Joe's father called all the Snuneymuxw people and made presents to them all. First he gave away the cow meat, then all the blankets."

"Do you mean to tell me that those blankets weren't for Ellen and her husband?" I asked.

"Oh, no! These were presents to Snuneymuxw people from Ellen's relations and from Siamtunaat and me," he replied with pride.

"But the money?" I asked.

"Oh, they kept the money, and Ellen, she kept her bedclothes, and dishes—those things were for her home, but the other things were for the Nanaimos, because she was a Cowichan and had married a Snuneymuxw man.

"Well," he continued, "that Indian wedding was at Easter, and now the priest told us that she must be married in the church, too, so just after Christmas everyone came to Puneluxutth' to see Ellen and Jimmy Joe married again.

"This time all the Snuneymuxw Indians and from away up to Comox came too—more than four hundred people. Siamtunaat and I got one hundred sacks of flour, and seven hundred ducks, and we took them over to Puneluxutth' for the wedding. Well, Father Donkele married them in the church, and Ellen had a new fine dress, and Siamtunaat, she had a new skirt and shawl. After the wedding we gave away all the flour and ducks to the Snuneymuxw people, and then everyone went over to Jimmy Joe's big house that he had at Puneluxutth' for a dance.

"Oh, it would make you laugh to see those people from Nanaimo and Comox dance. Their ways are not like ours, and they look very funny when they dance—like this."

Tommy Pielle—who might have been the original "Old Bill"[182]—put his feet together, held his hands palms outward, with arms slightly raised, and commenced jigging quickly up and down, from the knees, turning his body from side to side without moving his feet, smiling all the while in a foolishly sentimental fashion. It was quite the funniest exhibition I have ever seen, but funnier still was the miraculous change that suddenly came over his face. The smile faded, the jigging ceased abruptly, and Tommy Pielle stood staring over my shoulder.

I turned and saw Siamtunaat coming down the trail. With a muttered remark about "getting more cleaning done," Tommy Pielle faded away and I started off to meet Siamtunaat.

"I came to hear your story Siamtunaat," I greeted her, "but your brother was just telling me that you were away. May I come tomorrow and hear one?" Instantly her face was wreathed in smiles. "Tomorrow," she said, "yes, come tomorrow; I think I will tell you about some of our doctors medicine men, you call them."

I thanked her, promised to go early and hear her story, and hurried homeward, hoping that Tommy Pielle would have the good sense not to let her know that he had usurped her place for the afternoon.

Medicine Men—Indian Doctors[183]

As promised, the next time Beryl Cryer visits for a story, Mary Rice is ready to tell her about the practice of the shne'um, shaman, or "Indian Doctor."[184] She tells of her own experience with a female shne'um, followed by descriptions of two other healings, one she witnessed personally.

"TODAY," SAID SIAMTUNAAT, "I will tell you about our Medicine Men, the Indian doctors. Now these stories are quite, quite true. You may think the things I am going to talk about could not happen, but our Indian doctors know better than the white doctors, and I will tell you why that is."

She drew her chair nearer mine and leaned forward confidentially. "Your white doctors learn what they know out of books," she said. "But the Indian leaves all his people and goes away back in the mountains until he comes to some stream. There he stays, with no food, no place to sleep, only the water to drink and to wash himself with. All day and night he sings and shouts and washes his body. He has nothing to eat and he gets tired and thin, but still he sings and washes. Then one night, he's lying by the water; it's very dark up there, with the high rocks and tall trees all around him, and everything so quiet, only the little stream running, running over the stones.

"Well"—she lowered her voice to an impressive whisper—"there he lies, and after a long time he hears a Voice calling, calling. Listen! The Voice calls again, and now he calls back, and gets up and begins to sing and dance, splashing the water over his body and then, waiting, listens again.

"Now he hears the Voice near him, calling from the air! No one can ever tell what that Voice is, but it talks to the Indian and tells him everything, and he learns to do things that no other people can do."

She held out her arm and pointed to a scar on the withered old wrist. "See that mark?" she asked. "Now listen, and I will tell you how that came."

"Long ago, when I was a young woman, I used to go to ladies' houses to do washing for them. One day I was washing a dress, and a needle that had been left in it broke, and went right into my thumb. Right in it went; nothing could be seen of it. Oh, such pain I had, and the lady told me, 'Don't wait. Go quickly to the doctor!' Well, I put on my shawl and drove to a white doctor in Duncan. This man cut my hand and made it bleed a lot, but he could not find the needle. Next day my hand and arm were swollen and very sore. Then someone said, 'Why don't you go to that Indian woman who can suck sickness away? She will take that broken needle out for you.'

"I had forgotten about that woman. She was a good doctor, and had made lots of our people better. At that time she was working in a cannery at the Fraser River,

A Hul'qumi'num (?) shne'um ("Medicine Man"), mid-nineteenth century.

Image PN 7530 courtesy Royal British Columbia Museum.

so my husband took me over there and showed her my arm. It was so bad now I could not move it, and all black, like a burnt stick.

"The woman felt my arm all over, then she put her finger here, where this mark is. 'The needle is here,' she said, 'I can take it out for you.' 'What must we pay you?' asked my husband. Well, the woman looked at it and thought a little, then she told us, 'thirty dollars and thirty blankets will be enough.' 'Too much,' said my husband, 'we can't pay that,' and we got up to go. 'Wait!' the doctor called, 'I will take it out for twenty dollars and twenty-five blankets!' That was better, so we talked a little more, and at last she said that for twenty dollars and twenty blankets and two shawls, she would make my arm better.

"First she got a basin of warm water and a clean dish. Now she turned back her sleeves and washed and washed and washed my arm in the water, and all the time she was washing me, she was singing, sometimes very loud and quick, sometimes slow, slow, and so quiet that we could not hear her.

"For a long time she did this, then she put her mouth on the place where she said the needle was, and for a little time she sucked hard, then out on the dish she spat the broken needle! And in two days, can you believe it, my arm was quite well again, only this little mark left!"

Siamtunaat leaned back in her chair and chuckled heartily. "There is a very old man in Victoria now," she said, "who can suck away things like that; and long ago my husband had a relation who was a very, very good doctor. She lived at Kwa'mutsun, and she could take away sickness by pulling it out, and could suck away things, too."

"I 'member there was a man living at Xwulqw'selu who got two grouse bones stuck in his throat. My, how sick he was! All his friends tried to get the bones out, but they were too far down. At last they got the white doctor to come and see him. Well, that man pulled his mouth open and he looked inside. Then, do you know what he did? He put some 'big iron scissors' right down that poor man's throat, and tried to cut out the bones, but he could not find them—only cut the poor man and made him feel worse.

"Now the man was nearly dead—just lying in his house trying to get a little breath—when in came the Indian doctor.

"'What does that woman want here?' asked the white doctor. 'She can't help him: he's about dead now.'

"A white man who was watching said, 'I've seen this woman work and I bet ten dollars she'll get the bones out.' How that doctor laughed. 'Alright,' he said, 'I'll bet you ten dollars she won't: all her work is just a trick!' The woman doctor heard this, and oh! she was angry. 'A trick?' she called; 'I'll show you there is no trick!' and there, in front of them all, she took off her dress. 'Now,' she told him, 'see, my arms and neck have nothing on them. Now, come close while I work, and watch me.'

Mary Rice and Beryl Cryer

"She told the men to carry the sick man outside the house and to bring her a basin of warm water and a plate. 'Hold the plate,' she told the doctor, 'I will not touch it.' She dipped her hands in the water and rubbed the man's neck very, very carefully. 'Here are the bones,' she told the white doctor, 'right through here.' She put her mouth to the place she had touched and sucked, and sucked. All the people pushed close to see what she was doing, but no one spoke one word when, suddenly, the man gave a little cry, ah, ah! Like that, and, leaning over, the woman spat a sharp, crooked grouse bone on to the plate the doctor was holding. Again she sucked, and then on to the plate she put another little bone!

"For a little time the man lay very quiet, then he moved his neck, opened his mouth and sat up, twisting his head about quickly and coughing a little. Then he began to laugh. 'It's gone!' he called. 'It's gone! I'm well again!'

"The woman took a cloth and washed off some blood on his neck and, taking hold of the doctor's arm, she pointed to two small holes in the man's neck where the bones had come out, then, laughing at him, she went away to put on her dress."

Siamtunaat leaned forward, a hand on either knee. "I can tell you that white doctor had no more to say," she laughed. "He paid his ten dollars to the man who had bet with him, and went away as quickly as he could."

Here Siamtunaat fumbled amongst the many folds of her voluminous skirts and produced a handkerchief, with which she proceeded to polish the precious silver brooch she uses to fasten her shawl.

"You know," she said, "the trouble is, our Indian doctors ask too much pay." She breathed gustily upon the brooch and continued her polishing.

"Now a very, very clever doctor lived at one time at Kuper Island. His name was Tsilamunthut.[185] Ah, he knew all things! Why, when my sister who lived on Saltspring Island[186] got sick so that all one side of her could not move, we went to her house, carried her to the boat and took her to Puneluxutth', on Kuper. Then we got this Indian doctor. He came early in the morning, and all that day and night he sat beside her, hitting his drum and singing, and sometimes dancing a little.

"Next morning he called for warm water, and with this he rubbed her, and with his two hands he pulled and pulled, until he had taken out the sickness."

"Siamtunaat," I interrupted, "how did he pull the sickness out?"

"Well,"—she drew her chair up to the table—"he put his hands like this, one by her neck and one by her leg; then he slowly rubbed them along until they were near together. Now he shut his hands quickly, and pulled hard, and all the time he was singing, singing—and that day he made her better!"

"Do you mean to tell me he made her quite well?" I asked.

She nodded her old head gravely. "Pretty nearly better," she said. "She got up and she could walk a little, but he could not make her quite well—we could not pay enough."

"What did you have to pay him for that?"

She thought a moment. "He just came the one time," she said, "and we gave him twenty dollars, thirty blankets, a lot of plates and dishes, and two best shawls for his wife. Ah! That man was rich! He made people pay all they had, but he was a good doctor—the Voice had told him many things that other doctors did not know."

"And your sister was always able to walk after that?" I asked her.

"Not always," she replied. "She got sick again, and we took her to a doctor at Nanaimo. He said she had the 'rheumatiz' and he rubbed her, and very soon she was quite well and never was sick again."

"Are there many Indian doctors about here now," I asked. She shook her head, "None so good as that Tsilamunthut, but he is dead now. He was a very bad man and he was killed. Maybe some time I see you I must tell you how that same man made old Louis Chuhaasteenxun come again alive after most people thought he was dead. That is a story that no one knows, and I will tell you of the 'Thing' that no white people have ever seen!"

She pinned on her shawl with the shining brooch, and having once more discovered her pocket, tucked her handkerchief safely away and hobbled off to prepare her evening meal.

The Healing of Louie Chuhaasteenxun[187]

An elderly man who appears to be dead is revived by the famous shne'um from Kuper Island.

"YOU WERE GOING TO TELL ME MORE about your Indian doctors," I reminded Siamtunaat, as I drew my chair nearer to her little stove. There was a hint of storm in the air, and the warmth of Siamtunaat's kitchen was decidedly comforting after the drizzling rain outside.

The old woman was busy with her knitting and did not answer for a few moments, as, in some mysterious manner known only to herself, she counted her stitches and arranged them on the needles.

"Now," she said, when they were set to her satisfaction, "This story that I will tell you, is about something that no white people have ever seen—something that comes to help the medicine men!" She looked at me seriously as she spoke, and I nodded in silence.

"Long ago," she said, "a man called Chuhaasteenxun lived down at Hwts'usi'. The priest gave him the name of 'Louie,' and when he got old he was always called 'Old Louie.' Well, when this man was about twenty years old he went out one day to get some wood and he didn't come back! His poor mother looked and looked for him, and at last she found him lying under a tree—dead! She pulled him into the house, put him on his bed in the corner, folded all his blankets and piled them on top of him—as my people always do when anyone dies—and then went out to call all her relations. Now this was very long ago, when the priests had first been teaching the Indians, and they had all 'got religion.'

"All that night the woman and her relations sat around the man's bed and prayed and sang what the priests had taught them. Next day, just when light first began to come—I don't know what time it was, because none of my people had clocks in those days—the old mother saw Chuhaasteenxun's hands begin to move! Soon breath came back to him and he sat up: all the folded blankets falling off him to the ground.

"'Mother!' he said, and held out his hands, 'I've come back, God doesn't want me yet!'"

Siamtunaat paused dramatically.

"Now listen to this!" she said. "That man was never sick again until he was quite an old man; at that time I was a young woman, working here in Chemainus, and one day a man called me to go to Old Louie Chuhaasteenxun's house because he was very sick—'nearly dead,' the man told me. When I got there all the relations and friends were singing hard, and waiting for Tsilamunthut, the Indian doctor from Kuper Island."

"Very soon this man came, all dressed up in his coat of deerskin, with beads and skins of mink all over it. His face was painted red and black, with a little white, and he had, oh, such a nice hat! made of mink skins, with lots of little heads and tails and the mink's 'fingers' hanging down from it; and he carried two drums and sticks.

"Well, this man went into the house, and everybody went in, too, until no more could get inside. It wasn't a very big house, and Old Louie was lying on a bed in the middle. His head was hanging back and he was quite stiff, and it looked as though he must be dead, but in one place we could feel a little breath coming and going.

"Now when the relations went into that room each one took a little board and a stick, and now, some sat on the ground, some had to stand, and all were hitting their boards and singing and shouting; and over by the bed, Tsilamunthut began to sing and dance.

"Quicker and quicker he danced, and he got his sticks and hit Old Louie's hands: then he started pulling the sickness out of him, pulling, pulling with his two hands, and some men got the drums, and they hit the drums louder and louder: and still Old Louie just lay there!

"For five days everybody stayed at that house: some going out to sleep, some going in to sing and hit their bits of wood, and Old Louie never moved; He wouldn't live, and he wouldn't die! My! his wife was angry! She got so tired of all the noise, she said, 'Oh, he's dead enough, someone make a box for him!' but

Tsilamunthut told her, 'No one must make a box until the breath has all gone out of him!'

"At last Tsilamunthut got tired, too, and he called out, 'Has anybody got a slhuxun'?"[188]

"What is that?" I asked.

"Ah!" said Siamtunaat, "Not many white people know about that, but I will tell you. A slhuxun' is a long piece of cedar bark like that" (she pointed to a towel hanging from a nail in the wall). "But it's about two yards long, and it is cleaned and beaten very, very soft—like cloth."

"An old, old woman sitting by Louie's bed said she had one, and she went to fetch it. Now," here Siamtunaat lowered her voice. "Here is the story that I think none of our people have ever told before! But it is quite, quite true—I have seen this thing other times and this day we all saw it; but no white people could ever see it."

"Now listen to me! That old woman soon came back with her slhuxun' and gave it to the medicine man. Tsilamunthut took it and held it up high in front of him. 'Sing,' he called to the people. 'Shout loud as you can!'

"Oh, such a noise there was!"

"What did you sing?" I asked her. "What did your words mean?"

"Well, we had no words," Siamtunaat replied. "We just did what Tsilamunthut did. Suppose he shouted, 'Ah! Ah! Ah!' we all did the same, and if he called 'Hi! Hi!' all the relations called that, too.

"Now he held the slhuxun' in the middle, with his two hands, and pulled them to the ends very quickly; many, many times he did this, and, as he pulled the slhuxun' began to shake all over, soon it was shaking quicker than you can move your hands—just as though he had made it come alive! Then he took hold of one end and twisted it round in the air, ah, so quickly! and, do you know?"

She lowered her voice to a whisper.

"It came alive! Round and round it went in the air, until it made a large flat thing like a big plate. Tsilamunthut put one hand under it and slowly he rubbed his other hand all over the top. When he did this it shook harder than ever and began to grow and move about, changing, changing, until it turned into some kind of animal! It had a little head and ears standing up like the ears of a deer, only they were very long, and there were two legs with a long, long tail hanging down. Not for one minute did this thing keep still, it was shaking all over and its legs were moving—just as though it were dancing!

"'Now!' called the medicine man. 'This thing is ready to look and it will tell us if the man is going to die or if he will get well. If he is going to live the thing will show us in how many days he will wake and be well!' He took hold of the thing's tail and turned it up like this (forming a loop) and where he put it, there it stayed, stiff like a piece of wire. Then he called two big, strong men, and told them to hold

Mary Rice and Beryl Cryer

its tail. At first they didn't like to touch it, but after a bit they each took hold of it, like holding a big ring, so the thing was hanging between them.

"'You must do whatever this thing wants you to,' Tsilamunthut told them. He began to hit his chest and to sing and sing: the drums got louder and louder, and we all hit our boards and sang like the medicine man! And now the thing began to pull! At first the men were so frightened they tried to pull back, but they could not hold it, and Tsilamunthut called, 'Go where it takes you.' So, as it pulled, they followed, each holding by one hand to the round tail, and the thing going in front as though it was dancing in the air!

"Right up to the bed where Louis Chuhaasteenxun lay it went; and when it got there the thing pulled their hands down until it could stand on the blankets. For one minute it stood quite still on the blankets, and Tsilamunthut put up his hands for everybody to be quiet, then, very quickly it danced up the blankets, pulling the men with it, one on each side of the bed, right up to Old Louie's face. Now the thing put its hand down and sort of felt all over the face, and put its ears close to Louie's mouth. There it listened, keeping very still. When it had finished listening it turned round and, back to the end of the bed it danced; stood still one minute, and suddenly jumped high up in the air! Up it went as high as the men's arms could go, then down it came to the bed again, and danced a little bit.

"'Ici—one,'[189] said Tsilamunthut. He spoke in a very small voice, but everybody heard him, the people were so quiet, no one moving or taking much breath as the watched what the thing would do.

"Again the thing jumped, and the men had to reach their arms up and up until they were nearly breaking. Then down it came, but not to the bed this time; it fell on to the floor and Tsilamunthut whispered 'mox—two.'[190]

"There it lay on the floor and—" Siamtunaat looked about the room, her eyes filled with awe, as she whispered, "There—it—died!"

"Still everybody kept very quiet, in all that room there was no sound. Tsilamunthut went over and picked up the slhuxun', stroking it a little bit and then gave it back to the old woman.

"'Now, listen!' he called in a loud voice. "That thing has shown us what will happen to this sick man. It went up two times—you all saw that? And that means that in two days he will get well."

"Of course," said Siamtunaat, with a vigorous nod of her head. "No one could say anything, but it seemed funny! Old Louie looked dead and he acted like he was dead! but the thing had shown, and we must do as Tsilamunthut told us.

"For two more days everyone waited, and not for one minute did they stop singing and hitting their boards.

"All the first day Louie was dead, and his old wife got madder and madder. The next morning he was dead, too! but in the middle of the afternoon his eyes opened! and he looked round at all the people hitting with their sticks and singing.

Tsilamunthut was by his bed dancing hard and singing and, Oh, my! Would you believe it? That Old Louie Chuhaasteenxun sat up in his bed and he laughed and this is what he said:

"'Well, I've come back to you! I saw God, and he said to me: 'Go back to that land down there for twenty more years!'"

Siamtunaat waited a moment after this amusing announcement, then speaking in an impressive voice: "And do you know, Old Louie got up and was quite well, and after that he lived for just twenty more years, and then he died!"

"Siamtunaat, is that story quite true, every bit of it?" I asked her. Such a look of incredulity that I should doubt her appeared on her old face, that I felt quite ashamed of my question.

"True?" she exclaimed. "Yes, it's all true, every word. Why, I saw it all; with my eyes I saw everything as I have told you! Oh, didn't I tell you that our Indian doctors know more than your doctors? No white man could make a thing like that one I have told you about come to help him; but our men can do anything—that voice from the air tells them how to do all these things."

"How much did Louie have to pay?" I asked.

"Well." She thought a while. "I can 'member some of the things he paid. There was one horse, fifty dollars cash, five blankets and Indian blankets, and a lot of baskets and shawls. All these things and more Louie paid for his life for twenty years."

The End of Tsilamunthut[191]

Mary Rice concludes her stories of shne'um with a graphic account of sorcery and a revenge killing. According to Pamela Amoss, "there are many stories from this period [late-nineteenth to early-twentieth century] of the murder of arrogant Indian doctors by the outraged relatives of their victims."[192]

I FOUND SIAMTUNAAT SITTING on her doorstep and looking very sorry for herself, when I went to her cottage this evening.

"It's my legs!" she explained. "Oh, they're so bad I can hardly walk!" She held up a foot in a large carpet slipper, and drew aside her skirt to show me her poor old legs swathed in cloths from which some peculiar green substance was oozing.

"It's the rheumatiz, I guess," she said. "I put this stuff on, but it doesn't do much good."

"What is it?" I asked her.

"This? Why its 'erbs—I boil them and put them hot on my legs. By and by I'll take them off, and when my legs are dry, I'll rub some coal oil on them."

Mary Rice and Beryl Cryer

"And do you think that will make them better?"

She shook her head doubtfully. "Well, that's what they tell me," she said. She limped into the kitchen and brought me out a handful of new leaves and shoots of the elder tree. "These are the 'erbs that I use," she explained. "They're good for lots of sickness." She settled herself once more on her doorstep and I found a box nearby for myself.

"Siamtunaat, do you feel well enough to tell me one of your stories?" I asked her.

Immediately the smiles came back to her old face, and her earrings danced again and again as she nodded her head emphatically. "Oh, yes!" she exclaimed, "I been 'membering about the time that old Indian doctor Tsilamunthut was killed, so I could tell you. That man was very, very bad, as you know. Oh! He killed so many people! If he didn't like anyone, he would put something like a snake or a fish in them, and they would die!"

She patted her poultices tenderly, as she continued. "You know I told you that my father's father was Chief Xulqalustun of the Cowichans? Well, my mother's father was that old Chief Quyupule'ynuxw, [193] who everyone knows about. When that grandfather of mine got to be an old man he was so sick that his people sent for the medicine man Tsilamunthut to see whether he could make him better.

"For a long time he had not been very good friends with my grandfather and, instead of making him better, he pointed fingers at him, putting something inside the poor man, so that he died. Not long after that a man called Tommy Moses sent for Tsilamunthut to come and see his old father who was sick, and he killed that man, too! Then a whole family on Valdez Island got sick, the father and mother and three children and, what do you think? that bad man killed them all.

"One day me and my husband had just come home from hop picking and we were eating our supper on the beach at Puneluxutth'. We had made a fire and were roasting some deer meat, when this man Tommy Moses came along. He was a very good man, kind to everyone and all the people liked him. He came and sat down to have supper with us. By and by he said to my husband, 'George, is Tsilamunthut a close relation to you? Because I want to tell you, he's killing too many people. He killed my old father, and as soon as I get a chance I'm going to kill him!"

"I said, 'Ah, Tommy, don't kill him! it'll make trouble for you.' But he wouldn't change. 'No,' he told us, one of these days I'll kill him!'

"Now Tommy Moses had one boy. Oh, such a nice boy! Big and tall, and my! Tommy was proud of him! He sent him to the Indian school on Kuper Island, and the priests said he was a smart boy at learning, and would make a fine man.

"One day when this boy was about seventeen years old, he took his gun and went out to shoot some grouse. He hadn't gone far when he met Tsilamunthut walking through the woods.

"'What're you doing here?' asked the medicine man. 'I'm looking for grouse,' the boy told him. 'Well, you get home! I've got lots of sheep around here, and I don't want them shot!' This made the boy angry. 'I've got two eyes!' he said, 'can't I tell a grouse from a sheep?' and he started to walk past Tsilamunthut.

"'Look out!' called the man. 'You forget I'm a doctor and can do what I like to you!' He held his two hands out in front of him, and rubbed them round and round together. 'Now you get home!' he shouted. 'This'll make you sorry!' And as the boy turned to run from him, he threw something that hit the boy low down on one shoulder. Oh, such a pain he had, right through his back and chest! He was so scared he ran all the way home, and when he got there the pain was so bad he could not stand and blood was coming from his mouth. His poor mother got him on to his bed and ran out to call his father and uncle. They both came running, and after he had rested a little the boy told them what had happened, and how Tsilamunthut had thrown this sickness at him.

"'It hit me right here!' he said, and put his hand over his shoulder. His father and mother took his shirt off, and there, right in the very place where the sickness had hit the boy, was a big, black mark, just like a burn, and in front, where it had gone through, there was another black mark! That poor boy was only sick a few days, and then he died. Of course Tommy Moses and his mother knew what was the matter with him, but they could do nothing—only Tsilamunthut could have made him better, and, of course, he wouldn't try.

"What was the matter with him?" I asked.

"Well, I'll tell you. When Tsilamunthut held his hands out and rubbed them together, do you know what he was doing?" Siamtunaat's eyes were very round, and she emphasized her words with a withered, brown finger. "He was making a frog! And he threw that frog right into the poor boy! Oh, those Indian doctors can do anything.

"When the boy was dead, of course they had a big funeral, and that Tsilamunthut came to the funeral and he was 'Ah, so sorry such a fine boy had died!' But, when Tommy Moses saw him he left the funeral and went to get his gun: but his brother had taken it away and hidden it, and it was many months before Tommy found where it was hidden.

"Well, about a year after that I meet Tsilamunthut here in Chemainus, and he told me he would like to come and see my girl who was sick. I said I didn't want him, that a fortune teller from Ladysmith had been to see her and had told us she would soon be alright. While we were talking, I saw Tommy Moses coming along, so I went to my house on the beach, and Tommy came and sat on my steps and talked to me.

"'What d'you think?' he said, 'Tsilamunthut wants me to go home with him! He and his wife have got two bottles of gin in their canoe and he wants me to have some!'

"'Don't go Tommy!' I said. 'Don't have anything to do with that man!'

"'I'm going to kill him,' Tommy told me. 'Have you forgotten he killed my father and then my boy? That boy was all I had left. My daughter died long ago, and I just had that fine boy of mine—my only son!' And the tears came into his eyes and ran down his face.

"Again I told him, 'Don't go with those people. Think what will happen to you if you kill that man!' But he only laughed.

"'If I kill him,' he said, 'the police will catch me and hang me. Well, I don't want to live any longer, and that man must die!'

"We talked a little longer and he told me he had a lot of codfish in his canoe. 'Come and get some,' said to me. 'I don't want them all.' When we got to his canoe, I saw he had a lot of fish, some wool and his gun. 'Leave your gun with me,' I told him, but he laughed and, getting into his canoe, paddled away. Very soon I saw Tsilamunthut and his old wife start out in their canoe, and then a man called Jackson followed them."

Siamtunaat moved nearer to me along the doorstep, and lowered her voice. "They were never seen again!" she said. "Somewhere out in Stuart Channel, Tommy Moses shot them! He told me afterwards that he waited for the other canoes outside Bare Point, and they all had some gin, and then he shot them—Tsilamunthut, his wife, and Jackson! The canoes were found with holes in them where the bullets had gone, but no one ever found the bodies."

"Did he sink them, I wonder?" I asked.

Siamtunaat shook her head. "No, no; he told us he had buried them, but no one knows where, and so that was the end of that wicked man, Tsilamunthut."[194]

"And what happened to Tommy Moses?"

"Ah, poor Tommy! Of course, the police caught him, and he told them he had done it and asked them to hang him, but 'Put him in prison for all of his life,' they said, and that's what they did; but because he was such a nice, quiet man, never making any trouble, the men who kept the prison let him work for them, and he used to drive the prison wagon in New Westminster. He didn't live long, though; he was always so sad and wanting his boy, and at last he died; but he was always so glad he had killed that Indian doctor."

With many sighs Siamtunaat got up and, leaning heavily on her stick, shifted her weight with care from one foot to the other.

"My legs feel better," she announced. "These 'erbs are making them all right!" She looked gravely at me for a moment, then "You know," she said, "I always feel sorry the police got Tommy Moses, he was such a good man. Of course, he did kill too many, but that was the drink. He only meant to kill Tsilamunthut. Now, my father—Schu-thane (the priests named him Solomon Pierre)—he killed four men and was never caught; no one found out who done it! The first man he killed was at Hwts'usi'. My father was living there and he had got lots of good potatoes planted. Every year he would fill his big canoe with sacks of potatoes—thirty sacks he could put in—and he would paddle away down to Victoria to sell them. One night a man came and cut off all the tops, just when they were growing so nicely! My father knew what man would have done this thing, and the next night he took a big stick and killed him.

"Soon after that he got a nice, new canoe—the best canoe at Hwts'usi'. An old man living there liked that canoe very much and he wanted my father to trade it to him, but, of course, Solomon Pielle said 'No.' Every day that old man talked about it, and at last he got so mad he took his axe and he chopped that nice canoe all to pieces! When my father saw what he had done, he took his axe and he chopped the old man all to pieces, just like the canoe! Two more men he killed on the Fraser River, but no one ever caught him—he was too smart!"

She chuckled happily at the recollection of her father's adroitness in evading the law in those far-away days.

"Now," she said, "I'd better take these 'erbs off and rub my legs."

She sat herself down on the doorstep again and prepared to remove the bandages, and, feeling that it was an operation that should be conducted in the privacy of her doorstep—without an audience—I thanked her for her story and hurried home.

The Ceremony of the Singing Name[195]

Beryl Cryer is curious about the shulmuhwtsus rattle owned by Mary Rice, and questions her about it. Rattles such as this are "cleansing instruments" with special songs, and their use is hereditary and restricted to "only a few noble families."[196] Mary Rice explains its use in ceremonies performed when a young woman has finished her puberty training, and is ready for marriage. A young woman of "noble lineage" is syul'uw'a—"precious," a "pile of blankets."[197] When she has completed her training she is presented to the people with a special song, st'ul'mey'lh, using her new name, hence Cryer's title, "The Ceremony of the Singing Name." As Ellen White explains, st'ul'mey'lh embody "the form of presenting the energy that goes into the healing powers of that particular work that you're doing." As the anthropologist Homer Barnett observed, "the specific features of the celebration varied over the area; but all were the same in the sense that they were costly to stage; and the more costly and exclusive the better."[198] Mary Rice gives an account of a ceremony performed at Kwa'mutsun and her participation in it. This is followed by an amusing story about a woman's difficulty with the English language during the early days of Hwunitum' settlement at Nanaimo.

SIAMTUNAAT HAS ONE TREASURED POSSESSION—HER RATTLE. It was made by her grandfather Chief Quyupule'ynuxw, and is the crudest thing imaginable. An

Mary Rice wearing swuwqw'a'lh (goat's wool blanket) and holding a shulmuhwtsus (copper, formerly goat's horn rattle), circa 1920s. Photo taken by Beryl Cryer near Mary Rice's cabin, on Chemainus Harbour. Image PN 5923 courtesy Royal British Columbia Museum.

unpolished square of copper bent over to form a triangle, the sides laced together and a number of small stones inside. This is fastened to a roughly rounded wooden handle about six inches long and four and a half inches around.[199]

"When my grandfather first made it," Siamtunaat explained, "he used the horn of a mountain goat, but one day, when he was quite an old man, he found this nice piece of copper, so he took off the horn and made this one. It makes a better noise!" she added with pride.

I had been told by "one who knows" that rattles of this description are used only by chiefs or their descendants, and that their true use is in a mysterious and secret ceremony, but that anything regarding the nature of the ceremony, or even its correct name, no white man has, so far, been able to learn.

To my conceit I thought that Siamtunaat would surely tell me something of this ceremony, but when I questioned her she shook her head most emphatically. "No," she said, her face utterly blank. "Who told you such a story? This rattle is just for dancing and when I sing, and I use it when I help give a 'Singing Name' to a girl—that's all. There's no secret."[200]

She was so decided in her denial that I felt certain there must be some secret rite, but that a secret it would remain, so, wishing her to understand that I had no desire to worry her with questions, I asked whether she would tell me something about the giving of a Singing Name.

"Ah!" she said, with a contented chuckle, "that's something I like to tell you about. But that other story—someone has just been telling nonsense to you!" And I left it at that.

She turned her rattle about and gazed at it admiringly. "This rattle is very good for using when we give a name," she told me; "It always brings luck. She shook it, and the stones rattled wildly, with a harsh, grating sound.

"Now, let me see." She thought for a few moments, occasionally giving the rattle a little shake, then, "Yes, I think I'll tell you about the time I helped sing for William Michell's girl—that was at Kwa'mutsun, long ago.

"Now, when this girl was about seventeen years old, her father called all the people to Kwa'mutsun. I think that nearly five hundred men and women come—and he got two men and twelve women to dance and sing for him. I took my rattle, and I had my blanket of mountain goat hair, and we all wore paint on our faces. Some of the dancers had on big faces (masks) and had some dancing clothes, very fine ones! Well, Michell had a very big, long house at Kwa'mutsun, and when all the people had come, we went inside.

"At one end were Michell's four canoes, and in the middle of the house were three big fires blazing away up high in the air. When everyone had come in and all were sitting round the sides, the singing started.

"First a man got up and sang. When he had finished, all the women sang, one at a time, and after that the last man danced and sang.

"When that singing was done I began to sing again, and I held my rattle and kept shaking it while I sang. Then I took hold of one of the girl's wrists with my two hands and another woman took hold of her other wrist, so she couldn't get away, and we took her into a corner where blankets had been hung to make a little room. Here we took off the top part of her dress so that we could bathe her, and this is the way we did it.

"Now, you know, Michell's wife had got ready two pieces of cedar bark, all cleaned, with the outside bark taken off and the inside beaten soft and woven like two small mats. On the floor in the little room was a big pan of water, and I held one of the pieces of bark like this (doubled a little), then I dipped it in the water, and hit the girl on the face and head with the water that was in this piece of bark. Three times I did this, dipping the cedar into the water each time and all the time the other woman and I, we sang just as loud as we could sing!"

"What did you sing?" I asked her. "What did your words mean?"

"Ah!" Siamtunaat was very serious. "We had not many words, but they meant, 'Now we make you good and clean! Now you are a good girl! You will have great happiness and luck!'

"When the girl was bathed another woman came in singing, and she took the other piece of bark and dried the girl's face and hair. Now a fourth woman came in with a comb, and while we all sang, and I shook my rattle, she combed and braided the girl's hair, then, all singing happiness to her, we put on her dress and, taking her wrists again, we took her out to the people. Her father took her hand and called to all the people and said, 'See, here is my daughter. I give her the name of Tha-hut,' and everybody shouted, and we sang and sang 'good luck and be happy!'

She sat thoughtfully rubbing her dirty old rattle with a corner of her shawl, then, "you know," she said, "sometimes things are a little different when a Singing Name is given. Some people give more luck, some not so much. Now, when I gave my eldest girl her name, ah! she was given lots of luck: Why, do you know, I had two men who each poured a bucket of cold water over her? That was very good luck for her!"

I quite truthfully expressed my amazement, for I could not help feeling that luckier things might happen to one; however, each to his own taste!

"Yes," she continued, "while they poured the water I sang, and danced with my rattle, so that she would have lots of happiness."

Poor old Siamtunaat, for the moment she had forgotten the tales she so often had told me of the troubles and sorrows of this eldest daughter. Not even buckets of water, nor the spell of the treasured rattle, could drive away the cloud of misfortune which has apparently hung over the unfortunate girl the greater part of her life. Perhaps the same thoughts had occurred to her, for, as she got up and pinned her shawl about her, she said, "You know, sometimes luck doesn't come. Now Michell's girl, she had no luck, she died, and now Michell—he's dead, too."

She shook her head sadly, then a smile spread slowly over her face. "I'll tell you a story about the mother of Michell that will make you laugh," she said. She lowered herself into her chair once more, a laborious business today, for she is terribly crippled with rheumatism.

"Well, now," she said, "the time of this story is when white people first lived in Nanaimo. In those days the Indians used to do a little work for the white people, but they had not learned many English words and could not understand what was said to them.

"Now Michell's mother was just a girl, and she used to do washing for some of the ladies, but she was very frightened of them and could never learn their talk.

"One day she went to the house of a lady where she had done washing before. She leaned over the gate and waited until the lady saw her and went out to see what she wanted.

"'You want me wash?' she asked." Siamtunaat's mimicry of the shy Indian girl was delightful.

"The lady shook her head. 'You wash tomorrow,' she said. 'Alright,' said the girl; and she opened the gate and walked up to the house. The lady shook her head. 'Tomorrow,' she said again; 'You wash tomorrow!' 'Uh huh, wash tomorrow,' said the girl, and went round to the back of the house and got the washtub from where she had been told to put it the last time she washed for the lady.

"Now the lady took hold of the tub and pulled, and the girl pulled too, ' I said, "Wash tomorrow!"' the lady told her in a very loud voice. 'Alright! Me wash. You give me tomorrow!' said the girl, and her voice was very loud, too. Well, there they were, both very angry, and they both kept shouting: 'Wash tomorrow!' 'Alright, where tomorrow. Give me tomorrow, me wash.' At last the girl got so mad she put down the tub and went home.

"'What's the matter with that lady?' she asked her brother. 'She told me to wash "tomorrow," but she wouldn't give it to me, and how could I wash it?'

"When her family told her what 'tomorrow' meant, my! she felt so silly! 'I thought the lady must be crazy,' she said, 'and I suppose the lady thought I was crazy too! Now I know what she means, I'll go and wash her clothes tomorrow.' My how her family did laugh at her. They never forgot about that, and when she was an old woman she used to tell how silly she had been."

Siamtunaat shook with laughter at this joke, and she was still laughing as she hobbled off down the garden path.

Mary Rice and Beryl Cryer

Gold at Cowichan[201]

Frontier mythologies regarding gold are widespread in British Columbia. Mary Rice narrates an account, in which native people use gold found in the interior of Vancouver Island to make special bullets for their hunting rifles.

THERE ARE FEW PEOPLE WHO HAVE LIVED long in the district of Cowichan who have not at some time or other heard rumors of Indians in the old days using bullets made of gold. Many are the expeditions that have been made into the wilds behind Lake Cowichan in search of the treasure. At the present time there is, I believe, a man prospecting amongst the hills in the hope of finding some trace of this mythical gold, but so far Lady Luck has refused to smile upon any man.

Curious to find out what I could about this tale, I asked Siamtunaat whether she had ever heard of golden bullets being used by any of her people. She was interested at once.

"Why! yes, yes!" she exclaimed, "I know all about that gold. It's there, somewhere back of Cowichan Lake, and I know it, but no one can find it now: it's lost." She unpinned her shawl and, folding it carefully, pinned her brooch to the front of her sweater. When she makes these preparations I know that a story is forthcoming.

"You know," she began, when she had settled herself comfortably, "my other son—the one who is dead—he used to go every year, if he could get away, and hunt for that gold, but he never could find it."

"Did he know where to look?" I asked.

She shook her head. "Well, he knew what kind of place to look for, but he couldn't find anything. You see," she continued, "we know all about it because my son Charlie's first wife had heard all about that gold from her grandmother, and that old woman was the very one who found it when she was a girl!" Siamtunaat leaned back and smiled triumphantly. "You didn't think that story was true?" she asked. "Well, now, I'll tell you all about it and then you will believe."

"Now long ago there was an old man called Khy-Nhu-Latz, who was a great hunter. Every year he used to go hunting elk far behind Cowichan Lake. Well, one year his eldest girl asked him to take her with him when he went on this hunting trip. At first he said no, but every day she asked him, and at last he told her to get ready and they would start the next day. Now that girl was the grandmother of Charlie's first wife![202]

"Early the next morning the girl and her father started off. They went right up the Cowichan River and up the lake, then went into the woods and back and back, I can't tell you how far. At last they came to two high mountains standing together. They were very big and high, going up like two houses. The girl had hard work to walk as quickly as her father now, for it was all rocky and steep. Bye-and-bye they came to a place where, far up, the rocks were like this (she held up her hands, and bent her fingers over, meaning that the rocks overhung the lower part of the mountains) and under this place it was very dry, the ground deep with a kind of dust. Well, they had climbed and climbed, the girl was very tired, and still no sign of elk had been seen.

"'I must go further on,' said the man. 'The elk must be round the other side of the mountain.'

"When his girl heard this she began to cry. 'Oh!' she said, 'I can't go on! I am too tired. I must rest!' Her father was very angry. 'Why did you come?' he asked. 'I told you it was hard work. Well, you must stay here, and I will go on until I find where the elk are feeding.'

"He took the girl to the dry place where the rocks hung over, and there he left her. 'You can sleep here,' he told her, 'where it is so dry. I will not be away long, but never leave this place, or I may not find you when I come back.' Then he left her, and went on up the mountain.

"Well, the girl walked about a little, but she was afraid to go very far, and she was so tired she lay down in the soft dust by the rocks and went to sleep. Next day she woke up and ate some of the deer meat she had with her, and then she found a nice place to sit in the dry dust. There she waited for her father to come back to her.

"Bye-and-bye she picked up some stones that were lying near her and began throwing them up and catching them. 'What heavy stones!' she thought. She picked up more and they were all heavy. Then she began to rub one stone on the other, and where she had rubbed the dirt away she saw the stones very pretty, all yellow, and some a sort of red.

"'I will find a lot of these stones,' she said to herself, 'and give them to my father when he comes back; they are so pretty, and they are so heavy, they will make good bullets.' She took the bark from a cedar tree and made a little bag, and in this she put the yellow pieces of stone.

"That afternoon, as she walked about, she looked up to where snow lay upon the top of the mountain, and she looked about, the sun came to a place in the sky where it shone in under the rocks that hung over. As she watched, the girl saw all that part where the sun was shining turn a beautiful yellow, and in some places a red color, just like pieces of stone in her little bag. It was so pretty that she watched it until the sun moved higher up and went away behind the mountains.

"Well, you know, her father, after he left her, went on and on, far away, and at last he saw the elk feeding in a low place. He went very quietly down near them and, taking aim, he shot a big one. As quickly as he could he skinned it, and taking all the meat he could carry, he started off back to his girl.

"When he got near the place where he had left her, he shouted, but there was no answer. You see," explained Siamtunaat, "the poor girl was too frightened to answer, for she did not know who it might be! Well, he shouted again, and this time

Mary Rice and Beryl Cryer

he called her name. Then she knew it was her father, and ran to meet him. When he was sitting down resting, in the dry place under the rocks, she brought her little cedar bag and showed him the yellow stones. The man took them out and broke some, and he felt how heavy they were. 'We will take these back with us,' he told her. 'As you say, they will make good bullets!' So off they went, the man carrying the meat and the girl with her bag of heavy stones.

When they got home the man made the stones into bullets, and do you know, always after that he had good luck when he went to hunt. If he used the yellow bullets he never missed. Some of his friends asked him where he got those bullets, but he would never tell anyone, and he made the girl say that she would never tell. He would just point away back to the mountains and say, 'Oh, I just picked them up over there! 'Well, next year he went back to that place and took his girl with him, and they got more of the stone for bullets, and once more he went, but now he was very old and could not go far; but never would he tell any of the people where the yellow stones that brought such good luck could be found.

"When he was a very old man he died, but he told his girl that she was never to tell how to find that place, and she was always too frightened to tell even her husband."

"What became of the bullets when he died?" I asked.

"Ah, now!" Siamtunaat looked very mysterious. "There are two stories about those bullets," she said. "Some of the people say that he showed the bagful to a man and that man stole it all, but others say a man came to his house after he was dead and took the bag, and all the stones he could find. Charlie's wife didn't know which story was true; but we all know there is a place where these gold stones are. As I told you, my other son used to hunt for it, and lots of men have looked, but no one has got to the right place.

"You really think it was gold they found?" I asked.

"Oh yes! It was gold alright, but those old people, they didn't know about gold, they only thought it pretty, and would be good for bullets, and then they found out how lucky it was to shoot with."

She sat looking at me, and smiling to herself then. "Did anyone tell you that Nanoose Bob used gold bullets, too?" she asked.

"Nanoose Bob? That very old Indian who died a little time ago?" I said. "Did he really use gold bullets? Where did he find his gold?"

Siamtunaat laughed. "Well, now, it does seem funny, but both of Charlie's wives had relations (she pronounces it 'lelations') who found gold. You know," she explained, "after Charlie's first wife died he got another wife. Her name is Hilda.[203] Well, Hilda's mother was Nanoose Bob's daughter, and that old woman says that she can 'member long ago when her father used yellow bullets to shoot with.

"Where did he find his gold?" I asked her.

Siamtunaat leaned forward and spoke in a half whisper.

"Now, that's a thing he never would tell," she said. "Just like that other man, he found the yellow bullets were lucky, and when he killed anything he would cut the bullet out and use it again. But he never spoke about his gold. That old woman, her name's Qualla-chlam, she visited me last Winter and we both went to Charlie's for Christmas. Well, one night we were talking about the gold that old Whe-woth-al—that's Nanoose Bob—used to find, and this old woman said that she often saw the bullets and she knows that her father used to go away up Nanoose Mountain and that somewhere up there is a place where he had to get down to running water; the rocks were too high and steep, so he got cedar branches and twisted them together, making a rope. He fastened one end of this rope to a tree and climbed down to the water, and there he found the yellow stones. He always went alone, and never told anyone just where the place was."

"But later," I said, when he learned what gold was, why didn't he tell people, or sell some?"

"Ah!" She looked very wise. "You know Indians don't talk much, and I think maybe by that time he had lost the place, or when he got older he couldn't get down the rocks on his rope. Anyway, he died, and never talked, just like that other man, Khy-Nhu-Latz. But the gold is there, I know, and some day men will find it and will know that this story the Indians tell is quite true!"

Ye Olde and Merrie Game of X'atl'tul'[204]

It is summer, and Mary Rice has been making the rounds visiting relations. Back at her cabin, she calls on Beryl Cryer. The topic of "dancing" and "games" comes up, and Mary Rice describes a boisterous activity called x'atl'tul', performed at important social gatherings with the object of "showing strength, showing strength to one another, accumulating strength."[205] The subject changes with a description of traditional duck hunting with aerial nets at Hwts'usi' (Bonsall's Creek), wild carrot harvesting at Crofton, Maple Bay, and on Salt Spring Island, and the gathering of other plants and berries.

SIAMTUNAAT HAS BEEN GADDING. A week-end with her son Charlie and his family on their island;[206] then up to Nanaimo for a few days with a married daughter, after that to a dance at Duncan, back to Chemainus, and "so to bed." Not so bad for a very fat old person of over seventy. But don't think that she rested for long: dear me, no! In a few days she was up and away to Charlie's again and only returned two days ago.

As I watched her coming up the garden path this afternoon I fancied that she looked older, leaned more heavily on her stick, and walked more slowly. Evidently her recent dissipations had been too much for her.

After our usual greetings, she lowered herself into a chair with many moans.

"Ah," she shook her head sadly, "Ah, I'm so ti-erd; I'm getting old!" She rubbed her gnarled, work-worn fingers and screwed up her face as though in pain. "Do you know, I can't dance any more? No, I just sit now, I can't dance!"

"Never mind," I tried to cheer her, "you can think of all the times you have danced. Lots of people have not even that, you know. Tell me," I asked her, "who taught you to dance?"

This question appeared to cheer her wonderfully, for she chuckled as she answered.

"My aunt, she taught me. Oh, she was a nice dancer! My grandfather, he taught her, and he was the best dancer of all the Cowichans!"

"Siamtunaat, tell me what other things your people used to do for their fun besides singing and dancing!"

Immediately she was all attention.

"Ah, now wait!" she said, "that's a thing I was going to tell you, but I had forgotten. The women didn't play much, but the men had good games to play— lots of fun and laughing. Well, one was just the same as the white people play now—when all pull on a rope."

"Tug-of-war?" I suggested.

"Yes, that's it!" she said. "First, you know, the men had to make a rope. They went up the rivers and there they got the bark from the big willows. This bark they put in water, and then they rubbed and rubbed it in their hands, joining the pieces in that way until they had a big, strong rope, about as big as my wrist, and so strong that all of the strongest of the Cowichans pulling on it could not break it.

"I 'member when I was a little girl seeing the men playing a very good game. It was called x'atl'tul': that means 'pushing together'." She laughed softly to herself. "This time that I will tell about, the game made me so frightened that I held to my mother and cried and cried, but later I got like the others and thought it funny. Well, my grandfather called all the Cowichans to Puneluxutth'. I think it was to talk over things and then have a good time, and I 'member seeing all the canoes, some big, some small, paddling over to Kuper Island, and all the people coming up to the houses where the Puneluxutth' had lots of food ready for them.

"When they had eaten and had finished their talking, a good time began. There was running and jumping, all the young strong men from each village trying who was the best. Now they brought out the rope, and again the strongest from each place would pull and my! There was lots of shouting and noise. Then came the most fun. When everything else was finished, all the men played x'atl'tul'. First they put paint on their faces, and their feathers on their heads, and stood near together right along outside the houses. Now they were ready. First I must tell you that in front of the houses were big piles of clam shells where the people had thrown out the shells after eating. Now, all the men held their arms like this."—Siamtunaat put her hands together and stuck her elbows out—"When all were standing ready, one man would shout and the fun began, every man pushing hard with his elbow at the man standing next to him. Such a noise you never heard, all shouting and calling and making a noise, too! When a man pushed over the one next to him, that one would get up and, running to the pile of clam shells, begin throwing them at the rest as hard as he could!"

Siamtunaat was working herself up into a great state of excitement over this recital. She unpinned her shawl and threw it back from her shoulders and leaned down as though joining in the game.

"Now everybody's throwing clam shells!" she exclaimed, "heads down, so their eyes don't get cut, but throwing hard, so the edge goes first and cuts when it hits. Soon there's blood everywhere, cuts on their heads, their necks and shoulders, and all bleeding! Such a sight! but such fun—such a good game!"

She leaned back in her chair quite breathless, and shaking with laughter, and I waited until she had calmed down before I asked her, "What did your people find to feed all those Cowichans on?"

She threw up her hands. "There!" she exclaimed, "I'll tell you about the food we had in those long-ago days.

"Now you know that we caught lots of fish, and then there was clams—always lots of clams. Back in the woods were deer; sometimes the men shot them, and sometimes they found the trails where the deer went to drink at a lake or river, and on this trail they dug deep holes and covered them over with branches. Then they waited until the deer came along and fell into the hole, or sometimes they drove them through the woods and into the holes, and there they killed them.

"Now, in those days there were lots of ducks—you can't think how many! The Indians had a good way of catching these birds. They put big, high poles on the river flats, where the ducks went to feed—(there is one of those poles left now on the flats of Bonsall's Creek, down at Hwts'usi'. Do you know my grandfather and his son, my uncle, put up those poles? And there is one today)—and on the poles they hung strong nets made of a very strong sort of grass that grew away up the Fraser River. It's all gone now, but in those days the women used to weave it into mats and blankets. Well, there were the nets on the poles, and now the hunter would paddle very quietly up near the ducks, then, taking his paddle into his two hands and holding it in front of him across the canoe, he would begin tap, tap, tap, on the edge of the canoe. When the birds heard this noise they would get up to fly away, and as the men were behind them, they would fly right into the net, hit it and fall down. There the hunter hit them as quickly as he could, hit, hit, hit, faster than you can think, and very soon he would have a canoe full of good ducks to take home.[207]

"In those days my people went up on the Saltspring Island hills, and on those hills by Crofton and Maple Bay, and there they got very nice wild carrots, about as big

Mary Rice and Beryl Cryer

Pole (xwul'xwul'u) for attaching aerial nets used in duck hunting. Chemainus River circa 1930.
Image PN 6516 courtesy Royal British Columbia Museum.

as this"—(she held out a wrinkled brown finger)—"and there were lots of those things, I forget what you call them—some are red, some white, and they are hot."[208]

"Radishes," I suggested.

"Yes!" she said, "that's the name—radishers! Well, those were good, and the Indians used to get baskets of them, but there are none left now: sheep have killed them all. Down in the swamps were nice plants called 'dock,' and the young shoots of those are very, very nice. My people used to steam them. Lots of crab apples grew in the swamps, too, and everywhere there were salal berries, and up the Fraser River were blueberries. Those two kinds of berries we used to dry and put away in sacks made of rushes, and in the Winter we would eat them. Ah, they are good! Even now I always get those berries and put them away for pies."

She gathered her shawl about her and carefully fastened the treasured silver brooch. "Now I must go," she said, getting to her feet. "But before I forget, I must tell you a very good thing to feed babies on. My people always gave this to their babies to make them grow big and strong. After the priests came and gave my people seeds of vegetable for their gardens, the Cowichans always grew lots of punkins—they liked them best of all, and they found that punkin mixed with salmon eggs was the best food of all for their babies. I thought I'd tell you about it. Maybe, sometime you will see a baby not very strong, and you can 'member, salmon eggs and punkin will make it well!"

You may be sure that I thanked her for this valuable advice, and pass it on for those who would have healthy children—Salmon eggs and pumpkin, well mixed and, I hope, cooked!

The Cowichan–Bella-Bella Feuds[209]

Mary Rice relates four accounts of nineteenth-century conflict between Central Coast Salish people and northern people identified as Bella Bella. When Beryl Cryer began her series for the *Daily Colonist*, William Newcombe offered to help her access information in the Provincial Archives. On May 10, 1932, she wrote Newcombe a letter and enclosed a typewritten copy of what appear to be notes from her interview with Mary Rice.[210] Newcombe, unfamiliar with the histories Cryer was recording, was unable to provide her with any information.

It is interesting to note that Cryer was familiar with some of the individuals in the third story given by Mary. She tells Newcombe, "Mary's description of our old friend Skookum Tom, who used to sell us salmon in the old days—killing the woman and child is enough to turn one's hair grey." For some reason, Cryer changes his name to "Skookum Jim" in the following version.

"TODAY I WILL TELL YOU ABOUT lots of trouble between the Cowichans and the Indians from Bella-Bella," said Siamtunaat, as unpinning her shawl she folded it very carefully and hung it over the back of her chair.

"When my grandfather, Xulqalustun, was chief at Puneluxutth', oh, there was a lot of fighting, and always there was trouble with those Bella-Bella people. Why, once they nearly killed my poor grandfather! It was like this ...

"As I told you, Xulqalustun was a good friend of Governor Douglas, and one day he wanted to see the Governor about a little trouble, so he and his two brothers started off and paddled down to Esquimalt from Kuper Island. There they left their canoe and began walking to Victoria. They had not gone very far when a lot of Bella-Bella Indians jumped out from the bushes and there was a great fight. My people fought hard, but they were only three men and the Bella-Bellas were many. My grandfather called to his brothers, 'Go for help! I will stay and fight these men.'

"Away hurried his brothers and very soon they met a lot of men, who went back with them to help Xulqalustun.

"When the Bella-Bellas saw so many people coming after them they ran away, leaving my poor grandfather lying on the road nearly dead. His brothers carried him to Victoria, and there he had to stay for three weeks before he was well enough to go back to Puneluxutth'.

"Now the Cowichans were very angry to think that their chief had been nearly killed by those people. 'Those Bella-Bellas must pay!' they said. 'We will wait our chance!' Not long after this, a canoe full of Cowichans went to Victoria to trade fish and skins with the white people."

Here Siamtunaat stopped.

"Wait one minute," she said, "I will tell you the names of the people in that canoe. They were Loxa from Qw'umiyiqun', Charlie Qual-inah, Sam Thi-Thi-aone, and one woman, Suma'luya. Well, after they had traded all they had, they started home again and had got about as far as Ten-Mile Point, when far away they saw four canoes coming after them.

"'The Bella-Bellas!' shouted Loxa, 'Paddle hard!' How those people did paddle! never stopping until they had reached Saltspring Island. Now it was getting dark and they could not see or hear the other canoes. 'We will stop at the next village,' said Loxa, 'and with more men to help us we will kill all those Indians in the canoes.' Very soon they reached a village where more Cowichans lived, and when the people came hurrying down to the beach, Loxa told them the Bella-Bellas were coming. 'Listen to me,' he said, 'I have a good plan that will trick those people so that we can kill them all! First give me a big pan, then get your fighting things and follow us in your canoes.'

"Back into their canoe the Cowichans got and back they paddled to meet the Bella-Bellas, and behind them paddled four canoes from the village. Soon they came to a point the Bella-Bellas would have to pass, and here they paddled to the shore and hid the canoes, leaving only one on the beach. 'Now,' said Loxa, 'every-one must hide, and you,' he said to the woman, 'must give me your skirt, shawl and the handkerchief from your head.'"

"While the woman was taking off her things, Loxa gathered wood and made a big fire close to the water's edge. Then he put on the woman's skirt and shawl and tied the handkerchief over his head. He took the pan and, standing in the light from the fire, pretended to be busy making something to eat.

"It was very dark by this time and soon they heard the Bella-Bellas coming. Round the point they paddled and seeing a woman alone by the fire and just one canoe drawn up beside her, they gave a great shout and paddled to the beach. Out of the canoes they jumped and ran to catch the woman, but Loxa got behind the fire, and at the same time shouted to the Cowichans to fight. There in the firelight the Cowichans and Bella-Bellas fought, but not for long, for the Cowichans were the stronger and had taken the Bella-Bellas by surprise, and very soon there was not one left alive.[211]

"'Now,' thought my people, 'we will be left in peace!' But no! Can you believe it? Down came the Bella-Bellas again, and this time they fought the Snuneymuxw Indians, killing twenty! After that there was no more fighting for a long time, but the Cowichans were always watching for a chance to get even with the Bella-Bellas for killing all those Snuneymuxw; but no chance came for nearly three years.

"Now," Siamtunaat drew her chair nearer mine and her old face was very serious. "This is not a very good story of the Cowichans; but see, our people didn't know better in those days, and the Bella-Bellas had always been bad friends, killing all they could find.

"Well, three years later, there was a white man living in Victoria who was married to a Bella-Bella woman and they had one little girl. This woman was not well, and she longed to go and stay with her own people for a time, so her husband said she could go.

"One day her father, mother, brother and six other Indians came down from Bella-Bella to fetch her and the girl. They left Victoria early one morning and, paddling hard, were about ten miles from Sansum Narrows when the woman, looking back, saw canoes chasing them![212]

"'See!' she cried. 'The Cowichans are after us!' and holding her little girl closely to her, she crouched low in the canoe.

"On came the Cowichans and soon the Bella-Bellas saw that they could not get away. Now, the woman's old father called to his son, 'You are a good swimmer and must save yourself!' he cried. 'As soon as you can, go back to Victoria and tell your sister's husband of these Cowichans and see that they are punished. Go quickly!'

"The young man did not say one word, but, putting down his paddle and keeping low in the canoe, he slipped over the side and began to swim to the shore with quick, strong strokes. At last he was there and, crawling on the rocks, got between two logs, and there he lay watching his people paddling for their lives, but the Cowichans' canoes came closer, closer, until they were upon the Bella-Bellas. There, out on the water, the Cowichans killed all those people, even the sick woman and her little girl, and then they brought the bodies to the shore, quite near where the young man lay hidden. They tied the bodies together, two and two, and putting heavy rocks on the ropes, they took them out to a deep place and sunk them. Then away they paddled to where they had their camp.

"You know," said Siamtunaat, "all this story is quite true, for my aunt was in that camp and she often told me of that bad thing the Cowichans had done. Every year some of the Cowichans went to that place to fish for dogfish, and they would take the oil from these fish over to the American side and trade or sell it.

"When all the bodies were gone, the young man came out from his hiding place and ran and ran for many miles along the rocks, until he came to a place where he could swim across to the next island.[213] He rested for a time after swimming across, and then on he went, running, running; looking for some house where he could find people who would help him. All that night he walked along the shore, and very early in the morning he saw a woman coming over the rocks.

"Now, this woman was from Qw'umiyiqun' and was married to a white man, and after he had told her his story, she took him to her house and there her husband gave him dry clothes and something to eat. Then he took him to a place where the Government boat would come that day. This man walked with him and put him on the boat, and when the Bella-Bella man got to Victoria, my! How he did hurry to the house where his brother-in-law lived! He told the poor man what had happened to his wife and little girl and to all the Bella-Bellas. 'All are gone,' he told him. 'I saw it myself. Two men did most of the killing. They must be caught and killed too!'

"'We must tell the Governor at once,' said the brother-in-law, and the two started off for Governor Douglas' house.

"When Governor Douglas heard what the Cowichans had done he was very angry. 'We must find those men,' he told the Bella-Bella man, 'and if what you tell me is true, they will be hanged. Have the war boat ready to start quickly,' he told his people, and, taking the two men with him, he went on the war boat and told them to go right up to Puneluxutth' on Kuper Island. There he landed and went to see my grandfather, Chief Xulqalustun.

"'What do you know of this trouble with the Bella-Bella people, Pierre?' he asked. "You know," explained Siamtunaat, "Governor Douglas always called my grandfather 'Pierre.' My grandfather shook his head. 'I know nothing,' he told the Governor. 'The good priests have been here to my village, and we are all good, quiet people; we have all 'got religion.' There are other villages I know where the people are not so good; it may be that they can tell you of this killing.'

"'Well,' said Governor Douglas, 'those men must be punished, whoever they are, so keep your ears open, Pierre!' and away he went.

"Now, when those bad Cowichans who had killed the Bella-Bellas heard that they would be punished if they were caught, they took all that they had and paddled over to the American side, and there they stayed for many years; but one man—his name was Qleysuluq[214]—did not go away, and at last the police found out that he and his boy were in the camp at that time, and they put them in the prison at Nanaimo and said they must be hung.

"Now, my aunt always told me that Qleysuluq was not with the canoes that day, but that Johnny Yekoloas and Skookum Jim[215] had done most of the killing; but when Qleysuluq told the white men this, they said he was there and must die! For many days he and his boy were shut up in Nanaimo; then one day the policeman who looked after them told them, 'Tomorrow morning you both go to Victoria to be hung. Your wife is coming to say goodbye to you tonight!'

'It was very dark when the woman came to see her husband and boy for the last time. The policeman put her into the little room with them and locked the door again. 'Hurry up!' he called to her. 'You may only stay a few minutes!'

"Now this wife of Qleysuluq was a very clever woman. She took her husband into a corner where the blankets lay. 'See,' she whispered, 'I have brought you these.' She put her hand up her skirts and gave him a knife she had tied to her leg. 'Now cut these strings,' she told him, and showed him how she had tied one of those things that make round holes in wood (an auger) against her leg so that it could not be seen! 'Hide them under the blankets,' she said, 'and tonight you can cut a hole in the floor. Early in the morning get through onto the rocks under-neath—I will be waiting for you.' She could say no more; the door was unlocked and the policeman told her she must go.

"She put her hands over her face and pretended she was crying, and her husband and boy sat down on their blankets where the knife and auger were hidden and put their hands over their faces, too. The policeman just looked in to see that they were all right, and then shut the door again. That night, Qleysuluq and his boy worked hard making holes in the floor. It was slow work, for the boards were very thick, but at last there was a place big enough for them to get through. It was beginning to get light and Qleysuluq could see the rocks under the prison that they would have to jump on to. Suddenly he heard the policeman coming, and quickly he put his blankets over the hole and lay down. In came the man with some food.

"'Here you are!' he said. 'Here's your last breakfast; in two hours you and your boy go on to the boat to Victoria to be hanged!' Out he went, locking the door again.

"I can tell you those two poor people did not wait for any food. First, the man put his boy through the hole and, holding him by his arms, lowered him onto the rocks, then he jumped after him. Very carefully they crawled to the side and looked out. There, quite near them, was the good woman waiting. Qleysuluq made a little noise, and she nodded her head to tell him she had heard, but she did not look round.

"'Wait,' she said. "When I get up, come out and walk beside me.' For a little time she sat there; then, when there was no one to be seen, she stood up and picked up a basket from the ground by her.

"In one minute her people were out and walking by her, and, 'Hurry! Hurry!' said Qleysuluq; but she put her hand on his coat. 'Wait,' she told him. 'If you hurry, people will look at you—go slowly, look at the things and talk a little; don't hurry!' So they walked right through Nanaimo, past houses, past people, but no one looked at them, and at last they got to the beach. Here the woman had a big canoe filled with all their things.

"'Where are we going?' Qleysuluq asked. 'To the American side,' she told him; 'we will be safe there.' And there they lived for twenty years, and at the end of that time they came back to the Snuneymuxw people."

"What happened to Skookum Jim and the other man?" I asked.

"Skookum Jim and Johnny Yekoloas stayed away for a long time, and then they came back again, but very soon they were caught; but now the Bella-Bella man had gone and the police could find no one would would say that those two had killed the Bella-Bellas, and they had to let them go. They lived round here until they were very old men, and now both are dead."[216] My poor grandfather," she said, "he did try so hard to make his people good, but when they were bad he would never tell, because, you know, he had killed, oh, so many before he got religion."

"You know," she said in a confidential whisper, "I sometimes think maybe my grandfather knew something about that killing, but he never would tell!"

The Fish Charmer[217]

Once again, Beryl Cryer uses a photograph to coax a story from Mary Rice. This time, it is an old photograph of an aged brother and sister from S-amuna' (Duncan) that was often used as a tourist postcard in Duncan and Victoria. Mary Rice is preoccupied with family matters, but tells the story of the man's role as ritualist, and a certain control he had over the fish in the Cowichan River. Mary Rice continues the topic of fish when she relates a humorous story about cats and confusion over English words during the early days of colonization.

SEVERAL MONTHS AGO SIAMTUNAAT promised me a tale about two old Indians of whom I have a photograph, and armed with my picture I visited her cottage this morning.

I found the old woman in one of her gloomy moods, and, of course, before I dare produce the photograph I had to listen to her story of "Lots of trouble in our family." It appeared that a month or so ago her old brother, Tommy Pielle, took unto himself "a new woman," his wife having died last year.

"Such a nice, clean woman, this new one," mourned Siamtunaat, "and now, she's gone and left my brother! When he took her she had no clothes, everything was patched and worn out, and Tommy Pielle, he took her to Seattle, and for five dollars, he bought her such nice things at a second hand store! And now she's left him—gone away with one of her girls!"

She shook her head and sighed deeply, a look of mournful resignation on her face. I suggested that her brother might find another housekeeper to comfort him.

Tow-kau-ahl and Taul-kun of S-amuna'. Image PN 5920 courtesy Royal British Columbia Museum.

But, "No," she said, "he had gone to find her and take her back to Kuper Island. He told me that he did not want any other woman, that one was so clean, and such a nice cook!"

She smiled faintly as she told me this, and I felt that I might now show her my picture.

"Ah, those people!" she said as she took the photograph. I know about them. There were four in that family, three brothers, and one sister, and I think they never married, just all lived in one little house. This man here," she tapped the picture with a withered old finger. "He was called Tow-kau-ahl, and his sister, her name was Taul-kun. They were S-amuna' Indians and very, very old.

"Well, the story I can tell you about Tow-kau-ahl is true, because lots of people who knew him saw him do this thing, but I never saw him, only 'member my mother telling about him."

She held the picture at arms length and examined it carefully. Hm, hm, she grunted. "This man could do a thing that not many Indians knew about. He had 'bad' eyes, and no one could look at them for long, it made them frightened. Well, do you know, this Tow-kau-ahl never wanted anybody to fish in the Cowichan River. 'The fish are all mine,' he told the Cowichans. 'No one must fish in this place.' And he would look at the men who wanted to fish and they would go back to their houses and put away their nets and spears, and wait for him to bring fish to trade them.

"Do you know what that man did?" she asked me. "Well, I'll tell you. He charmed the fish!"

She paused for me to express my astonishment, "How did he charm them?" I asked.

"Ah!" she laughed, "now listen. That man had a rattle, it was like a bird made of wood. Oh, it was such a nice one, with pictures cut on it. Early in the morning, before the sun came, Tow-kau-ahl would take this rattle and walk through the woods until he came to the river. Here he would sit on the bank where it was high over the water, and he would sing and sing and shake his rattle, calling to the fish, telling what he wanted them to do."

"What did he say to them?" I asked.

"Well, I was told he called something like this. 'Oh fish! Go up the river, do not go down into the sea, but turn and go up, go up, go up! When you have gone far up where no people will follow, lie still and wait—I will come for you. Wait until tonight, then I will come! But turn now away from the big sea, and go up, go up!'"

Siamtunaat recited this in a curiously, toneless sing-song, and I could imagine the old man with his "bad" eyes, crouching on the river bank, shaking his rattle and charming the fish.

"Do you think the fish did as he told them, Siamtunaat?" I asked.

"Why, yes!" I know they did," she answered seriously. "When they heard that man Tow-kau-ahl singing to them, they all waited, listening to his voice, then, round they turned and up the river they went, swimming hard against the water that was coming down.

"All day long he would sit there, making his charm, and, when it was getting cool he would take his fish net and go far, far up the river to a place he knew about, and there he would catch more fish than he could carry."

"What net did he use?" I asked.

"Well, in those days my people used a net made of willow bark, or sometimes that strong sort of grass, that grew up the Fraser River (Indian hemp). The net that man had, was about one fathom long, or a little more (curiously enough, Siamtunaat generally gives measurements in fathoms), and it was made like a big sort of bag, with a big hole for the fish to go in. Tow-kau-ahl used to throw his net out in the river, and then he would throw stones as far up the river as he could, to frighten all the fish into his net, then quickly he would draw the hole shut with a line fastened to it, pull in the net and take out his big fish. Back to his little house made of rushes he would take them, and there he would smoke and dry them for the Winter.

"Now, as I told you, this man did not like any other person to catch the fish, and if he found other men had been fishing in his river, my, he was mad! He wanted to have all the fish for himself, so that he could trade them to the other Indians for blankets, clothes, and food.

"When Tow-kau-ahl was very, very old his sister died, and then he and his brothers went to live on an island near Seymour Narrows, and soon after that they, too, all died, and now there are none of my people who know how to charm the fish!"

Siamtunaat sat nodding her head over the picture, then she commenced chuckling to herself in a funny little way that she has.

"I 'member a funny story about fish, I will tell you," she said, as she settled herself more comfortable in her chair.

"Now first I must tell you that for a long time our people had no cats. The Indians on the American side had lots of cats, but over here we had none. One day, some of the Cowichans went to the American side with a lot of camas to trade, and they brought back four cats. My, the Cowichans were glad when they saw those cats! Everyone went to Kwa'mutsun, where the people lived, to see them, and everybody gave them lots to eat and they grew very big and strong. Pretty soon there were lots of kittens, and those people traded them with their friends for blankets! It was not long before there were too many cats—cats everywhere! Well, after the white people came to Fort Victoria the Cowichans used to trade with them, taking them salmon and deer meat and ducks, but they did not know much English, and the word they used for fish was 'salmon.' They never said 'fish.'

"One day a man from Kwa'mutsun went to Victoria with a lot of salmon. He soon traded all his fish, and was ready to start back home when a lady called to him. 'You got fish?' The man shook his head, 'No.' well, the lady told him, 'next time, you bring me fish! lots of fish!' She held out her hands to show she wanted a lot, and the man was very pleased. 'You trade?' he asked. 'Yes, yes,' said the lady, 'Me trade blankets, food, for lots of fish.' The man laughed, 'Yes, yes,' he told her, and getting into his canoe he paddled home to Kwa'mutsun. When he got there he went to all the people and told them, 'Give me all the cats you don't want, I want as many as you can catch!' He got a lot of baskets and mats, and then he helped them catch their cats.[218]

"My, what a time they had: everyone running after the cats and catching them! When they had caught them, they took them to the man, and he put them in the baskets and tied mats over them so that they could not run away. At last all the baskets were full, and the man and his woman put them into their canoe. There were such a lot! The canoe was quite full. Early the next morning those two people started off with all the cats for Fort Victoria.

"They paddled hard, for the cats were hungry and very scared, and tried to get out of the baskets. When they got to Victoria they carried as many baskets as they could up to the lady's house, and called to her. Out came the lady, and when she saw the man, she said, 'My, you've been quick, have you brought me lots?' He pointed to his baskets. 'Lots,' he said. 'Well, bring them inside.' They carried the baskets inside the house and cut the mats off them. That poor lady was so surprised, she just stood and looked.

"There were cats all over the room, big cats and little cats—all colors. 'More,' the man told her, 'lots more!' He started to go and get the other baskets but the lady stopped him. 'What are these for?' she asked. 'Take them away! no good!' The man looked at her, and when he saw how cross she was, he got mad, too. 'No good?' he shouted, 'that puss, you tell me, trade lots of puss?' 'No,' said the lady, 'I told you, trade lots of fish—salmon!' 'Ah, salmon!' said the man, 'salmon?—you say puss?' 'No,' she told him again, 'I said fish, not puss!'

"Well," laughed Siamtunaat, "they talked a long time and at last they caught all the cats and took them away, after the lady had given them some presents. They put the baskets in the canoe and started back to their home."

"What did they do with the cats?" I asked.

She shook her head. "Do you know, I never heard what happened to all those cats, maybe they took them back with them, but sometimes I think, maybe they put them all on some island to live.

The Woman Who Was Made Wrong[219]

A short anecdote about facial mutilation segues into a story about the frightening ordeal of a woman with a physical deformity, during the infamous Haida raid on Puneluxutth' in the first half of the nineteenth century. After this story, Mary Rice tells Cryer a Snuneymuxw Creation Story that her son-in-law, Jimmy Joe, gave her "to tell that lady."

POOR OLD SIAMTUNAAT HAS, AS USUAL, a house full to overflowing, with her "lelations"—Tommy Pielle, her brother, and four orphaned grandchildren all visiting her.

I was relieved to find that Tommy Pielle and the two bigger boys were just going off to pick cherries,[220] leaving the small Dorothy and Jimmy with their grandmother.

These two chubby, brown-faced imps were very busy trying to shut under a box a small yellow dog of that indeterminate breed seen only amongst the Indians. They were having but little success, and the small girl, losing patience, began hitting the unfortunate dog.

"D'othy!" Siamtunaat called. "Ah, D'othy!"

She hobbled to the door, and, standing there, read a lecture to the small culprit. As she talked with many gesticulations, I saw a look of absolute horror spread over the child's face; she gave a swift, side-long glance of fear at her small brother, clapped two grubby hands over her nose, and stood listening to her grandmother, dark brown eyes peering unblinkingly from between her fingers.

The lecture finished, Siamtunaat went back to her chair, chuckling. "Now maybe she'll be good," she said. "When D'othy gets bad I always tell her that story, and she's so scared that she keeps good until she forgets it again!"

"What did you tell her?" I asked. "Well, you 'member I told you about that man Qleysuluq who got out of the jail at Nanaimo? Now that woman, his wife, who helped him, was very, very ugly. Such a nose!"

Siamtunaat held up her hands in horror at the recollection of that nose.

"When she was a young girl that woman was very bad; no one liked her, and she had no friends. One day her brothers told her; 'You got to behave, or we'll punish you.' But it was no good; she just went on doing everything that was wrong. So, what do you think? One day her brothers took her in the house, and they got a sharp knife. Then one held her and the other cut her nose; two cuts on each side of her nose they made. I 'member seeing her when she was an old woman, and, my! she was ugly, the sides of her nose hung down. Oh, my!

"'There,' they told her, 'now when people see you they will know you have been punished and no one will look at you.' That's the story I tell D'othy when she bad. I say, 'Look out! Or your brothers will cut your little nose, and it will hang loose on your face like Qleysuluq's wife!'

She sat laughing and rocking in her chair for some time, then asked:

"Did I ever tell you about that woman with the big head at Puneluxutth'? No? Well, I can tell you that story today. You 'member long ago I told you how the Haidas came down and fought the Cowichans at Puneluxutth', when my grand-father Xulqalustun, was chief?[221] How all the women and children took food and hid in the woods, and my grandmother swam to another island with her two chil-dren, one on her back and the baby held in her teeth? Well, at that time there was a woman living at Puneluxutth' who was 'made all wrong.' She had six fingers on each hand, and each foot had six toes. Her head was two or three times bigger than any other Indian's head, and her hair was not like our hair; it was curly! She was very, very ugly, but my mother told me she was very kind to all the other women and to the little children.

"Well, when the Puneluxutth' saw the Haidas coming, as I told you, all their women ran away and hid back in the trees, but this woman had been so busy helping the children get ready that she was the last to leave. The Haidas were getting near the houses, when she crept out of the door and began to crawl up the hill to where the trees were thick and dark. All the other women and their children were out of sight; she was all alone, crawling, crawling up over logs and stones, trying, trying not to be seen. Behind her she could hear the shouts of the fighters, but on she crawled, through the long grass; for, if she was caught, she knew the Haidas would take her back with them to be a slave, and she would never see her people again. It was hard work for her to keep her big head down in the long grass, and very soon there was a great shout close behind her. She lay still, hoping she would not be seen, but up the hill came four Haidas, shouting for joy as they saw her lying there. Suddenly the woman 'membered how she was made, her big head, her hands and feet! Perhaps they would save her!

"She sat up and waited until the Haidas were quite close, then she held out her arms and spread all her fingers out for them to see. She put out her feet to show all her toes too. 'See,' she called to them. 'Look at me. See my great head! and all my big toes and fingers! No man may kill me, or take me prisoner!' She laughed at them as she sat there.

"When the Haidas saw such a queer woman they stood and looked at her, and she saw they were afraid. She stood up and held her arms high in the air, and shook her great head at them. The men watched her, and, as they looked she gave a loud cry and took one step to them, and as she came so they went back, back down the hill, never taking their eyes from her face.

"They were nearly down the hill, when the woman caught her foot in a hole and down she fell on her face in the grass. As soon as her eyes were off them, the fear left those men, and with loud shouts they caught her, and while three held her the other one took his knife and cut all around her head, taking away all the skin and hair. They did not kill her; maybe they were still afraid of her, but they left her lying there alone in the grass.

"After a long time the Puneluxutth' drove the Haidas away, and all the women and children came running down the hill, and there they found that poor woman nearly dead. They carried her down to the big house where she lived, and do you know what they did? They got lots of fish oil, and they put it all over her sore head, and then they got soft, grey, duck feathers—just the soft down that grows under the feathers—and they put lots of these on, patting them into the oil and then putting on more, until all the bleeding had stopped.

"For a long time that poor thing was very sick, often they thought she would die; but she was a very strong woman and bye-and-bye her head got better, a little skin came; but she never had any hair again. She always looked so funny, because she could never get those soft feathers off her head; they stuck all over it like little grey hairs growing, and my mother told me that all the little children would sit listening to her tell them the story of the Haidas taking her scalp and of all the ducks giving her their soft feathers to grow on her head, and keep it warm."

I heard the shouts of the cherry pickers returning, and, gathering up my parcels, prepared to leave. "How long are your people staying?" I asked her.

"Well," she said, "The two little ones are going to live with me, and I think Tommy Pielle will stay too. You see, he can't find that woman of his. He's been to Seattle looking for her, but she's gone; so now I think he will cut my wood, and I'll cook for him and this will be his home."

She laughed delightedly at this arrangement.

"Maybe he'll 'member some stories for you," she suggested. "Tommy Pielle likes you to make these stories about our people, and—Wait one minute!" she exclaimed. "The last time I went to Nanaimo my daughter's husband told me: 'Here's a story for you to tell that lady.' And I nearly forgot!"

She clucked her tongue vigorously and shook her head.

"Well, now this is the story he told me. It is the way the place where he lives got its name. The Indian name for this place is Hwsaluxal, and that means 'The Hay.' Now, long, long ago, there were no people living anywhere near Nanaimo, and at one place there was a big, flat piece of ground, and in the middle of this ground was a high pile of hay. One day, the sun, which, my people say, made all things, shone down on this hay and made a little man. For two days he lay in the hay, getting strong, then he climbed down and began walking along towards Nanaimo.

"Bye-and-bye he came to a spring and sat down beside it. Soon he felt thirsty and leaned over to have a drink. Well, of course, when he looked in the water, he saw the head of a little man looking at him and he thought this very funny. He sat and laughed and laughed and felt very glad to think he was not the only person in that land. But when he looked about for the man he could not find him. 'Where is that man?" he thought, and again he looked in the water. 'If I see him looking at me again, I will catch hold of him,' he said to himself.

"When he looked this time there was a little wind and he could not see the man; but deep, deep down in the water he saw another face, not like the first one; this was the face of a girl. Very carefully, so as not to frighten the face away, the man put his hand down in the water, and quickly he reached down and caught hold of the girl's hair. He pulled hard and at first he could not move her, then up she came and sat on the bank beside him.

"'What a nice place!' she said.

"'Will you stay here with me?' he asked. 'That is my house over there.' He pointed to the hay where he had been born. The girl looked at it and she went over and walked around it.

"'What a good house! But I can show you how to make it better,' she told him. She began pulling out the hay from the bottom of the pile until there was a big hole like a room. 'There!' said the girl. 'That is a better house. We will live here.' And there they lived for many, many years, and those two were the first of that tribe of Snuneymuxw Indians, and they got their name from the pile of hay where the little man was born.'

"As I said," repeated Siamtunaat, "my daughter's husband sent you that story; but I can tell you stories about names too! Next time I will tell you how Puneluxutth' got its name, and Xulel-thw. Oh, lots of places!"

I thanked her, and, seeing Tommy Pielle politely waiting outside until we had finished, I said good-bye, and left her, exclaiming delightedly over the cherries.

Legends Attached to Names of Cowichan Villages[222]

Mary Rice and Tommy Pielle make a special visit to Beryl Cryer's home in Chemainus to tell her the origin stories of Puneluxutth' and Yuxwula'us, two villages at the north end of Kuper Island.

THIS AFTERNOON SIAMTUNAAT AND TOMMY PIELLE visited me. They came slowly up the garden path, stopping at intervals to look across the lake and to talk earnestly together, finally arriving, breathless at the steps.

"Oh, you live so far!" my old friend exclaimed. "I think we'll sit out here," she added, seating herself on the top step, and pointing, with her stick, to a lower position for Tommy Pielle.

"You know," she said, "me and my brother we've been 'membering some of the Cowichan names, and this morning Tommy Pielle he said we'd better go and tell her right away. So I washed his shirt and, when it was dry, we had our dinner and came to see you!"

She smiled happily at Tommy Pielle, and he grinned back at her and rearranged his moustache at a more becoming angle. Tommy Pielle has, I am certain, been something of a beau in his day; but, to me he appears as the original "Old Bill."

"These stories," said Siamtunaat, "tell why our people, the Cowichans, gave the different names to their villages, and what the names mean. You know,"—she leaned forward and shook her old head sadly—"there are not many of our people left. Everywhere are empty houses, all broken, and fallen down. I can 'member when there were lots of people living in all the villages; now they are dead, and the villages are empty, not even the houses left; only a little cleared land and, sometimes, a few old apple and plum trees, gone wild. Soon the names of those villages will be forgotten like the people who lived there. That is why me and my brother want you to write about them, so that some people will read and 'member when the Cowichan Indians had many villages and were a great tribe.

"First, I'll tell you about the name 'Puneluxutth'. That name means 'two logs half-covered with sand.'[223] Longer ago than I can tell you, there were no people living in this land. Then the sun made a few people, one here, one there, in different places; but, 'member, they were not big and tall. The first men and women were very small, like this—she held up a mummy-like thumb—Well, as I told you, there was no one on Kuper Island, only the birds and animals; but the island looked just as it does today. At the north end was that long point that makes one side of a bay.

At the head of this bay, up on the bank, there was a spring of nice water coming right up out of the ground, and by that spring were two great cedar logs, lying on the ground and half covered with sand washed up by the waves when the water was high. I don't know how many years those logs had been there, with only the birds flying near, and the animals coming to drink at the spring. When, one morning, the sun was shining down oh, so hot, it shone down on those two logs and they got hotter and hotter. A maple tree was growing near and it gave a little shade to one of the logs, but the other was right out in the sun.

Bye-and-bye the bark on this log began to crack, and soon it began to move as though something in the log was trying to come out. Suddenly there was a loud crack! The bark split open, and out came a little man! He crawled out of the log and sat in the sun, getting strong. Now, the water was far out that morning, and as the sun got hotter and hotter the sand got very dry and hard; and as the little man sat up on his log watching the sun drying up the water, he saw the sand between the two logs open, just as the bark had done, and out of the sand came a little woman! My, he was glad to see some one who would be a friend. He got down from his log, and together they walked over the sand until they came to the spring.

Here they sat down and drank the fresh, clean water, and ate some blackberries, growing near.

"'This is a good place,' said the man. I think we had better make our house here.' So the two little people got busy, taking the bark off cedar trees and fastening it together until at last they had made a little house beside the spring. 'What name shall we give our house?' asked the woman. 'We will name it by those big logs where we were made,' he told her. So those two first people called their house 'Puneluxutth"—two logs half covered with sand.

"Have you ever been to Puneluxutth'?" asked Tommy Pielle. I shook my head, "Not for many years," I told him.

"Well, one day you must go and see that place; go to that bay, where the big houses are; seven of them, all big, big, standing by the water, and near them is that spring where the first little house was made, and near that are the two big cedar logs."

"Still there?" I exclaimed.

"Yes, still there, just as they always were, and they will always stay there, I think. Why, our grandfather, Xulqalustun, that old chief told us that his grandfather 'membered those logs, so we know that they are the same two logs that those two little people saw, and that out of one of them came that first little man."

"Listen!" said Siamtunaat, "When you go there, walk past those big houses, and there on the ground you will see the great pieces of wood that the old Indians made their houses from—great cedar logs. No man has ever found out how the people in those days made the long pieces like great shingles, to put on the roof. You look and you will see they are very old—more than one hundred years, I think; and they are made with deep marks all the way down them, for the water to run in. But how those shingles were made, no man knows."

"I must go to Puneluxutth' and see them," I decided and Siamtunaat and her brother nodded approval.

"Tell us when you go, and we will paddle over and show you our big house. It is not a very old one, but it is oh, so big," said Siamtunaat.

"And now I must tell you about another name. I think that Yuxwula'us[24] will be the next. That place is on Kuper Island, too, but it is not the same side as Puneluxutth'—not far from the Indian school. I can 'member when there were lots of houses there but they are gone now. Well, that name 'Yuxwula'us' means 'Eagle,' and I will tell you why it was given that name.

"As I told you before, the sun made just a few people; first the two at Puneluxutth', then two at this Yuxwula'us, and these two little people—just like those others—made their house by a spring of water. For many, many years these two lived alone in their house, and no little children came to make them glad, but at last, when they were getting quite old, a baby girl was born. My, how happy they were! and how proud they felt whenever they looked at that fat, brown baby. 'This is the finest baby in the land.' said the old father. 'Of course,' the old woman told him, 'but,' she said, 'there are no other babies! there are no other people!' 'I had not thought of that,' said the man. 'When we get very old who will look after our baby? Will there be no husband for her?' The two old people looked at each other and felt very unhappy, to think of their baby being left all alone. Then the woman said, 'Perhaps someone will come before we have to die. We can but wait.' The man nodded his old head and said, 'Yes, we can but wait.'

"Now, quite near their little house was a great fir tree. It was not very high, for the wind had broken off the top, one stormy night; but it was very big around, and up on the broken top a great eagle had made its nest. Every year that eagle came and made its nest, and the little people would sit on the rocks and watch the bird as it sat hatching its eggs, and they would hear the young birds crying for food, and see their little heads looking over the edge of the nest, waiting for the old birds to bring them something to eat, and at last, when they grew strong, the little eagles would fly away, and the old tree would be empty and quiet for another year.

"One day the old man and his wife were sitting watching the nest, and their baby, wrapped in the softest cedar bark, was hanging in its cradle on a low branch beside them, when their came a queer noise, 'Ya-a-a-a, Ya-a-a-a!' 'What was that?' asked the man. 'At first I thought it was our baby crying.' 'No,' answered his wife, 'it was not our baby, she is asleep, but I, too, thought it was a baby crying.' They sat and listened, and again came the cry. 'It comes out of the air,' whispered the little woman in a voice of fear. She ran to where the baby was sleeping and lifted it down. 'That must be a bad thing,' she said, 'I will take our child in the house!' Just then the cry came once more and, looking up, they saw the eagle flying round and round, coming lower and lower, until she settled, at last, on the edge of the nest. 'See!' exclaimed the man, 'the eggs must be hatched; she has food in her beak.' They stood watching whilst the eagle fed her little ones, then, as she flew away, again came that cry.

"It comes from the nest,' said the woman, "and it is the voice of a baby! Can the eagle have stolen some poor woman's baby? Are there, perhaps, other people in this land whom we have not seen?'

"'I will climb up and look before the eagle comes back,' said her husband, and, running to the tree, he quickly began climbing. When he got to the top he pulled himself over the broken edge and looked into the nest. 'Ah!' he called, 'you were right, it is a baby, a small baby boy, fat and brown as our own child. Bring me some bark to tie him in and I will bring him down from here.'

"He climbed down to meet his wife, who had quickly taken their baby from its cradle and was bringing the cradle for him to put the new baby in. It did not take him long to tie the child safely in the cradle and, hanging it on his back, he started down the tree. He had just time to reach the ground before the great eagle came swooping down upon him. Shrieking and clawing, the bird fought those two little people for her baby, but at last the woman got a long stick and with this she hit at the bird whilst her husband ran to the house with the child, and, seeing that she could not get into the house, the eagle flew up to her nest.

"Now those two were so happy with their two babies. 'Our child need never be alone now that we have this man child to take care of her,' said the mother, and she sat thinking of the days when these two fat little ones would have a house and babies of their own.

"One day, when the children were growing big and strong, just beginning to walk, the baby that belonged to the two old people crawled away from her mother and, sometimes walking a few steps, sometimes falling down and crawling, it got to the edge of the rocks and, rolling over, fell into the water. As it fell, the eagle, sitting on her nest, saw it, and, with a loud cry, flew after it, catching its little leg in her beak just as it went under the water. Holding the baby by the leg, the eagle flew up to the rocks beside the little house, and, as she put her feet on the rocks, what do you think happened?"

Siamtunaat looked inquiringly at me, but before I could hazard a guess, Tommy Pielle exclaimed: "I'll tell you what happened. That great eagle turned into a woman!"

He looked triumphantly at his sister, but she scowled at him and turned a broad shoulder on him.

"Yes, he's right," she said. "That eagle turned right into a woman. I can tell you those people were frightened; but the woman was so nice. She went up to the old woman and, 'We will be friends,' she said. 'Only give me back my baby boy. Oh, I have cried for him! She ran into the house and came out with her little boy in her arms. 'How fine he is!' she cried. 'Bring out your little one and we will see them together!'

"So those two babies played together and grew up together, and when they were old enough they built a little house of their own, where they lived until they were very, very, old, with their children and their grandchildren all living near them in the same place. And these two gave their home the name 'Yuxwula'us, the Eagle,' after the mother who had been turned into an eagle, but who turned back to a woman again when she saved that little baby."

Mary Rice, Tommy Pielle and Beryl Cryer

The Island of Xulel-thw[225]

After exploring the village and burial sites on Willy Island, the largest of the Shoal Islands located at the mouth of the Chemainus River, Beryl Cryer visits Mary Rice to learn more about the place. Following her account of Xulel-thw, the name of the old village that stood at the northeast corner of Willy Island, Mary Rice tells of the destruction of Sunuwnets village on Chemainus Harbour by a neighbouring people. She concludes the interview with a short account of the origin story of the village of Thuq'min' (Shell Beach), opposite the town of Ladysmith.

A FEW DAYS AGO WE SPENT AN AFTERNOON AT XULEL-THW, that lovely little island lying off the mouth of Chemainus River; the white shell beach gleaming in the sunshine against a background of fir and arbutus trees. Just another of those perfect spots which the Coast Indians seem always to have chosen for their homes.

The island is deserted now, all that remains are a tumble-down shack, a few plum and apple trees grown half wild, and one, mighty, roughly-hewn cedar log, evidently an ancient corner post—standing at one end of the clearing, but leaning at such a precarious angle that the winds of another Winter must, I feel certain, complete the ruin of what, Siamtunaat tells me, was long years ago, a fine, large lodge which housed the inhabitants of Xulel-thw.[226]

The owner of the dilapidated shack, Sulits'e', generally known as Old Willie, died many years ago. A generation ago, other members of the tribe moved elsewhere, but Old Willie remained faithful to his village; there he lived with numbers of dogs, and with his two wives, Mary Ann and Old Man.

Periodically the family would visit Chemainus, Old Willie leading the procession, stalking ahead, followed by Mary Ann, on her back a basket of salmon, oysters or crabs to be sold; and bringing up the rear would be poor old Old Man, hobbling along with the weight of the basket she carried on her back—the strap around her forehead.

No one knew Old Willie's age, but rumor had it that the older inhabitants of the district could recollect when Old Man was the young and favorite wife, and there was yet another old wife!

On the other side of the island, and facing the mouth of the river, all the old inhabitants of Xulel-thw and their descendants are buried. There on a curiously raised strip of land, with a swamp at the back and the salt water in front, stands the little old cedar house graves with their sliding windows and the usual plum trees growing about them; a veritable hedge of yellow tar weed fringing the white shell beach below. At a little distance are yet older graves, their roofs faintly showing through the dense underbrush.[227]

Looking curiously out of place in this primitive little burial ground is a stone pillar erected to the memory of Charles Stittin.

*Burial place (shmukw'ela) at Xulel-thw
(Willy Island).*
Photo by Beryl Cryer, circa 1930s.
Image PN 5958 courtesy Royal British Columbia
Museum.

I asked Siamtunaat about this stone when next I saw her. She was greatly troubled when I told her of the name.

"That's not right!" she said, "That man who is buried there was called Charlie Stuts'un. He was chief of Xulel-thw and had lots of money, that's why the stone was put there. Now that man and his family lived in that big house by the railway bridge at Chemainus River. He was an old man, about eighty-five, when he died, and they buried him at Xulel-thw because he belonged to that place. All these people are over there, the last to die was poor Louisa—you 'member—Pat George's wife? She was burned in her house. Well, her grave is over there, right by those little houses of cedar."

We sat in silence for a few minutes. Siamtunaat was thinking.

"See now," she said, "That name, Xulel-thw, means sort of marks—" She looked about her kitchen, evidently in search of something, then took down a carton of salt from her shelf. "See, marks like these," she explained, pointing to the lettering.[228] "As I told you, there was just one big house on Xulel-thw; it had no door in front, but at both ends there were doors: and do you know what those people had done? All along the front of that house, next to the sea, they had made a big, big picture—right along!"

"What was the picture?" I asked her.

"Well, it was a man catching a whale, and it was made very big. The man was in his canoe and there was the great whale swimming along in the water! The man who made the picture cut it in the cedar boards, and then he put color on it, red and black. My grandfather told me about it and said that whenever they had a big time at Xulel-thw Old Stuts'un—that was the grandfather of that Charlie

Mary Rice and Beryl Cryer

Stuts'un—would put more color on the marks, so that people coming to that place could see the picture from far away; and so they gave the place that name, Xulel-thw, marks, or sort of pictures!

"Not many people lived at Xulel-thw, only three families in the one big house. There were Stuts'un, the grandfather of Charlie, and his family; Sulits'e', Old Willie's grandfather, and his family, and then there was Hwslhuw'lhnenum, that name means a poor man.[229] That man was a hunter, every day he went hunting away back in the woods. My grandfather told me that that man was the best hunter he ever knew; he could dig those deep holes in the ground for the deer to fall into better and quicker than any other hunter, and he could cover them with branches and earth so that no man could tell where they were made. Now," Siamtunaat shook her head sadly, "there are no hunters like that, and there is no one left on Xulel-thw—all are gone—just the little houses of cedar left alone!"

A far away look came into the old eyes, and as she sat dreaming I thought of the little island as we had last seen it, with the mists of evening falling softly about the old shack, and the great cedar post standing gaunt and white in the twilight.

Siamtunaat sighed deeply.

"Oh, it makes me feel so bad, when I think of all those places empty—everybody dead or gone away!" she said mournfully. "Nearly every place I think of is like that. There are not many of us left! Right here, on this beach, there used to be a village, lots of big houses, with the sea in front and that water behind them. That place was called Sunuwnets, which means fresh water behind houses.[230] All those people of Sunuwnets were killed in a big fight, and about one girl!"

Siamtunaat laughed as though at a great joke.

"Now I'll tell you about that fight," she said, settling herself more comfortably with her knitting. "There were two villages of our people living near together, the people at Sunuwnets, in this bay, and another village at Chemainus.[231] These people were not very good friends, but a young man at Sunuwnets saw one of the girls at Chemainus and he wanted her for his wife. Every day he used to go and ask the girl's father to let him have her, but the old man wouldn't let her go.

"After a long time the young man told the girl's father, 'If you don't give her to me I will steal her, or kill her!' This made the old man so frightened that he said, 'Oh, take the girl and go away, but be good to her!' So the man took the girl back to Sunuwnets to be his wife.

"Well, for a time they were very happy, she was a good wife and her husband was kind to her; but his old mother did not like her.

"One day the old woman told him, 'That wife of yours is no good! She is too lazy. Make her do more work.' And every day she would tell him what a poor wife the girl was; until at last he said, 'If she is so lazy, you had better see that she has more work to do!' So that poor girl had to work all day and half the night, and always she was very unhappy.

"'Let me go back to my people!' she said to her husband. But he was afraid to let her go, for he knew that she would tell her father that the Sunuwnets had not been kind to her.

"One day the man was away hunting, and his old mother far out on the beach, digging clams; the wife was all alone! When she found that there was no one with her, she hurried into the house and got a rope that her husband had been making out of willow bark. Then she ran out and into the woods that in those days grew near the houses.

"When the husband came home, he called to his wife, but she did not answer. 'She's gone!' his old mother told him. 'I am glad, for now you can get a better wife who will not leave all the work for me to do!'

"My, that man was angry! Away he ran round to Chemainus, for, he thought, 'The girl had, of course, gone back to her people!'

"When he got near the village he saw his wife's father coming to meet him. 'Come quickly!' called the man, 'come and see what has happened to my poor daughter!' He took the young man through the woods until they got to the place where the hospital is now. 'See!' he said, 'there is your wife! She came back to her people and has killed herself, with your own rope!' He pointed to a tree near them, and there was the poor young wife; she had hanged herself with her husband's new rope.

"'For all that you and your people have done to my daughter, you must be punished—you, too, must die!' shouted the old man, and, with the great stick he carried, he hit the man on his head and killed him. Well, you see, that started a great fight. All the Chemainus Indians went over in their canoes to Sunuwnets, and how they did fight! So that before night there was not one man left alive at Sunuwnets. After that, the people from S-amuna' used to come right through the woods up to Sunuwnets, and there they would dig lots of clams, dry them, and carry them back to their own village. After a bit, the big houses fell down, and now there is nothing to show that there was at one time a big village there."

There was a long pause whilst Siamtunaat counted her stitches. "Now," she said, leaning back and smiling at me, "I can tell you about one more place, before my family come home wanting their supper.

"Do you know that nice, white beach of shells across from Ladysmith? That place is called Thuq'min'. It means 'spear the fish!' Long, long ago, when the first little man lived there, he sat on the beach with a sharp stone and a long stick in his hands. All day long he sat there, scraping away at the stick, just because he had nothing else to do.

"Bye-and-bye he looked at his stick and thought, 'What a nice sharp stick I have made! It looks as though it would stick into things nicely!' He looked about, but there was nothing to throw it at, on the beach; so he thought, 'Perhaps I might see something in the water I could throw it at!' He got a log and, taking his sharp stick, he paddled out a little way: then he looked down in the water. There he saw a great big salmon swimming along by his log. Very carefully he took his stick and pushed it hard down at the salmon. Straight to the fish it went, and stuck in its side, and after putting it in the sun to warm a little, he ate it. Every day after that, he would take his stick and catch all the fish he wanted; and because the fish were always waiting for him, and the stick never missed, he called that place Thuq'min', spear the fish.

Siamtunaat's Story [232]

Beryl Cryer comes in search of another story, interrupting Mary who is hard at work making sweaters, an important home-based business.[233] Mary Rice accommodates Cryer, and relates a series of stories from her childhood as she works. She begins with a recollection of her great uncle, Swilhultun, and his participation in a "dog-eating" performance, followed by an account of a time she and her brother hid in a longhouse at Puneluxutth' while it was searched by British sailors and marines. She continues with a recollection of visiting Victoria with her parents to trade, and a story about moving to Saanich as a young girl to live with her aunt. Beryl Cryer then asks her, out of the blue, if she remembers seeing any slaves. Mary Rice tells her about a slave owned by her maternal grandfather, Quyupule'ynuxw, and a story about a Songhees girl named Eliza, who was captured by the Bella Bella, and then the Haida, and lived as a slave until she was returned to her people.

WHEN I STOPPED AT SIAMTUNAAT'S COTTAGE this morning, she was carding wool: beside her a pile of unsightly, matted lumps of fleece, which she had washed and dried in the sun.

It seemed incredible that from this mass she could produce anything that would be suitable for spinning. But, as I watched, she took a small piece of the fleece, put it on a carder, and, after a few deft strokes of the second carder, dropped the whitest, fluffiest piece of wool—light as thistledown—into the deep basket at her feet.

In one corner of the kitchen I noticed another basket piled high with scarlet wool, carded and ready for spinning.

"What is that for?" I asked her.

"Oh!" she said, "I'm so busy! Lots of people want sweaters. That red wool is to make a sweater for a man in Vancouver who wants to wear it for hunting—he's in a hurry for it, so maybe I'll do that now, not this white one."

She carried the white wool into that bedroom of hers—which always appears to be bursting with things tied up in mysterious bundles, piled on the floor and hanging from the rafters—and dragged the basket of red wool across to her chair.

"I can spin while I talk to you," she explained. "Now where's that thing gone? She fumbled on a shelf amongst various odds and ends. "Ah, here it is! Here's my spinning wheel!" She laughed, and showed me a pointed and rounded stick through the centre of a round of tin—taken evidently from the top of a lard tin.

"That's what I spin with," she said; "see now, it's very easy!"

She took a piece of fluffy wool in her left hand, twisted the pointed end of the stick in one corner, and, with a quick, deft twist, had pulled the wool out into a long strand, at the same time twisting it on the stick. It was all done in the twinkling of an eye, and in less than five minutes she had her spinning wheel wound in a cone-shaped ball, with a rope of red wool. It was all very easy—until I tried!

"Now, what can I tell you today, I wonder?"

Siamtunaat thoughtfully rolled a piece of wool between her hands.

"S'pose I tell you something of when I was a little girl?" she asked.

"Just what I would like," I told her, and she laughed and nodded her old head.

"I was a very, very little girl when I can 'member my mother hiding me. She was very scared, and she took me and put me under our sleeping place, and told me I must make no noise or I would be eaten right up!"

"What was going to eat you, Siamtunaat?" I asked her.

"Well, now, I never like to talk about this, and I never told my chilrun—but do you know!" (She lowered her voice and her old eyes grew very round), "my grandfather, that Xulqalustun, had a brother. His name was Swilhultun[234] but when the white people came they all called him 'Captain Very-Good.' This man was a great dancer. He was always called to dance at any of the big times our people had, but sometimes he danced too hard. He would shout, and sing, and up to the great fires he would dance, jumping high in the air, and if he went on too long he went mad, and anything small that he saw he would tear to pieces and eat! Lots of little dogs were killed and eaten by Swilhultun,[235] and all the women would run and hide their little chilrun when he danced, because sometimes the very little ones were never seen again after a big time—that's what they told me!" She added; "That's the first thing I can 'member—my poor mother pushing me under the high place where we all had our beds, and telling me to pull some of the skins and things over me, and to lay very quiet.

"Next I 'member, me and my brother were playing together, when we saw a big boat—the biggest one I had ever seen. It came slowly through the water and stopped out in front of Puneluxutth'.[236]

"All the men ran to the beach, but the children stayed with their mothers near the houses.

"By-and-by we saw a small boat coming from the big one, and when it came to the beach some men in smart coats got out and everyone talked a lot. Soon my father came running back to our house.

Mary Rice and Beryl Cryer

"'It's the man-o'-war!' he told my mother. 'The soldiers have come to hunt for some bad man who has got away from them. They are going to count everyone, and we must all stay in our houses!'

"When me and my brother heard what our father was saying, we got very scared, and we ran into our house and we crawled under the beds where our mother hid me when Swilhultun danced. Even after such a long time I 'member that there were lots of potatoes and some deer skins under there, and we got behind them.

"Very soon we heard the people coming in, and my grandfather say: 'As I told you, there is no one in this house: all my people are outside!' Then a white man talked a little and my grandfather said, 'All right, you may look, but you will find no man hiding here!' I peeped out and I saw two soldiers take their guns and, walking together, beginning at one end of the house, they poked with those guns along under the high place—(raised platform)—where all the people had their beds. Along those guns came, poking, poking, and very soon they got close to us. My, how frightened we were!—too frightened to crawl out, so we started to crawl along behind and over the things that were put away under the beds, and no matter how quickly we crawled those big guns came just behind us all the time. Of course, we could not go quietly, and pretty soon those soldiers heard us, and I s'pose they thought the man they were hunting for was there, because they came along quicker than before, and suddenly one of the guns poked my brother! Oh, how he shouted and cried! and, of course, I cried, too.

"The soldiers looked under, and when they saw us they reached back and pulled us out! One big man held me up by the back of my neck.

"'What's this?' he asked. 'Does this belong to that bad man?'

"'No!' my father told him. 'that's mine! Give it to me!'

"The soldier laughed and sat me up on the bed, and I stayed there until he had gone." Siamtunaat's vast body heaved with laughter. "Oh, it makes me laugh to think of that man holding me up like that!' she chuckled. "It would take a lot of people to do that now!"

"Now, when my people went to Victoria I always wanted to go, too. Early in the morning we would start, the canoe filled with skins, and duck and deer meat, and sometimes potatoes. I used to sit amongst these things and often go to sleep, for it was a long way down to Victoria. When we got there I stayed and played with Indian children, whilst my father and mother carried the things round to the houses and sold them. We often stayed the night with some of our people who were living in Victoria, and would paddle back to Puneluxutth' the next morning.

"When my father died, my mother took me to Saanich to my aunt, and she kept me until I was getting to be a big girl. One day I 'member I had a fight with my aunt's big boy, and I ran away from their house.

"At that time there were only a few little houses at Victoria, but there were lots of Indians there, and I thought if I could get there, I would find some of my friends who would take me home to Puneluxutth'.

"For five days I walked and walked, but it was all trees, and I could not tell where I was and I couldn't find any houses. I had eaten all the dried fish and clams I started with, and oh, I was so tired and cold and hungry! You see, it was about March, and there were no berries for me to pick, and I had to sleep under trees without any blanket. Early one morning I got to a farm (I think it must have been out by Mount Tolmie), but I was afraid to go to the house—I was so dirty—so I hid in the bushes and watched.

"Soon I saw a man come out of the house, carrying two buckets. He was going to milk the cows, and he had a dog with him. Well, that dog soon found out that I was near, and it came after me. I was so scared I ran straight to the man, and when he saw how thin and dirty I was, he took me to the house, and a lady there was so kind to me. She helped me wash and gave me a dress and shawl, and she sat me by her kitchen fire and gave me something to eat. After that I went to sleep by the fire.

"By-and-by the man came in and woke me and said he was ready to drive me to Victoria. He had two horses hitched to a wagon, and my! how I did like that drive. We found a Puneluxutth' woman at Victoria, and when she and her husband started for Puneluxutth' that afternoon, they took me with them.

"My poor mother cried when she saw me, and my grandfather said I had better stay with them. The next year my grandfather Xulqalustun, gave a big potlatch, and he gave me my singing name—Xalunamut. That name means, 'Not seen before.'

"All the people from Nanaimo down to Victoria were called to that potlatch, and there were ten women and five men to sing and dance. Oh that was a big time.

"Do you remember seeing any slaves, Siamtunaat?" I asked her.

"Well, not many," she replied. "I can tell you about the time I went with my mother to stay with her father, Chief Quyupule'ynuxw, and there was a slave at his house. You know, the priests had been telling my people that it was wrong to keep slaves, and they had made everybody send their slaves back to the places they had stolen them from. Quyupule'ynuxw sent away all his slaves, but this one man would not leave him. 'No', he told the priests, 'this man and his woman have been good to me, and I have no other home; I will stay here!' And he stayed until he was an old man. That man had not been stolen like other slaves. Quyupule'ynuxw's wife had found him, thrown away. He was not a big, strong baby, so the people he belonged to 'threw him out.' Well, Quyupule'ynuxw's wife carried that baby home with her, and she got a lot of 'erbs and steamed him, and by-and-by he grew quite well, and when he got bigger he worked for Quyupule'ynuxw and was his slave."

She sat spinning busily for a minute.

"Oh, yes!" she exclaimed, "There was Eliza, she was a slave, too; I had forgotten her! Now she belonged to the Songhees, and she lived with her uncle near

Victoria. When she was a little girl the Bella-Bella people caught her and made her a slave. Then, when she was about eighteen years old, all the slaves ran away, whilst the Bella-Bellas were fighting far away. When these people got back they found no slaves left, and they went after them and caught nearly all again. Some they beat and worked harder than ever, and some they killed, but that girl they traded with the Haidas, and she went to their homes to be a slave. There she lived until she was about forty years old. One day some of the Haidas were going to Victoria and they told her: 'We will take you with us, but you must not get out of the canoe.'

"You see," explained Siamtunaat, "the Haidas did not know that she was from Victoria! When they got to Victoria they made the slave lie down in the canoe, and they tied her and covered her with an old mat; then they anchored the canoe out in deep water and went away leaving her alone.

"Soon a Songhees man came along in his canoe, and as he passed the Haida canoe the slave inside it heard him, and tapped against the side, hoping he would come and find her. The man paddled up to the canoe and 'Who are you?' he asked the woman. Now that poor thing had been away so long that she had forgotten how to speak Chinook; all she could say was the name of her uncle, so she said this to the man and he made her understand that he knew her uncle and was going to tell the Chief about her.

"When the Chief heard about that slave, he called all the people and they went on the beach and waited for the Haidas to come. When it was getting dark, just one or two came to the canoes, and the Songhees chief, Squameyuqs, said to them: 'Where is the Chief of this canoe? Tell him to come quickly, for I must talk to him!'

"When the Haida Chief came, Squameyuqs told him: 'We want no trouble with you, but in that canoe you have a woman who was taken as a slave by the Bella-Bellas many years ago. How many blankets will you take for her? The Haida chief said that he would take twenty blankets and one gun; so, in the morning the Songhees chief sent those things to the canoe, and the Haidas gave back the woman. Her uncle took her back to his house, and he paid back to Chief Squameyuqs, the gun and blankets.

Well, do you know, very soon a Portuguese man came along and married that woman. They went to live at Nanoose, where they had a big farm, and I think some of that family are living there now.

Indian Games[237]

Beryl Cryer watches Tommy Pielle make gambling sticks, which leads to a general discussion about gambling. Mary Rice interrupts the conversation to teach Beryl Cryer some Hul'q'umi'num' village place-names, and introduces her to an account of Xeel's, the Transformer, and sturgeon on the Fraser River.

TOMMY PIELLE WAS VERY BUSY. For some time I had been watching him at his work wondering what he was making. First he had gone into the woods and cut several long sticks from an elder tree. From one of these he cut four pieces, each one about two inches long; these he carefully peeled and, with a lead pencil drew a black line around the centre of two, the others he left white. The remaining sticks he cut into a number of short lengths.

"What are you making Tommy Pielle?" I asked him. He grinned cheerfully at me. "Oh this? It's a game. I make it for these children." He pointed to Siamtunaat's grandchildren playing on the beach.

Siamtunaat shook her head at him. "Now, Tommy Pielle," she said, "Don't you teach those little children to gamble!" She turned to me. "You know," she explained, "that's a big gambling game, its name is slhe'lem[238] All Indians play that game, and lots of white men, too! My brother likes to go to Yakima, they always have a big game there, and sometimes he makes a little money; sometimes he loses, but it's lots of fun!"

"Do you play?" I asked.

She glanced out of the corners of her eyes at Tommy Pielle whittling down his little sticks.

"Well," she laughed, "Sometimes I play a little, I like to put in five dollars some days, but I never win much!"

"See now," said Pielle, "I'll tell you how we play this game. Now these two"—he held up the sticks with the black line round them—"these are women! and these"—he held up the unmarked two—"are men! Lots of people can play, you know, and everyone puts in money and has twenty of these sticks." He pointed to the other lengths he had cut. "Now!"—he passed the 'men' and 'women' rapidly from hand to hand—"now all bet and say what hand the women are in! Oh, it's lots of fun. As my sister said, Yakima is the place I like to go to when I play; the people all sing, and some have drums and hit on them with sticks, and everyone has lots of money to spend! This is a very, very old game, about as old as smetale'. Do you know about that?" he inquired.

"No," I told him, "I don't know any of your games."

"Well, smetale' is like this. It's played with four front teeth from a beaver. They are pretty big, and so"—he curved his fingers. "Here are two 'men' and two 'women' again. The 'women teeth' have black marks under them. A man holds them all four in his two hands and shakes them, then he throws them up in the air and they fall on to a blanket. If they fall so that the marks of the 'women' show, then you win! That's a very nice game to play, and so is a game with the same name as that other one—Scha-lay-hlen—but we don't play it the same way.

"First there must be two pieces of wood from that tree you call arbutus: they are cut round like biscuits, and are as thick as my finger. One is made black, and one is left white. Now there has to be a lot of cedar bark, scraped until it is very soft and small. Into this the 'man' and 'woman' are put and mixed about, and changed from one hand to the other very quickly. Now everyone tries to say where the 'woman' will be, and everyone bets big money on it."

"You always guess where the woman is?" I asked him.

He laughed heartily at this. "Yes." He said. "I guess the woman is always hiding and we have to find her!"

Here Siamtunaat interrupted us, no doubt feeling that Tommy Pielle had talked long enough. "I will tell you some more names of our villages, and what they mean," she suggested, as she seated herself on a log near us.

"Now, you know I told you that Sunuwnets[239] was 'Fresh water behind houses.' Well, there is Q'ulits', the place you call Chemainus Bay. That place is sometimes like Sunuwnets, only at Q'ulits' it is the salt water that runs back, not good water coming in, and that name Q'ulits' means 'Salt water running back.'

"Over on Valdez Island there is a village called Leey'qsun. Now that name is a little hard to tell you about, but it means 'Bark standing up.' You know that little island near Kuper Island—at the south end? We call that Hwtth'isutsun.[240] It means 'Dry at low tide,' because when the water went out, our people could walk across to Kuper. Another place is up at Yellow Point: that is Kwqwumluhwuthun 'Big roots,' because at that place there used to be a lot of very big roots close to the water. You know where 'Hwts'usi' is down at Bonsall's Creek? You see, 'Hwts'usi' means 'Little creek, or stream!'"

Here Tommy Pielle leaned forward and talked rapidly to her for a minute. "Ah, yes!" said Siamtunaat, "I forgot to tell you about Kwqwumluhwuthun. It was one of the men lying at that place who found out what happened to our people when they died!

"You know, long ago, our people knew that the sun, who we call Sum'shathut made everyone, but they did not know what happened, or where they went, after they died. Now there was a man living at Kwqwumluhwuthun whose mother got very sick and died, and he was left alone. A few days after the woman had died, this man came home from hunting very tired and hot. 'I will get in the water for a little while before I get my supper,' he thought, and went into the sea in front of his house. As he lay resting in the water he heard his mother call him and, forgetting that she was dead, he answered her. Again she called him, just as he had so often heard her, when it was time to go and eat. When he heard her voice again he stood up and looked at the house, thinking he would see his mother. Then suddenly he remembered: 'Why, my mother has gone, she is dead! Who, then, can be calling me?' As he stood thinking, he heard the voice again, and saw someone standing just inside his door. Quickly he ran to his house, thinking that maybe, somehow, his mother had come back, but when he got there he saw a great big owl standing and looking at him!

"He called out to it, 'Who are you? Are you my mother? The owl did not speak, but as it flew past him and out of the door, it called him again, and as before, the voice was his mother's voice. So the man knew that his mother was turned into an owl. And after that my people believed that the owls—'those birds that come and talk in the night time'—are really their 'lelations' who have died."

Tommy Pielle had finished trimming and peeling all the sticks. His game was ready for the children, and, gathering it up, he started off down the beach to show it to them. As he left he asked his sister, "Have you told about the time the sturgeon left the Fraser River?" Siamtunaat threw up her hands.

"Why, no!" she exclaimed, "I can tell you that story now, there is just time." She turned to me again. "You know," she said, "before the priests came, and my people knew no better, they talked of someone who could do everything. He could make people, and he could kill people, but he was the head of all, always doing good, and they called him 'Xeel's.'²⁴¹ Well, in those days my people, and all the people from Hwmuthkwi'um, used to catch lots of big sturgeon in the Fraser River. Every year they would all go there for the sturgeon fishing. One day two of the Hwmuthkwi'um people—a man and a woman—made a fire on the rocks and started to cook a piece of sturgeon with the head still on it for their dinner. Just as it was ready to eat, a man came along the rocks and sat down beside the two.

"'I am so hungry,' he said, 'will you give me a piece of your sturgeon?' 'No,' said the Hwmuthkwi'um people, 'catch some fish for yourself; we need all of ours!' Again the man asked, and again those two said 'No!' Get away and catch your own fish!'

"Then the man stood up, and he said to them: 'Look at me, and see who it is that you have been talking to, who you would give no food to.' When he said that, the man and woman looked up, and they saw that the man was Xeel's!

"'Turn to stone!' said Xeel's, 'that's all you are good for. Turn to stone and stay there forever!'²⁴²

"And there they are!" said Siamtunaat, "I have seen them myself, the stone man and woman, with the sturgeon's head between them, there on the rocks, and looking up a little to where Xeel's once stood. And do you know," she added impressively, "from that day all the sturgeon left the Fraser River!

"Well, after that all the people got together to talk about this thing: 'What can we do?' asked the Hwmuthkwi'um; 'how can we get the sturgeon back again?'

"At last one very old man got up and spoke.

"'I will tell you what you must do,' he said. 'You must take your most beautiful young girl and sink her in the river, and Xeel's will send the sturgeon back again!'

"'We will do it,' said the Hwmuthkwi'um, and they took the Chief's daughter, put a new blanket made of the hair of the mountain goat around her, and on top of her head they fastened a kingfisher, with the wings spread down both sides of her face, and around her head they put the bones of a deer, a bear, and a mink. Now they took a long rope made of mountain goat hair, and they put this white rope about her body, and fastened heavy stones to the ends hanging down. Then taking her out to the deepest part of the river, they put her down in the water. Down to the bottom of the river she went, and, do you know, in just about one hour the sturgeon had all come back!

"Well, now, the mother of that poor girl was very unhappy. Every day she walked along beside the river, calling, calling to her daughter. One day, as she sat beside the water, crying and calling to the girl, a large sturgeon came swimming up to her.

"'Don't cry, my mother,' it said. 'See, it is your daughter talking to you. I have been turned into a sturgeon and I live with the fish. But you must never cry for me, I am so happy!' Well, when she heard her girl talk like that, the poor woman felt better, and after that she would sit near the water every day, and every day her daughter would swim up and talk to her!"

Siamtunaat paused a moment. Then, "I'll tell you a funny thing," she said. Ever since that girl was sunk, with that long white rope around her, some of it hanging down, every sturgeon has a thing like that inside it—something white, and looking like that rope of hair after it got wet!"

The Last Big Fight of the Cowichans[243]

When Beryl Cryer asks about the famous battle that took place at Maple Bay on Vancouver Island in the first half of the nineteenth century, Mary Rice directs her to an elder who knows more about the subject. Beryl Cryer meets the elder's son, Ts'umsitun, who volunteers to tell her the story in the context of six other conflicts that were among the "wars" between the Central Coast Salish and various northern peoples between 1790 and 1860.

THIS IS THE STORY OF THE LAST BIG FIGHT between the Indians of the Cowichan tribe and their enemies, the Qhwimux, Haida, and Bella-Bella peoples.

I had asked Siamtunaat to tell me what she knew of this fight, but she was very vague about it.

"I'll tell you who knows that story," she said. "You know that man Ts'umsitun? Well, he has an old father down at Hwts'usi'. That old man knows lots of stories! You ask Ts'umsitun and he will tell you how to find that old man."

The following evening I went out to where Ts'umsitun lives with his wife and family in a neat cottage with flower garden about it and a potato patch at the back. I found him putting the finishing touches to a beautiful little dug-out canoe he had made—a very smart affair, the outside black, and inside pale blue. It was to be fitted with oars, and Ts'umsitun was sitting on the ground cutting braces for the rowlocks, whittling down pieces of oak for the purpose with his pocketknife. He showed me the one he had finished, as smooth and symmetrical as though turned out by some machine.

"Yes," he said, with a decided shake of his head, "my old father knows some good stories. Now, what kind of stories do you want?"

I began to explain, but he interrupted me: "Oh, I know! You want to hear about the time all the Indians made peace, and the great fight they had over there at Hwtl'upnets?[244] Well now, it was like this—" He pushed away his tools, leaned back against a stump, and launched into a graphic description of that final battle of the Cowichans, whilst I found a seat for myself on a maple log beside him.

"Those old Indians," said Ts'umsitun, "had nothing to do but hunt and eat, so I guess they were always fighting!" He selected a grass straw with great deliberation, and, tucking it in the corner of his mouth, sucked it thoughtfully. "Always fighting!" he repeated. "One time the Cowichans went to war with the Bella-Bellas, and they brought back as many slaves as their canoes would hold. Those old canoes were not like our little dug-outs," he added. "They were very big. Each canoe would hold twenty men, or maybe more. Then down the Bella-Bellas came after them and again they fought, but again, the Bella-Bellas were beaten. Next time the Cowichans went to the American side, but those people were great fighters, and they chased our people back, but they could not land, and had to paddle home again.

"Then Ts'uwxilem[245] and his men came to help the Cowichans. My! that man was a great fighter! He took the Cowichans right back after the American Indians and they had a big fight. When it was over Ts'uwxilem made a rope of cedar branches, and onto this rope he fixed the heads of all the men he had killed, and he put the rope up on poles in his canoe, and all the way home he was shouting and singing to the heads of his enemies. When he got home he put short poles in front of his house, and on every pole he put the head of an American Indian!

"Well, they had such a good fight with the American Indians that the Cowichans thought they would get Ts'uwxilem and go and beat the Bella-Bellas. So, one day off they paddled, with Ts'uwxilem's canoe going in front as leader.

"When they got to the Bella-Bellas they paddled quietly to the shore, thinking that they would take the people by surprise. Out of their canoes they jumped and, shouting and yelling, they ran up to the houses. But something was wrong! No men came out to fight, no women went running to the woods to hide! The houses were empty!

"'They are back in the woods!' shouted Ts'uwxilem, 'we'll hunt for them!' Well, they had all lost their senses by this time, and, still shouting and calling to the Bella-Bellas to 'come out and fight, not hide like women!' they ran all ways, back into the thick woods.

"Now you see," Ts'umsitun explained, "the Bella-Bellas had seen the Cowichan canoes coming, and they had taken their fighting things and had hidden back in the woods, keeping very quiet. When the Cowichans came running about and shouting like crazy men, out came the Bella-Bellas from their hiding places, and my! how they did fight! The Cowichans were nearly beaten that time and had to run for their canoes, leaving many behind: nearly every canoe had men missing.

"Suddenly a man shouted, 'Where is Ts'uwxilem?' He was not there. Somewhere back with the Bella-Bellas was that great fighter. You know," explained Ts'umsitun, "Ts'uwxilem was a pretty bad man, but he was the greatest fighter! Any man would go where he led!

"Back went the Cowichans, and again the fight went on, then, out from the woods came Ts'uwxilem with some of the missing Cowichans. They fought their way down to the canoes and, seeing that their leader was safe, and that they were not strong enough to go on fighting, the Cowichans jumped into their canoes and paddled home.

"After this my people saw that something must be done. They had been nearly beaten that time, and their enemies were getting stronger. One day they would come down and finish the Cowichans. So they called all the Indians to a big meeting at Leeyqsun, on Valdez Island. From Hwmuthkwi'um over to Esquimalt and Saanich, up the coast to Nanaimo, then down to Chemainus Bay and on to Valdez Island, they called all the fighters to come and talk about this thing, and see what could be done to stop those Indians from one day coming and beating them and taking all their women and children to be slaves.

"Well, the day came for that great meeting, and from all parts came the big canoes filled with the fighting men of the Cowichan tribe. The beach at Leeyqsun was filled with the canoes, and still there were more to come—the people from Hwmuthkwi'um and Esquimalt, and Saanich were not there yet.

"Now, that same evening, it was nearly dark, when two men who had not gone to the meeting, but had been out hunting for seals, were paddling along beside the big bluff near Hwtl'upnets (Maple Bay) when they heard voices coming over the water.

They paddled into darkness beside the high rocks, and waited, for those voices sounded strange to them! Soon they heard paddles dipping softly, and again the voices, very near this time, and the men could hear that they were not talking as the Cowichan did.

"'Bella-Bella and Qhwimux,' whispered one man. They sat low in their canoe and watched as the canoes came along, and passed quite near to them in the darkness. One passed, then another and another, more and more, all great war canoes, coming quietly through the darkness to take the people at Hwtl'upnets by surprise!

"Now, what could these two men do? They knew that most of the men were away at Leeyqsun, and the women and children left alone. They could only do one thing. They must paddle as quickly as they could all those long miles to Leeyqsun, and get help!

"Away they went, paddling through the night, across the channel, and on to Valdez Island!"

Ts'umsitun threw away his straw and leaned forward eagerly.

"Now!" he exclaimed, "over at Leeyqsun, great fires had been made on the beach, and round them sat all those fighting men who had been called to the meeting. It was late, late at night, and very dark. Suddenly, from far away on the water came a shout! Every man jumped to his feet and stood listening, waiting! Then, when the light from the fires showed bright across the water there came a canoe, with two men in it. They paddled to the beach and 'Come! Hurry!' they shouted. 'The Bella-Bellas are at Hwtl'upnets! Hurry, if you would save your wife and children!'

"It didn't take those men long to get into their canoes with all their spears and fighting things, and then out into the darkness they paddled. Not one word was spoken, but each man paddled with all his might, and the paddles in every canoe dipped as one, and far behind were left the great fires burning on the beach and the women holding their children close, and whispering together of those other women and children alone at Hwtl'upnets!

"On through the night those men paddled and not far from Hwtl'upnets they were met by the Esquimalt and Saanich canoes on their way to the meeting. Quickly they told the story of the Bella-Bellas, and the Esquimalt and Saanich people turned their canoes and paddled back with the others. It was just beginning to get light as they reached the point at Hwtl'upnets. There, drawn up on the beach were the Bella-Bella canoes, and as our people watched they saw many men running down to the beach; they had seen the canoes coming round the point!

"Quickly our men got ready to meet them, and this is what they did."

Ts'umsitun broke a stick from a bush growing near him, and with this scratched in the dusty grass a rough plan of the bay. "See now," he said, "on this side there's a high bluff! Well, a lot of the Cowichans landed there and ran up to the top of the rocks, and there they waited. Then the other canoes made two lines right across the bay, from the point on the far side, leaving a little space near the bluff. Well, the Bella-Bella canoes were ready to start, but the leader waited, not knowing what

Ts'umsitun and Beryl Cryer

to do. He knew he must come out and fight, and so, all shouting together, they started paddling out to the middle of the bay. Now the Esquimalt and Saanich canoes moved from the front line, in and in, circling the shore, shutting the Bella-Bella Indians between two lines of enemies and making them paddle nearer to the bluff.

"Suddenly the leader saw the space that had been left, and thinking that there was a chance that they might get out that way he paddled for it, twenty canoes following after him. This was the chance the Cowichans up on the rocks had been waiting for. Just as the first canoe got under the bluff those men took great rocks that they had collected and rolled them down right into the canoe breaking it to pieces. On came the next, and the next canoes! Too late now to stop, and no good trying to turn back, for our canoes were close behind them! Twenty canoes went under that bluff, and only three got through. The water was filled with Bella-Bella and Qhwimux Indians swimming for their lives, but not one was left alive. The men in those three canoes paddled hard along the shore, chased by canoes from Puneluxutth' and Hwlumelhtsu, on Kuper Island. When they got near where Crofton is now they upset their canoes and ran ashore and back into the thick woods, and after them went the Kuper men. But most of those Bella-Bellas got away, and after walking for many months they reached Comox and the people there helped them get back to their own homes again.

"After that great fight, the Cowichans gathered all the bodies of their enemies and took them to the point at Hwtl'upnets, and there they made three big holes and buried them. For a long time there were sticks put up to show where those holes were made," added Ts'umsitun, "but I think they are gone now, and most people have forgotten about that fight.[246] After that there were no more big fights—sometimes some little ones, but nothing very bad, and not very long after that the people made peace, but that is another story."

Baby That Brought Peace and Friendship[247]

Beryl Cryer returns to Hwts'usi' to meet with Ts'umsitun, who tells her how a marriage and the birth of a child established peace between the Qhwimux and Hul'q'umi'num'-speaking peoples. This event occurred sometime after the fight at Hwtl'upnets (Maple Bay).

WHEN I NEXT VISITED TS'UMSITUN he invited me into his house. Never have I seen a room more spotlessly clean; from the pale green linoleum on the floor, to the four beds—which the room contained—everything was immaculate. Here, indeed, was evidence that the patient teaching by those in charge of the Indian Industrial School, on Kuper Island, had born good fruit.

Ts'umsitun's wife came in and, after shaking hands with me, seated herself on the doorstep with her knitting. I was given a chair beside the sewing machine, that I might put my notebook on it, and we got down to business.

"Well, now!" began Ts'umsitun, rocking back and forth in his chair as he spoke, "The other day I told you all about the last big fight the Cowichan Indians had, now, I'll tell you about the way the people made peace.

"Some time after that fight at Hwtl'upnets , a chief from Cape Mudge married a Puneluxutth' woman, he took her back to his home with the Cape Mudge people, and when she got to know them, she found they all were nice people, not very different from the Cowichans.

A little later a Qhwimux chief called Thuth-Luth, married a woman who was half Snuneymuxw and half Puneluxutth', and of course, like the other woman she too went to live with her husband's people, and was very happy there. After a time a baby boy was born, and Thuth-Luth made great feasts and called all the Qhwimux Indians to come and see his son. And that baby, was taken out and shown to all the people as they came up to the big houses, and all said that there had never been such a fine baby born to the Qhwimux tribe.

"Well, the woman's father was chief of Leeyqsun, on Valdez Island, and when he heard that his daughter had a baby boy, my how glad he was! He said, 'This will surely bring peace and friendship between the Qhwimux and Cowichan people!' So this Leeyqsun chief gave a big potlatch. He called all the Cowichans from up and down the coast to come to it. 'We will make peace!' he told them. 'There will be no more fighting with those Qhwimux Indians!'

"Now he sent a message to his daughter and to her husband, Thuth-Luth telling them to come to his potlatch and to bring their baby—his grandson. 'This child,' he said, 'will bring peace to us all, and both tribes will be good friends from this time! Bring all your people,' he told the Qhwimux chief, 'for I have thought of a way to end the fighting between us!'

"So Thuth-Luth and his people got ready to go to the potlatch. All the big canoes were filled with men, women and children, and besides the people, there were good presents which they took to give the Cowichans—skin coats, furs and good blankets made of goat's hair. When all was ready they started off on their long paddle to Leeyqsun. When they got some way past Nanaimo they made the canoes into rafts."

Here, Ts'umsitun's wife, who had been following the tale with great interest, spoke to him, and he laughed. "Alright," he said, "I'll tell her."

"My wife," he explained, "says that you don't know how canoes could be made into rafts? Well, they weren't real rafts, but in those old days whenever there was a big time anywhere, and the people went in their canoes, they stopped, as these people did, before they got to the place where the potlatch was to be; and they put the canoes three in a row, side by side, with about four or five long poles going across and fastening them together, and so they would go along, one raft behind the other, and their name for these rafts was Stot-A-Lock. Well, all the canoes were made into rafts, and in the rafts they fastened up poles on which they hung the blankets and furs and other presents for the Cowichans. My they must have looked fine!

"Over at Leeyqsun the chief and his people were ready for the Cowichans and the Qhwimux Indians to come. They had killed and cooked many hundreds of ducks; there were great piles of fish and clams, and hanging from the trees, were many deer, skinned and ready to be cooked.

"All day great canoes filled with the Cowichan people paddled up to the beach, and the village was filled with the families from every village as far up as Nanaimo.

"It was late in the afternoon when the old chief, sitting on the beach, heard shouts coming from far away over the water, and very soon he saw the Qhwimux people coming in their big rafts.

"My old father used to tell me that he heard it was a fine sight all these big rafts, filled with Indians, the wind blowing the blankets and skins on their poles, and the sun shining on the paddle blades as they were lifted from the water and thrust down again, every paddle keeping time with those in the leading raft.

"Now, as the rafts got nearer, all the Indians began to sing and wave the blankets on their poles, and so they came close to the shore, but they did not land, but paddled into a line along the beach, and now, singing and shouting harder than before, they took all the presents of blankets and furs, and, unfastening them from the poles, threw them on the water. This was to show the Cowichan people that the Qhwimux were very 'see 'em rich.' As soon as the presents were in the water all the Cowichans ran in and brought them to the shore, and then all those people began shouting when they saw what fine, good presents the Qhwimux people had brought.

"'Now,' called the old chief, 'hold up the baby that I may look at my grandson.' And Thuth-Luth took the baby and held him out for the old man to see.

"'Never have I seen such a fine child,' called the grandfather. But before you bring him up to the house there is something we must do. Now, this child has come to make peace between us, and so I think it would be good if we all had a little war—our last one—and this to be, not a real fight, but pretend.' Then turning to his people, he called out, 'Get your spears and come, follow me.' To the Qhwimux chief he called, 'Lay that baby out on the raft, where all can see it, and now, come with your men and play at fighting.'

"Well, such a time there was! The Qhwimux men, taking their spears jumped into the water, and the Cowichans, running at them, would not let them get to the beach; but not one man was hurt, and all were shouting and laughing like good friends. Very soon the Leeyqsun chief shouted, 'This is the end.' And every man shook hands and put away their fighting things.

"Now the old grandfather called for the child to be carried up to the houses, and he called by name every man who was to go on the raft to get the baby.

"After that they had the potlatch, and the Cowichans gave so many presents to the Qhwimux people that their canoes were filled with the skins and blankets. Never had there been such feasting, with great fires burning in the houses, with the flames leaping up to the high roofs of cedar, and men and women dancing about them every night. For more than a week the Qhwimux Indians stayed, making friends with the people whom they had always fought as enemies, each learning the ways of the other, and finding out many things. When they left for their homes at Qhwimux, there was great friendship in all their hearts, and ever since that time those people have been good friends, and when Thuth-Luth's baby boy grew up to be a man, he was made chief. His name was Chief Charlie Tch-Ossier, the one who brought peace to the Cowichan people."

Ts'umsitun crossed to a bed in one corner of the room, and after rummaging underneath it for some time, dragged out a basket. "This," he said, "is a very good Indian blanket." He shook out a large blanket made of mountain goat hair, and spread it on the floor beside me. "We call these blankets 'swuqw'a'lh,'" he told me. "This is old and not very white now, but when they are new these Indian blankets are very white, and I'll tell you why.

"Now, first, to make these blankets, the Indians used to take the hair off the skin of mountain goats. Then they got a black mud. There is a place I know of," he explained, "where in the old days the Indians used to dig this mud. I only know of this one place, and the Indians would come from all parts to get it. It is very, very black and sort of greasy when you rub it in your hands. Well, they made this mud into balls, then made a little hole and in it they put a fire of alder. When the fire was red and very hot, no flames, they put sticks across the top of the hole, and between the sticks they put the mud balls, and kept turning them round and round to bake. As they baked, they got white until, when they were quite baked, they were as white as snow.

"After they were cold the Indians broke them up into small pieces, put them on a mat or blanket and mixed the goat hair with them. Now they took a long, strong stick, and for a long time—more than an hour—they beat the hair and the baked mud together; after that it was ready for the women to spin into white blankets."

Ts'umsitun folded up his blanket with great care and again reached into the basket. "Now," he said, with pride in his voice. "Here's something my wife wants me to show you. She dug this out of the ground at Puneluxutth' many years ago. It is a great treasure of my wife's."

He handed me a knife, fashioned like a hunting knife; the rusty blade, about four inches long, was slightly rounded on one side and flat on the other, with a rounded tip. This was fastened between two pieces of white bone, the same length as the blade, with a large oval ring of brass or copper to hang it by in the opposite end.

The handle was dotted on both sides with small round marks, as though made with some kind of punch, and the brass handle had roughly cut marks around it.

"All these marks, " exclaimed Ts'umsitun, "show how many men were killed by the man who had this knife. This," he touched the ring, "is made from one of the rings that people in those long ago days used to wear around their ankles, and these marks show how many men he killed, too."

"But he must have killed hundreds!" I exclaimed.

Ts'umsitun nodded and laughed. "Sure," he said, "They were always killing in those days."

He twisted the ring about, and finally pulled it out from the handle, the ends coming unfastened in some manner, and I saw that it was a great deal longer than I had supposed.

"My wife will never sell that knife," said Ts'umsitun. "Lots of men have wanted to buy it, but she keeps it always." He put it back in the basket and tucked it in the blanket.

"I have some more things to show you if you come again," he said, "and I will get you some of that black mud I told you of—the mud they used to mix with goat's hair for the blankets."

I thanked him, and promising to visit them again before long, I left them sitting on their doorstep and examining the knife, which had again been taken from the basket.

The Haida Slave[248]

When Beryl Cryer calls on Mary Rice for another story, she finds her grieving the death of a grandchild. The deceased child's physical deformity reminds her of the slave, Agnes, who cared for her as a child. Among the Central Coast Salish, slaves, skw'ukw'iyuth, were uncommon, and were only found in wealthy households.[249] Mary Rice continues working as she narrates the story. Near the end of the visit, Tommy Pielle arrives and contributes a narrative about Raven, which is overlaid with Christian symbolism.

WHEN I KNOCKED AT SIAMTUNAAT'S DOOR this afternoon, it was opened by her small granddaughter, Dorothy. Siamtunaat called a welcome from her corner beside the stove, where she was busily carding wool.

"Come in! Come in!" she invited, and, reaching forward, swept a pile of wool from the chair near her. "Sit here," she said, "where I can talk to you while I work. Oh, how glad I am to see you!" She sighed deeply.

"What's the trouble, Siamtunaat?" I asked, for I had noticed at once that things were not right with her. Her hair, usually so neatly tied away under her handkerchief, was hanging in long, white wisps about her old face, and her eyes had lost their twinkle—looked, in fact, as though tears were not far away.

"Oh, such trouble!" She laid down her carders and clasped her hands. "My daughter's youngest girl—she's died!"

The old lips quivered, and those suspected tears brimmed over and rolled down her cheeks and on to her withered fingers. She sat looking at the drops for a moment, then wiped her fingers against her dress. "Oh, I'm 'shamed for you to see me like this!" she said, "but I feel so bad! That poor little girl!" She rubbed her sleeve across her eyes and pushed the hair back from her face.

Small Dorothy, guessing her need, brought a black silk handkerchief with which she dried her eyes, then folded and tied about her head.

"There!" she said, "now I look better!" She smiled up at me, but her brown eyes still looked dull and sad. "You know," she said, "that poor little girl was always sick; she had a bad back. I think one of the children dropped her when she was a baby, and her back got a hump, just like Agnes had!"

"Who was Agnes?" I asked.

"What!" she exclaimed, "don't you know about Agnes? I thought I told you about her!"

I shook my head. "Do you feel well enough to tell me now?" I asked.

She actually smiled cheerily. "I'll tell you while I card this wool," she said, and deftly worked black and white wool together until a mass of softest grey fell from the carders into her basket.

"Now, this story begins long, long ago—before I was born. At that time the Cowichans had been away fighting the Haida Indians and they beat them and brought away lots of slaves. You 'member I have often told you about my old grandfather, Chief Xulqalustun? Well, of course, he was with the Cowichans at this fight, and his brothers were there, too. One of his brothers, a man called Tch-Clo-Mun, found a woman hiding in the woods, with her little girl who was about two years old. Tch-Clo-Mun laughed when he saw that woman, for he thought she would make a good slave for him. He caught hold of her, to drive her down to the canoes, but the poor woman threw her arms round a young tree and would not let go.

"Well, Tch-Clo-Mun pulled and she held tight to that tree, and he could not get her. He could see some of the Cowichan canoes starting off from the beach, and could hear the cries of the slaves they were taking away with them. Soon he knew that his canoe would be ready, and if he did not hurry they would leave without him, thinking him dead. What was he to do? He could not pull the woman away, and he did not want to leave her! At last he got mad, and catching hold of her he killed her. Then he picked up the little girl and ran down to his canoe, leaving the poor mother dead beside the tree. When he got to the beach he threw the little girl into the canoe just as he would throw a dog, and there she lay until they got back to Puneluxutth'.

"When the women saw the Cowichan's canoes coming home, they ran to the beach to welcome back their men, and to look at the slaves they had brought. Now, Tch-Clo-Mun's wife was a woman from Kwa'mutsun, called Leed-Tha—a nice, good woman. When she saw that poor baby girl lying at the bottom of the canoe, she held out her arms, and Tch-Clo-Mun laid the child in them. 'Take good care of her,' he said; 'the mother was a fine-looking woman; maybe this baby will make a good slave for us.'

"Leed-Tha took the baby and she fed and washed her, but the poor thing just lay still, crying a lot, and on her little back was a mark where she had hit the canoe when Tch-Clo-Mun threw her down.

"My grandfather would walk into the house and look at her, and he would say to his brother, "Why do you keep that thing? She will be no good to you. Better throw her out!" But both Tch-Clo-Mun and his wife, Leed-Tha, liked that tiny girl, and they said, 'No, we will take care of her, and some day she will make a good slave!'

"After a bit that baby began to grow strong, but she was always very small, and the poor girl grew a lump on her back, and was a little 'humpy back.' Now," said Siamtunaat, laying down the carders, "my mother told me that when the little slave girl was about four years old, I was born, and my! how that little humpy did like to play with me! My mother had a stick made of very strong, hard wood, bending over at the top. This stick she would put in the ground near where she was working, and then she would fasten my little cradle—'Cha-cut-un' we call it—on to it, and it would swing in the wind and put me to sleep. All the Indians did that, and I did the same for my children when they were babies," she explained. "Now, sometimes there was no wind, and my cradle would be still, and I would cry. Then my mother would call to this little girl, 'Swing the baby for me!' and that little humpy would run up, and putting up her tiny hands she could just touch my cradle, and there she would jump, and swing, swing me, and sing, 'Don't cry, little baby, don't cry!' until I went to sleep again.

"When she was about fourteen years old, Leed-Tha's brother, who lived at Cowichan, saw her and wanted her for a slave, so Tch-Clo-Mun let her go, and that is when she went to live at Kwa'mutsun. She stayed there for many, many years. Just once her 'cousin' took her to live at Nanaimo, but she was not happy and soon went back to Kwa'mutsun. When the priests came they taught the Cowichans that it was wrong to have slaves, and made them give all their slaves up, and they were sent back to their own homes, but when they asked Agnes—(that is the name the priests gave her)—if she wanted to go home, she cried and would not leave. 'No,' she told them, 'my home is here, with all my friends. I cannot even talk as my own people do. I only know the Cowichan's way of talking!' and she would not go. So she stayed on at Kwa'mutsun until she was a very, very old woman, but all who knew her were her friends, she was such a kind, good, little woman.

"You know," the old voice began to tremble again, "Old Agnes was my very good friend; all my life we were friends, but she's dead now, and I'm getting to be an old woman, too!" Tears were threatening once more, when, to my relief her old brother, Tommy Pielle, came in from fishing. He shook hands with me, and then made himself comfortable on the wood box, where he proceeded to fill a wicked-looking pipe and to smoke it with tremendous enjoyment.

When it was drawing to his satisfaction, he began to chuckle.

"Did you ever hear the story about the Raven's voice?" he asked, looking at me through dense clouds of smoke. Without waiting for an answer, he continued; "I mean, why the raven has such a bad voice that no one likes to hear it? This isn't a very old story, but I think it's a good one. Some of it's true, because the priests told me, but some—well, I guess they haven't heard it all!" Again he chuckled. "Now," he said, "you know God made the world? He made everything, earth, and roots, and trees with berries on them! Good berries! Some red, some yellow, and all good to eat! Well, there were all those berries but no one to eat them! So God said, 'What's the good of all those things if there's no one to use them?' and so he made just two people." Tommy held up two grimy fingers. "Just two," he repeated, shaking his fingers at me. "This one here's named Adam, and this little one's named Eve! 'Now,' said God, 'don't you two fellers eat those big red berries on that tree in the middle of the garden. Eat all the others if you like, but if you take those big ones something bad'll happen to you!'

"Well, of course!" said Tommy Pielle, with a knowing wag of his head, "of course that woman Eve thought those berries were just the kind she wanted. She stood under the tree and she looked at them, and up in that tree, do you know what she saw? A great snake! It had an awful face! I know, because I've seen a picture of it in a big book in the church house at Puneluxutth'. I went in and I looked one day! Well, that snake bit off some of the berries and the woman took them in her hands, and she thought how nice they looked, then she put some in her mouth and gave some to her man. Now Adam stood there chewing those berries, and suddenly God came along. 'What are you doing?' called God. That man Adam was so scared that he tried to swallow his berries and they stuck in his throat, and all he could do was make a noise just like we hear the raven making today! And God punished him by making him turn into a raven, when he died. And we know that all the ravens are really bad men who have died, and they have to fly about making that noise, and nobody wants them! The raven's a bad fellow, always making trouble. I saw a picture of him in that book in the church house, too." Tommy Pielle leaned forward and tapped the ashes out of his pipe. "That church house belongs to me!" he said, "It's mine, Tommy Pielle's!" He thumped his chest impressively. "Me and Father Donkele, we paid for the big bell—fifty dollars we paid, and now Father Donkele's dead, so the bell's mine. There'd be no church house without that bell. It's all mine!"

He warmed to his subject "I'm the biggest man at Puneluxutth'," he exclaimed. "Other people say, 'We'll make a big house, the old houses are falling down!" So they get to work, maybe ten men, or more, and they work two or three days, get it half done and there they stop! Leave it! Never finish it. Now me and my sister, we say 'We'll build a new house where our house fell down. So we get the money together, get the boards; pretty soon that house is finished, the biggest house on Puneluxutth', and we give a big time in it! The other house still stands there, never finished! Oh, I'm a big man!" He laughed heartily and stamped about the little room, and Siamtunaat laughed with him.

"Tommy Pielle," I thought, "with due apologies to Mr. Longfellow, your name should be, not Tommy Pielle, but 'Iagoo, the great boaster'!"

The Good Priest, Father Rondeault[250]

Beryl Cryer is summoned to Mary Rice's cabin where she meets an elderly man, Quon-As, who provides her with a history of the early days of the Roman Catholic Mission of St. Ann's, established at Qw'umiyiqun' (Comiaken) in 1858. He and Mary Rice introduce Beryl Cryer to the subject of xwult'up "flying men." However, in the interest of propriety, they refrain from too many details.

A MESSAGE WAS BROUGHT to me this morning by Siamtunaat's small granddaughter: "If you will come and see my granny, she has an old man who will talk to you!" This was delivered in a high, breathless voice, and after that not one word could I get from her.

"Who was the old man? Where was he from?" To all my questions she was dumb, until the sight of a rosy apple unsealed her lips in a whispered "Tank you."

Siamtunaat's visitor was indeed an "old man." I found him sitting in the sun, deep in conversation with his hostess.

"Ah!" Siamtunaat smiled at me; "you have come, that's good! This man, Quon-As, is old, old. He can 'member things I don't know." She spoke rapidly to the old man, and he peered at me from deeply sunken, bleared eyes, and nodded his head several times.

"Aah! Haaa. I tell you stories, eh?" he asked. "Well, I been talking to her—(he pointed to Siamtunaat)—and she tells me you not heard much about that good priest who came to our people long, long ago, that Father Londo (Rondeault).[251] Now that's a story I must tell you because I, Quon-As, know all about that man."

Siamtunaat interrupted him. "You 'member," she said to me, "I told you about the time the priest showed my grandfather, Xulqalustun, how to make counting balls, using the bark from willow trees and tying knots, that he could tell the days and weeks and months? Well, that good man was Father Londo; he taught my grandfather many good things."

"Well, now, I'll tell you!" Old Quon-As evidently felt that Siamtunaat had talked long enough. He pushed his high-crowned brown felt hat to the back of his head, and rested a trembling hand on either knee. Such hands! bent and weathered with age and rheumatism, they were exactly like the claws of some great bird!

"Now see!" he began. "That good man came when I was a little boy. My people told me how he paddled all alone from Saanich up to Qw'umiyiqun'. He had nothing with him, just a sack of flour and his Book, a gun to get food with, and maybe a blanket.

"When the Cowichan people heard he was coming, everybody went down to the water to look at him, and to tell him how glad they were that he had come! and everybody wanted to shake his hand. All that day Father Londo was shaking hands and talking to the people. My father's friend, Tsulchamel, who the priests by-and-by called Gabriel—he told Father Londo to come and live in his house at Qw'umiyiqun', and there he stayed until he could make his own house.

"Now there wasn't any church house in those days, but the Qw'umiyiqun' chief, Loxa, he was called, told the priest, 'Take my lodge for a church house,' and there Father Londo said Mass everyday.

"Now the Indians began to come from all parts to hear the priest and see him in the church house. From the islands they came, and from all parts of the coast— big canoes full of men, women and children. He likes best to see the little children come. 'Bring them all,' he told the old people, and he held them and washed (baptized) them and gave them names like the white men.

"One day Father Londo called the people and told them, 'It is time that we had a church house of our own. We will all work together to build one!'

"High up on the rocks he found a place to put it—not where that old stone church house stands now, but near it, and near where the people are buried. 'From this place,' he told my people, 'we can look far out over the water, and see far over the land.' But in those days," added Quon-As, "there were great trees everywhere, and we could not look very far.

"Well, now they began to make the church house. 'We will make it very strong and warm,' said the priest, 'and we will use logs cut from the woods.' So far back they went to find the best logs, and after cutting them down they carried them all the way back, sometimes as far as half a mile. High up on their shoulders the carried them, many men carrying each tree, and in that way they made a big strong house. After that was finished they made a house for Father Londo. It was very small, only one room, and there was no floor, just dirt. For this house the Indians gave one board from each village: one from Qw'umiyiqun', one from Kwa'mutsun, one from Yuxwula'us and Puneluxutth' on Kuper Island, and so on, and in that way every place helped to make a house for that good man.

Quon-As and Beryl Cryer

When the new church was finished, everybody went to hear him talk and sing, and he taught the people how to sing and do as he did. Oh, so many went to hear him—sometimes six hundred, sometimes eight hundred: the house was too small, and many had to stand outside waiting to hear his voice.

"Very soon he taught the people to be clean and to wash themselves, to wear clothes like the white men, not dress in blankets, and he showed them how to keep their children clean, and not to drink the whiskey that brought them madness and made them kill.

"Then he told them, 'Every man may have one wife, no more,' and he made them send away their other wives, and they all did as he taught them. By and by he made a garden and showed the Cowichans how to clear their land and gave them seeds, so that they, too, might have potatoes and carrots and good vegetables.

"Now he got some cows and had milk and made butter."

Here Quon-As appeared to be lost in thought for a while. "Tell me," he asked. "Have you seen the old stone church at Qw'umiyiqun'? Yes? Well, Father Londo built that after he made the house of logs—Father Londo and Louis Gabourie[252] made it, with Indians to help, and a white man from Victoria to put the stones together and to make the windows. Now, do you know how the money came to pay those Indians for their work? Well, I'll tell you. As I said, Father Londo made butter and he sold that butter to people living about there, and with the money he got from his butter he paid those Indians. That is why lots of the old people call that the 'Butter Church'!

"Father Londo was always working, some times paddling many miles to see some of his people, coming home late and wet and tired, but always doing good, always working!

Very soon he began another house of logs. This was for a schoolhouse, and to this house came two good women—St. Ann's sisters. Those two Sisters lived alone in that schoolhouse and they had a lot of Indian girls who lived with them—forty girls, I think there were—and the Sisters taught them as the children are taught now in the big schools. These girls did not understand the white man's food, so they brought their own berries and fish, and ate that food, but by-and-by the good Father made bigger gardens and he grew grain. Then he made a little mill where he made that grain into flour. Now the Sisters showed the girls how to make bread and the Indians learned to eat that, and other things made with the flour.

"So now all my people began to be like the white men. They could eat white man's food and could put on clothes like the white people, but they still liked their own big times—the dances and potlatches, and times like that. The North Indians were the same. Up there it was hard work for the priests, for those Haidas and Bella-Bellas and all the others were bad people; they did many bad things that the Cowichans did not do, and the priests tried to stop some of their dances. By-and-by the Gov'ment made a law and told them that those dances must stop or they would be punished. One day I will tell you of those dances!"

Quon-As pulled his old hat over his eyes and sat lost in dreams once more.

"See now," he said, "as she," with a wag of his head towards Siamtunaat, "told you how the priests had to stop those people from the North flying?"

"Flying?" I exclaimed. He nodded his head, screwing up his old face as he did so.

"Yes, those people could fly, long ago. I have never seen them, but this woman, she knows about them."

He explained to Siamtunaat, and she threw up her hands and clucked her tongue, in a way she has when she is annoyed.

"Ah, how foolish!" she exclaimed, "I forgot to tell you that! Yes, what this old man says is quite true. Those North people used to fly, not so very long ago. I know, for I have often heard my family talk about them.

"Now I will tell you about one time when a flying man was seen. This was before my mother was born. My grandfather Xulqalustun, went with other Puneluxutth' to the Fraser River to do trading. Well, he had a house up a slough, where he stayed with my grandmother and their three children, two boys and one girl, and some other Cowichans. One morning all the people went out to do trading, leaving the three children alone.

"Don't go outside," my grandfather told them, "Stay in the house all the time we are away!" For a long time they stayed inside, then the two boys got tired of waiting and they went outside.

"At first they played near the house, then they went back into the trees. Suddenly they heard a shout! Who was that calling? They could see no one! Again came that shout. It was up in the air. They looked up through the trees, and there, high up on a branch, was a man! He was lying along a branch, his arms and legs hanging down. He had cedar bark round his legs (loin cloth), and round his neck, with pieces hanging down, and the same round his arms and legs. My, those little boys were scared! They started to run back to the house, but they had only gone a little way when they heard the man shout again, and there they saw him flying away over the tops of the trees, and out to the sea!

"When their father came back they told him about the flying man and he said that a lot of the people who were trading had seen him too, and he flew so near that they could see that he was a Haida from the North!

"Oh, yes! I know lots of people who have seen the flying men! They used to fly all over the world."

"Oh, yes" echoed old Quon-As, "all over the world they would fly, lots of the old people saw them, but the priests stopped them. They said that it was bad, that it was the devil made them fly."

"Could they all fly?" I asked.

"Oh, no! not all! Just some of the medicine men, and the dancers; not every-body!"

"And the Cowichans—could they fly, too?"

"The Cowichans?" They both looked at me in horror. "Our people fly? Why, no! The Cowichan Indians were good people: it was the devil made those North Indians fly! The Cowichans never tried to fly!" I made my apologies, and they laughed heartily to think I had been so foolish.

"Come again," invited Quon-As, "and I will tell you about that dance—the "Tomanawas."[253]

"Yes," said Siamtunaat, "and I have a story of how my poor Uncle Sch-Lun-As was tied up by the North Indians until he died. That is a good story."

I promised to visit them soon and hear their tales, and left them talking earnestly together, recalling, who knows what memories of their good old days!

Xwult'up—The Flying Spirit-Men[254]

As revealed in letters she wrote to William Newcombe, Beryl Cryer, by November 1932, was interested in marketing native-made sweaters with "original Salish designs."[255] Her acquaintance with Ts'umsitun's wife, Latits'iiya, appears to have inspired this idea. Having expressed interest in their work, Beryl Cryer is invited to their home at Hwts'usi'.

Ts'umsitun is busy digging potatoes when Beryl Cryer brings up the subject of xwult't'up. Ts'umsitun stops his work to explain the concept of guardian spirit power, and his wife and family provide additional comments.

Ts'umsitun's wife, who, I have at last discovered is called Latits'iiya, had asked me to call and see the sweaters she is making, so, taking advantage of a fine afternoon, I called at their house.

The front room, spotless as usual, appeared to be filled with children when I went in, but at a word from Ts'umsitun they all scurried outside like a lot of rabbits. Latits'iiya came forward to greet me and to shut the door upon the children. "I have a housefull today," she explained. "My married daughter and her children are with us."

A good-looking young woman, very smartly dressed and with beautifully marcelled hair, got up from her seat on a bed and bowed and smiled shyly. The youngest girl then came in with an armfull of Indian sweaters, which she spread out on one of the beds for me to admire. The ladies of the family had evidently all visited a hairdresser recently, and they all wore silk dresses and smart shoes and stockings. I felt quite overcome at their appearance, but we were soon deep in discussion of the really beautiful sweaters which they had made. White or grey, with patterns worked in black or brown, stars, butterflies, birds and flowers—all very handsome. To my way of thinking these patterns, which they tell me they copy from books on filet crochet, are not to be compared with their own original and most decorative designs.

The married daughter had just finished an especially handsome one, with a quaint bird design—typically Indian—across the front, and was commencing another one which, she told me, was to have blue butterflies on a white ground.

"It's hard to sell them now," said Latits'iiya. "No one has much money. This year we have to make them cheaper than ever before! But we have lots of wool." She pointed to a row of boxes against the wall, all filled with enormous balls of black and white wool. "And lots more outside," she said, "and lots more sheep, if we can find the people to buy our sweaters!"

Ts'umsitun laughed. "These women!" he said, with greatest scorn, "they just sit round all day making sweaters and talking, talking. They like to do it! No matter how many they sell, every day they make more sweaters! Now, me! I'm working outside digging my potatoes. I'm busy: but come again when I am not working; I have lots of good stories to tell you!"

"Ts'umsitun," I said, "I want to ask you one thing before you go. The other day an old woman told me about some people who used to fly about the world. Have you ever heard that story?"

From her rocking chair beside the stove Latits'iiya nodded her head.

"Yes, yes!" she said, "everybody knows about those people flying." Ts'umsitun drew forward a chair and sat down. Forgotten were the potatoes and the hard work outside!

"Now see," he began, "I'll tell you about that flying. That is called xwult'up. First I'll tell you how, long, long ago, our people used to believe in lots of different spirits—one for the fishing, one for the hunting, another for medicine men, and for dancing. There were lots of them, and to talk to those spirits—to get them to listen—the man used to go far away where there were no other people. He would find a stream away in the mountains, and there he would stay without food or blankets, and he must pray all the time. He must not sleep for long at a time.

"Every night he must wash in the fresh water; four times he must do this washing. Four times each night he must dive into the water, and when he dives he must call to the spirit he wants to help him. Then, when he gets so weak that he can hardly walk, the spirit comes to him. And when he gets back to his people he is a good hunter, or can catch lots of fish—he is helped by the spirit he has called to.

"Well, this xwult'up is something like that. If a man wants to fly he had to be clean, good, pure. The spirits will not listen to a man who is not all clean! He must leave his wife, and talk to no woman for many months; then he goes, as I have said, back in the mountains, all alone; and after the spirit has come to him he must get cedar bark, clean it and beat it for a long time, until it is very soft, and has long pieces falling down from it, and at the top of these long pieces, near the bark, he ties knots (like a fringe). Now he puts one piece round his neck and some on his arms and legs, all with the long fringes hanging down. Then he lies down beside the stream again, and waits until the spirit comes to him. Sometimes he waits many days, sometimes the spirit comes to him quite soon. This is what happens when he feels the spirit in him. His arms go out on each side of him, quite stiff, and his legs go out stiff, too, and then, pretty soon, his body begins to lift up and up, and he is flying through the air! Later he goes to the Fraser River, or some other place where there are lots of cranberries, and he makes a sort of belt of those cranberries, and he wears that belt all the time he's flying—that's all he has to eat!"

"Have you ever seen one of these men flying?" I asked him.

Ts'umsitun shook his head. "Well, I've never seen one close!" he confessed, "but long ago I was out in a canoe, going to Kuper Island, and suddenly I heard a funny noise! Well, just as soon as I heard that noise I knew what it was, because I'd often heard my father and other old people talk about the xwult'up, and I'd heard them make the kind of noise those men make when they're flying!"

"I've heard them, too!" said Latits' iiya, "and my father often used to see them flying over, making that noise. It sounded just like the noise the airplanes make now, but they made it with their mouths as they flew along!"

"Wait till I tell this story," said her husband, not pleased at being interrupted.

"Now, I heard that noise and I felt kind of scared! I wasn't very old at that time, but I thought it would be fine if I could go back and tell them that I had seen a man flying, and I began to look for him. I listened to hear where the noise came from, and I looked and looked, and then I saw him!

"Right on the end of Kuper Island, next to Tent Island, there was a tall, dead cedar tree with some of the top broken off, and not many branches; and there, right on the top, lying stretched out, and making that noise, I saw a man! There he lay, and he kept turning, first round one way then round the other, as though the wind must be blowing him! I was a long way out on the water, so I could not see the cedar bark on him, but I could hear that noise going all the time!

"After a time he kind of dropped down off the tree and went behind some tall trees growing on the point, and I never saw him again."

"My husband's father saw them lots of times, when he was a boy," said the fashionably-dressed married daughter. "The priests stopped the xwult'up. They said it was a bad spirit that made the people fly. But I don't! I think that people are not good enough now—that the spirits won't come!"

"How did they fly?" I asked; "did they use their arms as a bird uses its wings?"

"No!" laughed Ts'umsitun. "They were stiff, just like an airplane. It was the spirit in them made them go along. Not many of our people did it, though. My father told me often about a boy who lived at Kwa'mutsun. I forget his name. He lived alone with just his father and mother, they had no other children. He never went hunting, never went fishing like the other young men; he was always sick and weak.

"Maybe it would be good for him if he was a dancer!" said the old father. So he called all his people to talk about it. They all came to see him, and there were big fires burning hot and bright down the middle of the lodge, and each one did his own dance and his own song. Well, the boy just sat looking at them, and by-and-by he lay down, never said one word, and the spirit came out of him.

"Well, there he lay, just as though he was dead! They put him on the bed and put his blankets on him, and they all began to sing and dance, calling to the spirit to come back to the boy! For three days he lay there, and then"—Ts'umsitun lowered his voice—"something came to him!"

"My father means a spirit came to him," explained his daughter.

"Ts'umsitun nodded his head. "That's it!" he said. "A spirit came to that boy. He got up from his bed and he held out his arms and he began to dance. Along by the fires he danced, and all the other people sat quiet, watching. By-and-by he made a song, and until it was nighttime he danced and made that song! More logs were put on the fire that he might see to do his dance, and all kept quiet as he sang that song of his!

"At last they could tell that he was near the end of his song, and as they waited the boy began to lift, up and up, until he was high in the air, over the fire!

"'Ah!" shouted his father, 'catch my son.' Everybody ran about trying to catch the boy, who was now flying round beside the fires, his arms stiff and straight, and his legs the same! At last they got him and pulled him down, and taking two ropes of cedar bark, they tied them around his arms and then to one of the great posts of the lodge.

"Well, even then, do you know that they could not keep him down! His arms were tied, but his legs kept going up in the air, backwards, making him fall on his face. So they made the ropes loose so that he could fly a little way. You see," explained Ts'umsitun, "his father did not want him to fly, for, he thought, 'If he goes away, we may never see our son again!'

"Now the boy felt better when he found he could fly a little, and he began to dance a bit every day, and to make songs.

"One day he was dancing and singing his own songs, and some of his people were watching him, when they saw him stand up on his toes and begin to swing back and forward, and his arms went out stiff! Then he started to cry, and while he was crying his feet left the floor and up he flew; up and up, round and round the fire, and the people watching him saw that the ropes had been broken from his arms. They called to the father, and as he came running in he saw his only boy fly out of the big hole that is made in the roofs of our lodges to let the smoke go out!

"Away he flew, and all those watching heard that noise like an airplane, coming from his mouth!

"Now his old people had to get his home clean and ready for him to live in when he got back. Every day that house must be cleaned and there must be food put ready for him, and a lot of pitch put in a pile ready for a quick fire. Every day they must listen for him, and when they hear him coming they must hurry to have the fire burning and the food cooking. All these things must be done or he would never come back!"

"How long did they stay away?" I asked.

"About one year, most of them stayed, but some a little more, and I have heard the old people tell how all the long fringe pieces of the cedar bark were gone—worn away in the winds—when they came back, only the little knots left along the edge. But no matter how long they were away, everything in the house must be ready for them to come to."

Latits'iiya put down her knitting for a moment.

"My husband forgot to tell you," she said, "that the house for a man who is 'xwult'up,' must be away from all other houses, and when he comes back he is like a wild man. He shuts himself up in his house and prays and sings all day. No married people may go see him, must not go near him, and no woman may talk to him. He has to keep himself clean and pure, not spoil himself in any way. And so he lives for the rest of his life."

"Does he tell where he has been, things he has seen?" I asked.

Latits'iiya shook her head. "No one must ask," she said, "and a man who has been xwult'up talks very little; he only prays!"

"And that is quite true?" I asked. The entire family looked at me in amazement.

"True? Oh, yes!" they all exclaimed. "All our people, and the people from the West Coast, and from the North, all will tell you the same. They all had men who were 'xwult'up,' only they had other names for it, but after the white men came our people learned bad ways and now the spirits won't come."

I looked at that family sitting round on their beds, with their marcelled heads and silk dresses, educated from earliest childhood in the local Industrial School, two generations of them, and a third playing outside the door. Yet deep in their hearts the old superstitions persist, never to be eradicated.

Loxa, Chief of the Cowichans[256]

Curious to find out more information about Loxa, the Qw'umiyiqun' (Comiaken) leader whose photograph she found displayed in the Indian Agent's office, Beryl Cryer visits his daughter, Kathleen Stockl-Whut, who narrates some of his history.

AMONGST MY COLLECTION OF OLD Indian photographs, I have one of a Cowichan chief, in uniform, with a medal pinned on his coat, and holding in both hands a crucifix. The inscription beneath this picture reads, "Lohar, Chief of the Comeaken band, wearing a medal presented to him by the Governor-General for special services."

This Chief Loxa was not only chief of the Qw'umiyiqun' band of Indians, but the big chief—head of the Cowichan tribe—when the first white men settled in the Cowichan Valley.

For many months I had been hoping to learn something of the chief of the "special services" for which he had been decorated; but it was not until quite recently that opportunity offered, and early one morning I set out in a cold and drizzling rain to drive to Qw'umiyiqun' to visit Chief Loxa's daughter, Stockl-Whut, or Kathleen, as she is more generally known.

Not even the mist and rain could dim the golden glory of the maples that lined the roadsides, and scarlet-leaved branches of dogwood gleamed in vivid contrast amongst the more sombre-hued firs and cedars as we drove the twelve or more miles to Qw'umiyiqun'.

Stockl-Whut's home stands on a small, grassy knoll, overshadowed by the little stone church, built by the late Rev. Father Rondeault as a place of worship for the Indians and early settlers.

As we walked to the door numbers of cats scattered before us, and hungry-looking dogs barked a welcome. Stockl-Whut opened the door to us, and, when she had learned the reason of my visit, shook hands warmly and invited us in.

Such a room! Quite large and very high—for it had no ceiling and every imaginable object hung from the rafters and from clothes lines that were strung across the room at intervals. There were two beds, one on the floor and a white enameled one in a corner, and at one end a table piled high with dirty dishes and remnants of food. The entire place seemed to be hung about with clothes of every size and color. In the centre of the room stood a small heater, or rather, the remains of one, for the pile of ashes inside appeared to be all that was holding it together. However it was burning cheerily and we were glad of the warmth after the cold drive.

The usual family portraits, enlarged and in gorgeous frames, without which no Indian's home would be complete, were hanging round the walls, and amongst them I saw the duplicate of the small picture I carried with me.

Loxa of Qw'umiyiqun', circa 1887.   Image PN 5935 courtesy Royal British Columbia Museum.

This appeared to be the first time Stockl-Whut had been asked for the history of her father, and she was more than delighted to tell all she knew about him.

Never have I heard a more dramatic story-teller, nor seen a more expressive countenance than hers. At one moment fierce, with eyes sparkling and arms akimbo, a regular Amazon; the next, her lips trembling, eyes filled with tears of supplication, which soon disappeared, as, head held high, a look of pride on her still handsome face, she told of the presentation of the medal to her father as a "big Tyee!"[257]

"My Pappa Loxa was always very friendly to the white men," she told us. "He wanted them to come and live in our land, and he liked the priests and always tried to help them; they were good friends.

"Well, you know that Indian reserve you drive through just outside Duncan, the one by the Cowichan River? Well, that is the S-amuna' Reserve." (The district of Somenos, although several miles distant, was named after this tribe). "Well, long ago, an Indian of the S-amuna' people killed a white man, and of course there was a lot of trouble and a man-of-war was sent up to Cowichan with lots of soldiers to find the murderer.[258]

"The captain of the man-of-war came and talked to my father and said to him, 'Some of your people are hiding that bad man. If you don't give him up I will take my big guns and will blow up all your villages.

"Now Loxa knew where that S-amuna' man was hiding, and as he did not want all his people's houses to be broken, and wanted to help the white men do what was right, he went to the place where that bad man was to be found.

"'Come out!' he called to him. 'Don't be afraid; it is your friend and chief, Loxa.'

"The man came out from his hiding place, holding his musket behind his back with one hand.

"'We are friends,' said Loxa, and held out his hand. The S-amuna' man took the hand held out to him, and, quickly, Loxa pulled him closer, and reaching round behind him, caught the musket, and took it from him. Now he shouted to other men who had gone with him and they ran up and took the S-amuna' man and tied him so that he could not get away. Later on, the white men took him, put a black cloth over his head, a rope around his neck and hanged him. Up where the English church now stands they hanged him.

"Now the Indians saw that it would not do to harm the white men; that if they did so, they would be punished, and for some time there was no trouble.

"Now the government began to mark out land for the Indians to live on, to be called their 'reserves,' and three men came here to mark the lands. This made the chiefs of the different tribes very angry, and they talked together and made plans to kill all the white people. My Pappa Loxa heard of this plan and got very angry. He called all the chiefs of the tribes and talked to them, telling them that they must not touch the white men; that if they did so, the soldiers would come and blow up all the houses and kill everyone. All day he talked to them, and at last they saw as he did, and said they would leave the white men in peace and would do them no harm.

"In time the good Queen across the water heard how my pappa had saved her men and had been good friends with all the white people and she sent him a present with a message on it by her 'big Tyee.'" (The Marquis of Lansdowne, Governor-General of Canada). "And this is how the Queen's present was given to my pappa."

Stockl-Whut smoothed her skirt, cleared her throat in an impressive manner, and drew herself up proudly. She had arrived at the most important part of her narrative.

"One day there was a big time at Cowichan Bay. Many Indians came in their canoes from all parts, and the big ships came from Victoria, and there was racing in boats and canoes, and swimming. Oh, a big time! By and by a message was sent to Chief Loxa and all the Tyee Indians, and they all went on the man-of-war. There they found all the big men from Victoria were on the ship, and there before them all a big Tyee white man pinned the good Queen's present (the medal) on my pappa's coat, just as you see it in that picture!"

O the pride in Stockl-Whut's voice as she held herself very erect and described that presentation!

She pointed to the picture dimly seen through many coats of grime."There he is," she said. "There is my pappa, Chief Loxa, just as he looked that day they gave him the present.

"Ah! he was proud of that medal. On one side there was the good Queen's picture and on the other the message sent him, telling how good he had been to the white people."

I have had the good fortune to be shown one of the original programmes of this "big time" at Cowichan Bay. It reads in part:

"Indian Jubilee Sports at Cowichan Bay on the 28th June, 1887. Indians of the Coast tribes are cordially invited to attend and compete in the sports, consisting of foot, boat and canoe races. By the kindness of Admiral Sir M. Culme-Seymow and Captain Oxtey, H.M.S. *Conquest* will be present to assist."

"Ah, yes," said Stockl-Whut, "Loxa did all the priests asked him. At one time he had only one wife, and they had two little boys. Then I was born. After that he took another wife, but one day the priest came to him and said, 'Loxa, how many wives have you?' Loxa said that he had two klootchmen.[259]

"'That will not do,' said the priest. 'You must send one away.' So Loxa kept my mother, for she had two boys, and he sent away the other woman, for she only had three girls. After that Loxa and my mother walked up to the stone church and the priest married them."

"What happened to your father's medal?" I asked.

"It's lost," replied Stockl-Whut in a tragic voice. "I will tell you about it."

She drew her chair nearer the crazy stove, disturbing several sleeping cats as she did so. "Now when my pappa died," she began, "I was just twenty years old, and not married yet. Well, Loxa left a paper (a will), telling the priests to bury his medal with him, but when I married his grave was to be dug up and the medal taken from his coffin and given to me. So the priests buried him with his medal pinned on him.

"About two years after that I got married to Johnnie Tshos-o-Lok, and one day we went to my pappa's grave with the priests and Mr. Lomas, the Indian agent, and the head men of the tribe, and the coffin was opened and the medal taken out and given to me.

"Ah! I was proud to have that medal and to be able to show it to people and tell them what a fine man Chief Loxa had been. For a little time I had it, then," Stockl-Whut's voice shook and her eyes filled with tears. "That man I married, that Johnnie Tshos-o-Lok, took another woman and went to the American side, and here I was left alone.

"Well, one day when I was not here Tshos-o-lok came back with that woman and her baby and they came into my house. Old Quale-Sloch saw them drive up in a buggy. He said they opened the door and came in and by and by they drove away again.

"When I came home Quale-Sloch told me and I looked and found that Tshos-o-lok's dancing mask was gone and my medal—Chief Loxa's present that the Queen sent him—that was gone, too. Tshos-o-lok had stolen it.

"I went to Indian policeman Tom about it, and I told the Indian agent, too. 'Catch that man!' I said. 'Catch him and make him give me back that medal!' But Tshos-o-lok was a relation of Policeman Tom, and he and the agent talked to me like this:

"'Wait,' they told me; 'wait until the dances begin, then watch for your husband. If he wears his dancing mask, then we will know that it was he who went into your home, and that he must have the medal and we will go after him.'"

Stockl-Whut shook her head sadly. "Of course I went to all the dances, and that man was there, too, but never did he wear his dancing mask, and so nothing was ever done to get my medal back for me."

"Do you think he still has it?" I asked.

"Now, now," she said. "I know he did have it; that woman of his told one of my friends that he had got it, but his house has burned down three times and I am afraid he has lost my medal in the fires. Now see me." Tears again welled up in her eyes. "I have nothing left. My pappa was Chief Loxa, the big chief of the Cowichans, and I live here."

She pointed dramatically to the unevenly spaced boards and the broken window over which a flimsy curtain had been fastened to keep out a little of the wind.

"I have no money to buy food or clothes and I am looked down upon by these Indians whose men have money, but those people were poor—not even big men when my pappa was their chief!"

She rubbed her arm across her eyes and sniffed dismally. Poor Stockl-Whut, she apparently was suffering, even as many of her white sisters suffer.

"Perhaps you will get your medal back," I suggested hopefully, "then you can show it to all these people who seem to have forgotten that you are the daughter of their chief."

The idea appeared to cheer her, and we left her smiling from the doorway and inviting us to visit her again.

The Death of Sch-Lunas[260]

Visiting Mary Rice for another story, Beryl Cryer finds Tommy Pielle making toys for his grandnephews and nieces. Rice invites Cryer into her cabin where, taking up her knitting, she tells her about the time the Puneluxutth', acting on false information, attacked and killed a party of Haida visiting Nanaimo. She describes how her great uncle was captured and killed in a retaliatory Haida raid, one year later, "outside Nanaimo."

TOMMY PIELLE HAS MADE A MOST fascinating toy for Siamtunaat's two grand-children. When I went to see them last week, I found the old man sitting on his sister's doorstep with a pile of rushes and willow sticks beside him.

Little "D'othy" and Jack were crouched at his feet, watching with earnest faces while he sorted among the sticks and finally chose a fairly thick one, which he bent and bound into a circle about two feet in circumference.

Next he tore apart the rushes with great care, and commenced winding them around the stick, keeping them perfectly smooth and tight. This he continued to do until the layer of rushes measured almost two inches across; making a small and wide, green hoop.

Until then we had all watched in silence, but, as he laid aside the hoop, my curiosity could wait no longer.

"What are you making, Tommy Pielle?" I asked. He ignored my question for some moments, as he sorted and bent his willow sticks, at the same time chewing at the juicy end of a rush.

"Ah!" he said, as he at last found a stick to his liking. "This will make the bow! This game," he now condescended to explain, "is a very, very old one. When the

Indians of long ago had only their spears and bows and arrows to kill with, they had to shoot straight or there would be no food, and in a fight they would have no chance—all would be killed! So they made these toys for their children to play with, and in that way even the very small boys could shoot straight, and hit a thing as it moved. You wait now and I will show you.

In a few minutes he had made a tiny bow, and from a strip of cedar has cut a thin, beautifully shaped arrow.

"See now," he said, "this hoop is a deer running, and I, Tommy Pielle, will kill it!" With great precision he arranged the bow and arrow beside him, then, taking the rush hoop he rolled it swiftly away from him in such a manner that it rolled in a wide curve. Then he snatched up the bow and arrow and, holding it as a cross-bow, took quick aim and shot at the rolling hoop.

The first time he shot high, but with his second attempt the arrow sped true to its mark, and through the centre of the hoop.

"Ah, Haa!" chuckled Tommy Pielle, "my deer is dead!" He gave the toy to "D'othy" and commenced making a second, for little Jack.

Siamtunaat, who I guessed had been busily setting her house in order, now threw her door wide and invited me in.

"Leave him," she said, with a scornful nod of her old head at Tommy Pielle. "All day that man does nothing, just makes toys! Come and sit here, and listen to my story about an uncle of my grandfather Chief Xulqalustun, and how he was killed by the Haidas."

She closed her door upon the frivolous Tommy Pielle, and, taking up a sock she was knitting, began her story at once.

"I think I told you how my eldest girl married a man named Jimmy Joe? Well, this story begins about Jimmy Joe's grandfather. This man was of the Snuneymuxw, and he was named Sugnuston.[261] One day he saw a Haida woman he wanted for his wife, and after a time he took her and married her, and brought her back to live with the Snuneymuxw people.

"The woman was very happy with her husband, and sent messages to her people telling them to no longer be enemies, but to come as friends and visit her.

"One day three canoes full of her people paddled to Nanaimo, bringing many presents, and with friendship in their hearts. Well, that was all right, but there was one Snuneymuxw man whose brother had been killed by the Haidas, and my, he was angry when he found these people feasting with the Snuneymuxw. That night, when all were feasting and dancing, this man took his canoe and paddled away to Puneluxutth'. Pulling his canoe up on the beach, he ran swiftly to my grandfather, Chief Xulqalustun.

"'Get your fighting men!' he called, 'And come quickly! The Haidas are at Nanaimo!'

Mary Rice, Tommy Pielle and Beryl Cryer

"Then there was hurrying and calling from house to house, as the braves came out, their faces painted for battle, and carrying their fighting things. Pulling their feathers on their heads as they went running to the beach, to put their great war canoes in the water.

"Now they were away, leaving their women on the beach, crying brave words after them, bidding them fight as the Cowichans had ever done, and to bring back the heads of their enemies to put on poles about the houses!

"Darkness had come again as the Puneluxutth' canoes drew near to Nanaimo, and now, at the call from Xulqalustun, their leader, the paddles were lifted from the water and all the braves stayed as they were, resting and listening.

"For a time they waited there in the darkness, hearing the voices of the people, and the barking of dogs in the village, coming over the water. Suddenly the voices grew louder, and soon the sound of paddles could be heard coming nearer and nearer. The Haidas were leaving Nanaimo!

"Now the Cowichan canoes moved, some paddling silently, nearer to the shore, the others waiting where they were.

"On came the Haida canoes, the braves calling and talking to each other as they paddled, never thinking of the danger that was waiting for them in the darkness.

"At last they were between the Cowichan canoes and, at a shout from Xulqalustun, his braves thrust their paddles deep into the water and, with the loud war cry of the tribe, paddled hard at the Haida canoes. The fight was soon over, for no matter which way the Haidas turned, they found the Cowichan canoes. Out there on the dark, quiet water, the Cowichans killed every Haida, but one! This man, whose name was Hy-As-Thtun, jumped into the water and swam to shore, carrying his spear with him.

"My grandfather's uncle, Sch-Lunas, who was one of the Cowichan's greatest fighters, saw him swimming, and went after him, and as the man ran along the beach, Sch-Lunas waded to shore and chased him, calling him to wait and fight!

"Light was coming into the sky, as those two men on the beach began to fight, each man using the spear which he had carried with him.

"For many years men talked of that fight amongst the rocks, for both men were mighty warriors, and it was not until the red blood was running from many wounds that the Haida fell to the beach and, leaping upon him, Sch-Lunas cut his throat.

"Now in the morning light Sch-Lunas began to sing, and, as he sang, the sun came into the sky and shone down on his brown body marked with red where blood ran from spear wounds, and showed the black and white paint upon his face and the feathers on his head as, holding his spear high in the air, he danced about the body of his enemy, singing, singing, and these are the words that he sang:

"'Ah! Ha! You man, you enemy. You can't beat me!
My name is Sch-Lunas, and your name is Hy-As-Thtun, and you can't beat me."
Ah! Ha! I am a great fighter, no man can beat me!"

You Hy-as-thtun are dead, I have beat you!'"

Old Siamtunaat swayed her body as she chanted the warrior's song, and her fat, genial old face looked positively fierce.

"Well," she continued, "the Snuneymuxw people heard all this noise and came along the beach to see what could be the trouble."

"Xulqalustun went to meet them, and, not knowing that he was speaking of their friends, told the Snuneymuxw people how he and his warriors had killed all the fierce Haidas.

"'They will trouble you no longer,' he said, 'for we have shown them that the Cowichans are greater fighters than they, and show no mercy.'

"The Snuneymuxw people listened until Xulqalustun had finished, and then they told him that these people had come as friends, not to fight and kill. Xulqalustun said, 'But how could I know? One of your own tribe came for me. Now, what can I do?'

"'There is nothing you can do,' they told him. 'It was no fault of yours. Go home to Puneluxutth', but be ready to help us when the Haidas come down, for they will think that it was the Snuneymuxw who killed their men.'

"So Xulqalustun called his braves to the canoes, and, with great trouble in their hearts, they paddled home to Kuper Island. But there was one man amongst them who felt no sorrow at having killed the Snuneymuxw friends. Sch-Lunas carried with him the head of Hy-As-Thtun to put on a pole in front of his house, and as he paddled he shouted his fighting song.

"Well, about a year later, the Haida came down, and there was a great fight outside Nanaimo. All the Puneluxutth' Indians went to help their friends, and many were killed and taken prisoners, and lots of Snuneymuxw women were taken to be the slaves of the Haidas. My grandfather's uncle—Sch-Lunas—was in that fight, but he was not killed. The Haida chief told his men, 'Take this man to the canoes, for he is one of their greatest warriors, we will not kill him now, but will take him back to our own place.' So they tied Sch-Lunas and threw him into a canoe and took him away with them.

"When they reached their own village, they tied him up on a post, so that his feet could not touch the ground, and they tied his arms around the post behind him, and there they left him.

"For three weeks that poor man lived, tied up on his post. He was given no food, and he had no water to drink, and when it rained he would turn his face up to the sky and open his mouth to catch the rain as it fell.

"My grandmother used to tell me how, long after, when the Cowichans fought the Haidas and carried home again some of their own women who had been slaves of the Haidas, how these women would tell about Sch-Lunas, tied up to the post, and each morning they would go to him and say, "Do you still live, Sch-Lunas?'

and he would answer, 'Yes, I still live.' Then one morning they ran to ask their question, but there was no answer—the great Sch-Lunas was dead."

Qwulsteynum's Reminiscences[262]

Beryl Cryer seeks out an elderly man, Qwulsteynum, for a story and, after a false start, when she questions the authenticity of his story, he lectures Cryer on the impact of colonialism and its effects on the culture and the environment. He then gives details regarding seasonal food gathering, fish weirs, duck hunting and a hunter's training place on Sansum Narrows.

QWULSTEYNUM, BAPTIZED MOSES, BUT GENERALLY known as Captain Moses, by the white population, or Captain Moyez by the Indians, is one of the last of the old Indians in Chemainus district to peddle his salmon from door to door. A picturesque old figure, in his faded red sweater, his large head with its thatch of thick, white hair and strong, clean-cut features, set on broad shoulders, he is, I consider, quite the finest type of Coast Salish that I have met.

When it was explained to him that I wanted to hear stories of the old days, he immediately pulled up a chair and, sitting down opposite me, leaned forward, elbows on his knees and his chin on his hands. For a long time he sat, thinking deeply, a faraway look in his eyes. At last, without moving, he commenced to talk.

"This story that I will tell for you to write in the newspaper," he said, "is very, very old. It happened before my grandfather's time, and before his father's, but I know it is true!"

"Here's a piece of luck!" I thought. "Siamtunaat has always told me that Captain Moyez would know many old stories. She was right!"

"Now, in those long ago days," continued Qwulsteynum, "all this land was wild. All animals were wild, and all the people were like the animals!" He looked sideways at me, to learn the effect of this statement, and, evidently satisfied that I appeared sufficiently impressed, continued his story.

"One day there came to this wild land a large ship—not like the canoes—bigger and high above the water. There were men with white skins on the ship—lots of them—forty, I think, maybe more, and they were all on that one ship! The chief of the ship had a good name, he was called Columbus." Columbus! My hopes were dashed! Qwulsteynum's story was nothing less than the discovery of America by Christopher Columbus!

"You know," he continued, "that Captain Columbus was the first white man to come to our land!"

"Who told you that story, Qwulsteynum?" I asked.

"A white man told me," he confessed.

He told me all about the big ship and the men on it. "Our country was better before the white men came," he said, and launched into an account—only too true—of how the white men sent boats trading amongst the Indian villages, selling whiskey to the natives.

"That fire-water made my people mad," he said, "and they wanted to kill all they saw; then, when they had killed, the white men came and put ropes about their necks and hanged them!"[263]

Poor old Qwulsteynum, he is rather bitter against the white man. Many years ago, he was sentenced to a month in prison, for some small crime, and he has never recovered from the insult. All the same, he confesses, he did not have too bad a time. "There were loads of other men in the 'Skookum house'," he said. "We all had little house on a street (cells opening on a corridor). We had no work to do, everything was done for us. We did not even have to open our own doors! In the morning when we all went out, a man, sitting at one end of the street, pulled a handle, and every door opened and we walked out, and when we came in again the man shut all our doors for us, in the same manner!' He appeared to be immensely impressed with this attention. "Such good food! And every day a doctor came to see that we were quite well, and there was no money to be paid to him!"

"Now," he said, "when the priests first came, my people wore little cedar bark pants (loin cloths) and blankets made from the hair of dogs and from 'white mowich' (mountain goat).[264] 'Now,' said the priests, 'you are not wild people any more, you must cover your bodies, and wear pants and shirts.' But for a long time the people said, 'No' they would not change. 'We can't walk in these long pants,' they said, but the priests told them, 'if you don't wear those things, you will go down to the devil!'

"So they got frightened, and put on the clothes given to them. But some of the old men would never change. There was the old Chief of Puneluxutth', Xulqalustun, the grandfather of that old woman, Siamtunaat, he never wore white man's clothes, always he had his blanket fastened about him; but he was a good man and helped the priests in many ways.

"Have you heard that our people—the Cowichans—were always moving about finding food? Some time about May, they would go to places where the Camas— 'speenhw'—grew, and would dig lots of that root. Then next month they would pack and move to the Fraser River for the salmon and sturgeon there; they would smoke and dry thousands of these fish to be put away for the Winter months. At the Fraser River were the blueberries and cranberries, these were picked and dried too. Oolichans—'Stsa'mat' is our name—were caught at the Fraser River, but no Indian eats that fish, they are just caught for the grease. Another time the men would go after seal and porpoise; there was lots of good grease in those animals, all to be put away, and the meat dried for keeping.

Qwulsteynum and Beryl Cryer

"I remember when I was a young man, we had a very good way of catching the ducks. I will tell you about that. This was done at night time, when it got dark. Two men would take a canoe and paddle out to the flats, or to any place where they knew there would be lots of ducks. Now, in the stern of the canoe, behind the man steering, there was put a flat piece of wood or a stone, and on this was made a fire. At the other end of the canoe, a man stood waiting with a duck spear. Bye-and-bye the birds, being frightened, would fly at the light, and then the man with his spear would be busy, catching those birds as they flew to the light of the fire. Ah! That was good hunting!" He laughed heartily at the recollection of this sport.

"See, now," he continued, "here is the spear that we used."

Taking my pencil, he drew a rough sketch of a long stick, at one end of which was a small arrangement resembling nothing so much as a closed umbrella without a cover, the stays being made of willow sticks, each stick having a barbed tip. "These catch in the feathers," he explained, "so that the bird is not spoiled. In those days there were many, many hundreds of ducks, and when they flew it was like a great cloud moving, so many birds together. Now they are gone, and soon the salmon will be gone, too.

"See, now, when I was a boy, we would go over to Hwts'usi'—Bonsall's Creek—for the salmon, and, do you know, we could not sleep at night, there was such a noise. Swish! Swish! The salmon going up the creek, all pushing, pushing, to get far up. There were so many that the water was full, and the salmon next to the shore would get pushed far out of the water, on to the grass. Every river was the same, full of salmon. I can remember when the Cowichans had thirteen weirs on the Cowichan River, and I know that we used to catch just as many salmon in the weirs at the upper part of the river as we caught in the lower ones, and now, the white men say our weirs stop the fish."[265]

He laughed scornfully at this absurd idea.

"Those weirs," he explained, "do not belong to all the tribe. Any man may not get his fish from them. When they were first put in the rivers they belonged to just a few families, and now, in these days, they are the same, belonging only to the children and grandchildren of those first families—no other men may use them, or there is much trouble. When I was young, I remember they used a salmon trap in the in the creek at Hwts'usi'. This was made of willow sticks, like this (a toboggan-shaped basket). It was three or four feet each way, and was sunk in the bottom of the creek. In those days there were big times when the first salmon came up the rivers. All the Cowichans would be gathered at their fishing camps and there would be great fires in the lodges and much dancing and singing, after which the salmon feasting would begin. Many hundreds of salmon would be eaten at those feasts, for all would feed until they could eat no more."

Once again he rested his head in his hands and thought. "Have you heard of the duck nets that the Cowichans used?" he asked. I told him the account that

Siamtunaat had given me one of those great nets made of wild hemp that used to grow about the Fraser River, and how the ducks were caught. Qwulsteynum chuckled.

"That old woman only told you of one way," he said. "Now listen, and I will tell you of the best way those nets—which we called t'akum—were used. First, as you know, there were two high poles—forty feet high—set in the mud of the river flats, about fifty yards apart. One of these poles, as you have seen, is still standing down at Bonsall's Creek.[266] At the top of those poles was fastened a ring made of bone or of cedar. Now a strong rope of willow bark or cedar root was put along the top of the net, the ends going through those two rings and down to the bottom of the poles. Round the poles were put branches of trees, that the hunters might hide and not frighten the birds.

"Now the best time to catch the ducks was in the very early morning before the fighting; at night, when there was a big moon, or on days that were dark and stormy; but best of all was in the morning.

"The hunters would watch how the birds were flying at that time; if low, they would let the net down a little, if high, pull it up to the top of the poles. When the birds, flying out, hit the net, the man hiding at the bottom of the pole would let go of the rope, and drop the net on top of the ducks as they fell to the ground. Then there would be quick killing and many hundreds of ducks would be taken back to the villages.

"Sometimes a man would climb to the top of the pole, to watch the birds coming, and this man would drop the net on them." Qwulsteynum shook his head despondently. "Not much hunting now!" he sighed.

He pushed back his chair and walked to the door. Our interview was evidently ended? But no, he had thought of something more, for he closed the door again and returned to his chair.

"Has anyone told you about that place where the young braves used to shoot their arrows?" he asked. "No? Well, I can tell you about that! You know, long ago, all the people used to try different things to find out if they would be lucky, or what thing they were to do to be a fighter, or a good hunter, or good at catching fish—anything like that. Well, you know that place—Maple Bay—Hwtl'upnets we call it? Now, outside Maple Bay, around the point, there are some high rocks, and far up on these rocks there is a little hole—quite small. Long ago, the young braves would take their canoes and paddle out in front of that little hole, and, standing up in the canoes, they would aim, and shoot their arrows at the hole. It was along way to shoot, and standing up in the canoe, which was always moving, was not very easy; but the braves who got their arrows into the hole knew that they would be lucky and would always be good hunters. That hole is high up, but I think, maybe, if a man could climb up, he would find some of the arrows still there, far back in the hole, where they were shot by the braves, so long ago."[267]

Xeel's—The Sun God[268]

Once again, when Beryl Cryer visits Mary Rice for a story, a topic of general conversation leads to an account of Puneluxutth' ethnography. This time, the subject is Xeel's, the Transformer, a supernatural being who embodied the creative energy of the sun, and travelled the land in ancient times creating biodiversity, and shaping the land in ways to remind people of his works. Many places throughout the traditional native territories are associated with Xeel's' deeds. Mary Rice describes Transformer sites at Active Pass, Kuper Island, Kulleet Bay, Dodd's Narrow and Nanaimo.

SIAMTUNAAT HAS IMPORTED ANOTHER GRANDCHILD to help her, Tommy Pielle, her old brother, having decided to return to his house at Puneluxutth'.

Whether the truant wife has returned to him or whether he has taken another woman to keep his house I did not like to ask, but I am certain that it is a change for the better from Siamtunaat's point of view, at any rate. This new grandchild, Martha, had the house looking cleaner than I have ever seen it. Even the mounds of garments which usually overflowed both bedrooms had been hidden away, and the beds were neatly made.

Whilst I asked after Siamtunaat's various aches and pains, Martha wrapped up a newly-made sweater and, taking the small D'othy with her, went out to deliver it for her "granny."

As she closed the door behind her, Siamtunaat shook her head sadly. "Oh, that poor girl!" she sighed. Did you see her little hand, and the way she walks?"

"She is lame?" I asked. Siamtunaat nodded.

"Lame," she repeated. "Yes, that's it. When she was a little girl she was very sick and all one side of her died! Her hand, and her arm and her leg! Now, if only Xeel's[269] was here, he would make her better!" Again she sighed and shook her head sorrowfully.

"Who is Xeel's?" I asked.

"Didn't I never tell you about Xeel's?" exclaimed Siamtunaat. "Well, now listen! Long, long ago, all the people thought that the sun—who was named Sum'shathut—made all things. He made the world, but he didn't finish it, and there was nothing on it—just ground and water. Then Sum'shathut came down to the world to finish things. He came looking like a man, and his name was 'Xeel's.'

"Well, he went about fixing things, making lakes and rivers, and all things that grow, and then he made animals and all things like that. In just a few places he made people, not many though, as I have told you before. Now there were some places where he could not put a river or lake for the people to drink from, and so, do you know what he did? He put his foot down on the rocks, and he told the water to come up and there under his foot, the fresh cold water came bubbling up! I have often got water from some of those springs made by Xeel's.

"Over at Plumper Pass, there is one of those springs, I have seen it, it is just the shape of a big, big foot—about two feet long, and wide and deep enough to dip a bucket; but even in the very hot Summers that spring is always full of water.[270]

"There is another spring over on Thetis Island, but that has been changed, made bigger.

"Well, after Xeel's had put a few people in different places, he went over near Nanaimo, to a place called 'Jack's Point,' and there one day, when the water was far out, he went along the rocks, and made a big salmon. That fish is there today, made of stone, living against the rocks, with its mouth a little open, as though it was swimming. Now, you know that black bird, the raven?—Spaal' we call him. Well, when Xeel's was making that fish, Spaal' came along and said: 'What are you making that thing for?' Xeel's told him!

"'Before long, poor Indians will come this way looking for food to eat, and when they see this salmon, they will know that here is a good fishing ground; and this salmon I am making will bring other salmon here, so that there will always be lots of fish to be caught, and, do you know!" added Siamtunaat, "that has always been a good fishing place, the Indians can always catch salmon by Jack's Point!

"Now, as that man—Xeel's—went along he saw all sorts of people, sick ones, and blind ones, humpy, and lame ones like that poor granddaughter of mine, and he made them all well—if they were good, but if he saw any bad people, those he turned to stone—all bad animals were turned into stone, too. All along the Islands, wherever you go, if you look at the rocks, you will see stone people, stone fish, stone animals—why there is a stone dog in a little hole up on the high rocks of Kuper Island, and where ever those things are seen, there you may know that Xeel's passed, long, long ago.

"He went to all the little islands, and into every bay, no place was passed by. One day, as he was going along, past Q'ulits' (Chemainus Bay), he saw a man very busy on the beach.

"'What are you doing?' he asked. The man showed him two big knives that he had made. 'I am making these knives very sharp!' he said. 'There's a man called Xeel's, coming this way, he is turning all the people into stone. I don't like the way he acts, and I'm going to wait here for him, and kill him!'

"'You are going to kill this man?' asked Xeel's, 'and you have not even seen him? Maybe the stories that you heard are not true!'

"The man laughed, 'I don't like the sound of him!' he said, 'a man like that is better dead, as soon as I see him I will kill him!' Then Xeel's got angry. He took the two knives that the man had made, and put them, one on each side of the man's head. 'Now,' he said, 'because of the boldness that is in your heart, you will always wear these things on your head and, as you get older, they will grow longer, and small ones will grow from them like the branches of a tree. Go now! From this day you must always jump as you run, and your name will be Ha'put; and all people will hunt you that they may kill you for food.'

"As Xeel's spoke, the man turned into a great buck, with long, sharp horns coming from his head, where the knives had been put; and, as Xeel's gave him his name, he bounded away into the bushes, the first of all the deer.

"Then Xeel's went on and he came to those narrows near Nanaimo, Dodd Narrows. At one place along there was a spring of good water, but no one could go near it, for it belonged to a great devilfish that lived beside it. Not far from this spring there lived an old man and his grandson, a boy, fourteen years old, but very small, for he had never grown. These two had to paddle a long way to get their water because the devilfish tried to kill them if they went near his spring. One day they were out fishing, when they met a man.

"'Can you give me a drink of water?' asked the man. The old man shook his head. 'There is a spring just over there,' he said, pointing to the rocks, 'but no one may use it, as a devilfish kills all who go near!' 'I will drink from that spring!' said the man, 'can you lend me a bucket to carry some water in?' 'We have no bucket,' said the old man, 'and you must not try and drink or you will surely be killed.' But the man laughed and paddled to where the spring bubbled its cool, clear water among the rocks.

"'Since I have no bucket, I will use a large clam shell,' he said, and picked some big shells from the beach. Now he dipped them in the water, but, every time he brought the shell full of water up to his mouth, a hole came in the bottom and all the water ran out. Then, out from the rocks came the great devilfish. Straight to the man he came, holding out his long arms to catch and kill him, but the man did not move, only reached out his hand, and taking the great creature, tore it in pieces and threw them back into the sea. 'Come and drink!' he called to the old man and the boy. 'See! The devilfish is dead! I have broken him in pieces.

"'Who are you?' questioned the old man, as he and the boy paddled to shore. 'How is it, that you, a man alone, could kill that wicked devilfish? Many together have tried, but no man has been able to catch him! Surely you must be that Xeel's, who we have heard was coming this way, helping those in trouble, and punishing those that are bad!'

"The man nodded his head. 'Yes!' he told them, 'I am Xeel's.' He looked at the small boy, and he turned him into a big strong boy, who could help his old grandfather, and not have to be taken care of as though he were a small child."

Siamtunaat nodded her old head thoughtfully. "All the way along it was the same," she said. "Xeel's took away the bad and helped the good."

"Where did Xeel's go when he had finished down here?" I asked her.

"Well, I never heard for sure," she replied, "but my mother told me she thought he went back to the sun again, and there he stays today."

The Burial of Tsa'athmun[271]

When Beryl Cryer calls on Mary Rice, she finds her nursing an injury. The "Indian Medicine" that she intends to use reminds her of a "whiskey feast" that took place at Puneluxutth', probably in the 1860s. One of the protagonists in the story is later given a premature burial. The interview concludes with more discussion of traditional herbal medicines.

SIAMTUNAAT WAS FEELING VERY SORRY for herself; she has had a bad fall, and had to rest in bed.

"My granddaughter, Martha, has rubbed me," she explained, "but it makes me feel worse."

"Don't rub," I told her, "use hot cloths!"

Siamtunaat shook her head. "Such good white stuff, to rub with!" she said sadly, "and it cost so much money, I must use it!" Presently she brightened a little, "When my son Charlie comes, he'll fix it for me! He knows where to find Indian medicine that mends bones; that's what I want!"

"Where does he get it?" I asked.

"It's green stuff, and it grows in wet places," she explained, "He'll put that on, and it will make me better."

I looked in a few days later and found her sitting up in a chair.

"I can't stay in bed," she said, "so much to be done! The doctor came and he said, 'Put on hot cloths,' just like you did; and then Charlie came, with the Indian medicine, so I'm better now, but I can't knit. Oh, I am sore!"

She seemed anxious to talk however, so I drew my chair up to the rickety old stove, that appears to be held together with odds and ends of wire; and waited for her to begin.

"The first time that I saw that Indian medicine," she began, "was long ago, when I was a little girl. As you know, I was living at Puneluxutth' on Kuper Island. Well, at that time all my people were having a lot of trouble about an Indian from California, who came to stay with his sister, who was married to a Puneluxutth' man. This man said he was a doctor, but all the people died when he gave them medicine! Some of the Puneluxutth' people liked him and wanted him to stay, but others talked together, and said that he made a lot of people trouble.

"One day there was a big time at Puneluxutth'. A trading-boat came in and brought a lot of whiskey to trade with my people, for skins and meat. Of course, you know, when the Indians got that bad drink they went mad, and started fighting and trying to kill each other. I 'member I went away along the beach with two other girls, to get clams. We had our canoe and clam sticks for digging, and we were busy getting lots of clams, when my grandfather's wife, her name was Tsulaastun, came running along the rocks, calling to us to hurry back 'Get your clams, and come back quickly!' she called. 'Don't you know everybody is drinking that hot whisky and they have killed a man!' We were all excited! 'Who have they killed?' we asked. 'That man from California. His brother-in-law Tsa'athmun has killed him,' she told us; 'But come, hurry before there is more trouble!'

"My how we did throw the clams into our canoe! Pushing it out into deep water, we climbed in and paddled hard all the way back to the village. All that night there was so much noise, no one could sleep; all the men quarreling and fighting, and the women and children hiding from them. Next morning, a woman came to the house where we people lived together, and she told my grandfather's wife that the medicine man was not dead, but very badly hurt—all his body cut open and that before he got his cut, he had hurt Tsa'athmun, his brother-in-law, very badly. 'We think he will die too!' said the woman. 'I will go and see that California man,' said Tsulaastun, 'Maybe I can help make him better. We don't want him to die in our village, and make a lot of trouble for everybody.' So she took some of this green 'erb, like Charlie gave me, and started off.

"Well, I wish you could have seen my grandfather, that Chief Xulqalustun! He had had a long sleep and now, when he woke up he was hungry. 'Where has that woman gone?' he asked, 'doesn't she know that I have had no breakfast?' Oh, but he was angry! 'That California man is no good, he is better dead!' he said, 'why does she want to make him live?' Well, my mother came in just then, and she got her father some food, so he felt better, and while he was eating I ran out of the house and along to where the sick man was lying.

"I peeped into the house and there I saw the sick man on his blankets beside the fire, and Tsulaastun was putting some of the green medicine on the big cut, and trying to mend him by tying long pieces of cedar bark round and round his body, to shut up the cut. I had never seen so bad a cut—right down his body! After I had looked a little while, I ran home again for I knew there would be trouble if Tsulaastun found me there.

"Well, my grandfather's wife had all her trouble for nothing! That afternoon the man died. Some of his friends gave a biscuit box to put him in. At that time when anybody died, our people used to make a little platform—not very high from the ground—and on that they put the dead body, sitting up in a kind of box, and covered with blankets. Sometimes the traders brought biscuit boxes, and those boxes were very good to use for the dead people.

"Well, that Indian doctor was dead, but the other man, Tsa'athmun, was still living, but very, very sick. His wife got Indian doctors and everybody hit drums and danced and sang the medicine man's songs but it was no good. After three days Tsa'athmun too, died.

"Now, listen to this!" Siamtunaat who had punctuated her story with vigorous pokes at an enormous piece of wood in the old stove, now closed the stove door, and pointed her poker at me.

"Now before Tsa'athmun died, he called his old father and mother to him. 'There's something I want you to do for me,' he said. 'After I am dead, I want you to get my knife, and a piece of my tobacco, (they used to get pieces of hard, black tobacco from the traders) and put them on top of me, don't put them in the box, but on top of me, where I can reach them, if I want them. Then get my pipe, and the stones to make fire with, (flint and steel) and put them beside the other things. See that they are on top of me when you put me in my box.'

"Well, before that man died, all the Puneluxutth' were called to a potlatch at Kwa'mutsun and of course the old father and mother wanted to go, but they had to stay with their son and daughter-in-law, until Tsa'athmun should die. Now, nearly all the canoes filled with Puneluxutth' going to have a good time at the potlatch had paddled away, only a few people were left, and still Tsa'athmun was alive. Then came the morning of the potlatch. Early, early, his wife went to the corner where her husband lay on his blankets, and there she found him dead. She ran out to tell the old people, and they came hurrying up.

"'We must be quick!' they said, 'or it will be too late to go to Kwa'mutsun! We won't fix his box now, there is no time, we will put him in the ground, and later, when we have more time, we will fix him properly!' They quickly made a little hole and laid him in it; then they got some cedar boards to cover him, but, just as they put the first boards over, his wife came running out.

"'Wait!' she called, 'we must not forget the things he wanted. See, I have them all here!' She laid on his chest, the pipe, tobacco, knife and stones for fire, just as he had asked them.

"Now they put the boards across the hole, so that they were above, not touching him; and on top of the boards they put two feet of earth. Then they got ready as quickly as they could, and away they paddled to Kwa'mutsun.

"Well, they all stayed there about a week, and there was a big time, great fires burning in the houses every night, lots of singing, and oh! such good dancing! My grandfather, Xulqalustun was a very good dancer, and some of the Puneluxutth' had the finest dancing clothes, finer than all the other Cowichans, and great hats and faces. Oh, it was a good time. Presents were given, and songs were made, and there were feasts, in a different house each night. Well, when it was all finished, everybody went back to their own homes, many carrying presents, and all feeling tired, they had danced so hard, and had eaten so much good food.

"When they got back to Puneluxutth', Tsa'athmun's wife said to her husband's old people. 'When are you going to bury my husband properly?' 'Oh!' they told her, 'there is no hurry, he is happy where he is, for he has all the things he wanted beside him!' So they left him in peace. 'Someday,' they said, 'when we have more time we will fix him up!'

"Those were poor sort of people," said Siamtunaat. "They were never ready for anything, always waiting. Too lazy to do things, and then having to hurry to get things done."

She attacked the smouldering wood in her stove, with such vigor, I was afraid it would prove too much for the stove but, beyond shaking on its old legs, and the crack around the middle showing a wider streak of firelight, it appeared none the worse, as she slammed the door shut once more.

"Well," she continued. "About two years after Tsa'athmun had died, I was walking in the woods behind Puneluxutth', and I met those two old people. 'We have just seen the place where we buried our son!' the old man said. 'We think it is about time we fixed him up properly, so we are going to see Xulqalustun, your grandfather, about it.' I walked back with them, and we found my grandfather, and told him about moving Tsa'athmun. He told them he thought it would be a good thing to fix the grave, so they got a man to go with them and help them move Tsa'athmun.

"Now, what do you think!" Siamtunaat's eyes grew round, as she tapped on the stove with her poker, to emphasize her words. "When they had taken away the earth and the boards, what do you think they saw? Tsa'athmun had his knife in one hand, and in the other a small end of the tobacco, the rest was cut into small pieces, and in his mouth was his pipe, half full of tobacco! and that tobacco was burnt! Poor Tsa'athmun had been smoking.

"Had they buried him before he was really dead?" I asked her. Siamtunaat nodded her head, her lips pursed up tightly.

"They had buried him too soon—before he was dead!" she said. "The poor man had waked up, and when he found he could not get out he had cut his tobacco and had a smoke. But that taught the Cowichans a lesson, and after that they got frightened, and always waited two days before burying or putting out their dead."

Siamtunaat sighed deeply. "I'll have to get Charlie to bring me some more of that medicine," she said, "I'm not better yet!"

"What name has the medicine?" I asked. She shook her head. "I never heard the name, but Charlie knows what I mean when I tell him its for mending bones. The Indians use lots of things for their medicines. The roots of the hemlock tree make medicine when they are boiled, and those little seeds on the cedar trees, are good for some things, if they are hammered and broken up, and cooked; then those little seeds on that sort of cedar tree (Pencil cedar), are very good for a cold if they are boiled, and salal leaves and the roots of the dogwood tree. Oh, there are so many! Our medicine men know all medicines for all kinds of sickness, and people pay me a little money for the medicines I can give them."

From the window I could see her grandchildren paddling in, in their little canoe, but before I could tell Siamtunaat, her keen old ears had heard their voices.

"Here come the 'chilrun'," she said. "Martha will make me go to bed again, so you come another day, and we will talk together about those old days."

I hurried off before the family arrived, but, as I went along the beach I could see the small boy carrying a fine large salmon to the house, and guessed that there would be a good meal of fish for old "granny" that evening.

Iichnawmukw"'s Story[272]

When Beryl Cryer goes to visit an elder at Hwt'susi', she discovers her reputation precedes her. The man, Iichnawmukw', recognizes her name and knows that her work appears in the newspaper. But before he tells any "old stories," he begins with a speech criticizing Hwunitum' fishing laws. After this commentary, Iichnawmukw' gives a detailed description of traditional communal deer traps, which use nets and pits. "It was no trouble to get food in those days! No white men! No laws!" As Loraine Littlefield points out, the elder was using Beryl Cryer to convey a powerful political message to a large Hwunitum' audience, where native voice was seldom heard.[273]

HWTS'USI' IS BY FAR THE MOST PICTURESQUE Indian village that I have seen. To reach it, one follows a narrow road—thickly hedged on either side with rose bushes—which winds round and down a hillside to the flats of Chemainus River. Here the road runs along the bank of Bonsall's Creek, and it is beside this creek that the Indians have chosen to build their homes.

Some dozen or more neat cottages, many of them with a garden in front, cluster close to the road which, in some places, runs perilously near the edge of the creek. The creek itself appears more like a canal at this point, with its slowly-moving water and the green fields stretching away from the opposite bank.

A few boathouses are built out over the water, and drawn up along the banks are canoes and boats of all sizes.

About half way down the "row" live Iichnawmukw' and his old wife. Theirs is the most pretentious house in the row, additions having evidently been built on from time to time.

Iichnawmukw' came to the door in answer to my knock, and stood peering out at me through large, dark glasses. At first he seemed rather doubtful as to the advisability of letting me in; but when I had introduced myself he recognized my name and, taking me by the hand, threw his door wide.

"Come in! Come in!" he invited, and placed a rocking chair close to the red-hot stove.

The room was quite large, with a very high ceiling, and the usual enlarged photographs around the walls, and a lot of flowering plants in the windows.

Iichnawmukw' had evidently been having his lunch, for, through a doorway I could see his wife finishing her meal at a table set in a bay window with frilled cushions and more flowers. The whole place was beautifully clean and neat.

"Iichnawmukw', I want some stories about the old days," I told him.

"Ah!" He nodded his head and pulled his old brown hat lower on his forehead. "I know, my boy has told me!" he said; "Ankuty[274] stories, eh?—and for newspaper?" He was greatly impressed, and settled back in his chair to think. But not for long. He had troubles of his own to be told, and I must listen to a long and only partially understood tirade against the fishing laws.

He pushed back his chair and stood over the stove, talking and gesticulating with terrific fervor.

"There are three things a man must have to live," he said. "First, he must have fire to warm him. Then he must have water to drink, if he is thirsty, and last, he must have food to eat if he is hungry. And there should be no laws to stop people having those three things, so that all can live.

"We old people," he said, can't work for pay any more—we are too old, and so we can't buy much food. And the young people can't help us. They have their own families to feed. We old people don't catch more fish than we want for ourselves, to eat and to dry for the Winter. We don't waste the fish. Before the Jap men came there were so many fish, more than I can tell you. All our creeks and rivers were full. But now—where are they? The white men think that they will make it right again, and they say, 'The Indians must not put nets in this place! Must not spear fish in that creek!' Ah!" He took off his hat and threw it onto the table.

"How will we get enough fish for the Winter?" he demanded of me; and as I had but the foggiest idea of the fishing laws I could do no more than shake my head and try to appear sympathetic, at the same time hoping that he would soon come to the end of his tale of woe and get down to business.

He produced a very black pipe, and, having filled and lighted it, smoked in silence for a few moments.

"Ankuty stories, eh?" he asked once more and sat puffing contentedly at his pipe. "Has any man told you about the hunters long ago?" he asked.

"I know a little, but would like to hear more," I replied.

"Well, now, I'll tell you about the deer. Sometimes the hunters would catch those deer and elk in nets, and sometimes in big holes in the ground. Those deer nets were very, very long, it would take three men to carry one net, and they were made out of the strong pieces that go down the legs of the deer (sinews) and that big, strong piece in his back. It would take a lot of pieces to make one net. Now this net would be carried by three men to a good trail made by the deer or elk as they went to get water, and they would fasten it across this trail. They had to be very careful to put it up from the ground a little, so that the fawns were not caught, but could run underneath, and then the top would be tied to a tree about as high as a man, so that the deer could not jump over.

"When the net is ready, the hunter gets his dogs and starts out to hunt for the deer. That does not take long: there are so many! When the dogs get one, they drive it through the bushes and down the trail to where the net is hung. The deer gets scared and does not look much where it is going and jumps right into the net and gets tangled up in it! Then the hunter takes a hammer made from a stone and hits it on the head and kills it! To kill an elk was harder work. That would take two, or sometimes three men with their hammers!"

"How did they dig those big holes for the deer to fall into?" I asked him." Ah! Iichnawmukw' laughed. "That was a lot of hard work, more work than we would do now; those deep holes that they used to make on the deer trails, covering them with branches so that they could not be seen, were, how deep do you think?" He leaned forward, and, taking off his glasses, looked at me with painfully bloodshot eyes, as he put his question.

"I've no idea," I told him.

"Well," he said, "I'll tell you. They were ten feet deep! and just about as long as a big deer! Not too long, though, or the deer would jump out. And now I'll tell you how they made those deep holes. We called them lup'a. All the hunter had to dig with was a strong stick and a very big clam shell (sweem).[275] First he would work with his stick, then, as the earth got loose, scrape it out with the clam shell and throw it away. When the hole got very deep, with the hunter working down in it, he would throw the dirt out with his hands. Oh, it was hard work! And it took a lot of days, but the hunters had nothing else to do—lots of time for digging."

The old man chuckled away to himself, then called to his wife, who had been clearing away the lunch things. She came hobbling in and, as Iichnawmukw' told her my name, and what I wanted, she shook my hand in both of hers and held it over her heart, making a curious crooning noise as she did so.

"My wife, she is glad to see you!" explained Iichnawmukw'. She was a fine-looking old woman, dressed in the usual sweater and voluminous skirt, but she wore on her head, and pulled so low over her face that I could not see her eyes, a summery-looking brown straw hat, trimmed with brown ribbon bows and blue flowers. She brought her basket of knitting up to the stove and, drawing a chair beside mine, showed me the socks she was knitting—white, with a bright green stripe around the tops, beautifully soft and warm, and a good deal finer than the usual Indian socks.

"Has he told you how the old people used to keep the deer meat?" she asked me.

Iichnawmukw' slapped his knee. "I forgot! Well, now, all the meat from the deer and that elk would be cut in long strips and hung up to dry. I can remember when I was a boy, seeing all the houses with all the roofs full of deer meat, clams and salmon, hanging up to dry! Ah, the roof would be so full that not another piece could be hung up! It was no trouble to get food in those days! No white men! No laws!"

We were on dangerous ground once more, and I wondered how I could change the subject. By good luck I glanced out of the window, and there, stretching across the flats, and out over Xulel-thw and the neighboring islands, I saw a rainbow.

"See, Iichnawmukw'," I said, "what do you call that?"

The old man crossed to the window, and stood for some time looking up at the rainbow. "That," he said, "is called thuqul'shunum." As he returned to his chair he added. "I think that thing was put in the sky by God, to show everybody that He made everything! When men see that thing they remember. I think that is the way to find God—up under that arch. When a good man dies he flies up, under that thing of colors, and there is God, sitting on his throne! Not all men think that," he explained; "some men see that and they say, 'Ah, it is going to rain!' But me, I think you go up and under that to see God!"

"Who told you that?" I asked, wondering who could have put such a romantic idea into his head.

"No person told me; I just think that myself!" he answered.

"Now you know, long ago, all the tribes used to go to the Fraser River to meet and trade their things. From the Islands they came, and from along the coast. Oh! they did great trading!"

"What had they to trade, so long ago?" I asked.

"Well, see now, the Cowichans had deers' meat, and blankets, and mats made of the hair of dogs and of mountain goats. The Nimpkish had good red paint for putting on faces. The Nootka[276] and Makah people made good canoes, mats made of cedar bark, and sometimes hats made of roots of the spruce tree—they were good to keep off the rain! Then the Sannich took clams, wild onions and crabs. Other tribes took clover roots, Camas—we call it speenhw—dried berries and mussels. And, of course, sometimes the different people took slaves they did not want, and sold them.

"Oh, it was a great time! Everybody talking a lot, and sometimes at night, there would be feasting and singing. Any man could have feasts then! There was so much food, so many fish and deer! No laws in those days!"

"But Iichnawmukw'," I protested, "long ago you worked for the Government— helped the Indians keep the laws made by the white men?"

The old man drew himself up. "Ah, yes!" he replied; long ago I was an Indian policeman, and everybody knew me, but I only helped the Indians keep good laws, not like these about hunting and fishing!"

He was off again, so, gathering up my belongings, I said, "Good-bye" to the irate old man, leaving him to finish his harangue with his old wife as audience.

Ki'et'sa'kun of Nanaimo:
Telling How Governor Douglas Renamed Him "Coal Tyee"[277]

Mary Rice assists Beryl Cryer in her quest for more stories by directing her to visit two very knowledge Snuneymuxw elders, Joe and Jennie Wyse. The elders shared a special relationship, skw'ukw'il'us, "co-parents-in-law,"[278] and were authorized bearers of oral traditions. Beryl Cryer drives up to Nanaimo, and is welcomed into their home at Xwsol'exwel, in Nanaimo Harbour. Joe Wyse narrates in the Snuneymuxw dialect, while his wife translates for Beryl Cryer who takes notes.

Joe Wyse names the different communities that make up the Snuneymuxw, and describes how the discovery of coal in 1849 brought them irrevocably in contact with the Hwunitum'. He joins the discussion in English when the Douglas Treaty of December 23, 1854 is mentioned. His father, Sugnuston, was the lead signatory in the list of 159 men from Solexwel, who affixed their marks to the agreement. Joe Wyse himself was present as a small child. They remind their guest that "there was some mistake made at that meeting" regarding the agreement.

On the Xwsol'exwel[279] reserve at Nanaimo live "Joez" Sugnuston and his wife Tl'utasiye'. They are a tall, thin, old couple, both speaking good English. Tl'utasiye''s brown face is exactly like a shriveled apple; her twinkling black eyes almost disappearing amongst innumerable wrinkles when she laughs—which is often.

Her husband is a good many years older, but, in spite of his great age, is remarkably alert and welcomed me with the usual warm hospitality that I have met with amongst all the Cowichans.

These people all know one another—for the Indians are great visitors, and Sunday usually finds entire families setting out to spend the day, and often night, with distant friends—and I find the magic name of my friend Siamtunaat is the "Open Sesame" to many a door, she being apparently related to half the tribe.

Tl'utasiye' led me through her kitchen, with its shining stove and atmosphere heavy with the smell of smoked fish and oil, into the living-room, a large, square room which seemed to be filled with rocking chairs of every size and description, whilst brightly-colored artificial flowers were arranged on shelves and table.

I was given a chair at the centre table, and the two old people settled themselves on either side of me.

"Now," said Tl'utasiye', "My man, he can talk English, but I talk it better, so he will tell me, and I will tell you!"

Here she was interrupted by Sugnuston, who stood up, and, with many gesticulations, made a long speech, after which he shook my hand vigorously and sat down again.

Joe Wyse, Jennie Wyse and Beryl Cryer

Ki'et'sa'kun, also known as "Coal Tyee." Image PN 5908 courtesy Royal British Columbia Museum.

"He says," Tl'utasiye' interpreted, "that he thanks you, kind, white lady, for coming to hear his stories. Always he has wanted to tell what he knows to the white people, but nobody has time to listen. If you will write it for him, he will tell you of the time the Indians took coal to Victòria to show to the white men. He says "everything we tell you will be true, because me and my wife never do nothing wrong, except we are right!"

"Now, this place where we are living is called by the Indians, 'Xwsol'exwel' but the white people call it the Nanaimo reserve; that name is not right. You must know that long ago, before any white men came, there were lots of Indians living about here. At Departure Bay there was a strong tribe, so many that there were three rows of houses, and the place had three names. At the north end it was called T'iwulhxun, in the middle Enwines,[280] and at the south Yeshexen. Then out on that big island that you can see from our window, there was an-other tribe, they were called the Tl'eeltxw, and down where the coaling wharf is now, there were the Solexwel.

"Well, at Departure Bay, we call that place Sti'ilup, it was always very cold in the Winter, great waves coming in and, Oh! such winds! and after a time most of the people moved here to this place. Those were my people, my grandma was with them when they moved, but I was born here at Xwsol'exwel. Then most of the people out on the island were killed in a fight—I will tell you of another day, and those who were left moved here, too. Later, when the white men came and took the coal, they moved the Indians, my man's people, down from Solexwel, the name of the place where they lived, near the coaling wharf, down here to Xwsol'exwel, so that all the Snuneymuxw were together. Now, that is the way to say our name, 'Snuneymuxw,' not Nanaimo, as the white people call it."

"Well, long ago, before there were any white men in our country, the Indians were all very afraid of that great black fish, the whale, we call it Quon-as. There were lots of those big fish here then, but no man touched them.

"Now all the people living here knew about the black rocks that were round the shores, for they could see them all black and shining beside the water, and, in lots of places down deep in the water: and do you know what those silly people thought? Such a funny thing!"

Here Tl'utasiye' shook with laughter and her withered old face became more wrinkled as she enjoyed her joke.

"They thought that rock, all long and black and shining, must have something to do with the whales, for they were long and black and shining, too! So the head men said, 'Never touch that black rock no matter where you see it, for it belongs to the great black fish, and if we touch that rock, all the fish will surely come and kill us.'

"One day some of the tribe made a fire on the beach, and soon one said, 'What a bad smell! Then others smelt it, and it made them feel sick, the smell was so bad! Bye and bye some of them found that it was the smoke that smelt so bad. 'It must

Joe Wyse, Jennie Wyse and Beryl Cryer

be something in our fire: they said, and they got sticks and moved the burning logs. There right where the fire had been was a big piece of the black stone, and it was burning just like wood; but oh, how it smelt!

"All the tribe was called to look at it, and there was great tasting amongst the head men, for they were afraid the black fish would be angry and come to do them harm! So, for a long time after that they had men to watch the waters. Day and night a man stood out on the point of rocks that you can see from here, listening and looking for the whales to come. Of course none came very near, and after a time the Indians felt that they were never to touch the black rocks.

"Now, after a long time, people from Stth'amus[281]—that was the Indian name for the place where Victoria is now—came in their canoes with tales of white men in great ships coming, and they told how these men cut down the trees and built houses, and, oh! I can't tell you all the funny things they told about the white people! The clothes they wore, covering their bodies right up, and the queer food they ate!

"After the Stth'amus people had gone home again, everybody talked of those funny white people, and some of the young men said:

"'We must go and see for ourselves what these people are like!'

So about twelve young men took a canoe and paddled down to Stth'amus. When they got there they walked about looking at everything, at the men and the houses and the big boats, everything was just as they had been told!

"In one place they saw some barrels that had been thrown out behind a sort of store, the barrels were all broken, but the iron hoops were there, and the men picked them up and put them in their canoe. They found other things, too, that they kept to show their families when they came back. One man had some old boots, and cans—any old rubbish that had been thrown away they put in their canoe: for all these things were new to them.

"While they were walking about they came to the blacksmith's shop and there they watched him hitting an iron bar, making it flat at one end, and they saw how he put it in the fire and made it very hot before he hit it.

"When they had seen everything they came home and, as they paddled to the shore, they shouted to their people: 'Come and see what we have brought from Stth'amus!' and they showed the old boots and tins and hoops. All the tribe stood round looking at the things that those strange people had used. My father was there, you know, for he was the chief of that tribe.

"'There,' said the young men holding up the iron hoops. 'These we will put in the fire as we saw the white man do, and then we will hit them with rocks and make them into knives like the white men use.' And they all began breaking up the hoops and making them into sharp knives. While they were doing this, one of the young men said to his friend 'Did you see anything funny in the house where that man put the iron in the fire?' His friend, whose name was Hwe'o'kwen, shook his head. 'No,' he said, 'I saw nothing much, what did you see Ki'et'sa'kun?' Well,' Ki'et'sa'kun told him, 'I looked at his fire and I saw that he was burning some of that black rock that we say belongs to the Qwunus! It was just like our black rock, and do you remember, long ago, some men made a fire and burnt some here?' Then the two young men talked together, and they made a plan, but told no one else for they were afraid of what the head men would do to them.

"Some time after this a lot more of the tribe thought they would go and see the white men and maybe trade meat or skins with them; so they got ready to start. This time about twenty men went in two big canoes, and in the first canoe were the two young men, Ki'et'sa'kun and Hwe'o'kwen.

"When the men went down to the canoes they each carried things to trade with the white men, but Ki'et'sa'kun and Hwe'o'kwen carried between them an Indian blanket with something heavy in it; and this they put in the stern of their canoe and Ki'et'sa'kun sat beside it.

"'What is that you have?' asked the others, but the young men would not tell.

"When they got to Stth'amus they carried the blanket into the blacksmith's shop, and putting it on the ground, uncovered the black rock and sat down beside it, waiting for the white men to come and see.

"Very soon the blacksmith saw them and he called out asking what they had.

"Now, of course," explained Tl'utasiye', "they could not understand what the man said, but they saw that he was pleased when he saw the black rock. First he broke a piece off and put it in his fire, and it burned better than the rock he had. Then he talked a lot to them, but they could not understand, so he ran off and got a man who could talk a little to the Indians. This man asked them, 'Where you get this rock?' 'In our country.' they told him. 'How far?' 'About two days' paddling.' 'Bye-and-bye we come and see.' They said, 'Now you come with us.'

"They took Ki'et'sa'kun and Hwe'o'kwen carrying their blanket of coal between them, to see Governor Douglas.

"'See!' they told him. 'These men tell us they have lots of this coal where they come from, and it is only two days' paddling from here!' Governor Douglas was oh, so pleased! He shook the young men's hands and then he said:

"'Which of you thought of bringing this coal to show us?' They told him it was Ki'et'sa'kun. 'Then I will give Ki'et'sa'kun a new name!' he said. 'But first I will give him a present!' And he gave him a long coat and a high hat.

"When Ki'et'sa'kun had put them on, Governor Douglas said to the others— for by now all the Indians of that place were standing about watching: 'Now I give this man the name, Coal Tyee! and that will be his name for all of his life, because he brought the black rock that we call coal to us. Now, take him, put him in the middle of your canoe, for he must do no work, and paddle him home. Tell your chief that soon I will come with my big ship, and with men to look at this coal that you have.' Then he gave every man from this place a present of a nice shirt and some tobacco, and they got into their canoes and paddled away.

"My father often used to tell the story of how he went to the beach to meet the canoes, when he saw them coming, and how he saw Ki'et'sa'kun sitting in the middle of the canoe doing no paddling, just sitting with a great tall hat on his head, looking sort of proud. My father called to the men, 'What does this mean? Why does this young man do no paddling?'

"Then they told him of all that had happened, and of the great name of Coal Tyee that the white chief had given to Ki'et'sa'kun. Then Coal Tyee got out of the canoe, in his funny clothes, his high hat and his shirt, and would not even carry his blanket, but walked up to the big house where he lived and sat down, and never after that would he do any work, just sat and waited for people to do things for him: for was he not Coal Tyee!

"It was not long before a ship came with white men on it, and my father went to meet them.

"'What do you want?' he asked them, 'We want a man—called Coal Tyee,' they told him.

"My father called the young man, and the men told him that they had come from Stth'amus to look at the coal. So Coal Tyee put on his long coat and high hat and took the white men down to the water to see the shining rocks. They walked everywhere. looking and hammering the rocks and at last they went away.

"Well, one day a Hudson's Bay man came to see my father.

"'We want to talk to you and your people about this coal,' he said. 'We will have a meeting. You and all your people, and you must get another chief and his people, and on a certain day we will all talk this thing over.'

"So my father, Chief Sugnuston, called all his people, and he told another chief, whose name was Chief Shuna'h'un, to call his tribe, and together they went to the meeting.

"Now, you know, where the big wharf is now—where the steamers come? Well, down there is a rock, in the water. In those old days it was part of the land, and at that place was a very big house. To that house there went all the Hudson's Bay men, and the two chiefs with their people.

"Here Sugnuston interrupted. 'I was at that meeting,' he said. 'I can remember all the people in that house, and lots outside, but I was only a small boy standing beside my father.'

"Then the Hudson's Bay men talked to the Indians. 'This coal that is here,' they said, 'is no good to you, and we would like it, but we want to be friends, so, if you will let us come and take as much of this black rock as we want, we will be good to you.' They told my father, 'The good Queen, our great white chief, far over the water, will look after your people for all time, and they will be given much money, so that they will never be poor.'

"Then they gave each chief a bale of Hudson's Bay blankets and a lot of shirts and tobacco, just like rope! 'These are presents for you and your people, to show we are your good friends,' they said. The chiefs took the things, and they cut the blankets, which were double ones, in half, to make more, and gave one to every chief man, then the shirts, and to those who were left they gave pieces of the rope tobacco; so that every man in the tribes had a present.

"'Now you know,' said Tl'utasiye', 'we think there was some mistake made at that meeting, or, maybe, the people could not understand properly what was said; but later, when our people asked for some of the money for their coal, the Hudson's Bay men said to them, 'Oh, we paid you when we gave you those good blankets!' But those two chiefs knew that the man had said, 'The Queen will give you money.'

"And now the white men began to come and fix houses to live in, and they made a sawmill and cut down all our trees. Then boats called 'schooners' began to come for the coal.

The Indians did a little work then; they used to carry coal out to the schooners in their canoes—not little canoes like the ones we use now, but big, big ones that could hold twelve or more men; and the white men would pay fifty cents for one canoe load of coal.

"At first my people did not understand the money, and used to throw it away into the water—they only wanted blankets or clothes, but they soon found that money was good, and liked it better than the blankets.

"I remember my uncle went to work for a man who had a sawmill near Esquimalt Lagoon. I think his name was McKay; and after working for one month, he was paid one double blanket, a pair of shoes and a shirt.

"Can you remember any of the names of those white men, long ago?" I asked.

Sugnuston thought a little while, then: "There was McKay[282] and Cameron, and Work—I think he was called Doctor Work—and there was a Frenchman, the first white man I ever saw. I don't know what the white men called him, but we called him Chil-Qunlam. Those men were all down at Fort Victoria.

"Now that is all I can tell you of the first coal," said the old man. "But come again in a few days, and I will think of lots of other stories—of how all the first tribes started about here, and of how the S-amuna' Indians went to their home near Duncan. Lots of good stories!"

Origin of the Snuneymuxw[283]

On Beryl Cryer's second visit to interview the Wyses, Joe Wyse is unavailable, and Jennie Wyse is hard at work spinning wool with a homemade machine. Jennie Wyse takes up her knitting needles and tells Beryl Cryer the origin story of the Snuneymuxw people and the creation of the first swayxwi mask.

As I opened Joez Sugnuston's gate, I heard a most curious noise—an unceasing rumbling, with an occasional loud knock, which grew ever louder as I approached the house. As the path led straight to the back door, I knocked there first, but felt that nothing short of hammering could possibly be heard, so great was the noise within.

Getting no response at the back door, I went round to the front which faced the water. Here the noise as positively deafening and, going to a window I looked in. This was the room where I had been received on my previous visit and, over in a corner, I could see Tl'utasiye' sitting before an old sewing machine, spinning wool.

As my figure darkened the window she looked up and saw me. In a minute the front door was opened and Tl'utasiye''s wrinkled, brown hands drew me inside.

"Oh, such a noise I make when I spin!" she apologized. "See, my son made this for me, it makes such good wool!"

She showed me her wool, carded and rubbed on her knee, as Siamtunaat does hers, but, instead of the old and tedious method of "spinning" with a pointed stick driven through the lid of a lard pail, used by my old friend, Tl'utasiye' had her machine. It was an ordinary treadle, but across the top was a short, heavy stick— the peeled branch of a tree—along which were screwed six little hooks. Beneath this stick was a large spindle, so fastened to the machine that it turned rapidly. One end of the wool was put over the first hook and round the spindle. Tl'utasiye' then worked her treadle and the appalling noise commenced, as the spindle rattled round and the treadle banged violently upon the floor. As soon as the first few inches of the spindle were filled the wool was hooked over the second hook, and so on, until the entire spindle was full, the wool worked in this way being finer and more evenly spun, but not nearly so soft and warm as that produced by the old-fashioned method.

After she had demonstrated on her machine, Tl'utasiye' was ready to talk.

"My man—Joez—has gone out," she explained, "but we have talked a lot about your stories, and I can tell some that you will like."

Now that morning, before going to Xwsol'exwel I had been to call on one who knows our Indians better than any other I can name—who has worked amongst them for many, many years, and to whom they go for help with all their troubles and difficulties. Therefore when I explained that Sugnuston was to tell me some stories of the early days, I was delighted to be told "You couldn't find anyone better. They are a splendid old couple, and anything they tell you will be authentic, and what Joez doesn't know isn't worth knowing!"

"Now I can tell you one good story that is what you call a 'fairy story,'" said Tl'utasiye', knitting rapidly as she spoke. "But first I will tell you about the beginning of our people up here, and how they grew to be a great tribe."

"In the beginning—as you know—the Sun, Sum'shathut, made little people in different places—sometimes one, sometimes two. Now away back at the foot of Tetuxutun (Mount Benson) the Sun made a man and his wife. There they lived, all alone, and after a time they had three sons. At about the same time another man and his wife were made at Sti'ilup (Departure Bay), and these people had three daughters. They lived in a little cabin made of split cedar, with one small door, and in the roof was one board left loose, so that it could be lifted up to let the light in and the smoke go out—'kweyulutstun' we call it.

'One day, when those girls were nearly grown up, the man at Sti'ilup heard a Voice in the air calling to him!

"'Get some cedar wood,' said the Voice, 'and make for yourself a swayxwi.'

"That," explained Tl'utasiye', "is a mask—a very good kind of mask. Only certain people may use it, and it must stay in the same family always. It has a big face, and has swan's feathers standing up from it; and hanging down over the shoulders is an old-fashioned Indian blanket. It was easy to get the swan feathers in those days, for every year lots of swans would come and feed at the mouth of this river.

"Well, the Voice told him to make this mask, but he must never let anyone see it or know what he was doing. So every day the man would send his wife and three girls out to find food; then he would shut the door of his cabin and get to work.

"Now, up at Tetuxutun the three boys were getting grown up, too, and one day the eldest said to his brothers,' I wonder whether there are any more people in the world? Let us go and see what we can find!' So the three began getting ready to go and see the world. Now these people did not know how to make blankets; they used no clothes, but, as the boys were going away they thought they would cover themselves a little. They got deer skins to hang on their backs, and on their legs they put the skins of deer. Then they took the little hard, black toes (hoofs) of the deer, cleaned them and made them shine, and these they put down the sides of their leggings like buttons. Then they started off. By luck they went in the direction of Sti'ilup, and, after walking for some days, they came to the beach.

"Bye-and-bye one said, 'Listen! What's that?' All stood quiet, listening.

"Soon the noise came again. 'It is something being hit,' said the eldest. 'Come quietly!' On they went, and soon through the trees they saw a little cedar cabin. They had come to the house at Sti'ilup!

"Now the noise was louder, coming from the house, and the three boys walked around it, trying to find some way of looking inside, but there were no holes in the cedar boards. Then, looking up, they saw that a board on top of the cabin was lifted up, so very quietly they climbed to the roof and, lying flat, looked down into the cabin.

"Now that day the man had, as usual, sent his wife and daughters out to dig for roots that he might be alone and get on with his swayxwi. He lifted up the board in his roof to let light come in, and getting out his things set to work. As he held up the mask to look at it a shadow fell across the big face! Quickly he took a skin, lying near and threw it over the swayxwi and—'Ahn! Ahn!' he called loudly."

Here, Tl'utasiye' paused. "I never heard what that 'Ahn' means," she said, "But I remember, I used to ask my old grandmother when she told me this story, and she said it was something the 'Voice' had told the man to say if at any time he should be seen making the big face!

"Not until he had covered the wooden face, did the man look up and there he saw the boys looking down at him.

"Ah, but he was troubled! Going outside, he called to them, 'Who are you?' he asked. 'We are your nephews,' the eldest boy told him. 'Come down that I may look at you,' he said, and he took them into his cabin.

"'Now,' he said, ' I am the first man ever made—I am the head of all. Your father must be younger than I, so he does not matter much.'

"'No,' they told him. 'Our father is older than you—he is the head of all.' Well, they talked about this for a long time, and, as it was growing dark, the boys said they must be going home again. 'We are looking at the world,' they said, 'to see how many people there are in it, now we will go and tell our father of this place, and then we will start off again.'

"The man shut his door and stood beside it. 'You cannot go from here,' he told them, 'because you have looked upon the thing that I am making; you must stay.'

"Now in the cabin were four beds, one for the man and his wife, and one for each daughter.

"'Which of you is the eldest?' asked the man. 'I am,' one told him. 'Then go and sit over there,' said the man, pointing to his eldest girl's bed, 'and which is the middle?' 'I am,' said another. 'Go and sit there,' pointing to the middle girl's bed. 'Now that you have come here, you must marry my three girls, and make your homes here with us, for you must never tell any man of the thing I am making.'

"So the three boys married the man's three daughters, and all lived in the little cabin.

"After a time when the man had finished making his swayxwi, the boys thought they would like to take their wives back to Tetuxutun for a visit. 'We will soon be back,' they told the man, 'for we will always make our homes down here.' So the man let them go.

"Well, they started out, the three brothers going first, and their wives coming behind, and after they had been waiting for a long time, they came to a little trail and followed it.

"Now, some time after these people at Tetuxutun and Sti'ilup had been made, the Sun made a man in a place not far from Tetuxutun. This man had no woman; he lived all alone, and one day, when he was out searching for food, he, too, heard a Voice, calling from the air.

"'Listen,' it said. 'I will tell you how to make a spear.' Then the Voice told him to cut a pole and make it smooth and round, and it told him how to make a good spear head to fasten on the pole.

"The man did just as the Voice told him, and worked every day at his spear until the pole was the right size and the head shaped and very sharp. Then the Voice told him to light a fire, that he might burn the handle to make it smooth.

"Now, the man put his fire close to a pile of shavings that had been taken from the pole, and it was not long before it had crept along the ground and started to burn the shavings, Suddenly the man saw the whole pile of shavings begin to move. Up and down they went, as though there was something underneath. Then, from the air, clear and loud, came the Voice.

"'Quench the fire,' it said. 'Be careful not to touch the shavings, but spit upon the fire and quench it.'

"Quickly the man reached up to a branch beside him, and taking the leaves from it, he put them into his mouth and chewed them. When they were well chewed and wet, he threw them upon the burning shavings. More and more leaves he chewed until at last the fire was out.

"Now the shavings moved and shook harder than before, and out from amongst them there jumped a man and a woman.

"The man was frightened at first, but after a bit he felt so glad to have friends, and he asked them to live with him, and they all stayed together in the man's house. They were still living there when those three boys and their wives started out to visit Tetuxutun.

"Now, as I told you, the boys found a little trail, and as they walked along, they heard a funny noise. All stopped to listen. 'What can it be?' 'Sounds like men's feet stamping,' they whispered. Very soon they saw through the trees a small cabin, and through the open door could see people standing in a row, stamping with their feet.

"'Let's go and see,' said the youngest boy. 'No, better not, our father would not like it. We know nothing of these people.' The others told him, and they turned back on the trail. But the youngest would not leave. 'We will go and watch,' he told his wife, so they walked up to the door of the cabin and stood looking in at those strange people—the man who had made the spear and the man and woman who had come out of the fire.

"There they stood in a row, holding their hands up and elbows at their sides, and jigging from their knees, turning their bodies about, and sometimes stamping with their feet. Those were the first people to make that dance, and they called it 'Schuck-Hyuka.'

"For a long time the young people watched, but at last they went on after the others.

"Now the two eldest brothers and their wives at last got back to Tetuxutun and were welcomed by the old people. 'Where is our youngest son?' they asked. 'He and his wife stayed behind to see some queer people dancing,' replied the others.

"The old father threw up his hands. 'My son has gone to look at those people,' he exclaimed. 'Does he know no better than to mix with such low class. Why, they cannot be friends; these people were brought from a fire.'

"You see," explained Tl'utasiye', "the old father and mother did not think people made from a fire were as 'good class' as people made by the Sun."

"After some time the youngest son came home with his wife, and would have walked into the house, but, 'No,' said the father, 'You are no son of mine! Go away! Go back to those friends of yours who are making that dance.' So the two young people went away, and they walked and walked for many days and nights, looking all the time for a good place to make a home. At last they came to a big river, and walking along its banks, they found the best place that they had seen in all their journey. 'Here we will stay.' They said, and there they made their house. They named the place S-amuna' 'a resting place' (Somenos). Later on, when children were born to them, they, too, built their houses at the same place, and so grew the tribe of the S-amuna' Indians, who ever after have made their home beside the Cowichan River.

"Some time after, the other brothers and their wives went back to Sti'ilup, and the old mother and father went, too, so that there was no one left at Tetuxutun. But, as I told you in my last story, the tribe at Sti'ilup grew so big they had to build three rows of houses and have a name for each row, but the name for all the place was Sti'ilup.

"Those people," added Tl'utasiye', with a look of pride, "were my own people— my tribe. My old granny lived at Sti'ilup before they all moved to this place where we now have our homes. So you see, those people at Tetuxutun, and the man and woman at Sti'ilup, were the very first of our tribe that is now called the Snuneymuxw tribe."

Rock writings (xuxulul's) at Thuxwum ("Petroglyph Park").

Image PN 11783 courtesy Royal British Columbia Museum.

Sch-Weys, the Shaman[284]

Beryl Cryer visits Jennie Wyse with a particular subject in mind—the rock art (xuxulul's "writing") of the Hul'qumi'num/Snuneymuxw people. Jennie Wyse relates a story associated with a rock art site on the Nanaimo River featuring a competition between a shne'um (Indian Doctor) and Xeel's, the Transformer.[285]

TL'UTASIYE' AND HER HUSBAND, SUGNUSTON, appear to have as many relatives as old Siamtunaat.[286]

"You see," Tl'utasiye' explained. "'I am Jo-Ez Sugnuston's second wife. His first wife had lots of children, and I have had six girls, so we have lots of grandchildren! Oh, so many! They all go to school over there!"

She pointed across a strip of ground covered with dead bracken and hummocks of coarse grass, to where the small schoolhouse stood. As we watched from the window, the school door opened, and down the steps tumbled Indian children of all ages. Across the rough grass and up Tl'utasiye'"s steps raced at least a dozen of the smaller ones. In at the back door they crowded, to stop in wide-eyed embarrassment as they caught sight of me.

"Ah!" laughed Tl'utasiye'. "Those little ones! They know I have a box of apples in the kitchen! They all come to see old Granny when they smell apples!" She drove them before her into the kitchen, and in a few moments away they all raced, each carrying a large apple.

"Now we can talk!" said Tl'utasiye', unrolling, as she spoke, yards of soft grey wool from the largest ball I had ever seen, and shaking out a sweater fairly bristling with knitting needles. (All the Indians knit their sweaters as one works a sock—so that there are no joins, about eight short needles being used for the widest parts).

"Can you tell me what these are, Tl'utasiye'?" I asked, showing a picture of petro-glyphs, or Indian rock carvings, uncovered a year or so ago at Kulleet Bay.[287]

"Ah, yes." She took the picture and looked closely at it.

"I know about those things; those pictures are the same as the white man's prayer."

She stopped knitting and spoke very earnestly. "You know, in our tribes are men called 'Shamans.' Those are the men who go far away from all people, eat nothing, only wash and sing and pray, waiting for the Voice or Spirit to come to them. Sometimes, while they are waiting, they make these prayers on the rocks, but more often it is after the Voice has spoken.

"Any things that the Shaman wants he cuts on the rocks, sometimes for himself, sometimes for all his tribe, like this:

Tl'utasiye' raised her voice in a peculiarly monotonous wail:

"We are wishing and hoping for deer for our tribe, for no sickness and for good luck in fighting. Whatever is in the prayer, that is what the Shaman wanted for his people, and often in the prayer he would make a picture of the Spirit that his prayer was for.

"Now, up the river here at Nanaimo, there is one of those prayers, and Jo-Ez will show you another he knows of, but we must wait until the warm days come, then we will take the canoe and go to it."

She knitted for a while without speaking, then:

"I can tell you a story about the man who made those pictures up the river, He was a very good Shaman, and for many, many days he worked hard making that prayer to bring good luck to his tribe.

"This man Sch-Weys had a wife and one son, a boy of about fourteen years, and they lived along the beach nearer to the river.

"One day Sch-Weys came home and told his family; 'I hear a lot of talk from all I have met today about same stranger coming this way. Some say it is a 'thing,' some say a man, and it calls itself Xeel's. It is making a lot of trouble, changing things. We must look out for it, for if it comes this way, I must deal with it.'

"Before I tell you more," said Tl'utasiye', "I must speak of another thing. In those days when the people wanted to roast fish or a bit of meat, they took sticks, made them very sharp and round and smooth, so that could be run through the fish and then stuck in the ground before the fire. Some people still have those sticks and use them, and the name for them is "uya'thqsun.'[288]

"One day Sch-Weys said to his boy, 'I am going out to catch some flounders; you stay close to your home, and if that stranger comes, bring him to the beach and call me; but before you come to the beach run and get two 'uya'thqsun and bring them with you.'

"Now, just out in front of Sch-Weys' home was a good fishing place for flounders, so, taking his small canoe, the man paddled out a little way singing his fishing song that the Voice had told him as he went:

'Ah, fish! I Sch-Weys am here to get you! Many fish must I have to feed my people. For I, Sch-Weys, am a great fisherman. I, Sch-Weys, must get you today, fish. Ah-hhr.'"

Rocking back and forth in her chair, Tl'utasiye', chanted the fisherman's song, beating time on her knees with the sweater she was knitting, her wooden needles clicking a soft accompaniment to the weird tune.

"Sch-Weys had been fishing about one hour, when a strange man came out from the trees and walked to where the boy sat beside his home,

"'Are you alone?' asked the man. 'Have you no father?'

"'My father is out fishing,' the boy told him. 'He is not far from here. Come to the beach and I will call him.'

"Quickly he picked up two 'uya'thqsun lying beside him, and they walked to the beach together.

Jennie Wyse and Beryl Cryer

Now the boy called his father, and, Sch-Weys, taking up his paddle, started back. When he had come near the shore, he stopped paddling and called out, 'Who are you? Are you that man who is going about changing things to stone?'

"The man called back, 'Some things I have changed.' Sch-Weys said to the boy, 'Give this man a 'uya'thqsun and tell him to hold it pointing straight up. Now, if he is so wonderful and can do all the things he has spoken of to people, he will catch this flounder when I throw it.'

"Picking up a flounder from the bottom of his canoe, Sch-Weys threw it, but, ah, no, the stranger missed it and it fell on to the stones at his feet.

"'Try again,' called Sch-Weys, laughing. Once again he threw a fish, but again it fell to the side of the 'uya'thqsun.

"'Come,' Sch-Weys called to his boy, "You take the 'uya'thqsun, and let me see what you can do.

"Taking one of the sticks the boy held it pointing up, his arm straight out in front of him. 'Now!' Sch-Weys threw a flounder, and chk! straight to the 'uya'thqsun it flew and stopped, the sharp point catching its head and going straight through the body. Again he threw a fish, and, as before, it was caught.

"Now Sch-Weys paddled to the shore, and, pulling his canoe out of the water, he said, 'Come to our house and have food with us, you must be hungry.' Now in front of the house there was a fire burning, and, taking a 'uya'thqsun, Sch-Weys ran it through a big flounder and gave it to the stranger.

"'Here is one of the best for you,' he said. 'Stick it here in front of the fire and we will put ours beside it.'

"The stranger thanked Sch-Weys and taking the 'uya'thqsun, he tried to stick it into the ground, but wherever he tried, there he found rock. Sch-Weys laughed aloud: 'What things can you do, I wonder?' he asked. 'Here, give it to the boy; he can stand it up, for we always have our fire here.'

"The boy took the stick and at once pushed it down into the sand in front of the fire, and beside it put many more fish to cook. Very soon the fish were ready and all sat beside the fire and had their food. When they had eaten, Sch-Weys said, 'I have nothing to put water in that you may drink and wash, but come with me and I will show you a pool of water near my canoe; there you can drink, for it is good, fresh water. Together they walked down to the pool and the stranger knelt down and leaned over to drink. Suddenly two great arms like those of a devilfish came up out of the pool and caught the man round his neck.

"Ah, how Sch-Weys did laugh, because, you see, he, being a great Shaman, had made the rocks about the fire to make fun of the stranger and to shame him, and he had made the devilfish arms to kill him.

"'Now,' he shouted, 'show us how wonderful you are! Show us some of those things that you can do! You can no nothing against me, for I am this tribe's great Shaman, and nothing can harm me!'

"The stranger made no answer, but he reached up his hands and, taking hold of the two great arms, he broke them off as though they were sticks, and threw them back into the pool.

"Now he stood up, and Ah, he was angry! 'Sch-Weys,' he said, 'stay where you are and listen to me. What have I done to you or to your people that you should make fun of me, and now try to kill me? You have heard that I am changing things—turning people and animals to stone, but did no one tell you that it is only the bad and wicked, those better out of the way, that I changed? Did no one tell you that I had done good too? Made well the sick and lame people, helped all who were kind and good? Why do all people think of me as Xeel's the bad? Why not Xeel's the good, the helper? Because you have listened to all those wicked stories, and because you have tried to kill me, you must turn to stone, you and your canoe!'

"As Xeel's spoke, Sch-Weys slowly turned into a stone man, and behind him his little canoe became stone too.

"'One day," promised Tl'utasiye', "Jo-Ez and me will take you to see that stone canoe; it is still there—a very small one, for, as it turned to stone, it grew smaller."

"What became of the stone Sch-Weys, is he there too?" I asked.

"Tl'utasiye' shook her head. 'No, he has gone; the water has washed that stone away, but the little canoe stands just as Xeel's left it. And that is the story of Sch-Weys, the Shaman, who made that prayer on the rocks at Nanaimo River.

Tl'utasiye' peered anxiously from her window. "Time my man was back," she said. "Jo-Ez has gone to see about some money; we are all very poor, but the gov'ment helps us a little,[289] and I do my knitting.

"'When you come next time my man will be here, and he will have stories to tell you. After you came the first time we talked a lot about the old stories that our grandfathers and grandmothers told us, and we know so many that we will tell you. One day, when the Summer comes, we will take you in our canoe out to the big island—we call it Tl'eeltxw,[290] and there are many stone people and animals, and good stories about all of them. There is the place where you can see the girl and her uncles; there they sit, one little stone in the middle and four big stones around her. This girl was to marry a big chief from another place and she did not want to leave her own people, so her four uncles came and tried to coax her! Ah, that is a very nice story, but I must not tell you more, not until Jo-Ez Sugnuston can show you the stones, then we can sit in the canoe and talk.'

I thanked the kindly old woman and, who knows, one at these fine Summer days I may find myself setting forth with Tl'utasiye' and Sugnuston in their canoe to view the stone figures of Newcastle Island—or Tl'eeltxw—and to hear the legends concerning them.[291]

Origin of the Solexwel Totem[292]

Knowing that Beryl Cryer was able to locate a photograph of Mary Rice's grandfather Xulqalustun, Joe Wyse asks if she knows of any photographs of his father, Sugnuston. She says that she will look for some. He then proceeds to tell a story about Xulqalustun and his skill in catching sturgeon. Then, he narrates an origin story of his own people, the Solexwel of Nanaimo. The latter account is particularly valuable for its detailed description of a carving his father commissioned to adorn his house. The details of his description correspond to the imagery of a housefront photographed at Nanaimo in the nineteenth century. The similarities between Wyse's description and the well known photograph point to the likelihood this is, in fact, Sugnuston's house, and that the man in the photograph is probably Joe Wyse's father, Sugnuston. Cryer's conscientious recording of Joe Wyse's narration allows us to identify both a photograph of Sugnuston—the famous leader and signatory to the 1854 Douglas Treaty, and the iconography of his unique nineteenth-century Coast Salish housefront.

Tl'utasiye' and Sugnuston were both at home when I next visited Xwsol'exwel. I had told them when to expect me, and could see that preparations had been made in my honor.

The front room was spotless, with freshly laundered curtains framing polished windows, and an enormous fire roaring in the stove.

On the centre table, with its red cloth, was a very handsome Indian basket filled with leaves, and flowers quite ingeniously contrived from the papers in which oranges had been wrapped.

"How nice you have made your room look, Tl'utasiye'!" I complimented her. The old face creased into a hundred wrinkles as she laughed delightedly.

"Ah, you like it?" she asked, "Me and Jo-ez we work this morning getting ready, and see, we have made some flowers!" With immense pride she took the basket from the centre table and held it for me to admire. Each pinkish paper had been taken by the centre and given a tight twist, the edges being creased and cut to form petals, and really the effect was marvelously good.

"Before we talk about stories," said Sugnuston, "I want to ask, Have you seen a picture of my father—that Chief Sugnuston who I told you went to the coal meeting with the Hudson's Bay men?"

"No." I replied, "I have never seen one. Do you think there is a picture?"

He nodded his fine old head emphatically. "I think there must be," he said; "I think there is one in the Parliament House, and me and my wife here thought maybe someone would make another picture and send it to us. Our friend Siamtunaat has that nice picture of her grandfather—the one you gave to her, but we have no picture!"

Sugnuston and unidentified female in front of his house with painting and sculpture portraying the origin of the Solexwel, circa 1858. Image A-16-153 courtesy Vancouver Archives.

"Perhaps somebody will send you one—if there is such a thing. I will ask for you," I promised, and the old man leaned back contentedly in his chair.

"Did you know Siamtunaat's old grandfather?" I asked.

Sugnuston opened his eyes wide, in amazement at my question, "You mean, did I know the old Chief Xulqalustun of the Puneluxutth'? Yes, I knew him well. We often went to Kuper Island for big times, and the Puneluxutth' came here to our dances and potlatches, I will tell you a funny thing about that old man. As you will know, he was always a good friend to all priests and white men, and did everything the priests told him and made his people do the same, but there was one thing he would never do—he would not wear white men's clothes! Always he dressed in just his blanket, fastened on one side as he has it in his picture! See now!" He moved his chair nearer mine. "Has anyone told you how that man caught sturgeons?"

Now, long ago, Siamtunaat had told me of a peculiar power or gift that Xulqalustun had possessed by which he could spear sturgeon as no other man could, but the story had sounded so improbable that I had paid little attention to it. Now here was Sugnuston also suggesting that there had been something unusual in Xulqalustun's method of catching sturgeon, and, anxious to hear his version of the story, I asked him to tell it to me.

Sugnuston spread a hand on either knee and cleared his throat impressively, "This is a story hard to believe," he said, "but when I was a young man I remember seeing Xulqalustun doing this thing. There were four brothers—Xulqalustun, the chief, and three others. One of these brothers could catch the sturgeon as Xulqalustun did, but often he missed. Xulqalustun could always catch them, but the other brothers never caught in that way, nor any other man that I know of!

"Well, they would go out in their canoe, just two men, Xulqalustun and one other to do the paddling. Xulqalustun would stand up holding his spear, which was very long, with a spear head that had two sharp points. This head fitted onto the end of the pole and could be pulled off: this had a long line fastened to it. We call that spear tl'luqt sunum. They paddled out until they got to a good fishing place, then Xulqalustun would put the spear slowly, slowly down into the water, holding it straight up with his ear against the wood. When it was deep down he would move it along, feeling and listening!"

Here Sugnuston got to his feet and stood as though holding the pole against his ear.

"Ah! He feels one! Slowly now he moves the spear long until—Scrrrr-rr! his ear hears the spear points going over a rough piece of skin that sturgeon have near the head. Here is the place to spear it! Aha! He pushes down the spear, hard, hard! The great sturgeon is caught! When that fish feels the spear points go through it he swims and plunges, but now the paddler has the strong line which is fastened to the spear head, and very soon he and Xulqalustun kill that fish and paddle to another place for more.

"You know," the old man explained, as he seated himself once more, "the sturgeon is a soft fish and its skin is smooth—just that one rough place, and it did not seem to mind the spear points touching it carefully; it just lay still on the bottom until the spear went in it. No other man could do that, though many have tried, but no man could feel the fish and none could hear as Xulqalustun did!

"Did Siamtunaat never tell you the story?" he asked. "Yes," I admitted, "long ago she told me that story just as you have told it, so now I know that it is true."

Sugnuston tapped the table with a bony thumb. "All that I tell you is true!" he said soberly. "Some things the white people will call fairy stories because they do not know about those things. They cannot see as our people could, and their ears are not as ours. But we, the Indians know that many things are true that white men can not believe!

"Now, today I want to tell you about my own tribe, the Solexwel—the people who lived down where the coaling wharf is now. They were all moved along here to Xwsol'exwel when the white men came to take the coal, as we told you in another story.

Solexwel, 1858. *The centre lodge is probably Sugnuston's house. Watercolour by James Alden.*
Image PN 6405 courtesy Royal British Columbia Museum.

Joe Wyse, Jennie Wyse and Beryl Cryer

"About the same time that the people were made at Tetuxutun (Mount Benson) and Sti'ilup (Departure Bay), a man was made over at Solexwel. That name means 'The straw or hay'—"

"I remember," I told him. "Siamtunaat told me that story about the man who was made by the sun in a pile of straw, and of how he looked in a spring of water and found his wife! Siamtunaat called the name Hwsaluxul."[293]

Tl'utasiye', who had been listening intently, laughed. "We say lots of our words a little differently," she said, "but we can all understand each other."[294]

"Your son Jimmy Joe, who is married to Siamtunaat's daughter, sent me that story long ago," I explained.

"Ah, ah!" Sugnuston was delighted. "You know the first of it! Now I will tell you some more. After those two people had lived in the straw for some time they made a little house out of split cedar boards, and on the top they put rushes. There they lived alone, but they had no children to make their home a happy one.

"One night there was a very big storm. The two little people sat in their house, and all about outside they heard noises in the air, like lots of people talking— naan'um'[295] we call it! Bye-and-bye the woman went outside to look at the storm. 'Come,' she called to her husband, 'come out and listen.' The man went out, and the wind was so strong that be could not stand, but had to kneel on the ground. Well, there he was kneeling down, his hands on the ground and looking up to the sky. Never had he seen such rain: and the lightning—s-hwu-hwa'us is our name— kept coming like great fires! Suddenly there was a loud noise! Something like iron fell about the man, and bad pains went all aver him and down his arms into the ground, then he fell over like a dead man!

"When he woke up the rain had stopped, the lightning had gone away, and he was kneeling again and holding to each of his hands was a little child! They were both boys—just what he and his wife had always wanted! They carried the boys into the house, and to one they gave the name Slhumuhw[296] which means 'rain,' and the other they called Schy-As-Thun, or thunder, and the man gave himself the name Thq'ulhxw,[297] because he was kneeling when all that happened!

"That story has been told in our tribe by every father to his sons, down, down, down through the years.

"Long after, when my father, Sugnuston, was a very young man and was made chief, he got a man who could do such things to make a totem to stand in front of his great lodge. That totem was a man kneeling down, his arms hold up and then down—like this." With great difficulty old Sugnuston got to his knees and, with elbows raised and forearms hanging, showed me the position of the totem.

"There the man was, kneeling, and holding to each hand was a little boy, and under each arm was a door where the people went in to the lodge. When that totem was finished, Sugnuston gave a great potlatch and called the people all the way from Stth'amus (Victoria) and Saanich right up the coast. From every village they came to his potlatch and, when all the big canoes were pulled high up—on the beach and great fires were burning in all the lodges, with the women hurrying about cooking their meat and fish for the feasting, then my father, the chief, stood on a platform, high up in front of his totem, and pointing to it, he talked to all those people in a loud voice, telling them this same story as I have told it to you, and saying that the totem was there that old and young might see it, and so never forget how the first children of their tribe came out of the sky in thunder and in rain."

Last Fight of the the Tl'eeltxw[298]

Jennie Wyse narrates an account of a devastating Yukw'ulhta'x attack on the people of Tl'eeltxw of Gabriola Island, and a retaliatory raid by an alliance of Hul'q'umi'num'-speaking warriors. The events took place sometime within the first half of the nineteenth century, within the lifetime of Joe Wyse's father who was a participant in the expedition.

"TODAY," SAID TL'UTASIYE', AS SHE PLACED a chair for me, "I am going to tell you the story of the last big fight over at Tl'eeltxw. Now the Tl'eeltxw lived on a big island, I think it is now called Gabriola Island.[299] They were a large, strong tribe living in fine houses down by the water's edge. Such big times they had! Such feasting and dancing, and for those times the hunters would bring in so many deer, sometimes as many as fifty or sixty, and canoes full of duck and fish. It was easy to live then; no money, no trouble, not even clothes!

"Well, I can't tell you how many years the Tl'eeltxw had lived on that island, growing stronger in numbers and winning many fights until, my man's father told him, there were heads set up on poles all about the houses. But at last the end of that fine tribe came.

"Very early one morning before it was light, an old hunter waked up suddenly. He lay very still listening, but there was no sound to be heard only the people about him breathing and moving in their sleep.

"What had wakened him? He felt very troubled and could not go to sleep again. At last he got up and went out to the beach, listening, listening! It was very quiet out there, no wind, and the water was very smooth and still. 'Ah!' thought the old man, 'I was mistaken. There is nothing here!' He turned to go in again, when a sound came softly over the water and, as his quick ears heard it he dropped to his knees looking into the darkness; listening for the sound to come again.

'Ah, there!' Again and again it came. He knew what it was. The sound of water against quickly moving canoes, of many paddles dipping deeply, and now voices were heard—enemy voices. The Yukw'ulhta'x were coming!

"The man thought quickly; he was very old; it would take too long for him to go inside every house and waken the people, they must be warned quickly. He gathered up a lot of large rocks and threw these hard against the walls of his lodge, and as he threw he ran on to the next lodge, and the next, throwing his rocks and calling as he ran. 'Come out! Come out! The Yukw'ulhta'x are here! The Yukw'ulhta'x are upon us!"

"Inside the houses all were hurrying and shouting. The women calling their children to them, giving each child a handful of dried fish or clams to carry with them as, clinging about their mothers, they crept through the thick woods at the back in the hills. For, should the fierce Yukw'ulhta'x catch them they would be carried off as slaves and possibly torture and death would come to them.

"The braves had no time to help their women, they were putting paint upon their faces, finding their fighting things, their clubs and spears, their knives of stone with which to cut the heads of their enemies, that they might prove to all what great fighters the Tl'eeltxw were. And as they got ready they shouted of the heads they would take, and of how they would teach the Yukw'ulhta'x to come disturbing their rest.

"But they were too late. Already the great war canoes from the North were upon the beach and more and more coming in every moment whilst the cruel warriors in their feathers and war paint rushed upon the lodges shouting their war cry of the Yukw'ulhta'x.

"Never did Indians fight more bravely than did the Tl'eeltxw, but they had been taken by surprise and there were three Yukw'ulhta'x to every Tl'eeltxw, so that it was not long before the fighting was finished and the only sounds to be heard were the shouts of the Yukw'ulhta'x as they hunted the woods for the women and children and for a few of the old men who had gone to hide when they found the enemy were too strong for them.

"The Tl'eeltxw had good hiding places for their women and not many were found. So, growing tired of hunting, the Yukw'ulhta'x went back to the beach and there they broke down the houses, and made great fires of them, and not until they were burned away did they get into their canoes and, taking the women and children that they had found, leave for the North again.

"Now three of the Tl'eeltxw were away fishing when all this fighting happened, and not long after the Yukw'ulhta'x left, these men came paddling home, their canoes filled with fish. But what did they find when they got to the Island? No friends shouting to them from the houses, only the bodies of those friends lying on the beach, and the houses, smoking piles of black logs! What enemy had done this?

Where were their families—their women and their loved little ones? Nothing was left alive—not even a dog.

"With sad hearts they started towards the woods hunting and shouting to the women and children, hoping that a few might have been left by their cruel enemies. Soon the poor little ones and their mothers began coming out from their hiding places, a few here, a few there, and with them came the old men, until the three had quite a lot following them to the beach. There they fed them with the fish they had brought back, and whilst they sat eating, talked of what they would do.

"'We will leave his place,' said the men, 'and start a new home together in a place that we know of.' The women thought this a good plan, and so the next morning they took the canoes and paddled over to this beach. Along near where the coaling wharves are now, and near Solexwel, the village where Sugnuston's people lived, they made their homes.

"Well, some time later, news of the killing of the Tl'eeltxw got to the Cowichans, and all these people got together to go and punish the Yukw'ulhta'x. I can't tell you how many canoes there were, but every village sent three or four, each filled with their strongest and fiercest fighting men. When they were all ready, away they paddled and g˙⸱ to Yukw'ulhta'x early, early in the morning.

"Was there a village o that name?" I asked Tl'utasiye'.

She nodded emphatically. "Yes, there was a village called Yukw'ulhta'x," she said. "It was built on a piece of land with the sea in front and water running around to the back, like a lagoon.[300]

"Very quietly they paddled close in to the shore, and waited. Nothing moved. All was quiet. Everybody inside the houses was asleep.

"Now the Chief of the Cowichans[301] had told all the men what they were to do. To Chief Sugnuston, the father of my man Jo-Ez, he said, 'Take your canoes round to the back, the rest of us will stay here in front. You must go past the houses where they stand beside the water, and leave your canoes where the trees begin. Every canoe must have one man left in it. Hide in the bushes until you hear me shout, then run to the houses and we have them all, even as they killed our friends, the Tl'eeltxw.'

"Well, very quietly Sugnuston took his canoes round to the back where the water ran in, and, leaving one man to guard each canoe, as the Chief had told him, crept with his men through the woods until they could see the houses. There they lay waiting for the shout to come, when a lodge door opened and an old man came out. He had his head thrown far back and was spitting into the air, and sniffing.

"'Ah, ah!' he shouted. 'What do I smell? It is a strange smell! This will be a bad day for the Yukw'ulhta'x!' He began to jump and shout, making a great noise.

"'Something's going to happen!' he called; and as he turned round and round Sugnuston jumped at him and cut his head off.

"The old man made no sound but fell backwards into the water—dead. Sugnuston jumped in after him; got his head and threw it into one of his canoes. Just as he did this a loud shout came from the other side of the houses. Ah, such a noise there was—every man shouting and running to the houses! The doors were broken in and nearly every man at that place was killed, and the women taken for slaves and many of the children. They were driven down to the canoes and made to sit with their backs to that piece that goes across the canoes (thwart), we call it lhxulwulhtun, and to that piece of wood, their long hair was tied, so that they could not jump into the water.

"Indians always tied the women like that," explained Tl'utasiye', with a laugh. "Then they had them safe."

"Now they got the women belonging to the Tl'eeltxw, Cowichans and Snuneymuxw, who had been taken prisoners in other fights, and they put them into one canoe by themselves. Next the great houses of the village were burned and all the Yukw'ulhta'x canoes smashed. All the heads were gathered and thrown into the canoes, the canoes all got close together ready to come away. Suddenly there was a great shouting, and out from the trees came running a kw'akw'i-uthut."

"What is that?" I interrupted her.

"Well," replied Tl'utasiye', "that is a rich man's son who has been living back in the woods hearing the Spirits talking, and voices in the air. He was jumping up and down, up and down, high in the air, and his mouth was all white foam. He had nothing on his body but his head was covered with oil, and down from the breasts of birds.

"One of the Cowichans called out, 'Who will shoot him?' You see," said Tl'utasiye', "some of the Cowichans had old muskets—Si'kwul'esh is our name. 'That man must be shot,' the Chief shouted.

"Now there was one man who was called Squal-Chtun, and he said, 'I can shoot him!' Still the kw'akw'i-uthut was jumping up and down, never stopping.

"Now all sat very still waiting for Squal-Chtun to shoot. The Yukw'ulhta'x women tried to lift up their heads to watch, too, but their hair was tied too tightly, and they could only lie back waiting for the noise of the musket.

"'Now!' called the Chief, and Squal-Chtun shot. Down fell the kw'akw'i-uthut, with a hole in the middle of his forehead. Now the Yukw'ulhta'x were punished for what they did to the Tl'eeltxw, and feeling that they had had a good fight, the Cowichans left the burning village behind them and paddled away to their homes.

A Sti'ilup Legend[302]

Joe Wyse has gone fishing, but Jennie Wyse narrates a detailed story from her own family in which a man's wife is taken under the sea by a whale. He goes to rescue her and must use his wits to overcome several obstacles. An abbreviated version of this story was recorded by Franz Boas in December 1886.[303]

THIS LEGEND ORIGINATED WITH the Indian tribe who for many years made their home at Sti'ilup (Departure Bay) later moving to Xwsol'exwel and forming one of the Snuneymuxw band of Indians. It was told me by Tl'utasiye', as she sat, very erect, in a straight backed chair, her fingers busy with knitting needles and wool.

I had again missed Sugnuston: He was out fishing. Tl'utasiye' told me, but, "Next time you come he will be here," she said. "Today I will tell you a story that was told me by my old granny, and her mother told it to her, when she was a little girl, so that it is very old."

"Well now, out in the gulf there is an island, my granny never could remember the name, but on this island there lived a man, with his wife and family.

"One day, a man from a different country came to stay with these people, and, after a time he married the youngest girl, and they made their home on the island, near the old people. This man, whose name was Chum-Wist, was a good fisherman and a great hunter on the water, killing duck and sea-lion and seals, all things like that.

"On the bottom of his canoe he had fastened a flat board of cedar, and round and round on this he laid his lines, made from skin cut in thin pieces and fastened together.

"Whenever he went after seals he would paddle back with three or four, then he would call their friends and there would be a great stl'un'uq, or feast. When it was finished and all had gone back to their homes, Chum-Wist's wife would take the skins of the seals and walk out in the water to clean them. Up and down, up and down she would walk, rubbing them until they were quite clean and ready to be dried.

"They had been married about a year when a baby was born, after that Chum-Wist would sit on the beach with the baby on his knee watching while his wife washed the seal skins. One day as he sat watching, he saw a great whale swimming close in to the shore. Nearer and nearer it came and still the wife went on washing the skins. Chum-Wist was just going to shout out to her to take care, when the whale caught hold of her and dived under the water taking her with it.

"Chum-Wist ran to the water's edge to see which way the great fish had gone when, up it rose out of the water, holding the woman for him to see, then down it swam, out of his sight.

Jennie Wyse and Beryl Cryer

"Loudly Chum-Wist shouted for the other men, telling them what had happened. Then he got into his own canoe, which was a very fast one with which he chased the seals, and fixing his strong line to the bottom of the canoe, away he paddled, calling to the others to come after him as he could follow the track of the whale.

"For a long way he paddled, following where his quick eyes could see the track that the whale had left as it swam under the water, but at last he came to high rocks like a wall and could go no further. Suddenly he saw bubbles coming up, and knew by these that the whale had dived deep down.

"'Ah!' said Chum-Wist, 'down there the whale must have its home. I will go after it.' He tied the line about his body and called to his wife's brother, who was paddling after him. 'Stay here with my canoe. I am going after my wife. If I shake the line hard, you begin paddling as fast as you can and pull me up.'

"Taking his fish spear in his hand, down he dived out of sight amongst the great rocks where the whale had gone.

"Now," said Tl'utasiye', with a little laugh, "this is just a story you know, but my old granny said it was true, and she said that when Chum-Wist got to the bottom of the water he found he was in a new country. It was such a nice place with lots of trees and good things growing. It was the home of the things that swim under the water. You know," Tl'utasiye' explained, "our people always tell that long ago, all animals and birds were really people who could change into other shapes when they liked, and down where Chum-Wist was the swimming things could change and walk about and live like real people."

"Well, he took the line from about his body and tied it to a stick, then he began to walk about looking at things. Bye and bye he heard a girl laugh, and going a little further he saw three girls digging for clover roots. Very quietly he stole up beside them, and as he stood watching he saw that they were blind.

"'I am hungry,' said one, 'Give me something to eat.' 'Here is some dried fish for you,' the biggest girl told her, and held it out for the girl to take. Quickly Chum-Wist reached forward and took the fish. 'Where is the fish?' asked the first girl. 'Why you took it,' was the answer. 'No, you must have dropped it.' 'Well, here is another piece,' and the girl held out a second piece of fish.

"Again Chum-Wist took it. Now the girls began to feel frightened. 'There must be someone here,' said one. 'Perhaps he will help us, we are so poor, and we can none of us see.'

"Still Chum-Wist said nothing.

"Then the girls said, 'We know there is someone here, if you will help us, we will try and help you.' When Chum-Wist heard that he spoke to them.

"'If you will help me find my wife,' he said. 'I will make you see again.'

"'Listen then,' said the biggest girl. 'The whale has taken your wife to his house, and tonight he will eat her! Now, this is what you must do to save her. Walk along until you come to the first house, in there lives a man who is one of the whale's slaves. His name is Smuqw'a'.'[304]

"That name Smuqw'a' means that bird with the long legs who is always looking about, the crane or heron," said Tl'utasiye'.

"'He is watching now, for you, and you must try to kill him. We can do no more than this to help you, now make us see again, and then go and find your wife.'

"Chum-Wist put his fingers on the girl's eyes, and as he did so they turned into ducks and their sight came back!

Chum-Wist walked along until he came to the first house and saw smoke coming from the hole in the roof. Very softly he opened the door and looked in. In the middle of the room was a big fire, and on the floor, at the other side of the fire and lying with his back to the warmth, was a man. Chum-Wist crept up to the fire and gave it a big push, so that the burning logs rolled off and fell against the man.

"'Sts'ets'uhw!' (you be quiet) shouted the man, and pushed the fire back again. Now Chum-Wist spoke, 'If you will help me. I will give you something,' and he held up his spear and told the story of his wife.

"Just then a voice was heard outside. 'Hallo, Smuqw'a',' someone shouted, 'are you all right? I heard you call.' 'Thank you,' called back Smuqw'a', 'I shouted because my fire fell upon my back. It was my own fault. I am going to sleep again.' 'Now,' he said to Chum-Wist, 'If you will give me that good spear, I will tell you what to do next.' The whale has only one other slave, a man called Stuqeeye' (the wolf) He is getting wood ready for a fire, so that the whale can cook your wife! If you can get past him and find your wife, I will have to chase you as you run away. Remember this. You must hold your elbows away from your body as you run, then, when I throw the spear it will pass between your arms and your body. Now go.'

"Chum-Wist went on and soon he came to where Stuqeeye' was 'wedging wood.' Now, this is how he was doing it. The tree was lying on the ground and Stuqeeye' would take his wooden wedge, and with a big hammer would drive it down through the wood, breaking off pieces for his master's fire. Well, Chum-Wist crept to the other end of the tree and stooping down, whispered words to it. As the tree heard him it opened and Chum-Wist crawled inside. Along and along he crawled until he came to the place where Stuqeeye' was working. There he waited.

"Very soon the edge of the wedge came down through the wood, and as it came, Chum-Wist caught hold of it and broke it in half. When the slave found that his wedge would go no further, he pulled it out and great was his fear when he saw that it was broken, for he knew how angry his master would be.

"He took a second wedge and drove it down where the first had been and again Chum-Wist took it, and broke it in half. This time Stuqeeye' was so frightened, he sat down and began to cry.

"Chum-Wist called out to him, 'What's the matter? What's your trouble?' 'I've broken my master's wedges and I will be punished' replied Stuqeeye'. 'I can mend your wedges, if you will help me,' said Chum-Wist and he told Stuqeeye' about his wife.

"'I know,' the slave told him. The whale has put a board across his door and has hung your wife over it, her arms hanging down on one side and her legs on the other. They are making a big fire so that she may be cooked tonight.'

"As they talked they heard voices, and soon three women slaves came along to carry home the wood that Stuqeeye' had ready. Along they came, holding each other's hands and sniffing the air, and Chum-Wist saw that, like the first women, these also were blind.

"'I smell a strange man,' they cried. 'We must hurry back to tell our master.'

While they were gathering up the wood, Chum-Wist crept out of the log and getting a lot of fine bark dust, he spread it over a rock that the women would have to cross on their way home. Then he watched them all start off with their wood. When they reached the rock they climbed over, then all cried out in pain and sat upon the ground, to try and pick the tiny splinters out of their legs.

"'Now they can not hurry back to tell of strange smells.' said Chum-Wist. He called to Stuqeeye'. 'Give me your wedges and I will mend them, then you must help me.' He took the broken wedges, rubbed them with his hands and they were mended, the edges being sharper than before.

"'Now I will help you,' said Stuqeeye'. 'Come with me.' He took two large baskets and filled them with water. 'Now,' he said, 'walk close behind me when we go into the house, and when I shout something, take your wife and carry her away.'

"'The two men walked up to the house, keeping close, one behind the other. Stuqeeye' opened the door and they went inside.

"The first thing that Chum-Wist saw was his wife hanging over a board as the slave had told him. Then he saw there was a big fire is the middle of the room, and in the fire were lots of stones getting hot; for it was by putting red-hot stones into pans of water until it boiled that our people in the old days did their cooking. Then he saw lots of people sitting round the house, and as he looked, the people saw him.

"Just then Stuqeeye' threw his baskets of water all over the hot stones, and at once the house was filled with steam.

"'Ah! ah!' shouted Stuqeeye', 'Someone pushed me! Catch him! Catch him!' How Chum-Wist ran! He went straight to the place where he had seen his wife hanging, took her on his shoulder and ran out of the house. Behind him ran all the people calling, 'Catch him. Smuqw'a'! Catch him!'

"Smuqw'a' took his spear and, as Chum-Wist ran past him he threw it, but Chum-Wist remembered to keep his elbows out from his body and the spear went through, missing him. At last he got to his line, and tying it about his body shook it hard. Up he went through the green water, holding his wife all the time, and into the canoe, his people pulled them, and away they paddled, the fish people following behind.

"Chum-Wist's wife was very soon quite well again, but for a long time great black whales kept swimming around the island, frightening all who saw them.

"After Chum-Wist's wife had been carried away by the whale, and saved by her husband, her father grew to hate Chum-Wist for, he said, if he had been a good husband he would have driven the whale away. Every day he talked about it and at last he said to his family, 'I cannot stay any longer with this man Chum-Wist. We will all leave this place and make our homes in a new country.'

"Of course, the poor wife did not want to go, and her young brother said that he would stay, too, but the old man would not listen to them, and one day he burnt the houses and, taking all their things with them, the whole family paddled away leaving poor Chum-Wist alone on the beach.

"That poor man! Every day he sat on the beach and he cried and cried for his wife and little boy.

"One day as he was sitting there he heard a little noise, like a squeak beside him, and looking down saw a big rat, a kw'et'un' standing near him. As he watched, the rat looked at him and squeaked again. 'What do you want?' he asked. 'The people in my house want to see you,' said the rat. 'Will you come with me?' He showed Chum-Wist a crack in the rock, and waited for him to go in. 'I can't get in there,' thought Chum-Wist but he pushed hard and at last got through.

"He found himself in a big house full of sick and hurt people. There were seals who had been speared and had got away. Fish that had been caught and the hook broken in them, the whole house was full of these hurt people.

"When they saw Chum-Wist they all called, 'Can you make us better? If you can, we will help you to find your wife.' So Chum-Wist began to make them better. He pulled and rubbed the spear holes until the skin grew together again. He took out broken hooks and put back eyes that had gone, and at last all were well.

"Now a big seal said to him, 'I'll give you a—'"

Here Tl'utasiye' paused, at a loss for a word. "Now!" she said. "I don't know what that thing is called, but we call it 'Swogh-Em.' It is a long thing inside a seal; he has it because he has no teeth!"

"Like a bird's gizzard?" I suggested, and she nodded vigorously.

"Yes!" she exclaimed, "I will call it that—a gizzard. Well, the seal said, 'I will give you a gizzard and will put you inside it, then we will take you near the shore where your wife is and let you go. If you feel anything knock against you, shake yourself, or some seaweed may catch you. Stay in the gizzard until you can hear the waves on the stones, then undo the top, where I will tie it, and get out and walk to the shore.'

Jennie Wyse and Beryl Cryer

"They put him in the seal's gizzard, tied up the top and pulled him through the water for a long way.

"'Here we must leave you,' they called. 'Stay inside until you hear the waves, then find your wife.'

"For a little longer Chum-Wist floated in the gizzard, then he heard the swish of waves against stones, and opening the top, got out. He found he was quite near the shore and walked along until he came to a rocky point. In the bay he could see people moving about, and knew they must be his wife's people. Quickly he went into the bushes and walked along until he was at the back of the houses: there he lay hiding and watching.

"By and by he heard a woman crying for her husband, and knew it must be his wife. Soon a little boy came out of the house. Chum-Wist waved to the boy and called, 'Come here, I want to talk to you.' The child ran up to him and Chum-Wist saw that it was his own little son. 'I am your father.' he said, 'Go and tell your mother to come out here, but to tell no one that I am here.' The boy ran back to the house and whispered to his mother as Chum-Wist had told him. The poor woman ran as fast as she could to where her husband was hiding.

"'Take me away with you,' she cried, but Chum-Wist shook his head. 'Not yet,' he said. 'Wait a little while. Now, I only want my tools, find them and bring them to me.'

"When his wife had given him the tools, he said 'good-bye' to her and to his boy. 'I will come back soon,' he told them and hurried away.

Now he walked many miles back in the woods until he came to a lake and there he stayed. Well, he got out his tools and cut down a tree, and for many, many days he worked at that tree, cutting it and smoothing it until he had made a great whale. When it was finished he put it in the water and told it to swim, but the whale gave one jump and then down to the bottom of the lake it went, and there it stayed. Chum-Wist knew that he had used the wrong kind of tree, so he walked about looking for a tuxwa'tsulhp (yew tree), for he knew that would be the best kind to use.

"At last he found one and again he worked, making a whale, and again he took it down to the lake and put it in the water. This time the whale went out into the lake swimming and diving like a real whale, and then back it came to him.

"Now, to be quite sure that everything was all right, Chum-Wist made one more whale from the tuxwa'tsulhp, and this one swam and came back to him as the other had done, so now he was ready."

Here Tl'utasiye' began to laugh, "I don't know how that man did it," she said, "but the story says he took that great wooden fish all those miles back through the trees to the salt water. Sometimes I think, maybe, it is what the white people call a 'fairy story.' Well, when he got to the salt water again he took his whale out onto the point and waited.

"By and by he saw some canoes come out of the bay where his wife's people lived. He put his whale in the water and said to it, 'Go after those canoes and smash them, but don't let harm come to the youngest man, for he is my wife's young brother and he was good to me. Now go.' Away went the whale swimming and diving after the canoes. With his great tail he smashed two of them and drowned all the people. But the last he only broke at one end, so that the young brother sat safely in the other.

"Now Chum-Wist hurried along the beach, until he came to the houses. There he found his wife and little boy alone. And so they made their home in that place and the young brother lived with them, but the whale swam far out to sea and was never seen again."

An Indian Battle at Alberni[305]

Joe Wyse narrates an account of warfare between a Snuneymuxw group, the Yeshexen, and the Tseshaht of Port Alberni, in which the sons of a Snuneymuxw warrior are killed, and then brought back to life. Jennie Wyse offers information about medicinal plants.

SUGNUSTON WAS READY WITH A STORY for me when I next saw him. He sat beside his fire, a small grandchild on his knee and another an the floor at his feet, listening to his tale, her black eyes fixed un-blinkingly on his fine old face, while opposite him sat Tl'utasiye', busily sewing upon a patchwork quilt and occasionally interrupting in a low voice when she thought he was forgetting some important part of his story.

"This," began Sugnuston, "is going to be a good story. It is about the time our people went to fight the people at Tseshaht (Alberni). Well, now, you remember we told you how long ago at Sti'ilup (Departure Bay) the tribes grew so strong that they had three rows of houses and three names? Now one of these bands—the Yeshexen, went every year to Qualicum to get the salmon—the thuq'i (white men now call that name 'Sock Eye') as they went up the rivers. There they would make their camp and catch and dry the fish.

"Well, one year those people were all camp-ing by the river when a band of the Tseshaht came over the mountain and down to Qualicum, and there they had a great fight, killing many of the Yeshexen and carrying away their heads.

"When the Yeshexen that were left returned to their homes and told what had happened, all the people gathered to talk about it and see what had better be done, 'for,' said they, 'that place has always been our fishing ground and why should those

Tseshaht people take it from us? We will take our best men and go and teach them a lesson.'

"So, early one morning away went all their big canoes filled with the finest fighters, each man carrying his tuxwa'ts (bow) and tth'umeen' (arrows), and many with their spears.

"Leaving their canoes at Qualicum, they started through the woods, following the little trail used by the hunters, and at last came to a xatsa (lake). Now on one side of this lake was a big, open place, all clear, where the men could see a long way. Our name for a place like that is Sput-Khn. By now it was late in the evening, so there beside the clear place they rested, starting off again, very, very early in the morning.

"Now they walked quickly, for they must take their enemies by surprise.

"Well, when they got to Tseshaht, all were asleep. Very quietly they crept to the houses, and then, with loud cries, opened the doors, and, rushing in, killed as many as they could.

"Not waiting to take their heads, they hurried away before the Tseshaht could get their fighting things, and not one of their number did they leave behind.

"When they got to the lake again one man said, 'I have been thinking about those Tseshaht, and I feel that we should go carefully, for they may follow us.' When he had spoken, they all began to make plans. Some said that it would be better to hurry on; some wanted to go back and fight again. But at last the man who had first spoken said, 'Let us stay here, hide in these bushes beside the lake and then, when they come hurrying after us we can again take them by surprise, and this time will be able to carry away their heads with us."

"They all thought this a good plan, and it was not long before all was quiet beside the lake, as every man lay still—waiting.

"Well, they had not been hiding long before the sound of voices and hurrying feet was heard, and the Tseshaht came on to the clear place.

"On they came, their faces painted, and all carrying their fighting things. Ah! Ah! How our people did fight! The Tseshaht had no time to shoot; they were too surprised, and it was not long before they were running back, back through the bushes, hurrying to their homes.

"Now our people gathered together to see how many of their number were hurt or killed. Some were a little hurt, but only two were killed. These two were the young sons of a great fighter called Tch-Wat-Ahs, and when he found that of all those men his boys were the only ones killed, he was very angry.

"'Why should my boys be killed?' he shouted. 'It must have been their own fault! Leave them where they lie. Don't bother about them. Ah! to think that they have both got killed. Come, let us go.'

"He was so mad, he would not go near his sons, but started off and very soon all had followed him, leaving the two boys lying dead in that open place.

"They had not gone very far when one man said to his friend, 'I don't like to think of those two boys left there, the Tseshaht who killed them will soon be back to get their heads. Let us go and see whether we can save them.'

"The two said nothing to the others, but walked very slowly and at last were left far behind. When they could no longer see their friends, they turned and hurried back to where the boys' bodies lay. Now, one got behind some bushes on one side of the bodies, and his friend went round to the other side and hid, and so they waited.

"Now, it was a very fine morning, the sun was shining and everything was very clear. After a time a little, very fine rain began to fall and, as the waiting men looked through the bushes, they saw a very wonderful thing!

Sugnuston moved his chair nearer mine, and settled the child more comfortably on his knee before he continued, his voice very solemn, his keen old eyes gazing at me over his grandchild's smooth head.

"From each of those bodies a kind of steam began to rise, and, as the men watched they saw the steam change into two small rainbows, our name is Thuqul'shunum. The colors of these rainbows were very bright, and now they began to go up and up, just as though they were growing out of the bodies! Up they went, getting bigger and brighter, until at last they reached all the way from the bodies up to the sky.

"Now the youngest boy began to move a little, he turned his head about, first one way, then the other, and then he tried to sit up, but was too weak and fell back on the ground.

"After a time the other boy began to breathe and move his legs, then he too, turned his head and saw his brother lying beside him.

"'Ah?' he said, 'So you are hurt too? Where are the others?'

"'I think we are the only ones left,' said the brother, 'The others have all gone and left us alone. How are you?' he asked. 'Ah!' the other told him, 'I am shot right through; How are you?' 'I am shot just like you. What can we do?'

"As they talked, the two men who had been hiding, ran to them.

"'We have come back!' they said, 'Your father was so angry to find he had lost both his sons, that he left you lying here, but we felt sorry and came back to try and save your heads!'

"The men got moss and put it in the holes made by the arrows and carried the boys under some bushes and put their backs against a tree. Now one man said to the other, 'We must let the rest of our people know that these boys are alive. You are a swift runner. Go as quickly as you can, and try to catch them before they reach Qualicum! Tell them that life has returned to these young men and that we need their help in carrying them to the canoes!'

"'I will go!' said his friend, and he started to run. He ran, and he ran, for all those miles, and reached his people just as they were getting the canoes ready for the paddle back to Sti'ilup.

"Standing on a small hill, he shouted to them: 'Come back! Come quickly! Life has returned to those boys who were killed! Spirits have come down to them from the sky!' Then all began talking at once, ask-ing how the Spirits had come and the man told them of the two rainbows reaching from the bodies to the sky. So back they all went to carry the two boys out.

"When they got to where the boys were sitting, two of the strongest men said that they would carry them on their backs, and in this way they once more started for Qualicum.

"They had gone but a little way, when those two strong men stopped, and said they could carry the boys no further. 'I have never carried anything so heavy before!' said one. 'This one I was carrying got heavier at every step that I took!' said the other.

"You see." Here Tl'utasiye' interrupted, "They say those boys grew very, very strong after they had been dead and the Spirits had come back to them again, and that is why they felt so heavy! It was the Spirit in them!"

"Well," continued Sugnuston, "They all sat round wondering how they could get those boys to the canoes. Then one man said, 'Make a big basket, put them both in it, and I will carry them on my back!' So they got busy cutting cedar branches and splitting and weaving them until they had made a great, strong basket, big enough to hold the two young men.

"'We are ready,' they told the man who was to carry the basket.

"Now, see!" said Sugnuston, "that man was what we call spulqwitthe'alx,[306] that means a kind of Spirit would come to him so that he could do things! Well, when he heard that the basket was ready, he started blowing into the air, and crying out—calling and whistling into the air to get the Spirit that would make him strong. Now he began to dance and shout, jumping up and down, crossing his feet and running round and round until he was half crazy.

"'I am strong!' he shouted, 'I can carry anything! Lift the basket on my back, and I will run all the way to the canoes! Ah, but I am so strong!'

"They put the basket on his back, with pieces of cedar bark about his body to hold it, and then some held the man still while others very carefully lifted the young men into the basket and tied cedar bark around them so that they could not fall out. All the time this was being done the spulqwitthe'alx kept crossing his feet and trying to dance and whistle. At last they were ready, and away ran the man, shouting and dancing as he went along the little trail, and not once did he stop until he had carried those two in their basket all the way to Qualicum.

"When they had all got to the beach they gathered some of the moss that grows on the q'ey'xulhp (Barberry tree),[307] and after washing the boys' wounds they chewed the moss and put it in the holes."

"Wait!" said Tl'utasiye', "I must tell you about that moss. Our name for it is q'uts'i, and it is a very good medicine. If you cut your finger, get some of that q'uts'i and put it in the cut and tie it up; very soon it will be quite well.

"Long ago, if a man broke his arm or leg, they would get lots of q'uts'i, put it all over the broken place and then wrap it up in soft, beaten cedar bark and leave it, just undoing it sometimes to wash it and put fresh q'uts'i on, and it would not be long before that place was mended. We use the bark, too, for medicine, and so do the white people, but I have never heard the name they call their medicine."

"The medicine we make is called 'Cascara'," I told her, and she repeated the word over and over to fix it in her memory.

"Now!" said her husband, impatient of this interruption. "I must get this story finished! When the two boys were ready they were put in a canoe, then all got together and paddled back to their homes.

"Those two boys got better again, very quickly; they seemed to be stronger than they had been before they died, and to have lots more power. One day they said to Tch-Wat-Ahs, their father: 'Let us go back and kill some more of those Tseshaht people.' Their father was so pleased to hear them talk like this, and he said that he would go with them.

"They got great bones from an elk and made themselves big, heavy hammers, and then the three of them started off.

"Again, it was very early in the morning when they reached Tseshaht and, quietly creeping into one of the houses, they killed as many as they could with their hammers, then, taking their heads, they hurried out, not stopping until they were many miles from their enemies. Now, while these three were away, all the people from Sti'ilup and all about there had gone back to Tl'uqtinus (Steveston) for the fishing. I must tell you that every year the different tribes from all about this part of the country went to that place for the salmon. There was a long piece of land, and all along it were the camps these people.

"One day, just as the men had come in from fishing, a noise was heard coming over the water—voices shouting! What could it be? From the different camps all came running to the beach to see.

"'That voice sounds like Tch-Wat-Ahs!' said one, 'but he will never come back. Only three of them to fight against all those Tseshaht; those people have their heads by now!'

"But now a canoe came in sight, and as it came near the shore Tch-Wat-Ahs and his two sons stood up in it, each man holding the head of a Tseshaht in either hand; and all to-gether they held them high in the air, and then down, up and down, up

Joe Wyse and Beryl Cryer

and down they held them, and 'Aa Hu! Aa Hu! Aa Hu!' they shouted. And from the beach all the people shouted back.

"Then Tch-Wat-Ahs brought his canoe to the shore, the heads were stuck on poles in front of the camp, and there, sitting beside them, the two men of the Yeshexen who had gone back to save the boys' heads told all those people how the Spirits had come down the Thuqul'shunum to the boys' dead bodies and had made them alive again!"

Chief Qapuluq's Stl'un'uq[308]

Joe and Jennie Wyse choose another "good story for the newspaper," and when Beryl Cryer shows up, Jennie Wyse describes her husband's attendance, as a young man, at a stl'un'uq ("potlatch") at Thuq'min', which was disrupted by alcohol and the intervention of police and a naval gunboat, HMS *Rocket*. Corroboratory records indicate that this event took place in early April 1878.[309] Jennie Wyse concludes with her own account of a stl'un'uq held when she received her grandmother's name.

"TODAY I HAVE A NICE STORY FOR YOU!" said Tl'utasiye', as she led me into her front room. "Last night Sugnuston was talking to me about the days when he was a young man, and he told me of the time Chief Qapuluq, of Thuq'min' (Oyster Bay), gave a big stl'un'uq for his girls."

"What is a 'stl'un'uq'?" I asked her. Tl'utasiye' held up her hands in amazement. "Don't you know that word?" she exclaimed.

Stl'un'uq at Kwa'mutsun, 1912.   Image PN 1401 courtesy Royal British Columbia Museum.

"Why, 'stl'un'uq' is our word for what you call a Potlatch.[310] That word 'Potlatch' was only made by some white man; the real Indian name is 'stl'un'uq'!

"Well," she continued, "when Sugnuston told me that story, I said to him. "That is a good story for the newspaper. I will remember it and tell it to the lady when she next comes; and now, here you are today!" She laughed delightedly.

"Now this is about something that happened when I was only a very little girl— I am not as old as my man, you know. He was a young man when this happened, and he remembers all about it.

"When I was two years old my father died, and my mother, whose name was Chul-Quohl-Sa-Mat, married a man from the S-amuna' people and they went to live up the river, here at Nanaimo. One day they were digging the ground for a garden when suddenly there was a great noise. 'What was that?' called my mother, running to the house, for she was very frightened.

"'It sounded like the big gun on the white man's warship,' said her husband. 'I heard it once and it made a loud noise like that. There must be trouble down at Thuq'min'. Qapuluq is having a big time there.' They waited at the house for a little while, but the noise did not come again and they went on with their work.

"Well, Sugnuston told me the rest of the story last night; he knows about it because, you see, he had been asked to the stl'un'uq and had gone with a canoe full of other young men. Now, I must tell you, that our people always have a 'big time' when the daughter of a rich man is old enough to marry. The father likes to show how much he has, what a big man he is, and often he gives his girl a new name."

"Siamtunaat once told me how the Indians give their girls a 'singing name,'" I said. Tl'utasiye' nodded her head.

"That is the same thing," she said. "Every place and every tribe has a little different way of giving a name, but today I will tell you of the way Chief Qapuluq gave his stl'un'uq.

"This man Qapuluq had two girls and he was a very rich man, so he called all the people from every village to come and see his daughters get their names and have a 'big time.'

"When Sugnuston got to Thuq'min' the two girls were sitting outside their father's house, with paint on their faces and lots of blankets about them, and with blankets over their heads. Four days they sat there for all to see, and every day more and more canoes full of people kept coming, until there were many hundreds there.

"Now you know, in the old days, when the Indians had a big time white men would hear of it and they would take their boats and a lot of whisky, and go amongst our people selling the whisky. For five dollars they would sell one coal oil can full, and, as you know, whiskey always meant lots of trouble.

"Well, the policeman at Nanaimo heard that white men were going to Thuq'min' with whisky in their canoes,[311] so he got a big canoe and six men, to

Jennie Wyse and Beryl Cryer

paddle him, and they went to Thuq'min'. There they found the beach full of canoes pulled up out of the water, and more coming in all the time. First they looked in the canoes on the beach, but could not find much whisky, so they paddled out into the bay and there they waited, and every canoe that came along they stopped and made the people move their blankets and mats to show whether they had whisky with them or not. In this way the police got a lot of cans of whiskey and very soon some of the men began to make trouble about it. They got their canoes and started out after the policeman.

"Sugnuston and his cousin got their paddles and started to go, too, but Sugnuston's uncle, Ts-Quhal-Mt, saw them.

"'What are you going to do?' he asked them. 'Take the whisky away from the policeman? Ah, yes, I know. Now listen to me! You will only go and set yourselves into trouble. Don't go. Stay here on the shore, and wait until the policeman wants help: then, if yon want to fight, go and fight for him!'

"Well, there was lots of trouble. Some of the Snuneymuxw helped the policeman, but there were too many of Qapuluq's friends against them, so the white man told his men to paddle him back to Nanaimo with all the whisky cans he had taken. When he got to Nanaimo he found the boat that carried the mail once a week was just leaving for Victoria and he got on it and went for help.

"The day after this trouble with the policeman, Qapuluq was to give his girls their new names: but before he could do this some of the young men from the different villages had to run a sort of race, and Sugnuston was going to run with the others."[312]

Tl'utasiye' waited a moment, and screwed up her eyes in a quaint way she has when she is thinking deeply.

"Now," she said, "I will try and tell you how they did that race."

"In one place Qapuluq had a big, hot fire with sticks laid across it, quite close together. Near this fire was a big basket nearly full of cold water, set in a hole in the ground so that it would not fall over. About one hundred yards from the fire were two men, holding in each of their hands two stones. About one hundred yards from the fire were two men, holding in each of their hands two stones. About one hundred yards from these men, the first four young men stood ready to race. This is what they had to do:

"When Qapuluq gave a shout, the four ran to the men with the stones, each took one stone and ran as quickly as he could to the fire. The first two to get there put their stones on the sticks that went across the fire. Now, they were each given a long stick that had been split at one end and, holding this with both hands out in front of them, they danced back and forward in front of the fire, and while they danced they sang, 'Xwaxwi' smunmeent', 'xwaxwi' smuneent', 'xwaxwi' smuneent!' That means my stone is getting hot! My stone is getting hot! Three times they had to sing this, then they danced again, four times without singing, and then each caught his stone in the split stick and, leaning over it, whispered a si'win',[313] a sort of prayer, to it. After that they turned round, danced up to the basket and away, again three times, holding the stone in the stick, and then dropped the stone into the water.

"As soon as the first two running had put their stones on the fire, four more young men were ready to start running, and so on and on until a lot of stones were in the basket and the water was very hot.

"Now, Qapuluq had said that when the water was hot enough, some of the men were to dance and others were to set the girls and bring them down to the fire; there the women would wash them and he would call their names. But, poor man, everything was spoilt.

"The water was nearly hot enough, and some of the young men were dancing with their stones and Sugnuston and three others were getting ready to run. Everybody was watching, sitting with their backs turned to the water, and so no one knew what was happening behind.

"Suddenly, just as Sugnuston was starting to run, there came a loud shout, there, coming up the beach, were a lot of soldiers, and out in the bay was the great man-o'-war waiting.

"When the Indians saw the soldiers they began to run away into the woods, but a white man shouted to them.

"'Stay where you are. No one is to move. These are orders from the white chief. Now!' he shouted. 'The white chief is going to show you that he must be obeyed, and that when his policeman wishes to search your canoes for the whisky that will do you harm, you must help him, and not make trouble. If you will not do this you will be punished, and your villages will be blown to little pieces. Stay where you are. The white chief is going to show you how strong his great guns are. Now all look at those trees and listen!'

"Sugnuston told me," said Tl'utasiye', "that there was not one word from all those hundreds of people as they sat waiting, as the man told them. Many thought they were going to be killed by the great guns but not one moved or cried out, they just sat looking at the tops of the trees where the man had pointed."

"Suddenly there was a very loud noise, and everybody shouted and jumped up and started to run, some one way, some the other. The soldiers ran after them, calling to them not to be frightened, but to look at the trees and see what the gun had done. After a time, when they found that they were not hurt, they looked at the trees and saw that the tops were all broken and the branches fallen to the ground.

"'Now you see what will happen to your homes if you are foolish again!' said the soldiers.

"And so," finished Tl'utasiye' with a laugh, "poor Qapuluq never finished his stl'un'uq and I never heard whether his girls got their new names. But Sugnuston told me he was angry, to think he did not have time to run in the race before that big gun was fired!"

Jennie Wyse and Beryl Cryer

Tl'utasiye' gathered up the patchwork quilt she was making and began sewing busily upon it.

"Now, I would like to tell you about the time I was given my name," she said. "My grandfather was a very rich man—his name was Si'emtun—and when I was about fourteen he gave a big stl'un'uq and called all his friends to it. At that time another rich man lived here, called Que-Unum, and he and my grandfather, Si'emtun, worked together and built a very big lodge with a long open place like a field beside.

"When my grandfather said he would give his stl'un'uq for me, and I would have my grandmother's name, his friend, Que-Unum, said he would help, and his niece, a girl from the Hwmuthkwi'um people, would be given a name, too.

"Well, Si'emtun called twelve men and told them to take his biggest canoe and go and call the people from all the villages.

"Do you know how they did that? No? Well, I will tell you.

"First the rich man giving the stl'un'uq put all his blankets and skins that he had to give away in one big pile. Then he cut lots of little cedar sticks about three inches long, and made them all smooth and clean.

"Now he moved his blankets one at a time to another pile, and each time he took a blanket he put down a cedar stick, so that at the end he had cut as many sticks as he had presents. Then he tied the sticks in bundles and gave them to his men to take in the canoe when they went to call the people.

"Each person called to go to the stl'un'uq was given a stick, and when there were no more sticks, no more people could be invited. In that way there were always enough presents, and the rich man knew how many people were coming to his stl'un'uq.

"Well, Si'emtun and Que-Unum called all the people in that way and they got one hundred women to come and sing, and for me, my grandfather got a man to dance the swayxwi. Everybody cannot have the swayxwi, but I belong to the oldest people, to the ones who made the very first swayxwi!

"When all the people had come, the women painted my face and put a blanket of mountain goat hair over my dress; and took me down to the big, open place by the lodge.

"Everybody was sitting round on the grass, and on one side there were long boards for the people to hit with sticks, whilst the women sang their songs, and the xwaayxwi danced.[314]

"On the other side of the field the girl from the Hwmuthkwi'um was sitting on a high pile of blankets, with her face painted red and lots of blankets all over her.

"You see, the Hwmuthkwi'um people do things differently to our people.

The women took me behind some blankets that were tied to poles, so that they made a little room. This was where the man dressed for the swayxwi dance, and there I waited until the singing and dancing was finished.

"Now my grandfather called to all the people that he was giving me my grand-mother's name, Hallar-Tia. Then the xwaayxwi came behind the blankets, took my hands and pulled me out to the middle of the field, and there he danced with me, and all the women sang, and hit their boards.

"After the singing was finished I went on dancing with the xwaayxwi, and I sang my song!

"Shall I tell you what I sang?" she asked.

"I would like you to sing it to me," I told her, and she needed no second bidding.

"I won't dance it," she said, "but I will sing it for you," and she commenced rocking back and forth slowly whilst she sang, her voice very soft and low.

"Hallar-Tia utan now se sela
Ow utchase at un Hallar-Tia!"

"That means, 'My name is Hallar-Tia! Because I'm not a prince, my name is Hallar-Tia!'

"That song was what you would call just pretend!' laughed Tl'utasiye'. That part, 'Because I'm not a prince' is just pretend, because all the people knew that my people are the same as princes, and, of course, I knew it, too.

"When I had finished dancing with the xwaayxwi, the other girl was given her name, but she did not have xwaayxwi to dance for her and she did not dance, but lots of the women sang for her, and then a man went up to where she was sitting all covered with her blankets. He was carrying a box, and everybody was looking to see what he could have inside it!

"He put the box on the ground at her feet and opened it. Inside he had a lot of little mink; they were not really alive, but he made them look as though they were. He took them out of the box and made them run up the girl's blankets. All about her they ran, and as they went they made a loud squeaking noise.

"For a long time he let them run, then he took them, one at a time, in his hand and held them high in the air, and ran his hand quickly down their fur; this took the life out of them, and he put them back in their box and shut the top.

"That cost those people a lot of money, much more than the swayxwi and all the singing women coat my grandfather; but that is what the Hwmuthkwi'um people do, when their girls are given their names!"

Tl'utasiye' folded up her quilt. "It is getting late, and my man will be coming for his supper," she said. "Next time I see you I will tell you about the name I gave my son. Maybe I oughtn't to tell you but I would like you to have that story! If my man is away I will tell you, but if he is here——" She left the sentence unfinished, but I guessed from her expression that it was a story of which Sugnuston disapproved, and so, I am hoping, that perhaps he may be out when next I call.

Jennie Wyse and Beryl Cryer

Sugnuston's Ancestors[315]

Joe Wyse is away fishing when Beryl Cryer visits and Jennie Wyse feels free to tell her some of the history associated with the "Indian names" of her husband and son. Snuneymuxw and Hul'qumi'num people only bestow ancestral names on individuals worthy of carrying them; many names have ancient histories attached to them, which accentuate their power. Joe Wyse probably felt that the story associated with the names Sugnuston and X'um'tl'ilum would offend Hwunitum' sensibilities, but Jennie Wyse wants it to be on record. Before she provides the account, she discusses fishery depletion, and a hidden freshwater spring on a Galiano Island beach.

I FOUND TL'UTASIYE' SITTING UNDER one of her cherry trees, carding wool. "It makes too much dust in my house," she explained, "I always do this part outside, if it is not too wet, then, I can work quickly and have no dust to sweep up when I have finished!"

"Well!" she gathered up her great basket filled with its mass of fluffy, white wool. "That will be enough for today. Come in, and I will get my knitting, Sugnuston is away," she told me, as she began casting on stitches for a sweater. "He's gone fishing again. You know when he was a young man, Ah! he was a good fisherman. But he is getting old now, and there are not so many fish to catch. Sometimes he brings home lots of salmon, sometimes only one or two.

"I remember when we were young, I always went with my man when he went hunting or fishing. We would find a good camping place and, if he wanted to go far back in the woods I would stay at our camp until he came back. One year, it was very hot, all the springs and streams were dried up, only the big rivers had water in them. One morning, Sugnuston said, 'I am going hunting for grouse, do you want to come with me?'

"'How can you go?' I asked, 'Where will you camp, and where will you find water to drink?' Sugnuston laughed. 'Just get ready' he said, 'and I will show you where to find water.'

"Well we got our blankets and canoe and started off. Late in the afternoon we were paddling along by that big island you call Gabriola, when Sugnuston pointed to a bay. 'We will make our camp there,' he said, 'You can stay in the camp, and I will go back and hunt!' Well, the water was far out and, after we had paddled as far as we could, we got out and pulled the canoe up the beach.

"'Now, said Sugnuston, 'I will show you where to get water! This place was found by the old, old Indians, I don't know how long ago!'

"For a little time he walked about on the sands looking. Then he called to me. 'Bring your clam stick and dig here!' I could see nothing but I began to dig where he showed me. Very soon, water began to come, and the hole filled to the top.

"'Drink some!' said Sugnuston. I knelt on the sand and took a long drink. Never had I tasted such cold, good water. 'You must not forget where this place is, and you must remember to come every day when the water has gone out, and get all you want!' my man said. There is no other water left on the island, but you will always find plenty here if you dig a hole.' There are some other places that I know about, where springs can be found when the water is out, but they are easy to find, because they bubble up through the sand; but this spring did not bubble—the water came slowly. On Gabriola, there is another spring nearly opposite the brick yard, and at Englishman's River there is a big one."

Tl'utasiye' knitted rapidly for some minutes, then laid her work down and knotted the handkerchief more firmly about her head.

"Well, now!" she said thoughtfully, "I must tell you a good story." She went on with her knitting, and was busy for a time rearranging the stitches on her needles, but I could see that she was thinking.

"I like to get the story ready in my head," she laughed, "then I do not make any mistakes. You remember I had a story I would tell you, if my man was not at home? "Well now, I think I will tell that today. You know," she said with a little laugh, "I don't like to tell you this story, it is about such a bad thing that my man's relation did, but you must remember please, it was a very long time ago, and we do not like to ever talk about it—we are 'shamed of it."

"First I had better tell you how we gave my boy my man's name. You know my son was called by a very old name, X'um'tl'ilum and everybody said to me, 'Why don't you give your son your man's name?' 'When he is big, I might do that,' I told them.

"Well, when he got to be a big boy someone said to X'um'tl'ilum, 'Why don't you name yourself after your father?' And then others asked me, 'When are you going to use Sugnuston's name for your boy? If you don't use it, some one else will, for it is the finest name in the tribe, and must go on—not be forgotten.'

"We all talked it over, and I said to my man, 'I wonder? What do you

think? We are well off now and can do it and, as they say, maybe—some one else will take the name, and then it is lost to our son?'

"Sugnuston thought about it and then he said, 'You are right. He had better take my name—Sugnuston. I will see about calling the people!'

"Ah! Such a big time we had. We called all the people from round Esquimalt, Saanich, up to Cowichan, everywhere, every village was called; and then we called all the Hwmuthkwi'um, because those people are Sugnuston's relations. When they had all come, everybody went to one of the biggest houses on the beach, there were so many people the house was quite full, with everybody standing up. Then they brought in our son, to give him his name.

"Sugnuston had got a man who was a good talker, and he stood in the middle of the people and talked to them, telling them about my man's name and why we had

Joe Wyse's father, Sugnuston, and daughters/wives, seated in front of their house at Solexwel, early 1860s. Image PN 5929 courtesy Royal British Columbia Museum.

called them all to our stl'un'uq. Then I gave my boy his new name, Sugnuston, and the man told everybody that it was the oldest name in the tribe and so must be passed on always. After that Sugnuston and I, we gave every man fifty cents, and then the 'good time' began, Lots of dancing and singing, and good things to eat! Oh, we had a big stl'un'uq.

"Now," Tl'utasiye' put down her knitting, "Now, that I have told about my son's names, first, X'um'tl'ilum, and then Sugnuston, I am going to tell you a story about a relation of my man, who was called Sugnuston, and who lived a very long ago. Well, this Sugnuston was a very rich man. He always had lots and lots of wool for blankets, and had more blankets than any man in the tribe. I must tell you that it was this man who first made the sharp pointed sticks that our people used to fasten their blankets about them, and those sticks were called Sugnuston, after him.

"Most of the people were very poor at that time and had no wool for their blankets, and, as I said, this man, Sugnuston had more wool than he could use; but not once did he give any away. 'It is all mine,' he laughed to his son, 'I will keep it and some day all these fine blankets will be yours!'

"One Winter it got very cold. The old people of the tribe said it was colder than any Winter they had ever known; and many of those poor people had no wool. Sugnuston laughed at them and said:

"'I'll tell you what I will do. I will give you some of my warm wool if you will give me some of your most beautiful young girls to be my slaves!'

"He went to his house and told his son what he had done. Then he made a seat and put it outside his door, dressed his son in some of the best blankets, and put a cap made of long goat's hair on his head. Now this son was called X'um'tl'ilum and even now, when some of our people dress for dancing or for a 'big time' they wear a cap just like the one Sugnuston made, and it is called X'um'tl'ilum after that first one who wore it.

"When X'um'tl'ilum was dressed in his warm things, his father said to him, 'Sit out there on that seat, so that everyone can see your warm dress, then they will bring their girls, and we shall soon have lots of slaves.'

"So every day, X'um'tl'ilum put on his blankets and hat, and sat out on the seat; and all the people came and looked at him.

"'Feel how warm it is,' he would say, holding out a corner of his blanket. 'See, I do not shake with cold, although I sit out here in the snow and wind. My head is hot, where this hat covers it. You need not be cold, we have lots of blankets like these. You have lots of girls. Why not change? The wool or blankets would be useful to you, and the girls would be useful to us.'

"At last, one by one, the people began taking their girls and selling them to Sugnuston. For the most beautiful girls he gave blankets, and for those not so good to look at, he gave wool.

"At last he had nearly all the young girls living in his house, all working hard making more blankets for him. They were kept shut inside the house, for he was afraid of losing them if he let them out.

"One day when X'um'tl'ilum was sitting outside the house, waiting for the people to bring more girls, a young man with his blanket about him, came along and stood looking at X'um'tl'ilum. Now, for a long time this man had been waiting to marry, and that morning the girl's father had sold her to Sugnuston.

"After a time the young man walked away. He went into the woods and gathered a lot of small bushes, then he got a big club, and went back to the beach. When he got near the house where Sugnuston lived, he dipped his branches in the water, and walked up to the house. There was X'um'tl'ilum sitting outside. The young man went close to him and shook the wet branches in his face. X'um'tl'ilum jumped up. 'Why do you come splashing your wet branches over me?' he shouted, and hit the man.

"Quickly the young man lifted his club and hit X'um'tl'ilum on the head and killed him.

"Ah! Sugnuston was mad! He called all the men he kept as slaves, and he made them dig a big, deep pit—like a great room they made it.

Tl'utasiye' paused. "Ah!" she exclaimed, "I don't like to tell you this part, it is bad, bad! My man will never talk of it, but I say, well, it was long ago, we would not do such things now, and it makes a good story to tell to you, for it is all quite true.

"Well, then, when the big hole was ready, they took X'um'tl'ilum's body and put it in one corner, then they drove out all those poor young girls and made them climb down into the hole. When they were all in, the slaves got long planks of cedar and laid them over the top. Then they stood a thick pole up in the middle and put lots of dirt over all, until it was covered deeply with dirt. While they were doing this, Sugnuston had more slaves watching to see that the girl's relations did not come and try to save them; but they had always been afraid of that bad man, and he had always done as he wished, so that no one dare try to fight the slaves.

"When about two feet of dirt had been put over the boards the slaves pulled out the pole, leaving a round hole going down into the pit.

"Every day Sugnuston went to this hole and called down to the girls, "How are you getting on, eh? No, I can give you no water, the hole is too small to pour it down,' and every day before he left, he would ask, 'How many are left?'

"At last there was no answer, when he called down the hole, and for a long time he sat there—listening; but all was quiet down in that awful place, and he walked back to his house.

"'Get more earth,' he called to his slaves. 'It is all finished. Now, if the people want their daughters, let them come and take them!' But no people went near that place and no man spoke to Sugnuston. They kept away from him, and there he lived in his great house, with all his slaves, until he died, and no man ever talked to him again.

Wilkes James (Quil-Kay-Milth).   Image PN 6381 courtesy Royal British Columbia Museum.

Quil-Kay-Milth, the Carver[316]

Beryl Cryer visits another Snuneymuxw elder, Wilkes James (Quil-Kay-Milth), who discusses his work as a carver, and invites Cryer to meet his elderly mother. His mother asks James to tell Cryer another version of a Snuneymuxw origin story—one she had heard previously by Joe Wyse. Wilkes James continues with an origin story associated with his father's name, Tsul'quamut, the man who made the first swayxwi mask. He concludes with an account of the wedding between a half-sister and the son of Loxa of Qw'umiyiqun' (Comiaken). Cryer's unflattering physical description of Wilkes James' mother is somewhat mitigated by her depiction of an ancient woman with a keen mind, held in utmost respect by her family.

How many visitors to the town of Nanaimo have given more than a passing glance at the totem pole at the intersection of Albert and Commercial Streets? There are not many, I feel certain, who know the history of that totem and all that it represents.

The day I first met Quil-Kay-Milth, the carver, was one of those cold, windy days of which we have had so many this Spring. His wife led me down a narrow, muddy trail to the waterfront where stands the old lodges that housed the tribe in bygone days. There they stand, close to the water's edge, their great walls and roofs of split cedar shakes weathered to a silvery grey by the passing of the seasons. These lodges are all empty now, some being used as store houses, others kept in repair for use when a stl'un'uq (feast and dance) is given.

In front of the largest of these lodges a man was fastening the door with a large padlock.

"There he is," said my guide. "There's my man. He has his work in that house." She called to him, and having fastened the door, he came and shook hands, and, leaning against an old boat where we were sheltered from the wind, we talked.

"You saw my name on that totem?" he asked. "My Indian name, Quil-Kay-Milth. That was my grandfather's name, too; he was a very great carver and his father before him. My family have always been carvers; from the very beginning it comes.

"The first we can remember was my old mother's grandfather, then her father, Quil-Kay-Milth—whose name I have—next her brother, my uncle, Selakwiltun, and now, I am carving, too. But—too bad—with me it stops—I have no son— only two nieces, my sister's girls. They must try to carve, for there is no one else can do it.

"Come and see." He turned abruptly and crossed the road to the lodge. The padlock was unfastened and he led the way inside.

Such a vast place it was—quite the largest lodge that I had been in. The platform that is usually built up around the sides had been taken out and I, at first, thought the place quite empty, until my eyes grew accustomed to the gloom, for

Totem pole (sxt'ekw') carved by Wilkes James (Quil-Kay-Milth) to honour his father,
Tsul'quamut.
Image PN 6054 courtesy Royal British Columbia Museum

the only light was that which came through cracked boards and down the three smoke holes in the roof. Then I saw at one end of the room, an enormous peeled log lying on the ground, and, beside it, something raised on trestles and covered with a collection of papers and cardboard boxes.

"Here's some of my work," said Quil-Kay-Milth, as he led the way to the cedar pole on the ground.

"This one I'm just starting."

It was a wonderful piece of work seen in its rough state, without a covering of paint. At the top was a great eagle with wings slightly raised, its claws curved about a branch. Beneath this bird was the roughly cut figure of a man, holding in one hand a long stick and in the other a club.

"I've not done much of this one yet," said the carver. "I've been getting this other finished." And very carefully he lifted off the papers and boxes, showing me part of a newly painted pole.

He only uncovered about six feet, as the paint was wet, but I was able to see the figure of a man with beautifully executed feather headdress and his blanket falling in folds about him.

"This pole is pretty long," Quil-Kay-Milth told me, "but that other I am working on is much longer, that will be a fine totem."

"I suppose your uncle taught you to carve?" I asked. He shook his head and laughed.

"No," he said. "I never would try. When I was a boy I always wanted to be out playing, and then as I grew up I got work—I didn't want to stay at home carving. But my mother was always talking to me, telling me I must hurry and begin, that my people had always been carvers, and I must be one, too. Then my uncle, Selakwiltun, died, and there was no one left to carve.

"You see, my mother's people belong to Hwmuthkwi'um, and the Snuneymuxw had no carver; when they wanted carving done they had to send for a man from some other tribe, and so my mother's people have always been the carvers for this tribe. "Well, every day my old mother told me I must hurry up and begin, and that I must carve a totem for my dead father, Tsul'quamut. So at last I got my uncle's tools and I made that totem that you saw in Nanaimo today."

"Had you carved many things before you made that totem?" I asked him.

Quil-Kay-Milth shook his head. "No, I never would try; that totem is the very first thing I ever carved. My old mother sat beside me when I did it and told me what to cut and how to cut the pictures. She has told me what to put on these poles—(he pointed to the two beside us)—and how to color them, but she never carved anything herself. It took me just three months and three days, working seventeen hours a day to carve my father's totem. These others will take longer; I had to hurry with that first one, as I was going away.

"Come and see my old mother," he invited. "We can sit in her warm house and I will tell you the stories of my father's totem and of those others that I am making."

We went across the road and down a wooden plank to a house built as close to the water's edge as it had been possible to put it.

"My mother lives here with my married sister," he explained as he opened the door.

The house consisted of one large room, with beds around the walls and a table in the centre at which the family were finishing a meal. Quil-Kay-Milth introduced them to me, as his sister, her husband and their two daughters, and as we shook hands and I was given a chair, I wondered where the old mother might be. Then I heard a curious grunting noise behind me, and, turning, saw her on a bed in the corner beside the stove.

She was very, very old and very, very small. So withered and shrunken was she, it seemed impossible that she could ever have been a young and strong woman.

There on the bed she crouched in a semi kneeling position; a red flannel rag tied about her head; her skin, a strangely golden brown color, stretched tightly over her bones, and her sightless eyes turning here and there in her efforts to learn who had entered the room.

Quil-Kay-Milth seated himself on the edge of her bed and, putting his hand on her shoulder, talked to her in a low voice.

"My mother wants to shake your hand," he told me, and moved my chair nearer the bed, whilst I took the tiny claw like hand in mine.

Her son took a crust of bread from the table and put it in her hand, and she sat chewing it with her toothless gums whilst she talked to him in a husky little voice.

"My mother wants me to tell you that her name is Siamtunaat,"[317] said Quil-Kay-Milth, "and it must be put in your story. She says I may tell you the story of my father's totem, but that the stories of those other poles must not be told until I have finished and sold them. But my mother wants me to tell you that, if I do sell them, I will let you know the day they are to be put up in their places, and you must come and I will then tell you their stories. You see, we have always done as our mother tells us; and so—" He shrugged his shoulders expressively.

Here we were interrupted by an anxious cry from the old mother. She had lost her crust and clawed desperately amongst the bed clothes as though her greatest treasure were gone. Quil-Kay-Milth soon found it for her, and she crouched down once more to attack it with renewed vigor. Curious little creature! Blind and practically helpless, yet ruling her family of grown men and women like a veritable despot!

"Now, this is the story of the first totem I ever made!" Quil-Kay-Milth leaned his elbows on his knees and covered his face with his hands, and only once did he move from this position while telling his story. With minor alterations, it was the same tale as that told me by Sugnuston of the Origin of the Snuneymuxw.

"Long, long ago," he commenced, "this world was just rock. There was no grass and there were no trees. Well, one day there landed on this shore a man named Tsuk-Al-Hun. He wore no clothes but had a lot of tth'umeen' (arrows) going from his shoulder down, and across him to his side and at his knees were two slaves. This man looked to the east, and he looked to the north, but nowhere could he see any stl'eyuq'um (smoke), so he knew that he was the first man to land there. No man knows how long he stayed on the beach, but many, many years after he and his slaves had a home beside a little lake away, back near Tetuxutun (Mount Benson); and he must have lived there a very long time, for great trees grew up and grass and bushes, as it is now; and Tsuk Al Hun had three sons.

"The eldest of these boys was called Squal-H'noe, the next Hoch-Ut-Shun and the youngest Shuy-At-Hut."

From this point the story was much as Sugnuston had told it. The three boys set out to look at the world, and to see whether there were any other people living at that place. After many days they arrived at Sti'ilup (Departure Bay), where they found a man carving a swayxwi mask.

"That man's name" said Quil-Kay-Milth, was Tsul'quamut." As he pronounced the name slowly, for me, the little creature on the bed commenced speaking rapidly in her curiously hoarse voice. Quil-Kay-Milth laughed.

"My mother," he explained, "says I must tell you that Tsul'quamut, the name of the man who made the first swayxwi mask, has come down through all the years until it was given my father.

"Well, the three boys watched the man carving and, because they had seen the mask before it was finished, Tsul'quamut made them stay and marry his three daughters. After some time the youngest boy, with his wife, went to the old father at Tetuxutun, but Squal-H'noe and Hoch-Ut-Shun made their homes at Sti'ilup. There they learned how to make canoes and become great hunters, every day going out and killing kw'aant' (porpoise) and sweelum (seals), and those were the first game eaten by our people.[318]

"In time there grew a great and powerful tribe at Sti'ilup; and I carved that totem in memory of my father, Tsul'quamut, and of Squal-H'Noe, the first of this tribe to live at Sti'ilup.

"Look at my totem; at the top you will see a man; that is Squal-H'Noe. Under him is Yuxwula'us, the eagle, who was his guide and his spirit when hunting. Then there is the black bear, who gave his skin for a coat to keep Squal-H'Noe warm. And then, at the bottom, is the swayxwi mask as it was made by the first Sil-Kay-Malth.

"There are not many families who may use that mask, and those who do are very proud of it. That is why I put it on the totem, that all who see it will know that my father's people belong to those who may use the swayxwi."

Quil-Kay-Milth looked at his old mother. "I think that's all the story, mother?" he asked. She held her hands out towards him, and I thought she would fall off the bed in her eagerness as she talked and gesticulated.

"Ah, yes!" Quil-Kay-Milth pushed her gently back amongst the covers. "My mother would like me to tell you about the time my half-sister Tza-Lah-Mia, got married," he explained, "because that was one time when my people had the swayxwi to dance."

"Well, long ago my father, Tsul'quamut, who was a cousin of Joe-Ez Sugnuston, had another wife, and they had a girl named Tza-Lah-Mia. Now, you have heard of that old Qw'umiyiqun' Chief, Loxa, who was chief of all the Cowichans? Well, his son, Sueenchtun, wanted to marry Tza-Lah-Mia. One day Loxa came to see my father and settle about the two getting married. He came with two canoes full of Qw'umiyiqun' people, and there was a lot of talking, but at last everything was settled and they went home again. After some time, when my people were ready and had called all their friends, Sueenchtun came with Loxa and lots of Qw'umiyiqun' people, and they were married in the Indian way.

"My father and his wife made their fire in our big lodge here—the one I have my poles in—and they put blankets all along the seats, then they sat down before their fire and waited.

"By-and-by Sueenchtun came with a swuqw'a'lh (Indian blanket). He spread it on the ground near the door and sat down on it. There he sat for three days and three nights. On the fourth day he folded up his blanket. Two of his friends came in, took hold of his hands and took him over to my father's fire.

"'Sit by our side and share our fire,' said my father. So he spread his blanket on the ground and sat beside their fire.

"Now, my father's people brought in blankets—oh so many!—and made a great pile of them beside the young man. The door was opened and everybody came in.

"Now two woman pulled Tza-Lah-Mia into the house, holding her by the wrists, and they brought her to Sueenchtun's side and she sat on his blanket with him. More and more blankets were piled up beside the two—all to be given to the Qw'umiyiqun', to show what a rich man my father was—and then in came the xwaayxwi and began to dance, and lots of woman shook their rattles and sang. Oh, it was a Big Time!

"When it was finished and the Qw'umiyiqun' were ready to go away, some of the women took Tza-Lah-Mia into another house. There they put a very old blanket about her, and on her back they tied a little axe and a bundle of sticks. Then they put her in one of the canoes filled with blankets and covered her right over with a big blanket. The Qw'umiyiqun' got into their canoes and all paddled away."

"Why did the woman tie sticks and an axe on her back?" I asked.

Quil-Kay-Milth shrugged his shoulders. "Well, it's hard to tell why," he said. "But you see, my father was a big man in the tribe and he sent his daughter to her

Wilkes James and Beryl Cryer

husband, like that—looking as though she was going to a poor man's house where she would have to work hard and wear poor clothes. But Sueenchtun was a good husband to her, and she had a nice house and little work, and often he would bring her up here to see her people.

"Tza-Lah-Mia is still living at Qw'umiyiqun'. She is very old now, but she was a fine girl when she married and had the xwaayxwi dance for her."

Quil-Kay-Milth got up from the bed, and at once his mother began to talk, pulling the bed clothes about her shoulders as she did so.

"My mother says she would like you to come again another day," said Quil-Kay-Milth. "She is tired now and must sleep."

As I said "Good bye" to her she held my hand in both of hers and "crooned" over it, as so many of the old women do, and so we left her to rest and dream of who knows what by-gone days, for that old brain of hers must be filled with a wealth of stories, could we but get her to tell them.

Tl'utasiye"s Childhood Games[319]

Joe and Jennie Wyse have been discussing appropriate stories for Beryl Cryer to record. Today, instead of origin stories, Jennie Wyse describes some of the organized games she played as a child. Joe Wyse relates the myth of Beaver and Raccoon.

SUGNUSTON WAS LOOKING UNUSUALLY SMART, as he opened his garden gate for me. "He is going to a football match," Tl'utasiye' explained. "Our grandson is playing, so, of course, his grandfather must watch. Oh! we are so proud of that boy!"

Her husband laughed. "He's a fine boy," he agreed, "and that's a game I like to see. But it is early yet. I think I will stay and talk a little bit before I go."

He followed us into the house, took off his coat and hung it with great care over the back of a chair, placed his high crowned black felt hat on the seat and drew up a chair to the table where Tl'utasiye' and I were sitting.

"We often talk about you," he said, "and we think about stories to tell you." He leaned across the table and tapped it to emphasize his words. "You see, we both know lots of stories, but we only want to tell you the best. Some are not much good—might not be true—I can't tell." He shook his head doubtfully.

"Now," he turned to his wife, "you tell her about those stories we talked of after she went home last time."

Tl'utasiye' cleared her throat impressively. "Well, now," she began, "my man and me thought you would like to hear about the way the children played when we were small, and then we thought we would tell some stories about the little animals—the beaver, and mink and 'coon?

"Ah! you would like that? Well, then, first I will tell you of a game I used to like the best of all. I tried to teach my grandchildren this game, but they go to school and the teacher there tells them white children's games, so they won't learn these games of mine and soon they will all be forgotten.

"Now, this is a game we used to play in the houses when we couldn't go outside. My old granny liked to have the little ones playing in her house and she would help us in our games. Well, all the children who wanted to play would go into the house, then one would have to sit in a corner with eyes shut, so as not to see what the others were doing. Now, my old granny would spread rush mats on the ground and all the children would lie down with their faces hidden; round in a ring they would lie, with their feet together in the middle. Then my granny would take blankets and cover them right up. When all were covered, the one in the corner had to walk round and feel the heads and backs through the blanket and try and guess who it was. In those days our people used to get long dishes made of wood from the Indians up North and we children thought it good fun to take one of these dishes, turn it upside down under the blanket, and get a stone or something hard for a head and then hear what name the boy who was guessing would give to this funny child."

Tl'utasiye' chuckled heartily at her recollection of this joke.

"Now here is a game to play outside: First, you must remember that when I was young the big houses were all full of people; every village was the same. Lots of people everywhere, and oh! the children—so many. When we played a game and held hands, the children reached far along the beaches—oh, so many, and now I only know of one old woman who played in those games with me. Sometimes she comes here and we meet and we just hold each other and cry." Tl'utasiye"s old eyes quivered as she blinked the tears from her eyes.

"I was nearly crying," she exclaimed, "and I started to tell you about fun and games."

"Well, now, all the children used to hold hands in a big circle with two of the biggest standing in the middle. Now they would all dance round, then stand still and look up in the air and sing like this."

Tl'utasiye' stood up, and, holding to the back of her chair, jigged up and down singing softly: "Stem 'a' lu they tsitsulh? Stem 'a' lu they tsitsulh? (What is that up on high?)"

"'U smuqtulus. (I wonder if it is moss hanging down.)"

"'Uwu, 'uwu, 'uwu. (No, no, no, no)."

"Now all dance round again and then run away and sit in a long, long row, with heads down as though hiding. Now the two big ones would take a stick, and, holding it between them, would walk along the row and sing, 'N'stoum na khuk,

Joe Wyse, Jennie Wyse and Beryl Cryer

quoah chlav vehowdkh!'[320] 'My slaves, I wonder where they went?' Many times they would sing that until they had come to the end of the row, then all would jump up and play the game again."

Sugnuston held up his hand. "Wait, now," he said. "I want to tell you that name smuqtulus is what we call that kind of dry moss that you sometimes see hanging down from the trees. Now," he turned to his wife, "Tell about the game with the stone, and then I will tell one of our animal stories."

"Ah! Ah!" Tl'utasiye' nodded her head. "I will tell you just this one more, then:

"All children but two stand in a long row. Now one of those two shut his eyes and the other gets a little round stone and holds it between his hands. Everybody puts their two hands together and holds them out in front of them, and the boy with the stone puts his hands over every child's hands and gives the stone to someone. After that the boy who has had his eyes shut has to come and guess who has the stone.

"My grandchildren," she added, "tell me that the white children play a game like that; perhaps you know it?"

"Yes," I told her. "Their game is very like that, and I think they use a button instead of a stone."

Tl'utasiye' was greatly amused. "A button!" I heard her repeating to herself as she gathered up her knitting and prepared to work whilst Sugnuston took his turn at story telling.

"My story," said Sugnuston, "is about that animal with the funny tail—the beaver, and that other animal that is like a big cat, the 'coon. We call the beaver Squl'ew and Sxayukw'us is the 'coon.

"These two were never very good friends, but they always pretended that they liked each other.

"Well, one sunny day Squl'ew' thought he would take a walk, and it happened that Sxayukw'us thought he would take a walk that same morning. By and by they met and got talking together.

"After a time Squl'ew' said, 'Have you ever seen my home, Sxayukw'us?'

"Sxayukw'us shook his head. 'No, he said, 'I don't know where your home is.'

"'Well, would you like to see my house?' asked Squl'ew'.

"'Yes, I would like to see it,' said Sxayukw'us.

"While they talked they had walked along together and now were beside a lake. 'See that rock out in the middle of the lake?' said Squl'ew', pointing to a big stone sticking up out of the water, 'well, that is where I have built my home.'

"'I see,' said Sxayukw'us. 'How do you get there?'

"'I swim,' his friend told him. 'Can't you swim?'

"'Ah, yes. Of course I can swim,' said Sxayukw'us, who thought he could do everything. 'But I don't feel like swimming today.'

"'Well, then, I will carry you,' said Squl'ew'. 'Get on my back and I will swim there with you.'

"So Sxayukw'us got on his back and Squl'ew' carried him out to the rock. When they were close to it, Squl'ew' said, 'Here we are. Jump off and I will show you my house.'

"'It's a funny place for a house,' thought Sxayukw'us. But he jumped off and ran up the rock. As soon as he had jumped, Squl'ew' gave a loud laugh and dived under the water.

"By and by he came up a little way from the rock and laughed again; then he slapped his tail on the water, making a great noise. 'Good bye, oh, silly Sxayukw'us!' he called. 'Stay as long as you wish, and swim home when you feel like it.' Then he dived again and swam away.

"Well, that poor Sxayukw'us did not know what to do. He ran round and round on the rock and climbed down to the water and put his little hand in, but quickly he drew it back again, for the water was cold and very deep.

"For long months he lived on that rock, and every morning he climbed down and put his hand into the water, but every morning it was the same; he was afraid to get in and try to swim.

"At last the rain began, and Sxayukw'us felt that the water grew colder each morning that he put his hand in. One morning when he felt the water there was something hard on top—ice had come.

"'Ah!' he thought, 'now I can walk home on this,' but when he pressed on it his hand went through.

"Three days he waited, feeling the ice every morning, and on the fourth day he walked right out on it, and finding it quite strong, ran across to land and back to his home.

"Well, the warm days came and again those two went out for a walk, and again they met.

"'Hallo!' said Sxayukw'us, 'I have not seen you since my nice visit to your home. Did you see me swimming back the next day?'

"'No,' sald Squl'ew'; 'I heard you were staying out there.'

"'Oh, no!' laughed Sxayukw'us, 'I had to hurry back to finish a new house I had begun to make. Would you like to see my nice, new house?' he asked.

"Squl'ew' said that he would like to see it. 'Where is your house?' he asked. They were walking through the woods now, and Sxayukw'us sat down on a log and pointed to a great fir tree that had been broken off far up near the top.

"'My home is up there,' he said, 'at the top where you see those big branches.'

"But how do you get up to it?' asked his friend.

"'I climb up.' said Sxayukw'us. 'Can't you climb? Can you only swim and run?'

"'Oh, yes,' Squl'ew' told him, 'I can climb, but it is so hot today. Do you think you could carry me up to see your house?'

"Sxayukw'us began to dance and sing. 'Get on my back, get on my back, and I will carry you up to my house.'

"So Squl'ew' got on his back and he began to climb. Up and up they went, and each time they passed a branch Squl'ew' would ask, 'Is not this where your house is, Sxayukw'us?' And Sxayukw'us would laugh and say, 'A little higher, Squl'ew', a little higher.' At last they got to the top and Squl'ew' jumped off his friend's back and sat down where the branches forked.

"As soon as Sxayukw'us felt Squl'ew' jump off he called, 'Good bye, Squl'ew'. Stay as long as you like.' Then he ran down the tree and away through the woods.

"For a little while Squl'ew' sat there between the branches too afraid to move. Then he saw that the sun was going behind the trees and knew that he must hurry or it would be dark before he could reach his home. He crept to the edge and looked down, then he sat quickly back again and shut his eyes, he was so afraid. Again he crept to the edge and put one foot over, feeling—feeling for something to stand on. But there was nothing, and he sat down once more. The next time he crept to the other branch and put his foot down the other side of the tree, but there was nothing, so he sat down to think. 'Now,' he said to himself, 'when Sxayukw'us was on the rock, ice came to help him, but what is there that can help me up here? There is nothing,' and he began to cry, alone in the dark.

"All that night he sat crying, but the next morning when the sun came back to warm him, he felt better, and he thought, 'If there is nothing that can help me, I must help myself. Now, what can I do? I can swim, I can dive, but swimming and diving won't help me up here. I can gnaw and bite sticks and trees.' He stopped for a long time. He sat thinking.

"'I must gnaw this tree down,' he said at last. 'I will have to begin here at the top and gnaw right down to the bottom. It will take a long time, so I must work hard.'

"He moved to the side that was broken down lower than the other and began to bite the hard wood. All day and on through the night he worked, and in the morning he leant over and looked down, but sat back quickly and shut his eyes; but after a little while began to work again.

"So for a whole year poor Squl'ew' worked, gnawing down the tree, and every morning he would lean and look down, and then have to sit and shut his eyes, for looking down so far made him giddy.

"At last the morning came when he found that it was not very far to the ground, and he worked harder than ever. Then one afternoon he put down his foot and touched the ground, and it was not long before he was hurrying through the wood on his way home to the lake.

"After that, whenever Squl'ew' and Sxayukw'us went for walks, they went in different ways, or, if they saw one another, they would pass without stopping to talk."

Origin of the Qhwimux Tribe[321]

It is late autumn 1932, and Mary Rice has been away harvesting tules, the bulrushes that grow along lakes and estuaries. She has been drying the tules, preparing to make them into thul'shutun, large woven mats used for many things, particularly bedding. In her brief autobiography Cryer, states that Mary Rice taught her the technique, which may explain the attention to detail in the article. This story also demonstrates that in 1932, tules, used for hundreds, if not thousands of years, for bedding, screens and shelter, continued to be harvested and used by native people.[322]

The main part of this article, however, is a very detailed account about the origin of the Qhwimux (Comox) people. According to the account, an elder from Kuper Island asked Mary Rice to learn the story so that she could tell it to Cryer.

HEARING THAT MY OLD FRIEND SIAMTUNAAT had returned to her home on the beach, I walked down to see her.

"Ah!" she exclaimed, smiling until her twinkling eyes were almost lost to sight in her fat old face. "Ah! At last you come to see the old woman, eh?"

She dusted off a chair with a corner of her voluminous skirt, and set it beside the door for me.

"Sit down," she invited. "Sit down. Ah, I'm so busy! I've been away too long, and now look at these rushes, all to be made into mats for my beds." She pointed to masses of dried rushes piled in every available space.

"Do you know how we make our mats?" she asked. "No? Well, now, I'll show you, and while I work I can tell you a story an old man at Puneluxutth' on Kuper Island told me—for you. He told me two times, so that I could 'member it all."

"She gathered up a bundle of rushes and spread them out on her table.

"See now, here are my needles," she said, showing me four long sticks, most beautifully polished. "Old Reuben made these for me," she explained, as she handed me one. It was about twenty inches long, with one flat side, the remainder slightly rounded, and as smooth as a knitting needle. An eye at one end was threaded with coarse twine, the other end being sharply pointed.

With remarkable deftness she arranged the rushes evenly on her table, and threaded as many as possible on her needles, pulled the twine through, then unthreaded the needles and repeated the process until her mat was about a yard wide, with four inches between each row of twine.

When she had the desired width she worked back again, adding more and more rushes.

"This is how my people have always made their mats," she explained.

"Long ago, some of the old people did not bother making mats. They just put the rushes in a pile for their beds."

She leaned back in her chair and began to laugh.

"Do you know," she said, "I can 'member away back, when I was a very little girl, sometimes I had to sleep in my old granny's bed. Now, that old woman never wore white people's clothes— just had a blanket about her, and her bed was a pile of rushes. Well, when she went to bed she would take off her blanket, lie down on the rushes and spread the blanket over both of us. I can 'member now how I used to kick my feet about in the rushes. I never liked the feel of them, but I liked the sound they made. Then granny would slap my legs and tell me to keep still, but I just had to kick those rushes.

"You see, my mother's beds were soft, with lots of blankets, but my old granny would never have one like that."

Siamtunaat rolled up the mat she had finished, and commenced sorting out more rushes.

"Now," she said, "I will tell you my story. It is about the first people at Qhwimux—'Punt-Lutz' is the Indian name for that place."

"In the beginning, long ago, there were no people living at Punt-Lutz. Then, a long way back in the woods where there was a lake, a man was made.

"For a long time he lived there alone eating the roots that he found, and after a time he made a bow and arrows and killed animals to eat. Then, one morning, when he woke up, he saw a woman standing looking at him. She was a fine, tall woman, with long hair that reached right down to her feet; but she had no arms.

"The man jumped up and ran to catch her. 'Ah, I have been waiting so long for you,' he said. 'Come and live with me, and be my wife.'

"But the woman shook her head.

"'No, no,' she said. 'See, I have no arms. What if we were to have children? Perhaps they would have no arms, too. I must always live alone.'

"But the man would not let her go.

"'I will look after you,' he said. 'And why should our children be only like you? Why not like me too?'

"So the woman listened to him, and lived with him as his wife. Every day the man would go out to hunt, and he would come home with deer and elk, and cook the meat and feed his wife, and do all the work for her.

"'Where are you from?' he would ask her. But she would not tell him. 'I do not know,' she said. 'I walked a long way, but I can't remember.'

"Well, after a time, two babies were born to them, two fine, big boys, and both had arms like their father. The man took and washed them and looked after them, for the poor woman could not touch them.

"These two children grew up very quickly, as did all the first children long ago; and the man was kept busy looking after them and doing all the work at home, as well as hunting for food, and it was not long before he began to get bad tempered, and quarreled with his wife.

"'You are tired of me,' said the woman. 'Put the children on my back, and I will go and take them with me. You need never see me again.'

"'No, no!' said the man. 'I was tired and did not mean what I said.' But every day it was the same; there was always trouble, until one day while he was out hunting, his wife took the children and walked away into the woods.

"Bye-and-bye she came to a creek, and along this they walked, with her children following behind.

"When they had gone a long way they stopped for a rest, and to eat some of the dried meat they had brought with them.

"'I must have a drink,' said the woman. She stooped over the creek to drink, and, as she looked into the clear water, she saw her two arms grow from her body. They came down quickly, just as though they had been shut up in her shoulders all the time.

"'Ah! Ah!' she called to her boys. 'Come and see! Come and look at me!' And she sat down on the bank of the creek and began to laugh. Suddenly she sat very still and listened. From up in the air there came a man's laugh and a voice spoke.

"'Now you are all right, poor woman,' it said. 'Now you are all right, just like the other people.' 'Ah, yes,' she called, 'Did you do this? Did you give me my arms?' 'Yes,' said the voice, 'I gave you your arms. Now you can go back and help your man do the work.'

"'I will go now,' she said, and, calling her boys to her, she started back. When she got to their home she saw the man sitting looking into his fire. He had some cooked meat ready, but was not eating. Looking up, he saw her coming, carrying one of her children on her arm, and holding the other by his hand.

"'Ah, but they were glad to be together once more. And sitting by the fire, the woman told him how the Spirit from the air had given her arms to her. After this they lived very happily for a long time, the woman helping her husband do the work, cleaning and smoking the deer and bear meat that he brought in, and digging for roots and gathering berries to dry for Winter. In time they had a large family, for the children that were born to them were always twins, and grew to be fine, strong children.

"Now the woman loved her two eldest children the best and always helped them to do their work, until their father grew angry and quarreled with his wife, telling her that she made them lazy, that they were of no use to him, and, taking a stick, he whipped the biggest boy until he lay on the ground unable to move.

"That night the two boys talked together. 'Let us leave,' said the biggest. 'We are able to take care of ourselves now. Why should our father treat us as though we were slaves?' So the next morning, while it was still very early, they left their beds and started off through the thick forest.

Bye-and-bye they came to a river and walked beside this, following it down until they came to the sea. Now the water was a long way out, and as they walked over the sand they saw water spurting up all about them. 'Look!' said one, 'there must be something down there; we will find out what it is!'

"They got sticks and scraped away the sand until they came to a large clam. 'It may be good to eat, they thought, and breaking it open, tasted it. Ah, it was good! They both began to dig, and very soon had a large pile of clams. They carried them up to the beach and, getting cedar sticks, made a fire and put the clams beside it to cook.

"For many months they lived at that place beside the river, always having plenty to eat, for beside the deer they killed, they could always dig clams when the water went out. One day, when the water was very low, they saw something splashing in the river, and, hurrying to look, found more salmon than they could count, swimming up the river. The water was filled with salmon, and more and more were coming, all pushing and fighting to get far up in the fresh water.

"How the boys worked killing those fish—hitting them on the head and throwing them far out on the river bank! That night, when they had finished cleaning and putting the fish to dry, the two sat beside their fire and talked.

"'Do you remember?' said one, 'how hard our father used to work finding enough to feed us with?' 'And do you remember?' said the other, 'how our mother has often told us of the time when she had no arms and our father would do all the work, washing and feeding us, after a hard day's hunting? Let us go back, and tell our people of this place, and bring them all here to make their home with us!'

"A few days later, they took their dried clams and as many salmon as they could carry, and started back to find their people. Now, after they had quarreled with their father, and had left him, their poor mother cried and cried; and nothing that her husband could do made her feel any better, and the poor man did not know what to do. One day, as she sat beside the lake, thinking of her lost boys, she heard a voice, and saw a lot of people coming through the bushes. This was another tribe of people who had been made, far back in the mountains, and had left their home to look for a better one.

"'Stay with us,' said the man, 'for my wife has lost her two eldest sons, and is lonely and unhappy. Make your home with us, and help to cheer my poor wife.' So the new tribe stayed there, and made their home beside the lake.

"It did not take the boys very long to get back to their old home, for they walked night and day, they were in such a hurry to see their family again. One morning the mother woke to see two young men standing in the door of her little house. 'We have come back to you, mother!' they called. 'We have found a place where food is all about us—no need to hunt for hours for a meal. There is food that you have never heard of—more than a large tribe would need. See, we have brought some of the new food for you to eat.'

"All the people came up to look at the strange new food and to eat pieces of it.

"'Ah, my sons,' said their father, 'I did wrong. I beat you as though you were children that must be taught, and now it is you who can teach us.'

"'You were right,' the boys told him, 'for it was your beating that made us become men.'

"For a few weeks the boys stayed at the lake, then the little houses were taken down, the skins and all that the people had were packed, and together they all started down the river to the sea. There they formed the Punt-Lutz tribe, which grew to be a tribe of many hundreds, and ah! The fights there were between those people and the Cowichans, before the last battle was fought and peace came to all our people."

Visit of the First Ship to Sti'ilup[323]

Jennie Wyse gives an account of the first Hwulunitum' sighted in the Nanaimo area, as told to her by her grandmother. She then describes a special cedar cloth made for babies, which was given ritual treatment when it was no longer used. Joe Wyse concludes with a story about Mink.

"HAVE WE EVER TOLD YOU ABOUT the first time my old granny and her people at Sti'ilup (Departure Bay) saw a white man's ship?" asked Tl'utasiye', carding her wool rapidly as she spoke.

We were sitting out under the cherry tree. Tl'utasiye' busy as usual, while Sugnuston sat very upright on a box, his tall black hat pulled well over his eyes, as he puffed contentedly at an ancient black pipe.

"That old granny of mine was quite a young girl when the first boat came to this land," continued Tl'utasiye'. "All the tribes were living over at Sti'ilup, long before they moved here. One morning, very early, some of the men got up to go hunting, and as they went outside the houses and looked over the water, they saw something that they could not understand.

"'What can it be?' they asked each other. 'We had better call the others!' they said. And they ran along the houses, calling to the rest of the tribe.

"'Come out! Come out and see what is in the water. It must be a new island that has come in the night.' In a few minutes everybody was on the beach looking at the strange, new thing that had come to them. As they watched they saw things moving on that new island.

"'See!' they called, 'there are some sort of men on it, perhaps they have come to fight. We must go out and see what they are here for.' So they all began getting ready to go and look at the queer thing. The men painted their faces and put oil on their heads, got their fighting things, and when all were ready, four canoes, filled with men, paddled out to where the thing lay on the water. As they got near they saw it was a kind of great canoe, but far bigger than anything they had ever seen before.

"Now they saw a man sitting with his legs hanging over the side and, as they looked at him, he kicked his feet against the boards. 'See!' said one of our men, 'this is a new kind of man, look, he has feet made of wood! Listen to the noise they make!' Ah! they all thought that funny. They sat in their canoes and laughed to see the feet made of wood.

"After a bit, this man called out, and another man name and sat beside him; and this man was stranger than the first, for he was smoking.

"'See!' called the chief, 'what people are these? They have burning stomachs! Smoke is coming from their mouths!'

"The strange men threw pieces of biscuit into the canoes, but my people wouldn't touch them. Then one man got a tin and, tying a rope to it, let it down to the chief; and made signs for him to take it as a present. So the chief untied the rope and put the tin in the end of his canoe.

"Those strange men did not stay long, for a wind began to blow out from the land, and, putting up its sails, the boat floated away.

"Now the chief and his men paddled back to tell the women what they had seen, and to show them the pieces of white stick the men had thrown into the canoes, and the tin, which had been given to the chief.

"'What is it?' said one lifting the tin. 'There must be something inside it, it is so heavy.' The chief opened the tin and all crowded around to see what was inside.

"'Looks like soft pitch,' said one. 'It is pitch,' said another. 'It will do to mend our canoes with.' So the chief divided it, giving each man a little. 'I don't know what it is,' he said, 'but it may be as you say—a kind of pitch. Keep it for your canoes.'

"One man, who had a cracked canoe, hurried away and very carefully poured the stuff along the crack, but it did not dry, only ran all over the bottom of the canoe, and made a great mess. Suddenly one of the men gave a loud shout.

"'Put your fingers in it!' he called. 'Taste it! Eat it! I have never eaten such food!' At once, all began putting their fingers into the stuff and eating it. The women and the children all got some too. Everybody was eating it, only the poor man who had poured it into his canoe had none; but he got a shell and scraped a little out and ate it.

"For," laughed Tl'utasiye' "do you know what was in that tin? It was molasses! A big tin of molasses."

Tl'utasiye put down her carders and shook with laughter, and old Sugnuston pushed back his hat and joined in the joke.

"Ah!" he said, "it was hard for those old people. They didn't know much, all the men did was fight and hunt, and the women spent all day getting food and looking after their children."

Tl'utasiye' leaned eagerly forward and tapped my arm with one of her carders.

"When my man talks of what the women used to do, that makes me remember something we said we would tell you one day.

"You know how, long ago, the people used to clean cedar bark and weave it together to make a little covering for their bodies? Well, the women would get that bark and make it very, very soft for their babies. They would wrap their babies right up in the bark and put them in their little wooden cradles—our name for those cradles is Scha-Cutun. Well now, this is what I want to tell you: When white people have babies—and it is the same with my people now—the mothers make nice little baby clothes and, when one baby has finished with these clothes, they are put away for the next baby; but in the old days the mothers did not do that.

"When their babies had grown too big for the cedar wrappings, they never put them away for another baby, for every baby must have new ones. Those things that had been used were cleaned, the cedar rolled up and tied, and then taken away to a small sort of cave and put inside. Those things were always kept, they must not be thrown away or burned.

"My man and I, we know where there is one of those little caves nearly full of little rolls of cedar bark wrappings, and we want to take you in our canoe to look at it. When we talked about it, we could remember seeing all the little rolls of cedar under the rocks, but we had not been there for so many years, we thought maybe someone had taken them away; so one day Sugnuston took the canoe and went to look at them. 'For,' he said, 'it is no good telling the lady about them if we can't show them to her.'

"Well, my man found the place, and he saw a little of the cedar, but he says it is so high up he can't think how these women ever got to the cave. He is going another day to look for them—he thinks there must be some trail to the top of the rocks and a way down to the little cave, from the top. When he has found how to get there, we will take you to see them."

Sugnuston had for some time been showing signs of restlessness. He had taken off his hat, knocked the ashes from his pipe with quite unnecessary vigour, and cleared his throat several times, scowling at Tl'utasiye' as he did so, but not until she had finished what she had to tell me did she take any notice of him. Then she laughed, and nodding her old head at her husband, said:

"My man is in a hurry to tell you one of his stories about the little animals, but if I did not speak first, you would never hear what I have to tell, Sugnuston has so many of these stories for you!"

Sugnuston moved his box further into the shade and seating himself, folded his thin hands on one knee.

My story today," he said. "is about that little animal who is always trying to be so smart, and who always wants more than anybody else, Qeq'yux, the mink! Now, I must tell you that Qeq'yux is the name we have for him up here, but down at Cowichan and Puneluxutth' they call him Chuchi'q'un'.

"Well, one day, long ago, Qeq'yux was walking along the beach, up further North, looking for little crabs to eat, when he smelled a very nice, sweet smell. He put up his nose and smelt the air. Ah! the smell came in over the water!

"Quickly he ran to a little hill from where he could look out over the water, and coming towards him he saw a big canoe full of people. Now, these people had a big basket full of cooked speenhw (Camas) in their canoe, and that food smells very sweet when it is cooked. As the canoe got near to Qeq'yux he could smell that sweet smell better than ever.

"'What can that be?' he thought. 'Would those people give me some, I wonder?' He ran to the beach, and getting up on a high rock, called, 'Q'et'um s'haqw 'o 'ushul? What sweet smell is passing?'[324]

"'Yes, we do smell sweet,' called back the men. 'We will give you a little if you like.' And they paddled to the shore and gave Qeq'yux a little of their speenhw.

"Qeq'yux ate a little and he licked his lips and laughed. 'This is better than anything I have ever tasted,' he said. 'I must have some more, they did not give me much.' He hid what he had left under a leg, and running quickly, was soon in front of the canoe, and sat on the beach waiting for it to come.

"When the men were near enough, he stood up and called, 'What sweet smell is passing?' 'There is someone else smelling our speenhw,' said the men, 'Oh well, we'll give him just a little.' So again they paddled to the shore and gave Qeq'yux some of the sweet-smelling food.

"'That was easy,' laughed Qeq'yux. 'I will try again,' and he once more hid the speenhw and started to run ahead. Bye and bye he saw a burned tree in front of him and he stopped a minute in front of it, looking at it. Then he rubbed his little hands on the black wood and put them all over his face. He stood up and rubbed his front up and down on the black, and then turned and rubbed his back in the same way, until he was covered with the burned wood.

"'Now they won't know me,' he thought, and running quickly got in front of the canoe and lay down on a point to wait for it. Pretty soon the canoe came along and Qeq'yux jumped up and called, 'Halloo! What sweet smell is passing?' The men in the canoe were getting tired of giving away their food and one said, 'We've given away too much already, let's paddle past and not answer.' But the others said, 'Oh well, let's give just this once more.' So they paddled to the beach and gave the little black animal some of their speenhw.

"'I may as well get all I can,' thought Qeq'yux, 'I will clean myself and they will again think I am someone else.'

"So after he had hidden the speenhw, he rolled on the moss and he jumped in the grass until he thought he must be clean, then he ran as hard as he could to get in front of the canoe once more. He had been rolling so hard, trying to get clean, that the canoe had got far ahead and it took him some time before he got in front again. Then he ran to the beach just as the canoe was passing.

"'Ah!' he called. 'What sweet smell is passing? And I am so hungry.'

"Now the men in the canoe were tired of hearing that call, and they had given most of their speenhw away, so they paddled close to the rock to see what animals these could be that kept calling for their speenhw.

"'What is it?' said one. 'It looks like that little Qeq'yux we saw a long way back,' said another. 'But see how black he is.' They jumped out of the canoe and caught Qeq'yux and held him up by the back of his neck. 'It is Qeq'yux,' they said. 'And see how he has blackened himself to trick us. Getting all our good speenhw.'

"They took a stick and beat poor Qeq'yux, the black flew from his coat, and he cried to them, to let him go.

"So they threw him into the bushes and paddled on, and poor Qeq'yux got up and shook himself and hurried off to find the speenhw he had hidden, and to eat it, but he had learned a lesson, that it does not do to be too greedy."

The Magic Hole on Mount Tzouhalem[325]

At the north end of Galiano Island, on her way to interview John Peter, Beryl Cryer finds Qwulsteynum in front of his house. In conversation, he discusses the supernatural power of xwult'up, as well as a special site (the "Magic Hole") on Shquw'utsun (Mount Tzouhalem). John Peter joins the conversation, and recounts how he worked as a youth for Governor James Douglas in Victoria.

FOR MANY MONTHS QWULSTEYNUM had not been seen about our streets, and then I learned that, in all probability, the familiar old figure in his faded red sweater, with a basket of salmon on his arm, would not be seen here again—for poor old Qwulsteynum had gone blind.

"Him eye lost!" his wife explained. "Ahh, too bad!"

As a young man Qwulsteynum was known up and down the coast as a mighty paddler and, as captain of the Kuper Island racing canoe, brought his crew home triumphantly after many a race. Hence his title of "Captain" Mo-Yez.

During the Summer I saw him taking part in one of the Indian dances at the Sweet Pea Festival at Duncan. As he was led forward by his chief, Edward Hulbertsun,[326] and stood listening on a heavy walking stick, his fine old head turning this way and that as he sang the medicine man's song in a voice that was wonderfully true and strong, one wondered how many amongst those watching him realized that the plucky old fellow could see none of the swaying, shuffling figures about him and had no idea of the crowd of interested onlookers. It was not until his song was ended, the last dancer had disappeared into the tent, and Qwulsteynum was left alone, hesitating, while his chief came to lead him off, did one realize that he was totally blind.

I saw him a few weeks ago at Porlier Pass (Cowichan Gap), where he spends the greater part of the year, occasionally moving to Hwts'usi', the reserve at Bonsall's Creek, and it was while at the pass that I heard the story of how, not so long ago, Qwulsteynum woke one morning to find his old wife very ill.

Blind as he was, there was nothing that he could do to ease her pain. He must go for help.

Surely a Divine Providence watched over that brave old Indian as he felt his way over the rocks to where his canoe was kept, pushed it into the water, and set off to seek help at the gas station situated in Anchor Bay, half way through the pass.

How he guided his canoe through the treacherous tide rips and currents—for the tide was running strongly at that time—and how he avoided the kelp beds and knew at what moment to turn into Anchor Bay, will never be known; but the occupants of the station were roused by loud shouts and sounds of hammering, and hurrying out found Qwulsteynum sitting in his canoe shouting lustily and banging upon the wharf with his paddle.

I found him sitting out on the rocks in front of his house, an old hat pushed to the back of his head and his face turned to the wind blowing in from Trincomalee Channel.

"It's good," he said, as I seated myself beside him. "This wind makes me feel good. You know," he added, "my eyes are gone, but I see all the things in here." He tapped his forehead.

"Before you came," he said, "I heard a funny noise, and it made me think a long way back. When I was a young man I heard a noise just like that one, and do you know what it was? It was a xwult'up—a flying man, flying away to look at the world."

"Do you know about those flying men?" I asked him.

"Now listen." Qwulsteynum held up his stick and brought it down on the rocks with a bang. "Don't you talk about those people. We don't like them; we never talk about them. They used to eat the dead. Now—" he paused awhile to let this awful information to sink in, then—"do you know what a man had to do before he could fly—before the Spirit came to him? Well, now, first he would eat and eat until he could not move, and after that he would sleep. For four months he would sleep, and at the end of every month he would turn over. The first month he would sleep on one side, next month on his back, then on his other side, and the last month on his front. After that he would wake up so hungry, and he would hurry away and find some dead man and eat and eat. After that he would go back into the mountains and wash, and wait for the Spirit to come to him.

"Our people never did that," he told me. "Only those North people could fly; the Cowichans never ate their dead."

"Sometimes a Cowichan would marry a woman from the North people; then sometimes their boys would fly—a little, but the Cowichans got ropes of skin and tied them to poles, so that they could only fly round and round, and not get away.

"See now!" he suddenly exclaimed, "I don't like to talk about those xwult'up. You want a story, eh? Well, wait, I must remember."

He pulled his hat well over his eyes and sat very still, remembering. Then he put his hand on my arm.

"Listen!" He spoke in a whisper. "I will tell you of something that no white man knows about. Even our young people do not know of this." He leaned towards me, and I felt that he was trying—oh, so hard—to see my face. "You think that will be a good story?" he asked.

"Qwulsteynum," I told him solemnly, "I think it will be my best story."

"Aaha!" His face broke into smiles. "Now listen. You have seen that mountain near Duncan that the white people have called Tzouhalem?[327] Why do they call it that name?" he demanded. "That Ts'uwxilem was a bad man. No good Indians would have him at their houses. He was bad. He stole our women—once he had thirty of our women at his house—and he stole all that we had. He fought the white men and he fought the good Indians. He was bad, and so—" he paused dramatically—"so," he continued, striking the rocks with his stick, "the white men gave his name to that good land."

"Never mind. Qwulsteynum," I interrupted, "I want to hear that story of yours."

Instantly he laughed. "Ah!" he said. "I forgot. When I hear the name Ts'uwxilem it always makes me mad.

"Well, now, long ago, when my father was a young man, all that land at Qw'umiyiqun' was big trees, only Indians living there. Well, there was a little trail going through the trees, just big enough for one man to walk. That trail went from the Indian village through the trees up and up the mountain, until it came to where the rocks go straight up, and there it stopped. Now,"—his voice sank to a whisper—"do you know what was in the rock where the trail stopped? There was a little hole."

Again there was a dramatic pause. "That hole," he continued, "was very, very wonderful. It was a place where the young braves went to see if they would be lucky, to try their luck and to find out what would be best for them to do.

"No man would go alone to that place. Many would go together and try their luck. Now, this is how they would do it.

"There was only room for one man's hand in the little hole, so one at a time the braves put their hands in, as far back as their arms would go.

"The first man would put his hand in and feel about, pick up something and shut his hand tight. Then he would take it out and all the others would come up close to see what had been put in his hand, and all would try and guess what they would see when the man opened his fingers.

"Sometimes there would be a handful of white goat hair. That was very good luck, for that meant the man would have good luck hunting the mountain goat. Sometimes he would find a handful of fish scales when he locked his hand, then that man knew he would be a good fisherman. One day Ts'uwxilem went to try his luck. He put in his hand and brought out a handful of long, black hair. That is why he was such a great fighter, killing people and taking lots of heads with the long hair hanging down.

"Lots of different things they found in that hole, but the best of all was to find a piece of the skin of the mountain goat. The man who put in his hand and found that would be very rich, have lots of blankets and skins and be able to give good times with lots of presents—a great Tyee."

"Who put all those things in that hole?" I asked him.

"No one put them in," was the indignant reply. "They just came there when the man put his hand in. It was just as though there was someone inside that stone who saw the hands coming in, and put a different thing in each hand."

Qwulsteynum looked at me and nodded his head slowly. It was difficult to believe that he was blind. "That is all the story I can remember today," he said. "Soon I go to Hwts'usi' to live. It is a better place for me now that I have no eyes. You come and see me there one day, and I will have another story for you, maybe a better one than the one I told you today."

We were interrupted by a shout, and climbing across the rocks came Saytchletsu.[328] What age Saytchletsu may be I have no idea, but he is a good many years older than Qwulsteynum.

"What are you doing?" he asked after we had shaken hands. "Aha! Telling stories. Well, I can tell you good stories too—old, old stories." He sat down beside his friend and looked steadily at me for some time.

"Now," he said, "did anyone ever tell you how I worked for that fine man Jim Douglas? He was Governor Douglas, and I was a little boy, maybe ten years old. Well, one day I was going along past a nice house and began driving some chickens out of the garden. I went in and helped him drive them away and he patted my head and said I was a good boy. Well, he said to me, 'How would you like to work for me keeping those chickens out of my garden? You come every day and I will pay you two dollars and fifty cents every month.'

"Well, I told him, 'All right, I will work for you.' So every day I sat by that garden with a can of feed, and when the chickens came I put a little feed down, away from the garden, and kept them out without having to work very hard.

"For one month I did that and then the man—he was Governor Douglas—gave me my money and a letter to the Hudson's Bay store telling them to give me a Chinaman's coat that would not be too big for me. Well, I went along and I had to pass a baker's store. The baker called to me, 'Here, boy, come and cut wood for me, and I will give you fifty cents every week and some cakes.' My, I had often looked at his cakes and wanted to eat them, so I told him all right, I would work for him. The baker gave me a buck saw and showed me a pile of wood, and I began to work. I forgot all about Governor Douglas and his chickens.

"For six days I cut wood and then the baker gave me fifty cents and some of his cakes. My, those cakes were good! For three weeks I cut wood for the baker. Then one day while I was working a man came and stood by me, and when I looked at him I saw it was that man, the Governor, and all that time I had forgotten about him. My, I was scared! 'How much money are you getting?' he asked me. I told him, 'Fifty cents every week, and the baker gives me cakes.' Well, Governor Douglas laughed and he laughed. 'All right,' he said. 'When you get tired and there are no cakes left for you, come back and I will find you some work.'"

Saytchletsu shook his old head. "I never went back to work for him," he said. "He was a good man. I often think of him, but those cakes were what I liked."

"Come another time," he invited, as we heard my boat whistling. "I want to remember some stories for you—good stories."

I promised I would come before long, and left the two old fellows sitting together looking away through the pass that they had known for so many years and dreaming their dreams of bygone days.

The "Moons" of the Cowichans[329]

For many months Beryl Cryer had been researching the names for the months, or "moons," of the Cowichan calendar.[330] Her research culminated with her visit to north Galiano Island, when she interviewed John Peter in August–September 1933.

Cryer discovered that, in general, many elders could not recall all of the months. This was due, in part, to the breakdown of the native economy, which was closely tied to seasonal resources. A new moon signalled more than just the arrival of a new month—it marked the appearance of a resource. Cryer was also a little perplexed that different people gave different names for the same month. However, as anthropologist Diamond Jenness noted in his own extensive research on the "Salish Calendar," "each community roughly equated its social and economic activities with a lunar period, and as these activities varied from district to district, and even in the same district, so also did the names of the 'months.'"[331]

Mary Rice, Tommy Pielle, Stockl-Whut, Edward Hulbertsun, Kli-Um, Joe Wyse, Jennie Wyse, Wilkes James, John Peter and Beryl Cryer

THERE ARE FEW OF US, I FEEL CERTAIN, who, at some time or other, have not "cried for the moon," but how many, I wonder, have set out as I did, to search for a moon, and not for one moon alone. I was looking for thirteen moons!

It was Siamtunaat who started me in my search, when, in the course of her story telling, she referred to "Our old-fashioned months."

Of course I had to ask her what she meant.

"Well," Siamtunaat put down her knitting and thought a little; then she took down a gaily-colored calendar from the wall.

"See now," she explained, "here are your months—all with names. Well, long ago my people had something like that, but they had one more than you, because they counted by the moons—thirteen moons—thirteen Lhqelts, and a name for every one!"

"Tell me about them," I begged, but she pursed up her lips and shook her old head.

"I can't memember," she said, and took up her knitting again.

I waited, knowing well that she must not be hurried, and before long my patience was rewarded.

"I can remember some," Siamtunaat exclaimed. "There was Wulhxus, the moon when the little frogs sing in the swamps. And then Liimus when the wild geese fly over."

Followed another long silence broken by the stamping of heavy boots outside, and Tommy Pielle opened the door.

"Aha! My brother will tell you those names!" said Siamtunaat, and, as Tommy seated himself in his favorite corner on the woodbox, she told him what I was wanting.

Tommy Pielle was at once all attention, and the two old people talked together for some time with much shaking of heads and gesticulating. Finally, Siamtunaat appeared satisfied and turned to knitting once more.

"My brother and me," she said, "Can memember a few, but some have gone. First there comes:

"Tl'eqtlhqelts—the long month. After that was—

"Mim'ne'lhqelts'[332]—the son of long month—the cold month. Now comes the ones I memembered, Wulhxus—Little frogs sing in then swamps. Liimus—the wild geese fly over. But some are gone." She shook her head dolefully.

"Just tell me any you know," I suggested, and after some arguing with Tommy Pielle, she continued. "The next we know are after summer time. P'uq'ulenuhw[333] —the moon when the leaves are turning color. Hwisulenuhw[334]—the wind shakes all the leaves from the trees.

"After that we can memember some names, but we don't know what they mean. There is Pune'q[335] and Shts'ul'we'sum[336]—

"Wait," exclaimed Tommy, "I know that one, now you say it! Shts'ul'we'sum—Put the paddles up—that means—put the paddles in the corner and stay in the houses. The moon when it was too cold outside and too much wind, when all stayed in the houses and the old men sat beside the fires and told stories!"

"When did that moon come?" I asked him.

"Well!" They thought for some time. "It was the same time as Christmas," Siamtunaat thought, but both agreed that it came first—was the first moon in the count.

"That is all we know," said Tommy, "but see now. You know that old man Saytchletsu, who lives at Cowichan Gap? He knows all things. Long ago he was a great hunter for the Puneluxutth', and he can tell you those moons—I have heard him talk of them."

"Ah, yes!" Siamtunaat nodded her head vigorously. "That old man is older 'n me. He is my uncle—my mother's own brother and he knows all those old things. Go and talk with him, about those old-fashion moons." I assured them that I would, but getting to Cowichan Gap was not an easy matter for me at that time, so in the meanwhile I decided to collect what I could in my own district, and went to see Stockl-Whut at Qw'umiyiqun'.

"You want those old-fashion months?" Stockl-Whut shook her head. "Now see, my Pappa Loxa, he was chief of all the Cowichans; long ago, he used to tell me all about those old things, but I never listened, I always wanted to be out with other young people."

I told her some of the names I had been given by Siamtunaat and her brother, but she did not appear to recognize them.

"Wait," she exclaimed suddenly, "I remember one that my papa used to say. It was like this, 'Punhwemun,'[337] time to dig the speenhw (Camas). That must be the same time as that month you call 'May,' for that is when the Camas is ready to be dug."

She could remember no more, so I added Punhwemun to my list and continued my search.

Four old people that I visited, around Cowichan, had heard of the moons, but in each case could only remember some of those I already had, Wulhxus, Liimus, P'uq'ulenuhw and Hwisulenuhw being known to all of them.

Some weeks later I went to the Hwts'usi' Reserve. Here Chief Edward Hulbertsun asked me into his house—two enormous rooms—the first practically unfurnished, but the second, where his wife was entertaining two of her friends, was crammed with furniture. There were at least four double beds, several dressing tables and smaller tables, with the usual rocking chairs fitted in where space would allow, and everything piled high with the most amazing assortment of oddments. Baskets and beaded bags of all sizes and of really beautiful workmanship. Several old alarm clocks, baskets of dusty photographs, dancing

260

Mary Rice, Tommy Pielle, Stockl-Whut, Edward Hulbertsun, Kli-Um,
Joe Wyse, Jennie Wyse, Wilkes James, John Peter and Beryl Cryer

masks, piles of wool ready for carding, and everywhere heaps of rags and clothes. The effect was indescribable.

On the walls were enlarged photographs in dingy, gilt frames, three huge clocks—none of them going—and, on a small table in the window, were two shining hand bells.

As I stood beside the enormous stove, having persuaded my hostess not to clear a chair for me, I asked Hulbertsun about his bells.

"You don't know those bells?" he asked in a shocked voice. "You're not a Shaker?" I had to admit that I was not, that I knew nothing about Shakerism.[338] "Well! Well!" Hulbertsun looked at me over the top of his glasses. "Well, maybe sometime you'll be a Shaker—like me. Ah! I am a good Shaker. I look after all my people!" He rearranged his bells and stood back to admire the effect.

"So you want to hear about those old-fashion moons?" he asked. 'Ah! Yes, yes! I know about all those things, and my wife, she knows about them too. Now,' eying my notebook, "you tell me what you have in your little book, then I'll tell you some more!"

I foolishly repeated the eight names I had collected, while the old rogue listened intently.

"Uh-huh," he said as I finished. "That's what you have!—Wait now, I'll tell you—" He took off his glasses and commenced polishing them on a corner of his grimy sweater.

"That Shts'ul'we'sum is all wrong!" He waved his glasses disdainfully. "All wrong! It's not 'Put the paddles in the corner and stay in.' It's 'Put the paddles in the canoes, go out with the paddles!' That moon comes when it is time to get the seals, when the men used to paddle far out, then put their paddles in the canoes and sit looking, looking for the seals to come." He crouched low in his chair and shaded his eyes with one hand. "Now, you put Shts'ul'we'sum like I told you—not that other; and see, that Punhwemun, the moon for speenhw, that's no good." He made some remark to his wife, in a low voice, and turned again to me. "The moon for that time is not Punhwemun. We don't know that word. We say 'Xwe'a'xwtn, the moon of the Oolichans.' And those others about the leaves falling down and the leaves getting another color. No good! All no good! See now," he lowered his voice confidentially, "you come another day and we'll tell you all those moons. Not now, I must think." So, realizing that the old fraud really knew nothing of the moons, I left him and called on old Klin-Um, who lives in a cottage nearby.

Klin-Um sat in his usual place, on a stool, behind the stove, his bare feet held to the warmth, and on the floor, on the opposite side of the stove, sat his old wife, also with no covering on her feet, and smoking a very old and black pipe. She scrambled to her fee, to place a chair for me, while old Klin-Um grinned a toothless welcome, and I could see him listening intently as he strove to learn where I would sit, for he is quite blind.

"Those moons," said old Klin-Um thoughtfully. "I know, I know long time ago, I know all those moons—now all are gone."

"Him too old!" explained his wife. "Too old! All has gone. Tooth gone, eyes gone, inside head gone. He forgets all."

There was a long pause, broken by the old man talking rapidly.

"My man knows just one, no more," said his wife. "He says 'Qwi'lus,[339] berries are ripe now.' But all the others are gone—too bad."

I now had ten seasons, three more were needed.

Tl'utasiye' and her husband, Sugnuston, of the Snuneymuxw, were the next people I questioned. Sugnuston told me he had heard his mother talk about the moons, and tell how the old people and the hunters would watch for the moon to change.

"Now," said he, "I can remember one name she had was Xwe'a'xwtn, the moon of the Oolichans,' but," he added, "my mother was from the Hwmuthkwi'um!"

I told him that Hulbertsun had given me that name, and he nodded his head. "Yes, yes," he explained. "My mother was Hwmuthkwi'um and Hulbertsun's wife, she is Hwmuthkwi'um too!" Here Tl'utasiye' had something to say. "I know one of those names," she said. "It comes after that P'uq'ulenuhw and Xwe'a'xwtn, it is 'Stul'at'luw'—'time to get ready to go for salmon,' the time when all went to the Fraser River for the fishing and for the berries."

"I have 'Qwi'lus' for that time," I told her.

"Not my talk," she said decidedly, "that is another country's talk. Then, after Stul'at'luw', come the two you have about the leaves, and then comes Suyum[340] dog salmon go up the rivers. Now we will think."

They thought and talked earnestly together for some time, then Tl'utasiye' said, "We know more names, but we don't remember what they mean. There are Pune'q, Thluntun, and Tthul'xhumutsun."

"I know!" Sugnuston slapped his knee. "That old woman Siamtunaat,[341] she is very old, I think she will know all these names."

So, on I went to call on the tiny old mother of Quil-Kay-Milth, the Totem carver. I found Quil-Kay-Milth on the beach and together we went to see the old woman. She appeared to be even smaller and more shriveled than when I had last seen her, but remembered me and immediately began to discuss the moons with her son.

"My mother says she can tell you a little," Quil-Kay-Milth told me as soon as the husky little voice ceased. "She says, 'In the Summertime, when it's hot, there was 'Qwa'nu, berries are ripe now.'"

"But," I objected, "I have Qwi'lus for that time!"

They talked it over for some time. "My mother says I must tell you that her names are from the Hwmuthkwi'um. She is not of the Cowichans, her people are a little different from the Cowichans, she thinks. Then, she knows 'Pune'q' that

Mary Rice, Tommy Pielle, Stockl-Whut, Edward Hulbertsun, Kli-Um,
Joe Wyse, Jennie Wyse, Wilkes James, John Peter and Beryl Cryer

means, 'All is put away—nothing showing.' That is in the cold time, but we don't know if it's before Summer, or after. You know," he explained, "My mother is very, very old now, and she forgets. She can remember one more, but says maybe it's not quite right. 'A'qwen, rain has come, water in all the creeks,' and there is Tth'ul'xwumutsun,[342] but she does not know what it means. She says, that is all today, but she will think."

I left feeling somewhat overcome. I had set out to find thirteen names, and here I was with fifteen and their meanings, also three with meanings unknown! However, with the help of Siamtunaat, Tl'utasiye' and Sugnuston, I succeeded in sorting them out and arranging them in their proper order, although there was a heated argument as to whether 'Shts'ul'we'sum' should be last or first on the list. Siamtunaat, however, won the day, the result being as follows:

Those names marked with (H) denote Hwmuthkwi'um, with (S) Snuneymuxw, a branch of the Cowichans speaking a slightly different dialect.

1. Shts'ul'we'sum—Put the paddles up and stay in.
2. Tl'eqtlhqelts—The long moon.
3. Mim'ne'lhqelts—Cold moon, son of long moon.
4. Wulhxus—Little frogs sing in the swamps.
5. Liimus—The moon when the wild geese fly over
6. Punhwemun—Time for the speenhw.
6. Whay-Ah-Whtyn (H)—Moon of the Oolichans.
7. Qwi'lus—Berries are ripe now.
7. Qwa'nu (H)—Berries are ripe now,
7. Stul'at'luw' (S)—Moon when the salmon are ready (Fraser River).
8. P'uq'ulehuhw—Moon when wind shakes the leaves down.
9. Hwisulenuhw—Moon when wind shakes the leaves down.
10. Suyum—Dog salmon go up the rivers.
11. Pune'q (Hwmuthkwi'um/Cowichan)—All is put away—nothing showing.
12. 'A'qwen (H)—Rain has come—water in all the creeks

I still did not feel satisfied with my list, and continued to show it to all the older Indians I met. Very few recognized the names—none could help me with the thirteenth. Finally I decided to cross to Porlier Pass (Cowichan Gap), and have a talk with Siamtunaat's ancient uncle, Saytchletsu, who I knew to be a splendidly reliable old fellow.

"Now wait!" he exclaimed, as I told him what I wanted. "I know all those old-fashion moons, but you must have them just right—no mistakes! Indian Law made the names of those moons—long ago Indian law; so they must go in your little book—right."

He tipped up his chair and leaned his head back against the wall to think; his mouth wide open, eyes shut, and steel-rimmed glasses on the tip of his nose.

John Peter (Saytchletsu) of Galiano Island.

Image PN 6474 courtesy Royal British Columbia Museum.

Suddenly he brought his chair down with a bang.

"I have them!" he exclaimed. "Now listen! These are the moons of the Cowichan Indians, and they are right!—the same as when Indian Law made them."

1. Tthul'xwumutsun—The moon when a little ice has come on the water.

2. Shts'ul'we'sum—Put the paddles up in the corners and stay in the house, too cold to do anything.

3. Pune'q—All things are put away (moon when the fire is put away in its cedar wrapping).

4. Wulhxus—In all swamps, little frogs sing.

5. Liimus—High up, the geese fly over.

6. Xwe'a'hwtn—Moon when it is time for the Oolichans.

7. Qw'asthun—The Lycamas [camas] is ready to be dug.

8. Qw'alantn—Moon when berries are ripe (crab apples).

9. Qalykun—Salmon have come, all creeks and rivers are full.

10. Tum'qwi'lis[343]—Everybody comes home.

11. Stul'at'luw—Rain has come, water in all the creeks.

12. P'uq'ulenuhw—Moon when all leaves turn color.

13. Hwisulenuhw—The wind shakes the leaves down

"Now," he tapped my arm with one thin, brown finger, "put those names like I told you.

"The first to count is Tthul'xwumutsun. The next, Shts'ul'we'sum, that is like Christmas time." He thought a moment.

"What name has this month?" he asked.

"September," I told him.

"Ah-haa," he nodded. "Well, the moon for this month is Stul'at'luw[344]—rain has come, water in all the creeks."

As I told him of my first list, he sat with eyes closed, listening.

"I know some of those," he said, "they are like mine, but some I don't know. You see," he continued, "people in different places speak a little differently, but the moons I have told you are the very old ones—the right ones! Now you told me Tschol-Mut-Son, and Tch-Whol-Honmatchun? Just names—no meaning? Well, I think they are the same as Tthul'xwumutsun, the first month, but maybe the people who told you had forgotten, or have a little different way of talking. Now you have the true Cowichan moons. Put them in your newspaper and say to your people that I, Saytchletsu have told them to you."

Xulqalustun's Fun'ral[345]

Beryl Cryer examines cultural syncretism in Puneluxutth' worldviews relating to the burial of the dead. She describes, somewhat intrusively, the burial of John Peter's wife at the north end of Galiano Island in 1933, revealing that she did not have respect for all native customs. Later, Mary Rice describes the traditional burial of her grandfather at Puneluxutth', circa 1886, and shares some of her own thoughts about the subject.

So MANY YEARS HAVE PASSED since the first missionaries commenced their faithful work amongst the Indians, and so inextricably have their teachings become interwoven with the natural superstitions and beliefs of the natives, that it is today practically impossible to tell where the one begins and the other ends.

As when Iichnawmukw' explained to me that the Rainbow was the entrance to Heaven. "When a good man dies he flies under that, and finds God, who lives in the Sun." And old Saytchletsu, undoubtedly a devout Catholic, told me, "Every Indian knows that Xeel's—what you call God—lives in the Sun (Sum'shathut) and that He made everybody. That is why, when one of my people die, we hold the body, and call—just like praying—to the Sun, 'You sent this body to this place. Now take it back again!' And everybody knows that all people are like the Moon, very small at the beginning, then getting bigger and stronger until grown up; after that getting smaller and not so strong, not so strong—until finished; but, just like the Moon, they come back and start growing again!"

Every Indian will tell how, in the days of old, Xeel's, the great Transformer, came down from the Sun and went about the world changing things, punishing those who did wrong and helping the weak and those who were injured.

Even Siamtunaat, who attends Mass regularly and who is apparently very religious, believes implicitly the story she told me of the healing of old Louie Chuhaasteenxun by a Medicine Man, and described most dramatically the manner in which he used a slhuxun', turning the strip of dressed cedar bark into some curious animal, which showed in how many days old Louie would recover; and how, at the appointed time, the old man opened his eyes and said, "Well, I saw God, and he said to me, 'Go back to the land down there and live for twenty years more.'"

So it is that in many of their ceremonies one finds that curious blending of paganism and Christianity.

When Saytchletsu buried his wife last year, a priest was in attendance at the graveside, but did he know of the ceremony which had gone before?

Scores of relatives and friends had gathered at the little shack which stands up on the rocks facing Porlier Pass, there to wail and mourn, crying to Sum'shathut, the Sun, to take again the body which he had sent to the earth. A bowl of water had been passed around, each person taking the water in his two hands and washing his face, signifying that as their faces were clean, so also were their hearts.

One wonders, did the good priest look inside the coffin, and if so, what must his thoughts have been?

Saytchletsu did not intend his old companion of so many years to set forth ill equipped on that last journey of hers.

There in her coffin she lay, in a new white nightdress literally ablaze with cheap jewelry. Gaudy colored brooches wherever they could be pinned, necklaces, bracelets and earrings. A new shawl was put about her shoulders, and she was then wound in yards and yards of white flannelette. A rifle and shells were laid to one side of her, and her paddle on the other side. Over all were packed dried herrings—scores of them—as many as could be pressed into the coffin. And so he sent her off, prepared for any emergency.[346]

When I last saw Siamtunaat she was feeling very depressed.

"I'm getting old," she told me. "Soon I'll be dead and this house will be empty. You know," she said, "I am having a little trouble with my children. Do you remember that nice rattle of mine, my shulmuhwtsus? Well, that was given to me by my old grandfather, not Chief Xulqalustun, but my mother's father Chief Quyupule'ynuxw. He took off the mountain sheep's horn and put on that nice piece of copper. Well, I tell my children that when I die I want my rattle to be buried with me, so that I can have it always. But the children say that it must pass on to one of them, and then to my grandchildren."

She sighed deeply. "I s'pose it doesn't matter what I say, they'll take it when I'm gone."

She finished the toe of the sock she had been knitting in silence, then turned to me and laid a wrinkled old hand on my arm.

"There's another thing I want to tell you," she whispered. "You know, I'm a good Catholic, and all my children are good Catholics too, but there is one thing I would like—I would like to be buried in the old-fashioned Indian way, like my grandfather Xulqalustun was. Have I ever told you about that fun'ral? No? Well now, this is what my people did in the old days, and the West Coast people still have their fun'rals like this."[347]

She reached into her basket for the mate to the sock she had just finished, rolled them together, and commenced casting on stitches for another.

At last they were satisfactorily arranged and she turned her attention to me.

"My grandfather was a very old man when he died," she explained. "But long before, when he was a young man, he had been taught by the priests and had 'got religion,' and so, when he died, of course my grandmother had to get the priest. But first she called all the people to the house where the poor old man lay.

"He was on his bed with all his blankets folded and put on top of him. Ah! So many blankets—I can't tell you how many; and all his counting balls that I told you about long ago were put on top of the blankets.

"When everybody was inside the house, the women washed the body and put him in a box, and all the people sat around shouting and calling to the Spirit in the Sun to come for the body. After that they carried him along the beach to the long point that runs out into the water at Puneluxutth', and there the priest buried him, with his counting balls beside him, and his people put a little house of cedar planks over him.

"Well, four days after he had been buried, everybody washed their heads, combed their hair and put paint in red and black stripes on their faces, and all went to the beach and sat looking at the grave, and all along in front of them were little fires.

"Now, all began to talk and laugh and tell stories of their old chief, and while they talked they cut off their hair until it was short to their necks, and burnt the hair in the little fires.

"There were three old women sitting there, holding rattles like that one of mine. One sat at each end and one in the middle of the people. By-and-by, after everyone had cut their hair, these women shook their rattles hard and called like this, 'Hoooo-whu! Hooooo-whu!' Everybody jumped up and turned, looking at the water, holding their arms out and with their hands turned up, and four times they bowed right down to the water. Then all threw off their blankets and ran right into the water, and washed and swam about. Then, when all were clean, they put on their blankets and ran home, feeling good and laughing.[348]

"I think that is a good way to have a fun'ral," she said, "That is how I would like to be buried, but I can't tell my family; I have taught my children to be good Christians, and they would laugh at me and say, 'Mother, you are crazy!'"

She knitted rapidly for a few moments, then gave a deep sigh. "Oh, well," she said, "I s'pose it won't make a bit of difference when I'm dead."

"No," I agreed, "it won't make a bit of difference."

Sugnuston Tried to Make Peace with the Haidas[349]

Joe Wyse provides Cryer with more details about the violence between the Puneluxutth', Snuneymuxw and Haida that probably took place in the 1840s, and which had been described earlier by Mary Rice.[350] When the narrator's father, Sugnuston, "was a young man," he had a Haida wife. She missed her family, so he arranged to host them with a special stl'un'uq ("potlatch"). False information, instigated by a vengeful man, led to a bloody Puneluxutth'-led attack on innocent Haida.

MANY MONTHS AGO, SIAMTUNAAT TOLD ME the story of a great mistake made by her grandfather, Xulqalustun, Chief of the Puneluxutth' of Kuper Island, which led to the capture and death of Schlu-nas, one of the Puneluxutth's finest warriors.

A Chief of the Snuneymuxw—for what reason Siamtunaat never knew—had taken a woman from his enemies, the Haidas, and had married her. This woman persuaded her husband to make friends with her people and invite them to visit her.

All went well until one of the Snuneymuxw grew angry at the idea of friendship with the hated Haidas, and, leaving the feasting, hurried to Puneluxutth', where he called upon Chief Xulqalustun to bring his warriors and kill the Haidas as they left for the North.

Xulqalustun, believing that the Haidas were upon a raiding expedition, led his canoes to Snuneymuxw. There they waited in the darkness for their unsuspecting victims, who were leaving for their homes that night.

As the Haidas' canoes left the beach the Puneluxutth' surrounded them, and it was but a short while before not one of the Haidas was left alive.

It was during a later battle, when the Haidas swept down upon the Snuneymuxw to punish them for their supposed treachery, that Schlu-Nas was captured.

Several days ago I heard a fuller account of the events which led up to the slaughter of the Haidas by the Puneluxutth'.

Sugnuston had just returned from a fishing expedition and was resting in a large rocking chair beside the kitchen stove.

"I don't have much luck now," he said with a dreary shake of his fine old head. "I'm getting too old to go far—I must be nearly ninety, I guess. You know," he said, "I can remember when, long ago, the hunters and the fishermen would get up early to hunt food for the tribe. Down to the beach they would go, put their hands in the water and call to Sum'shathut—the Sun—to give them luck, to show them the way, and to keep them safe. Not one man would go until he had made that prayer, and when they came back at night their canoes were always full, right to the top, with fish, deer meat and birds. Now maybe I get two, sometimes three salmon!"

He rocked back and forth, shaking his head sadly, until his old wife bustled into the room, carrying a large basket of carded wool.

"Now," said Tl'utasiye' in a businesslike voice, "who will tell a story today?"

Sugnuston roused immediately. "I will talk today," he said, "for I have a story all ready to tell."

He cleared his throat impressively, crossed his thin legs and settled back in his chair.

"Well, now, this story is about my father when he was a young man and chief of the Snuneymuxw tribe. His name, you know, was Sugnuston, just the same as mine. There has always been a man of that name in our family as far back as we can remember.

"Well, then, once when my father led the Snuneymuxw against the Yuxwula'us, he caught one of the Haida women and brought her back to his home, but he did not make a slave of her; he married her in the old fashioned Indian way.

"That old father of mine was a fine man; he was a good chief and good to his women, and the Haida woman was very happy, but, of course, she missed her own people. After a time a boy was born to them, and then she begged my father to let her go and see her family, to show them her baby boy. But Sugnuston would not listen to her.

"'No, no,' he told her. 'They would not let you come back to me, and I would never see you and our little son again.'

"'If I may not go to my people,' said his wife, 'will you ask them to come and stay with me in our house?' And because he thought more of her than of any of his other wives, he told her, 'Yes,' she could have her people to visit her and he would give a great stl'un'uq for them.

"So Sugnuston called a meeting of the tribe and he talked to his people, telling them that he was going to 'call' their enemies the Haidas to his stl'un'uq, and that there must be friendship and peace, not fighting, for, as they knew, the Haidas were the relatives of his youngest wife.

"Well, I can tell you there was great talking amongst the people, and the old ones shook their heads and said that no good could come of this foolish visit, but Sugnuston would not listen to them but set about getting ready for the biggest stl'un'uq he had ever given.

"All his blankets were carried out and counted into great piles—many hundreds of blankets he had—and beside them were put the cedar pegs—a peg for every blanket—that would be carried in the canoes when they left to call the people to the stl'un'uq, and that would be given, a peg to every man called, so that when the day came for the giving of presents there would be no mistakes made and every man would receive a blanket.

"In the biggest house a great Swha-Khwyn was made—" Sugnuston paused and looked at me inquiringly—"That word Swha-Khwyn, you know what it means?"

he asked. "Well, you see, my father had told the people that there must be friendship, but he was afraid that when all were singing and dancing and getting excited, some might forget his words and do harm to the Haidas; so he had great logs brought in his house and these were put across the middle of the room like a strong fence, with just one place to open and shut and that fence was called a Swha-Khwyn.

"Now Sugnuston took two of his biggest canoes filled with his finest men, and went himself to call the Haidas, and with him he took two canoes filled with presents.

"Other men he sent to call the people from Hwsanets, Leeyqsun, Cowichan, and so right up to Snuw'nuwús.[351] He called all the people to come to his stl'un'uq, and to come with friendship in their hearts for the Haidas. Only the people on Kuper Island, the Puneluxutth', the Hwlumelhtsu and the Yuxwula'us were not called, for they had been to a stl'un'uq given by my father some time before, and must pay back to him before being called again.

"All was ready and the people began to come. First came the Haidas in their great canoes, and at once Sugnuston and his wife took them to the big house and put them on one side of the Swha-Khwyn and shut the timbers so that no man could get in beside them. Then the Chief went to wait for the Cowichans to come, leaving his wife to talk to her people.

"Pretty soon the voices of the Cowichans could be heard coming over the water, all singing together, making hee'hwenuhw, as we call it, and then the canoes came in sight, fastened four together, making big rafts, and all with blankets hung on poles about them. More and more canoes came in until there were hundreds paddling hard to the beach, and everybody was singing and shouting.

"When all had come, my father made a long speech to his people, telling them once more that there must be no trouble or they would bring shame upon him and all their tribe.

"After that he took them into the big house to see the Haidas, and all together they ran in, shouting friendship to their old enemies, and on the other side of the Swha Khwyn the Haidas stood, shouting and shooting their muskets up at the roof to show that they would do no harm to the Cowichans.

"For three days all went well. Each day there was feasting and much talking, and at night the great fires were made in the houses, and there was dancing and singing—ah! that was the biggest time the Snuneymuxw had ever seen.

"The Haidas kept on their side of the Swha-Khwyn all the time, but they had their dances too, and Sugnuston gave them more food than they could eat, and, oh, so many blankets!

As I said, for three days all went well, but on the evening of the third day Sugnuston had the biggest feast and dance in the house where the Haidas were, and after a time one of the youngest men of the Cowichans—a great fighter, whose father and two brothers had been killed by the Haidas—got too excited and began jumping up and down beside the timbers dividing them and calling to the Haidas to come over and fight him.

"Now all the people had qwiqwmus on their heads; that is the name for sort of hats made of long hair tied at the top and falling down over their shoulders, just the same as the dancers wear now.

"Well, at first this young man tried to climb over the top of the timbers, but his friends pulled him back; but later on, when no one saw him, he crawled under the logs and got in beside the Haidas, calling out to them that he was come to fight them, as they had killed his family. The Haidas laughed at him, and some of them caught hold of him by his Qwiqwmus and pulled it up in the air, pretending to cut round his head to take his scalp; but my father ran up to the Swha-Khwyn and shouted to them to put the man back through the logs and he would punish him.

"So the Haida Chief pushed the man back, and before any could stop him he had run through the people who were all crowded together, and was outside in the darkness.

"There he quickly hurried to where his canoe was pulled up on the beach, and putting it in the water he paddled away to Puneluxutth', where he called to the Chief Xulqalustun to bring his best fighting men and hurry to help the Snuneymuxw, for the Haidas were even then in their houses! But not one word did he tell of the friendship between the Haidas and the Snuneymuxw—ah! that man made great trouble, but he was punished, for he was one of the first killed in the fighting.[352]

Q'ise'q and the Munmaanta'qw[353]

Beryl Cryer is directed to Johnny and Rosalie Seletze of Kwa'mutsun in her search to record a complete version of the myth of Q'ise'q. She arrives to find Rosalie Seletze making lunch and nursing her aged husband. Mrs. Seletze, a gifted storyteller, gives Beryl Cryer "the story from beginning to end," in close proximity to where all the events of the story took place.

THE FOLLOWING LEGEND OF Q'ISE'Q and the Munmaanta'qw is very generally known among the Cowichan Indians, the facts varying but little, although I have been given three names for the tribe—the Munmaanta'qw or Stoneheads, Kw'etk'um or Short People, and Smatth'sunts or Hammer Heads.

A curious feature of the legend is that, although the older members of the Cowichans insist that this tribe once existed, they appear to have no further knowledge of them beyond this one story. On several occasions I had been told portions of the legend, but there were gaps in the story; names and places confused or forgotten, and always a vagueness as to the ending. Then one day I learned that Johnny Seletze, of Kwa'mutsun,[354] knew the story from beginning to end, so to Kwa'mutsun I made my way.

I found the Seletzes in a one-roomed cottage built at the back of the great old lodges that stand along the bank of the Cowichan River.

Mrs. Seletze, a thin little old woman in a clean blue dress, with a blue handkerchief tied over her white hair, came to meet me as I picked my way across a series of small streams that ran past her door.

Close beside the cottage were the ruins of a lodge.

"My father's house," explained Mrs. Seletze; "my poor father's house! Blown down in the great wind this Winter. I like to be here, near the house where I lived when I was a little girl," she said. "For a time we have been living over at Green Point,[355] but," she sniffed disdainfully, "the Indian ladies over there were not very nice people, and my good English friends[356] have gone to England, so I have brought my man here."

Her husband was ill in bed. From the doorway I could see him propped amongst spotless pillows, as he ate an orange his old wife had cut up for him.

"He's very sick," she told me, as she broke three eggs into a pan and in some miraculous manner fried them over the top of an ancient heater. "It takes all my time to fix him up, that's why I'm so late with my lunch! Ah, well!" She gave a great sigh. "I take good care of him, then he'll last longer!"

She changed the blue handkerchief for a grubby white hat trimmed with a pink ribbon, which perched on the top of her head in a ludicrous fashion and, carrying her plate of eggs and bread with her, sat down beside me on the platform outside her door.

It was such a peaceful spot. The warm Spring air heavy with scent from the cottonwoods where they lined the river banks in the distance, their sticky buds leafing out into a lacework of softest green, with here and there a cherry tree standing out amongst them laden with snowy white blossom; and, as a never changing background, the murmur of the river as it rippled past.

But Mrs. Seletze had finished her lunch and was ready to talk.

"That story you want to hear," she commenced, tipping her hat over her eyes: "It's a very good one, and it's long, so I'll begin right away.

"Long ago a queer tribe of people lived over near that mountain people call 'Tzouhalem'.[357] They owned all the mountain and a big piece at the bottom called Xinupsum. These people were just like my people only they were short and their heads were made of stone, just their faces being left like ours; and the name they had was Munmaanta'qw, or Stonehead. Well, over on that point—Green Point they call it now—at the bottom of the mountain, there lived another tribe of people like the Cowichans, and the chief of this tribe had one daughter, such a fine-looking girl! One day the chief of the Stoneheads saw this girl and he stole her and took her to be his wife.

"This man already had one wife, a Stonehead woman, and when she saw how much her husband liked his new woman she got mad, and all day and all night she thought and thought of a way to get rid of that girl.

"One night, when all were asleep, she went out to the back of the house and threw herself down in the mud and rolled about in it, then she ran into the house and called to her husband: 'Come quickly and see what has happened to me!'

"All her people woke and ran to see what was the matter.

"'Where have you been?' called her husband. 'Why are you covered with mud?'

"'See,' she cried, 'see what the brother of that young wife of yours has done to me! I could not sleep and walked outside the house and he came after me! What are you going to do about it.'

"Her husband did not wait to hear more. He took his spear, pushed away his young wife, as she tried to hold him, and ran outside.

"Through the woods and out to the Point he ran, never stopping until he came to the house of his brother-in-law. With a great shout, he broke open the door and, as the man and his family woke from sleep, calling to ask, 'Who is it? What is the matter?' he killed them, one after the other, with his spear.

"Well, when the young wife heard what her husband had done, she ran away that same night, and went back to her father's house.

"'Let me stay with you!' she begged him, 'until after my child is born. After that I will make a home for myself.'

"'You may stay,' said her father, 'and if the child is a girl it may live, but if it is a boy, I will kill it, for no son of Munmaanta'qw shall live with my people!'

"When the girl's old grandmother heard this, she told her granddaughter, 'Come and stay in my house until your child is born, and if it is a boy, I will help you to save it!'

"So the girl lived in the old woman's house until one night a baby boy was born to her.

"'Give it to me!' said the old granny, 'give it to me! We must be quick, before your father sees it!' Taking strips of beaten bark, she bound them around the little body, then wrapped it round in bigger pieces, as all our people covered their babies in the old days. Then she took it to her son.[358]

"'See!' she said to him, 'see the fine granddaughter your girl has for you! What good luck that it is not a boy for we could never keep a son of the Stoneheads in our family!'

"The old man was pleased when he saw what a fine baby it was. 'Take it back to its mother!' he said. 'A good thing it is a girl; it would be a pity to have to kill such a fine child!'

"The granny hurried back to her house and called to her granddaughter, 'Come quickly! We cannot stay here, for we cannot always hide from people that this child is a little boy. We must make a home for ourselves far back in the woods, where no one can find us!"

"Well, now!" exclaimed Mrs. Seletze, taking a final scrape at her plate, "Well now, there was just a little light coming into the sky as the old granny, followed by the young mother carrying her baby, started out to find a hiding-place from the tribe.

"When light came they hid in the thick woods which grew close to the rocks where the old stone Catholic Church now stands, then, when night came, out they crept, and, going to the stream which runs below that church, they bathed the baby. The cold water made the baby cry, and some of the people heard it. 'Listen!' they said, 'it sounds as though a child were crying down by the creek!' And that," said Mrs. Seletze, " is why we call that stream Shxuxey'elu or 'Cry Creek,' and do you know"—she tapped my arm with a thin brown finger—"in the old days—and when I was a girl—no young wife would ever drink water from that stream; if she did, her babies would be poor, crying children!

"Well, so they went on, walking, walking at night and hiding in the daytime. The second night they stopped at another stream and again they washed the baby. Now the old woman had carried with her a big clam shell to dip water in, so that the baby could drink, and at this stream she left the shell behind and it turned into stone and do you know that all these years there has been a big stone up there beside the stream, just like a shell, but my husband tells me that now it has gone. I s'pose," she added with a shrug of her shoulders, "that some lady has got it in her garden to put a flower in. But because of that one shell, that creek has always been called Ts'e'witun—like a basin.[359]

"At last they got to a bigger stream, and up this they they walked until they came to a good clear place beside the water. Here they made a little house of cedar branches and began beating more cedar bark to wrap the baby in.

"'We will call him Q'ise'q, 'said his mother, 'and we will take such care of him that he will grow to be a fine man.'

"So every morning his granny took Q'ise'q down to the stream to bathe him. On the way she gathered boughs of hemlock and, dipping these in the water, she rubbed his little body all over—for hemlock makes a man very clean and strong—then she shook out the branches and piled them on a big rock. The first morning after she had washed him, she shook the branches as I have told you, and as the drops fell back into the stream they changed into big, fat trout!

"'We are sent here to feed you,' said the first trout as it fell, and after that there were always plenty of fish in the stream for them to eat. After a time the trout swam back and back along the stream until they came to a lake, and ever since then there have been trout in the stream we call 'Jaynes' Creek, and back in

Kwa'mutsun Lake.[360] And do you know"—she wiped her plate carefully with a small crust and threw it to some chickens scratching beside us—"do you know, ever since that time, some of the men of our tribe have gone up to that same place to bathe and rub themselves with hemlock, and they have always piled their branches on the big rock, until now there is a great, high pile of rotten boughs lying there. Even at this time there is an old medicine man, a doctor, who goes to bathe up there, and the big rock is still called Q'ise'q's Rock!

"When he was three or four years old, Q'ise'q's mother made him a little bow and arrows, and with these he killed small birds which they ate, but he always kept the skins, with the heads and the wings still joined on, and stretching them on sticks, put them in the sun to dry, then laid them carefully away.

"Later his mother made him a larger bow and he shot deer and elk. The skins of these animals he dried and put on poles, making a nice warm house, with a little fire on the floor in the middle.

"When they dried the deer meat he kept the sinews, and taking some apart used them to sew his bird skins together into a sort of cloak, with places for his arms so that when he held his arms out it looked as if he had wings. And, ah! this cloak was beautiful with so many bright feathers of every color shining upon it, and Q'ise'q felt very proud when he looked at it.

"He had now the feathers of every kind of bird but one sewn on it. That one was the eagle, and although he had tried many times, he had never been able to kill one of the great birds. But he felt he must have some eagle feathers, and at last thought of a plan.

"Taking his big bow he killed an elk, and, after taking out all the inside, he pulled it to a clear space near where the church called St. Peter's is built—and then crawled inside the animal's body and waited. Very soon an eagle, seeing the dead elk lying on the ground, came flying round. Lower and lower it came. Q'ise'q waited until it was close to the body, then he reached out and caught it by the neck, and very quickly killed it. It was a big white-headed eagle with a fine white tail, and when he had dried the skin, Q'ise'q sewed it on his cloak. Now the cloak was finished, and putting it on, Q'ise'q walked through the woods thinking."

Mrs. Seletze stopped abruptly. "Do you know what he was thinking?" she asked. "No? Well, I'll tell you. You see, whenever Q'ise'q went hunting his mother always said to him, 'Go that way,' and pointed back to the lake. 'Never go near the sea water.' But she would never tell him why he must not go. Then another thing, whenever he asked about his father and why they lived alone, never seeing other people, she would stop him quickly. 'Don't ask me,' she would say. 'Your father was a bad man. If his people saw you, they would kill you. We must always live here by ourselves.'

"So Q'ise'q walked along, thinking. 'Now I am grown and have my spear and my big bow and arrow, I'll go over that way and see what other people look like, and perhaps I will be the one to do the killing.'

"So he walked on until he got to the place where the old stone church is built, and there he saw a lot of men running about playing a game with sticks and a round piece of wood, and he saw that these men had heads made of stone. Well, he watched them for a while and then he went back to his mother and told her about them.

"'Ah!' she said, 'those are your father's people, the Munmaanta'qw. If they get you they will kill you,' and she begged him never to go there again.

"Now Q'ise'q made up his mind that he would kill all those Stonehead people, but he knew that before he could do it he must be very strong and well. So every morning he would bathe and rub himself with hemlock boughs and he would lie in the sun at that place where St. Peter's Church is now, and would think how he was going to kill all those men. Well, one day he put on his feather cloak and lay out in the sun, as I have said, and after he had been there a little time he heard a voice in the air talking to him.

"'Give me your cloak and I will give you mine,' said the voice.

"'No,' said Q'ise'q, I made this myself and I want it.'

"'Take mine,' said the voice again. 'Change with me, mine is better than yours.' But Q'ise'q would not listen, and went home.

"A few days after that, he was lying in the same place when he saw something away off, flying towards him. He lay watching it, wondering what it could be. It looked like a line of red coming across the sky. When it got near him, Q'ise'q saw that it was a flying man dressed in a cloak like his, but very red, and he knew that this was s-hwu-hwa'us (Lightning) who had been talking to him.

"'Try my cloak, Q'ise'q,' said the man. 'If you will wear it you can fly all over the world and no one can see you when you have it on, for it is a Spirit cloak.'

"'Well,' said Q'ise'q, 'I'll try it.' So they changed cloaks, and Q'ise'q found he could fly right up in the air just as s-hwu-hwa'us had done. 'It is a good cloak,' he told the man. 'I will change with you.' So s-hwu-hwa'us flew away in Q'ise'q's feather cloak.

"Now Q'ise'q in his new cloak flew high up over the trees and then down to Xinupsum, and there were the Stoneheads playing their game. Q'ise'q flew right down beside them, but as s-hwu-hwa'us had told him, they could not see him; they could only hear the noise he made going through the air.

"After that Q'ise'q saw s-hwu-hwa'us again, and this time the man showed him how to make all kinds of medicines—poisons to kill people, or to turn people to stone, and others which would make them come alive again.

"Now Q'ise'q was ready to go after the Munmaanta'qw; but first he must have a strong club. He got a piece of yew and made a great club; then, putting on his cloak, he flew up into the air and then down past a big stone, hitting it as he passed. Ah! the club was not strong enough; it had split in half. Now he got a piece of hard hack [spirea] and made another club. Again he tried it on the stone, and this time the stone split in half and there was no mark on his club.

"The next day he put on his Spirit cloak and, taking the club, he flew over Xinupsum, and, as before, the men were playing with the ball. Down flew Q'ise'q amongst them and quickly hit them as they passed him; right on the heads he hit them, breaking them in half as he had broken the rock. The Munmaanta'qw could hear the noise of his club, but they could not see him, and in great fear they ran away to their homes. Two or three times Q'ise'q flew over Xinupsum and each time he killed a lot of the men. Then those who were left talked together, trying to think how they could please this Spirit that came amongst them and killed so many. They agreed to give him one of their girls, so all the girls put oil on their heads and made themselves look nice and had to sit in front of the houses waiting for Q'ise'q to come.

"Well, there was one little girl sitting there who had no oil on her hair, so that it hung down over her face, and she had not washed and did not look nice. The girls made her sit at the end of the row, and all laughed at her, telling her that she would not be taken by the Spirit. While they were talking, Q'ise'q flew down by them and listened to their talk, and when he saw the dirty little girl crying, he picked her up and carried her off to his home.

"After that, he went over and killed all the other Munmaanta'qw and told his mother, 'All those people are dead now; there is nothing for us to be afraid of.' So for a very long time Q'ise'q and his wife, his mother and his granny, who was now a very old woman, lived in the house back beside the stream.

"One day Q'ise'q heard a noise of someone calling, and, following the sound, he went down by the old village of Xinupsum; from there he saw a canoe coming over the water without being paddled and in it were three men.

"Now, Q'ise'q had heard that a man called Xeel's was going round turning people into stone and changing the world, so when he saw the men, he flew home as quickly as he could to get his medicines.

"He told his family that he was going to fight Xeel's with the medicines; but he said to his mother and granny, 'First, I must find out whether my medicines will really turn people to stone. I will try it out on you,' and he shook some of the poison on to them.

"At once the poor women turned into rock, and, very pleased to find that his medicine was all right, Q'ise'q shook the life-making medicine on them and they came alive again.

"Now, the three men came along, and the first one called, 'Is that you, Q'ise'q?'

"'Yes.'

"'You staying here?'

Johnny Seletze, Rosalie Seletze and Beryl Cryer

"'Yes.'

"'Well, I'm going about turning people into stone, so that there can be more islands in the sea, and to make the rivers run in different places. I am going to try my medicines on you.'

"'Try my mother first,' said Q'ise'q. So Xeel's shook some on the mother and turned her into stone, and at once Q'ise'q turned her back. Now, Q'ise'q and Xeel's began fighting, throwing the poisons on each other, and all the time Xeel's drove Q'ise'q and his family back and back, until they came to Kwa'mutsun Lake, and their poor Q'ise'q found that he had no medicine left.

"'You have us,' he said to Xeel's. 'Put my mother and granny at the end of the lake, my poor wife in the middle, and I will be at the mouth of the stream.'

"And," said Mrs. Seletze, "I and my man have seen him. All our people know where he is. Deep in the water, there he is, just a big stone, and at that place the water never freezes, never, not even when the Winters are coldest. My man tells me that no one has ever seen that place with ice on it."

Mrs. Seletze got to her feet. "That is the end of my story," she said; "but if you will come again, I would like to tell you another. I have lots of good stories and my sick man would like to help me remember them."

She walked out to the river bank with me, and held my hand in both of hers as I said "Good-bye."

"I have a new friend," she said. "I will not forget you, and you have a new friend, too. That is good."

She laughed and waved her tin plate to me as she turned to go back to that poor, sick husband of hers.

Tales of Sheshuq'um[361]

Sometime during the summer of 1934, Mary Rice moved from her cabin at the edge of the Halhed property in Chemainus to be with her son's family. Beryl Cryer visits her one last time in her old home, and finds her preoccupied with work and her brother's domestic problems. As usual, she makes time for Cryer to record a Puneluxutth' version of an ancient myth connected to a place called Sheshuq'um 'wide open mouth' on Sansum Narrows, opposite Salt Spring Island.

SIAMTUNAAT HAS MOVED. "I'm too old to live by myself!" she said with a mournful shake of the head. "I am an old, old woman now! But," her eyes twinkled merrily, "I don't look so old; if I wasn't so fat, I guess people'd think I was a young woman!"

She spoke truly, for, although her hair is quite white, her cheeks are round and unwrinkled, and her eyes as bright as they ever were.

"I'm going over near my son," she said, "then my family can take care of me, and I can see my grandchildren every day." So, along with her feather mattresses, blankets and mats, her innumerable baskets, shawls and sacks containing who knows what treasures, Siamtunaat moved.

I saw her one afternoon before she left; her old brother was again visiting her, and Siamtunaat sent him off, as soon as I arrived, to gather wood from the beach.

"That poor man!" she exclaimed, as she watched him saunter slowly away. "Such trouble he has always had with his wives! You remember when his first old wife died, he came and lived with me? Then he went to Yakima and got himself a woman, but she was no good—so lazy! and, ah, so dirty! But he kept her and was a good man to her, but after he had bought her a lot of clothes at a secondhand store, she went away and he could never find her! And now, look at him!" She waved a wrinkled hand in the direction of the love-lorn Tommy Pielle. "Look at that man! He got another woman to take care of him; and what does she do?" She questioned fiercely, "Nothing!—just nothing! All day that woman sits making baskets! My poor brother comes in—'Where's my clean shirt?' he asks. 'There's no clean shirt!' She tells him.

"'Where's my dinner?' 'I haven't time to cook your dinner!' she says.

Siamtunaat put a hand on my arm. "What do you think of that?" she questioned.

"Did she make good baskets?" I asked.

"'Wee—ell!' Siamtunaat drew in her lips and raised her eyebrows. "Pretty good—yes, pretty good baskets, but Tommy Pielle took that woman to keep house for him, not make baskets. So now, she has gone back to her home, and that poor man has to do his own cooking. So I said to him, 'Come and stay with me until I get moved.' But I said to him, 'You will have to work for me, not walk about talking all day."

Siamtunaat shook out the sweater she had on her lap and did some careful measurements with her thumb, before repeating the handsome arrow-patterns she had worked into a band at the bottom.

"That's all right!" she exclaimed. "Now I can talk again."

Before I go away I want to tell you about a big stone thing that is near Maple Bay.

Now you must go in a boat through Sansum Narrows, to Maple Bay—Hwtl'upnets we call it, and that name means a deep bay.

You must go across the bay, and there on the point that is nearest to Cowichan Bay, is a great big stone.

"Well, you get out of the boat and look at that stone, and from one place, you will see that it is like a great stone face with the mouth all broken and gone. The name of that stone is Sheshuq'um.

"In the long ago days it was only the very bold Indians who would try to go past Hwtl'upnets, for, do you know!"—Siamtunaat's eyes were very round and she lowered her voice to a whisper, as, putting down her knitting, she leaned towards me—"Sheshuq'um was alive! Yes!" she nodded emphatically.

"That great head was alive! He couldn't move, but he was alive like a man. He could open his mouth and shoot out a great, long tongue that reached right across to Saltspring Island. If any Indians were foolish enough to try and paddle past, out would come the great tongue, curl around the canoe, and into Sheshuq'um's mouth it would go! And those Indians were never seen again!

"Sometimes they would wait until it was dark, and then, softly, the canoes would drift down with the current, keeping close to the rocks where nothing would be seen; but it was no good, that awful Sheshuq'um always knew, and just when they thought they were safe the canoe would be taken from the water and they were gone! Once, my old grandmother told me, as the great tongue took hold of a canoe, lifting it high in the air, one of the men jumped down into the water, but it was no good; the tongue threw the canoe back into Sheshuq'um's mouth and quickly dipped into the water and caught the poor man as he was swimming to safety!

"Now, over near the Fraser River there lived a very big man. His name was Smaqw'uts, that means; a strong man! He was the biggest and the strongest man that the Indians had ever known.

"This man heard one day that a strange person, a kind of spirit, called Xeel's, was going about the country changing everything; and he did not think that sounded right, so he told his friends, 'Just wait until that man comes! I will kill him.' So he cut a great branch of a yew tree and made himself a sling.

"One day the people told him, "That Xeel's is coming this way. He has been up near Shts'um'inus,[362] and over to Hwlumelhtsu[363], turning people into stone. Today they say he is going to Hwtl'upnets! Now, Smaqw'uts! Show us what you can do! Kill this man!

"So Smaqw'uts took his sling, and he picked up the largest stones that he could find, and, aiming in the direction of Hwtl'upnets, he shot.

"Now you see," explained Siamtunaat, "Smaqw'uts was so far away from Hwtl'upnets, that he did not really know just where to aim, so he turned his sling in different ways, and shot and shot, until all his stones were used up

"'Now!' he called to his friends, 'Let us go and see how that man Xeel's is feeling!'

"Away they went to Hwtl'upnets and, as they went, they saw the big stones that Smaqw'uts had shot, lying along the beaches.

Siamtunaat paused. "Now," she said, "whenever you see a big stone up on a point, or lying by itself on a beach, you will know that it is one of the stones Smaqw'uts shot when he tried to kill Xeel's.[364]

"Well, Smaqw'uts and his friends went along, but they couldn't see anything of Xeel's, but when they got to Hwtl'upnets, there they saw Sheshuq'um with his mouth all broken.

"'See what you have done!' shouted his friends. 'You have broken that Evil Thing's face! That is better than killing Xeel's!'

As they stood talking they saw a strange man walking along the rocks. 'Look!' said one, 'Maybe this man is Xeel's! Wait and see what Sheshuq'um does to him, for although you have broken his mouth, he is not dead.' Well, the man walked along until he got close to the great head.

"'Look out!' shouted Sheshuq'um. 'If you move I will put out my tongue and eat you!' Xeel's shook his head.

"'No!' he said, 'you will never put out your tongue again, but you will stay here looking across the water as long as men shall pass this way, but never again will you do harm to anyone!' And he put out his hand and turned Sheshuq'um into stone, and there he sits for all to see as they pass along that way, but, as Xeel's said, never again will he do harm to anyone."

Memories of Ts'uwxilem[365]

When Beryl Cryer visited Johnny and Rosalie Seletze to learn the story of Q'ise'q, Rosalie also gave her information about the famous warrior Ts'uwxilem (circa 1820–1849). In the 1930s Ts'uwxilem (Tzouhalem) was a well-known native historical figure among Hwunitum', and the subject of much popular writing.[366] Usually described as a maniacal Indian warrior, Hwunitum' writing reinforced racial stereotypes and overlooked much of the historical man—a powerful indigenous leader with strong guardian spirits. There are several W'sanec and Hul'qumi'num histories about him,[367] but Rosalie Seletze's account, recorded by Beryl Cryer, is the only Ts'uwxilem account given by a known relative.

After Ts'uwxilem's mother and brother are killed by Haida, his grandmother trains him to be a warrior. Some events in his life are described, including his death at Hwlumelhtsu on Kuper Island.

TWO MORE OF MY INDIAN STORY-TELLERS have gone. Johnny Seletze,[368] after a long illness, died during August, and his old wife, having nursed him faithfully to the end, followed him a few weeks later.

I last saw her in the Spring, when she told me the legend of the Munmaanta'qw—the Stonehead Indians; and, with great pride, claimed Ts'uwxilem as a relative.

"That poor man!" she exclaimed. "He was not all bad! Now you hear people say, 'Oh, that Ts'uwxilem, he was no good. Always killing people! Stealing woman; doing all things that are bad!' But it was not all his fault. I will tell you about him.

Ts'uwxilem's father was a Kwa'mutsun man, but his mother came from Qw'umiyiqun'. One night there was a great storm. Not as bad as the one we had last Winter. But there was thunder and the sky was like fire, and such a wind! Well, that night Ts'uwxilem was born.

"When his father saw him he shouted in anger. 'Ah! see what the spirits have sent me! This will never be a man. Throw it out on the shell piles.' And he tried to take the baby to throw it away, but his old mother caught his arm.

"'Leave the child!' she said. 'He is the strongest baby I have ever seen; indeed, he will be a man and a fighter. Leave him and see!'

"You know," Mrs. Seletze exclaimed, "that poor baby was not like other children. He was very small, but his head—!" She threw up her hands. "Ah, such a head! It was like the head of a child of two years—so big, and like a bad spirit to look at!"

"Well, when Ts'uwxilem was about three years old a baby brother was born, and, when this child was only a few months old, the Haidas, those cruel Indians from the North, who were always fighting with my people, came suddenly upon the village when many men were away, and, after some fighting, carried off a lot of women and children. Among them Ts'uwxilem's mother and little brother.

"Ts'uwxilem was not taken; for when the Haidas came he was back in the woods looking for berries with his granny, and they kept hidden until the great canoes had paddled away. My mother told me how the old granny said they peeped out when the canoes were leaving and saw the poor women sitting with their long black hair tied around the sch-wyltz (thwarts) of the canoes; for, if they were not fastened in that way, they would throw themselves into the water and drown, and the Haidas would be without slaves.

"Away they paddled, and, when they had got as far as Sansum Narrows, Ts'uwxilem's baby brother began to cry.

"'Stop that noise!' shouted one of the Haidas, and he kicked at the baby. Louder and louder the baby cried until at last a man caught hold of it by its legs and threw it far out into the water.

"How the poor mother cried when she saw her little one left behind in the water! She screamed and tore at her strong black hair, but it was tied tightly and she could not get free. Still she cried and struggled, and at last a Haida took his knife, cut her hair, and threw her out of the canoe, and on they paddled, leaving her to struggle and drown as her baby had done. Soon after that a great wind began to blow, and paddling to the shore, the Haidas camped for the night, waiting until the storm had passed. That night one of the women got away, and, after walking and walking, keeping near to the beach all the way, she at last got back to

Kwa'mutsun, and here she told them how the Haidas had thrown Ts'uwxilem's mother and brother away into the water.

"Well, Ts'uwxilem's old granny took him to live with her, and every day she told him how his mother had died, and made him promise that some day he would fight the Haidas and pay them back; and she taught him how to bathe himself every day, rubbing his skin with hemlock boughs, and to run in the woods and away back in the hills where the spirits would come and talk to him. 'You must be a fighter!' she would say to him. 'Trust no man!' And because he looked like a bad spirit with his big head and ugly face, everybody made fun of him, and I think that made him bad tempered, so that when he grew up he thought that everyone was against him, and he would fight or kill all those who would not do as he wished.

"Some say." She leaned towards me confidentially. "Some say that when he was very small he would get up in the night when all in the house were asleep, and would creep to the fire that was always burning in the middle of the floor, and he would take the hot ashes and eat them, and that is why he grew to be so fierce, and such a fighter.

"But," she laughed, "I don't think that can be a true story. But all know that he was a great fighter and never knew fear, and that he made much trouble among his own people, taking away men's wives, and killing those who had been his friends if they came after their women; so that at last the chiefs had a meeting and they said that Ts'uwxilem must leave the village. So he was turned out, and after that made his home up among the rocks of Cowichan Mountain and that is why that place is called Mount Tzouhalem.

"My mother often used to talk about Ts'uwxilem because he was her relation, and she told me how he wore his hair long, but used to fasten it on top of his head with sticks, and in his hair—Do you know what he had? A snake! There, twisted in his hair was a live snake! He said it was a spirit that helped him kill anyone who would not do as he liked. He would take the snake off his head and put it about his arms and neck, but nearly always it slept twisted in his hair.

"'Ts'uwxilem had another thing that I will tell you about, that he always carried, because he said it gave him good luck, and nothing could hurt him if he had it with him.

"One day he was going hunting up Cowichan Mountain and he put on his s'kwutsmin to bring him good luck, and, taking his musket and spear, started off. You know what s'kwutsmin is?" she asked. "No? Well then, wait and I'll show you."

She disappeared into her house and very soon came out carrying a kind of harness made of mountain goat hair. This she slipped over her head, put her arms through loops and adjusted it about her body. At intervals there were clusters of small black deer hoofs, polished until they shone in the sunshine. "We wear this for dances," explained Mrs. Seletze, "but Ts'uwxilem wore it to bring him luck when he went hunting.

"Well, he walked for many miles without finding anything to kill, and at last got right up to the top of the mountain.

"By this time he was tired, he had walked so far; so he lay down beside a log and went to sleep. He slept for a long time, and when he woke up it was quite dark, and a little rain was beginning to fall. He did not want to stay up in the woods all night if it was going to be wet, so he began feeling his way down the mountain.

He had gone just a little way down when right ahead of him he saw a light! Ts'uwxilem stood very still watching that little light and wondering what it could be. For quite a long time he waited, but the light did not move and, at last, Ts'uwxilem crept closer and closer until he could touch it. Very carefully he put out his hand, and in the darkness he felt what he thought must be a root of some kind. He took hold of it and pulled but it was held by a big tree that had fallen across it; so there in the darkness he began turning and twisting it until he had broken it off.

"For some time he sat there, holding the root with the little light on it, and wondering what it could be, and I guess he felt a bit afraid of it, too! 'It must be some kind of spirit,' he thought, 'and, as it has not hurt me, I guess it has been sent to help me!' And, holding it very carefully, he went down the mountain.

"When he got home, he stirred up the fire to make a good light that he could see what he was holding in his hand.

"The flames burned brightly and Ts'uwxilem knelt, where the light was brightest. Now, he saw that it was not a root he held, but a piece of rope made from cedar bark, twisted and woven together, and it was the thickest and strongest rope he had ever seen.

"For a long time he sat there in his house looking at that piece of rope and turning it over and over in his hands, wondering who could have made it, and why it had been taken to the very top of the mountain? Then he wondered whether the spirit was still living in it and he hurried out into the darkness. Ah! Yes! There was the little light! The spirit had not left him, and when Ts'uwxilem saw that, he felt so big and strong, and he knew that whatever he wanted he could have—that the spirit would help him, for he alone found it!

"For a long time he told no one about his piece of rope, but one night, when all the people were sitting about their fires, and the old men were telling their stories, one very old man began telling the story of the time when the great rains came and all the land was covered with water.

"'At that time,' said the old man, 'the people had seen three or four days of rain, but this time the rain came and it never stopped. For days and days the water fell until the houses were swept away and many of the people drowned. When they saw how deep the water was getting, the men got together and began making a great raft. They got the biggest logs they could find and fastened them together with cedar bark ropes, and with smaller poles across them; and on this raft they put their families and as much food as they could get together. Now they all worked together making a great long rope of cedar bark. It had to be very long and very thick, for one end they tied about the raft and the other they took to the top of Cowichan Mountain and there they fastened it about a very big stone. 'Now,' they thought, 'no matter how high the water comes we shall be safe!' There on the great raft the Cowichans stayed. They were always wet, for they had no covering; and they were always hungry, for they had not much to eat and they must make it last. And every day more and more rain fell, and every day the raft rose higher and higher up the mountain, and the Cowichans, sitting on their raft, went up and up until at last the raft was on top of the mountain and floating over the treetops.

"'At last the rain stopped and the water went lower and lower, leaving the raft resting on top of the mountain; and the Cowichans climbed down the mountain and started making their new homes; but for many, many years the raft could be seen up on the rocks, and the great strong rope lay on the ground beside it, until both had rotted away, and now, after all these years, there is nothing to be seen of raft or rope.'[369]

"Now Ts'uwxilem had been sitting with the other young men, listening to the story-teller, and when the old man had finished speaking, he jumped up and ran into the firelight, holding his piece of rope.

"'See!' he called. 'What is this? Come and look, you wise story-tellers! Who says there is nothing left of the strong rope? What is this that I have found high up at the top of the mountain?'

"Then everybody crowded around him, looking, and putting out their hands to touch the thing he held; but he would not let them near it.

"'Keep away!' he called. 'The spirit that saved the Cowichans lives in this piece of rope, and, as it helped my people before me, so now it will make me strong to fight my enemies and it will make me greater than any chief among you!'

"You see," explained Mrs. Seletze gravely, "I think the poor man was always a little bit crazy; his big head made him queer."

"Well, the old men all looked at the thing that Ts'uwxilem held and all said the same, that it was indeed a piece of the rope that had held the raft when the great flood came, and after that Ts'uwxilem carried that with him, for he said the spirit always saved him when he was in greatest danger."

For a little while Mrs. Seletze sat thinking, her old hat perched on the back of her head, and her eyes screwed up as though in pain. "I am thinking what to tell you about that man," she said at last. "Of course, you have heard what a great fighter he was and how he used to go to the North fighting those enemies of the Cowichans—the Haidas. Never did he forget how those people had killed his mother and brother, and every time he came home from the fights with Haida heads hung across his canoe. He would put the heads on pieces of cedar and fasten them high up on poles in the canoe.[370]

"I guess you have read in papers of the time he tried to fight white men when they first came to Fort Victoria? Ah!' She shook her head and laughed. "Ah! that's the time he found that the white men were better than Ts'uwxilem! Their great guns frightened him![371] But tell me, has anyone told you about the time he had a quarrel with a friend of his at Kwa'mutsun?

"This man had just got married to a girl from another place, and when he brought his wife home and showed her to his people, Ts'uwxilem saw her and thought that he would like to have her for himself. You see, he never liked other people to have wives; if he ever saw a good-looking girl, why, Ts'uwxilem had no rest until he had taken her off to his own house!

"Well, he wanted this new girl, and he told his friend, whose name was Tse-Multh, that he was coming to take her away.

"'You keep away!' said Tse-Multh. 'If you come here I will shoot you! That girl is my wife and no one else is going to have her!'

"How Ts'uwxilem laughed! 'Three days from tonight,' he said, 'I will come. Tell her to be ready to leave with me, and, look here,' Ts'uwxilem shook his fist in his friend's face, 'if you try to stop me I will shoot you!'

"'Do you think I will let you take my wife?' shouted Tse-Multh. 'If I find you around here I will surely shoot you!'

"'Alright,' Ts'uwxilem told him. 'Listen to me. Three days from today, I will come, just before it gets dark, and, if I see you about, I will shoot you before you can shoot me! Remember, three days from today, before it gets quite dark!' And putting his blanket about him, he went away.

"Well, for three days, Tse-Multh waited, and he told his wife to keep inside the house, never to go outside without him; but at that time Ts'uwxilem never went near the house.

"It was evening of the third day, and very carefully, and quietly, Tse-Multh crept from the house to watch for Ts'uwxilem.

"There was no one about, no noise of any kind, only the river running past, just as it does today, making a little singing as it touches the stones along its banks; the only things to be seen moving were a lot of dogs of all kinds over by the shell piles, looking for bits of food that had been thrown out; those dogs were always there, and the man just gave them one look and crept on.

"Now, Ts'uwxilem had been wondering how he was going to kill Tse-Multh before he was seen, and after a lot of thinking he got a plan that he thought would do.

"When the third day came, he waited until the sun had gone behind the mountain and darkness had begun to come, then he put his blanket about him, and, taking his musket, started out to find his friend and kill him. From shadow to shadow he crept, getting nearer and nearer to the big shell piles in front of the houses. Very soon he saw a dark shadow moving along the side of one of the houses and knew that just as soon as he could see that it was the right man, he would shoot; so he crouched low on the ground and crept a little nearer, and, as he crept along, with his blanket hanging about him, he put his musket between his legs and lifted it so that it stuck up in the air behind him.

"Now, as I told you, Tse-Multh was watching very carefully, but still he could see nothing that looked like Ts'uwxilem; only the dogs sniffing among the shells, Bye and bye a big dog left the piles and came slowly towards the houses. Tse-Multh thought that it looked very big, but he knew that in the darkness things often did look different, and, as he watched, he could see the dog's tail sticking up in the air as it walked along—and then, even as he looked at it, the dog's tail dropped, the animal stood up in the air, and Tse-Multh saw that Ts'uwxilem stood before him!

"'Ah! Ts'uwxilem!' he cried. But before he could say more Ts'uwxilem pointed his musket and shot him dead!

"When Tse-Multh's wife heard the shot, she ran from the house to see whether her husband was safe, and Ts'uwxilem, who was watching for her, caught her in his arms, put his blanket over her head so that her cries could not be heard, and carried her off to his house.

"And now," said my old story-teller, "I will tell you how Ts'uwxilem died!

"It was like this: Over on Kuper Island there was an Indian village where the Hwlumelhtsu lived.[372] Now, one of the Hwlumelhtsu was a man named Scheylumtun, and he had a big, fine-looking wife called Suma'luya. For many months Ts'uwxilem had wanted that woman, and at last he made up his mind to go and take her. One day he started off with his second brother, a man named Squae-Lem. You know what a second brother is?" she asked. "Well, it means that the two had not the same mother, for, as you know, in those days our men had many wives. Well, away they went, and when they got to Hwlumelhtsu, Ts'uwxilem ran to the house where Suma'luya lived and began singing and dancing, shouting to Scheylumtun to bring his wife out for the great Ts'uwxilem to take away.

"There were not many of the Hwlumelhtsu in the house, and when the heard Ts'uwxilem's voice they ran away and hid, only the brave Suma'luya waited, hiding behind a big post just inside the door. Pretty soon Ts'uwxilem came to the door, looked in, but could see no one. He turned to go away when, quickly, Suma'luya leaned out, and, putting a thick clam stick across his breast, held him from behind and shouted to her husband to come and kill him.

"It did not take Scheylumtun long to get his axe, and with one blow he cut off Ts'uwxilem's head. Later the Hwlumelhtsu sent the head back to Kwa'mutsun, but they kept the body on Kuper Island."

Mrs. Seletze got slowly to her feet and gathered up the shawl she had been sitting on. "I can tell you no more today," she said, holding out her hand. "I have talked too long, but before long I am coming to see you and tell you some more of our stories, for I know so many that my poor husband has told to me."

I never saw her again, for she remained faithfully at her husband's side until he died; and now she, too, has gone.

The Smilhu[373]

Sometime during the winter of 1934–35, Beryl Cryer attended a smilhu (winter spirit dance) held at Xulel-thw on the Chemainus River, and wrote the following account of what she witnessed. She was only vaguely aware of the cultural meaning of the "tamanous dance," as Hwunitum' called it, and had even asked Newcombe in 1932 if it still existed.[374]

In every person there are two entities: the dominant, cognitive, task-oriented side, called sta'al-kwlh; and another side called shts'ulehwum, the spiritual side, that makes contact with spirit power and allows the emergence of s-yuwun, "the Indian dancer's song" and power. Upon successful completion of training, the shtsulehwun becomes a permanent positive presence in one's life.[375] The smilhu, a public demonstration and witnessing of this achievement, became institutionalized in winter feasts. Unlike Homer Barnett and other early anthropologists, who relied on informants for descriptions of the smilhu, Beryl Cryer saw firsthand what she wrote about. Cryer's witnessing, and subsequent reporting, of the smilhu may have been her undoing as an amateur ethnographer.

Beryl Cryer and a friend are allowed inside the longhouse, where they are invited to sit with Ts'umsitun. When he learns that it is Cryer's first experience at one of these ceremonies, he explains some of the activities. In her account, she vividly describes the dances, paying close attention to the time signatures of the songs. As the evening progresses, she allows herself to be carried away into a romantic imagination of the past.

It is not known if Beryl Cryer brought her notebook to the smilhu, but misrepresentation of longhouse ceremonies by Hwunitum' writers, and concerns over the misuse of songs and speeches, had already led to a ban on any writing utensils, cameras or recording equipment in the longhouse.[376]

Even if she did not use any recording equipment in the longhouse, people may have objected to what Beryl Cryer published about this event, and, consequently, stopped speaking to her. Following publication of "The S'mee-Tha" (Smilhu) there was a sudden change in her submissions to the *Daily Colonist Sunday Magazine*. Following the March 3, 1935 publication of this story, Beryl Cryer began to submit old stories from the "Legends of the Cowichans" series, co-written with her sister, Maithal, years earlier for the *Cowichan Leader*. Only five original articles, apparently derived from earlier work, made their way into the pages of the *Sunday Magazine* over the next few years. It was almost as if she had been shunned.

A WEEK OR SO AGO I HAD OCCASION to visit old Quai-Sult, at the Hwts'usi' Reserve. He was not in his little house which stands by itself on the far side of the creek; and I was told that he was at the big dance house, "very busy."

At the dance house I found the old man with other members of his family, busily engaged about something inside the lodge. I was not allowed to go into the building, but from the doorway I could see mighty piles of split maple logs stacked against one wall and, away at the far end, dim figures moving about a smoky fire.

The old man was far too busy to talk to me. "Send me a letter," he said, as he politely edged me away from the door, "then I will stay at my house and talk to you. But here! no, no! I have too much business to do!"

"Are you getting ready for a 'Big Time'?" I asked him. He gave me a quick look and shook his head. "No, no," he said, "we're just busy! that's all." But I had seen one of the boys, standing near, give a quick nod of his head, and the old man's denial had been a shade too emphatic. There was no doubt that they were preparing for something. But so many white people have abused the privileges accorded them by the Indians in allowing them to attend their ceremonies, by supplying the natives with liquor and so bringing trouble amongst them, or by reporting what, to them, appeared to be unseemly behavior, to the police, that they are now regarded with suspicion by the Indians, and are no longer welcome guests at their festivities.[377]

Three nights later I went to their dance at the Chief's invitation.

The dance house is on the Xulel-thw Reserve. Many years ago the Xulel-thw had their home on an island off the mouth of the Chemainus River, the band consisting of three families living in one large house, along the side of which had been painted the picture of a man chasing a whale, and it was from this painting that the band took their name of Xulel-thw, or "markings." As the band increased in numbers some of them left the island and moved up the river and, in later years, when the Government apportioned lands to be reserved for the Indians, the Xulel-thw were given this tract near Westholme, and the combined bands in that district erected a great dance house.

It is no easy matter to become a dancer amongst the Coast Salish. The individual has, generally, been an invalid for a considerable period, or had severe illness and, after lying day after day with nothing of interest to occupy his thoughts, it is either suggested, or the idea comes to him, that he will "make a dance." He lies on his bed, thinking, can't eat, can't sleep, only thinks all the time of the dance he will make, then, when he gets very weak, a spirit comes to him and tells him of the dance he will do. There must now be a time of purifying, of constant bathing and praying, calling on the spirit to help him, until the day comes when the dance is finished, a stl'un'uq is given, and the new dancer is shown to his own people and their guests.

·   *Beryl Cryer*

Many are the spirits that come to the aid of the would-be dancers, and each dance bas its own particular song and rhythm, the dancer's face being painted to represent his patron saint. There are skalathan, the spirit of thunder; s-hwu-hwa'us, lightning; sthuqul'shunum, rainbow; xwult'up, flying spirit—an endless list. There are also spirits of birds and animals, the dance of the woodpecker being, I am told, especially interesting, but I have not yet been fortunate enough to have seen it.

The night was wretchedly wet and dark as we set out to drive the three or four miles to the reservation. Not a light was to be seen about the lodge, and we feared that something had occurred to prevent the dance from taking place, but we soon discovered cars parked in every available space in front of the lodge and along the roadside.

Feeling our way through the dark, we stumbled along a deeply rutted road to the dance house.

Little groups of men were standing about the door talking in low voices. As we approached a man flashed a light in our faces. "May we go in?" was asked. "Sure!" was the reply, and he stood aside for us to enter.

Imagine this great dance house, built of split cedar boards, the supports and crossbeams of enormous cedar logs, the earthen floor beaten flat and hard as cement, and, down the centre, three mighty fires which supplied the only light in the place.

Like all the lodges, it was open to the roof, which towered many, many feet above us. To the left of the doorway was the great pile of maple logs I had seen on my previous visit and here also was the first of the fires, with women moving about it, stirring huge iron pots set about the glowing embers.

Dividing this "kitchen" from the dance floor was a table of rough boards, which ran the entire width of the room, and was set with soup plates, spoons, cups and great piles of bread and butter.

Around the walls was the usual raised platform, divided at intervals by uprights, and seated along this platform were the Westholme Indians[378] and their guests, each band sitting together: the Snuneymuxw, Lhumlhumuluts', Kwa'mutsun, Xwulqw'selu and S-amuna'—some three or four hundred of them, men, women and children.

Several of the bands had hung their sections with marvelously woven swuqw'a'lh, the blankets of mountain goat hair, and all of them were arrayed in their best, the up-to-date dresses of the younger women looking strangely out of place amongst the painted faces, wonderfully beaded costumes and curious head dresses of the dancers.

In front of the platform, narrow boards had been nailed to stakes driven into the ground, and behind these sat men with short sticks with which to drum on the boards when the dances were in progress. Besides these men there were the regular drummers standing about with their shallow deer hide drums held in one hand.

Two enormous fires were built down the centre of the dance floor, the maple logs piled to a height of four or five feet, and about these fires men worked continually with long poles, ever heaping on more logs and keeping those already blazing piled in their place, and, as they poked the logs, great flames leaped up and myriads of sparks flew upwards to the rafters, until one felt that nothing short of a miracle could prevent the entire building from catching ablaze.

High up in the roof were two smoke holes, or kweyulutstun, to allow the smoke to escape, but so lofty was the building that it seemed to me very little smoke found its way to the holes: in fact, when we first entered, so dense was the smoke that it was practically impossible to distinguish figures at the far end of the hall.

As we went in I saw Ts'umsitun sitting by himself on a front bench close to one of the fires. He smiled a welcome and invited us to sit on his bench. I told him that this was the first stl'un'uq I had seen for many years—airing my Indian name for the dance with some pride. He appeared greatly amused. "That word 'stl'un'uq,'" he said, "means when the people are gathering for the dance; now, when they are all inside the house, we call it 'smilhu.'"[379]

Four women now walked solemnly around the floor, their arms slightly bent and held out in front of them, hands with the palms up and fingers curved, and, as they passed along in front of the drummers, they jerked their hands upwards three times, then moved on to the next group. "These women," explained Ts'umsitun, "are asking the drummers to help their dancer."

I had neither seen nor heard any given signal, when suddenly with one crash the drums commenced to beat, the drummers at the same time chanting at the top of their voices. From amongst the Snuneymuxw a man began to groan and wail. The drums clustered in his direction, until at length, the dancer, having worked himself into a sufficiently frenzied state of mind, was helped over the drumming boards by his friends and stood slowly swaying from side to side, all the time groaning as though in pain.

His face was painted in alternate stripes of red and black; on his head he wore his qwiqwmus—a headdress of human hair, falling to the shoulders from a height of about one foot above the face and topped by two large eagle's feathers. He wore a black velvet tunic and knee length pants, elaborately beaded and finished at the knees with large bunches of beaten cedar bark. His feet were bare, but from knee to ankle his legs were encased in tightly fitting leggings, knitted and beaded. All the male dancers in costume wore these curious leggings, some embroidered or beaded, others with a pattern knitted into them.

With feet well apart and knees bent, the Snuneymuxw commenced his dance, body rigid, feet scarcely lifting from the floor.

As I watched his feet, I became aware that there was a most marvelous rhythm in the drumming and chanting. In perfect unison the drums beat out their measure—boom, boom–boom, boom, boom, boom, boom! Over and over it was repeated, two–five, two–five, the men sitting behind their board were all drumming, and everywhere feet kept time, and hundreds of voices took up the chant as the dancer slowly circled the hall. At times he appeared to sway and hesitate as though exhausted, but spurred on by the drummers, he at length reached his seat, was caught by friendly hands and lowered to his place, apparently in a state of collapse, groaning and shaking as though in agony.

The drumming and chanting died away, boys wandered amongst the crowd with buckets of water and a dipper, offering refreshment. Then a girl from amongst the Kwa'mutsun cried out in a shrill, hoarse voice, and, stretching her arms before her, palms up, hands tightly clenched, was helped out to where the drummers gathered about her, shouting and drumming to encourage the spirit to come to her.

Her fawn colored dress was decorated with great bunches of beaten bark tied about her waist, and on her wrists and ankles; her head was literally smothered with enormous tufts of the cedar bark tied on top and falling over her face, which was painted red and black to represent the xwult'up, or Flying Spirit, which had come to her aid in the making of the dance.

There were no less than five dancers representing the xwult'up at this dance, the cedar bark adornments and manner in which the faces were painted alone denoting the Spirit, as in every case the dance appeared to differ. This dance is better known by its Chinook name of Tamanous,[380] but is a greatly modified version of the original performance, which included a disgusting orgy of feasting upon putrid human flesh and tearing apart of the limbs of small babies and sucking their blood, small dogs being also torn to pieces and devoured.[381]

The drums had altered their beat; it was no longer two–five, but had changed to two–three, two–three, and by listening carefully one could trace a weird air.

Slowly, slowly the girl moved, for all the world like a mechanical figure, her bare feet appearing to slip along the earthen floor as she turned this way and that, always with her palms upturned, and fingers curved, a curious tenseness about her entire figure, and, as she danced, the drummers followed after, singing and drumming to spur her on until she fell gasping and crying into her seat.

Between the dances two or three of the women made their rounds encouraging the drummers, and little groups of three or four wandered across to the table, where they were served with bread and butter, tea and a stew or soup made of potatoes, onions and clams.

Again the rhythm altered. It was three–eight, three–eight this time, the beats following more quickly one after the other. The singing grew louder and fuller, everyone who possessed a stick and anything to hit took up the beat until the very air appeared to vibrate. Three–eight! sounded the drums and out leaped a man in a wonderfully beaded suit—the eagle feathers on his qwiqwmus decorated with ribbons of red and white hanging from the tips. About his ankles and wrists he wore clusters of kwutsmin or deer hoofs, polished until they shone in the fire light, and with every move he made, these hoofs shook and rattled, making an extraordinarily sharp and piercing sound. Outlining his suit were hundreds of thin strips of cedar wood carved in a fancy pattern, and these swayed and rattled as the dancer moved about the fires.

The tempo of the drums increased, the chanting grew louder and louder as the dancer increased his pace, tossing his arms from side to side.

The heat from the enormous fires was almost unbearable, and steam was rising from the ground about them, until one felt that the bare feet of the dancers must be scorched as they danced close to the flaming piles.

The night had cleared and the smoke was finding its way through the smoke holes, but all about us ashes were failing, powdering the women's hair, and covering everything with a soft, grey dust.

A dancer from the Lhumlhumuluts was helped into the firelight. He was a broad, heavily built man, dressed in overalls and shirt, with painted face—another xwult'up dancer.

This dance was unlike anything we had seen. The man moved with greater abandon, dancing very close to the fires, springing towards them as though prepared to leap into the midst of the flames, only to fall heavily to his knees, legs apart, arms spread wide.

Over and over he repeated the movement until he had made the round of the lodge. This man possessed a very handsome dancing dress, but, having no intention of dancing, had not brought it with him. However, the Spirit "came to him," and dress or no dress, he had to dance.

In quick succession the dancers followed one after the other, the new dancers appearing time after time, apparently entering more and more into the spirit of the dance with each appearance.

I noticed a young girl smartly dressed in a silk dress of black and green, high heeled shoes and silk stockings, but with her face curiously painted, walking amongst the drummers, encouraging them.

"See that girl?"Ts'umsitun nodded towards her. "That girl was going to die. She was very sick, she just lay on her bed, too sick to get up. One day she was lying there when she heard a voice talking to her out of the air. It was Skalathan, Thunder—the Thunder Spirit. He told her about a good dance he would show her, and do you know, that girl got up and made her dance! She got well and strong, and last year she danced for the first time and showed off her dance to all the people. No, she's not dancing tonight; she doesn't feel good, but she's helping the other dancers."

I watched the girl as she came towards us, up the other side of the room. As she approached her own people I saw her stop, lift her head quickly as though she had been called, then, seating herself on the drumming board, she took off her shoes and stockings, pulled her hair about her face, appearing to hold the ends in her mouth, so that only her face was visible. An extraordinary cry came from her, shrill and nasal; her thin arms were taut before her and, as she got to her feet, the drums crashed out with redoubled vigor.

The beats were now three–five. By this time the spirit of the dance had spread to the audience. All around the walls bodies were swaying, men, with bent knees, were jigging, and all were shouting in time with the dancer.

Many of the men were so carried away that they were prepared to join in the dance and had to be held back by their womenkind, who grasped their belts from behind whilst they pranced and tugged like restive horses.

Watching and listening, we felt how thin was the veneer of civilization! In fact, I began to fear that my own layer was none too thick!

There was a lull in the proceedings, and I looked about me trying to picture the scene as it might have appeared before the advent of the white man with his so called civilization.

The interior of the building, with its raised platform, about fourteen inches high and four feet wide, would have been the same. But in those days the house was a dwelling place, and the platform was covered with mats made from the bulrush, in three or four thicknesses, and, running the entire length of the lodge, behind the platform, was another mat, made in one piece to keep out draughts.

In this mat was stuck the natives' arrows, wool spindles, mat needles, war clubs, etc.

Yet a third mat was spread on the earthen floor in front of the platform and was used to sit upon whilst working or eating, the platform being used as a sleeping place, each family keeping what possessions they had under their own section of platform.

Directly over the fires was a rack, built upon four posts about ten feet high, driven into the ground. This rack was fifteen or twenty feet long and four feet wide, and was made by placing two long poles from one post to the other, and then smaller poles across them, building them up, until fairly close together. On this were put meat, fish and clams, strung on sticks to dry, the rack bring sufficiently high to be out of the reach of dogs, and to catch the smoke without getting too much heat from the fires. To reach this rack a ladder was made by cutting deep notches in a large pole.

The old people love to tell of the days when game was plentiful and the entire building overhead was filled with these racks, laden with good food for the Winter months.

Hung about the walls were the implements used by the natives in their every-day life. Paddles, dip nets, cedar bark bailers, fish spears and herring rakes.

In those days there were no iron pots in which to prepare the feasts, but wonderfully constructed cooking boxes. These boxes were partially filled with water, which was brought to boiling point by plunging in stones which had been heated in the fires, the stones being lifted with the aid of wooden tongs. When the water was hot enough, the meat or fish was put in and left to cook.

As to the audience! The platform would have been filled with natives wearing short skirts of beaten red cedar bark and blankets or cloaks of the hair of mountain goat, or, possibly, similar garments woven from birds' feathers—those of the seagull being the most common. Here and there would be an ornamental cloak of brilliantly hued birds' feathers, but these were rare and only used occasionally. Possibly a few cloaks of the yellow cedar bark might be seen. These would have come from the West Coast, as they were never made by the Cowichan Indians. The dancers were in no case overburdened with clothes, cedar bark, and in some cases skins, being used. The men's hair hung about their shoulders, or was fastened in a knot on the top of their heads, whilst the women's well greased heads were often covered with the down from the breasts of seagulls.

I was roused from my dreaming. One of the dancing girls had brushed against me as she was taken to the table for supper, her headdress having been removed and her face carefully covered with a shawl that none should see her as she ate.

It was getting very late, several parents, having gathered together their families, had left for home.

Suddenly there was a stir amongst the people; more logs were heaped upon the fires, making the flames leap high in the air, the drums beat in quick succession, as all the new dancers leapt out on the floor, each one held from behind by a friend or guardian. Gone were the restrained movements of the previous dances. They all pranced about the fires, the guardians holding them in check with apparent difficulty.

This was, for us, the grand finale, for, as they sank gasping and groaning into their seats, we were told that it was time for us to leave, but as we stumbled back to the car we heard the drums break out again and the chanting rise and fall in time to a new dance.

The Punishment of Spaal'[382]

Beryl Cryer reintroduces her readers to Xeel's, the Transformer, quoting the late Johnny Seletze, and then reprints the story about Xeel's, Qwuni (Seagull) and Spaal' (Raven) from the "Legends of the Cowichans" series, originally published in the *Cowichan Leader* on July 26, 1928. Although Mary Rice provided the story, the narrative style is entirely that of Cryer and her sister, Maithal Ross. As such, the text highlights the considerable difference in style between the earlier material (which is not included here, but will be the subject of another publication) and the articles that appeared in the *Daily Colonist* between 1932 and 1935. The story preserves the key components of the myth to reveal teachings regarding self-interest, greed, the origins of death and other human issues. The anthropologist Diamond Jenness was only able to record fragments of this myth, which appears here in its entirety, as told by Mary Rice.[383]

MANY ARE THE STORIES THAT OUR Coast Indians tell us of Xeel's, that wonderful spirit man, the great transformer, who was sent from Sum'shathut the sun spirit, the maker of all, to go about this world changing things, rewarding the deserving and punishing the wicked. At times he appeared alone, at other times one is told of two, or sometimes four of these spirit men.

"Now that we have been taught," Johnny Seletze explained to me, "we know that those men who came to this land changing things must have been the Disciples, but we have no name for any but Xeel's, who we now think was Jesus Christ."[384]

This story of how Spaal' the raven was punished by Xeel's, was told me by Siamtunaat, whose stock of old legends appears to be well nigh inexhaustible.

One morning, many, many years ago, Qwuni, the Seagull, got up very early to go fishing for herring.

Light was beginning to come into the sky as he pushed his canoe out from the beach, and, as he paddled across the fishing ground he knew that Sum'shathut the sun god, would soon be coming over the mountains, far away, where the sky comes down to meet the water, his colors of red and gold were preparing the way for him, as they moved across the sky, driving the dark night clouds before them.

For some time Qwuni fished busily, plunging his herring rake through the water and shaking the glittering fish into the bottom of his canoe. Suddenly there was a whirr of wings and a great black bird flew down and, perching on the canoe, began filling his beak with the fish.

"Who are you?" cried Qwuni. "Why do you come here stealing my fish?" "My name is Spaal', the raven," the black bird told him, "and I have a family of hungry children at home, I take these herring for them!"

"I, too, have a family to feed," cried Qwuni, "eight little ones waiting for me to return with their breakfast. Go! Catch your own fish, I need all of mine!"

Qwuni flew at the thief and tried to drive him away, but Spaal' was so big and strong that Qwuni could do nothing, and at last was forced to stand on a piece of drift wood and watch while Spaal' carried off all his herring.

It was now too late to try and catch more fish, the herring were all gone, and poor Qwuni flew to his empty canoe and paddled sadly home again.

Every day the same thing happened, Qwuni would get a good catch of herring, and, just as he was ready to paddle home with them Spaal' would fly down and carry off the lot. The little seagulls grew more and more hungry and cried so hard for food, that at last Qwuni's wife set off to see whether she could not plead with Spaal' to spare them even a few fish.

"My little children are starving!" she said. "They will die if they do not get food soon!"

Spaal' only laughed. "Tell your husband to get up earlier!" he told her. "Then he will have time to catch enough herring for his own family as well as mine."

The next day one of the little seagull boys died of hunger.

Qwuni was desperate, and hurried off to Spaal's house to beg for a little mercy.

"Ah, Spaal'!" he called to the raven, "My boy is dead, my little boy! He died because we had no food to give him! And why? Because you, whom I have never harmed in any way, have eaten all our fish, and I had nothing else to give him!"

Spaal' laughed, "I can't help it!" he said."My children must have food, and if I can't catch enough for both families, then yours must suffer! There is nothing I can do about it!"

"There is one thing you could do," replied Qwuni. "You are big and strong, and you can fly anywhere; will you go and fly about the world, and find Xeel's, that great man who can make the sick well and the dead live again? Find him and ask him to come and give my little boy his life again!"

At this Spaal' laughed louder than ever. "Why should I look for him?" he asked. "If I go where men are living the smoke from their fires will get in my eyes and I shall go blind. If you want this Xeel's to help you, go and get him yourself!"

"Who would look after my family? They would all die before I got back, and, think of this, Spaal', who would catch fish for your family if I were to go? You would have to fish yourself!"

But Spaal' only laughed once more and flew away, leaving poor Qwuni to fly back to his house. He took his little dead son and buried him sat beside the little grave wondering how he could possibly find food for his children without Spaal' knowing of it. Suddenly an idea came to him. He took his knife and after a time succeeded in making a bow and arrow such as he had seen men carving. The next morning he set out early, long before Spaal' would be up. Very quietly he crept through the forest, his feathers getting damp and draggled as he stole under the bushes from which the dew still dripped. He had not gone far when he saw a great buck step daintily through the grasses on his way to drink at a nearby stream.

Qwuni took careful aim, as he had seen men do, and shot. To his joy the animal fell dead! Qwuni ran forward and was about to cut off the buck's head when he heard the crackling of branches, and saw a man coming through the woods towards him.

"Good morning, Qwuni!" called the stranger. I see you have shot a fine buck, that is good luck for me, for I am hungry! Let me have the heart and kidneys, and you may keep the rest."

Now, as everybody knows, the heart and kidneys are the best parts of a deer. Qwuni would have liked them for himself and his wife, but the stranger had asked for them, and, after all, thought Qwuni, I can shoot another deer tomorrow, and there is more than enough meat on this great animal for my family for several days. So he cut out the parts that the man had asked for and gave them to him.

"Now, listen to me," said the stranger. "Because you have given of your best to me, I will do good things for you!" and picking up his meat, he disappeared into the bushes.

Qwuni cut off as much of the deer meat as he could carry and hurried off to his home. As he neared the house, he saw his wife running to meet him.

"Ah, Qwuni! come quickly!" she called, "come quickly, for our little son who died has come back to us!" and as she spoke, Qwuni saw the boy whom he had buried the day before come running from the doorway.

"Now I know who the strange man was, who I met in the woods!" he exclaimed, "It was Xeel's! and because I gave him the meat that he asked for, he has given my little son back to me!"

Every day, after this, Qwuni went went hunting and his children grew big and strong, for there were always more than enough to eat in the seagull's house.

In time Spaal' came to hear of Qwuni's hunting and, taking a basket of herring, he went to the seagull's house to exchange his food for deer meat; but Qwuni would not trade with him and threatened to shoot him if he did not leave at once. This made Spaal' so angry that, as he took a herring from his basket to eat it on the way home, he snapped at it so quickly that he bit off one of his fingers! As he reached his house he held up his bleeding hand. "Look!" he called to his wife (for he was a great liar), "See what Qwuni has done! I offered to trade some of our fine herrings for a small piece of meat and see! he flew at me and bit my finger right off!"

As Spaal' could not get Qwuni's meat he decided to shoot some for himself; so he made a bow and arrow as Qwuni had done and set out to hunt for game.

It was not long before he, too, saw a buck feeding under the trees, and, aiming carefully, he shot it through the heart. Drawing his knife, Spaal' was about to skin the animal, when the same man whom Qwuni had seen, stepped out from behind a tree.

"What a fine buck, ah Spaal'!" he cried, "will you spare me the heart and kidneys for I have had nothing to eat and I am hungry."

Spaal' laughed and shook his head. "Why should I feed every beggar who asks for food?" he jeered. "Go hunting for yourself, I have none to spare for you!" and, putting his knife in his belt, he threw the deer over his shoulder and started off for home.

How heavy the animal was! At every step it grew heavier and heavier, until he was forced to stop and throw it on the ground whilst he rested. When he tried to pick it up again he could not move it, so heavy had it become, so he cut out the heart and the kidneys to take with him." I have enough for one meal here," he said to himself, "and later on my wife can come and carry in the rest of the meat."

Spaal' hurried along and when he neared his house he shouted to his family, "See children, what good meat I have brought home to you!" Come and carry it in for your mother to cook!" And he threw the meat to his children as they ran to meet him. But as he did so, he gave a loud cry and shuddered with a great fear, for, as the meat left his hands it turned to stone, and hitting his children, killed every one of them!

As Spaal' and his wife gathered up their poor children and carried them into the house Spaal' remembered that Qwuni 's dead child had been returned to him, and, he said to his wife, "There is nothing we can do for our little ones, but Qwuni got his son back all right, so he will tell us how we can make ours alive once more. Before we go to ask his help, you had better carry in the rest of the deer I shot or Qwuni will have stolen it." And he told his wife where she would find the meat. Spaal''s wife searched thoroughly through the forest but no sign of the meat could she see, and at last she had to return to the house and tell her husband that she could not find it.

"Qwuni must have stolen it, as you feared he would," she said. "It must be there," said Spaal'. "I will go with you and show you the place!" So together they hunted all about, where Spaal' had thrown down the deer, but the only thing they could find was an old rotten log covered with moss. "I don't remember that log!" said Spaal', "I know it was not lying there when I passed through here before, for it was in just that place that I put the meat!" As he spoke he remembered the strange man who had asked him for food, and again he shivered with fear, for he knew that the man must have worked magic with his meat!

"Well!" said Spaal', "we had better go now and find out from Qwuni how he made his boy come alive again. So together they walked to the seagull's house.

"Ah, Qwuni!" called Spaal', "my children are all dead! I want you to come and work your magic, and give them life again!"

"I can do nothing," replied Qwuni. "But when your boy died, how did you make him come alive again?" asked Spaal'.

"I told you," said Qwuni. "I did nothing; it was the great and good Xeel's who made my child live again, but where he is now I do not know!" "Go and find him for me!" begged Spaal'. But Qwuni shook his head. "How can I do that?" he asked.

"When you took all our food and my little one died of hunger I asked you find Xeel's. What did you say? 'That the smoke from men's fire would blind you.' How about my eyes, Spaal'? If I went blind who would feed my family? No! Go and find Xeel's for yourself! I must stay at home!" And Qwuni went into his house and shut the door.

So Spaal' and his wife went sorrowfully back to their home and buried all their children; but they would not let Qwuni rest. Day after day they went to the seagull's house, calling and asking him to help them find Xeel's. And even to this day we hear them calling and begging Qwuni to save their children.

The First of the Shtsuw'athun[385]

This account by Beryl Cryer was probably recorded three years prior to its publication, during one of her frequent visits to Nanaimo in the winter and spring of 1933. The style of writing is quite different, closer to her "Legends of the Cowichans" material, and bears none of the "contemporaneity" and dialogue of voices of the earlier *Daily Colonist* series. Joe Wyse narrates a myth demonstrating the Shtsuw'athun (Tsawassen) connection to Active Pass in the Gulf Islands. Of minor interest are Cryer's hyphenated transcriptions of the English name "Barnacle" and "Shaman" to reflect the way she wrote Hul'q'umi'num' words.

THIS IS SUGNUSTON'S STORY of how the Bar-Nacle man got his wife, and so started that great band of the Cowichan tribe,[386] the Shtsuw'athun Indians at Plumper's Pass.[387]

Longer ago than any can remember, when all this land was forest and no white people had some to take it from us—a large band of the Cowichans lived on the banks of the Fraser River at Chilliwack. Each year this tribe grew in strength until they numbered many hundreds. The hunting all about the village was good, and at no place on the river was the fishing better, so that the roofs of the houses were filled with salmon and deer meat drying in the heat and smoke which rose from the great fires ever burning in the centre of the floors, and there was always food in plenty for the Winter months.

But one year great trouble came to them. The Winter was harder and longer than any they had ever known, and while there was still ice on the river the people found that their piles of food were gone. The snow was higher than a man, and no hunter dare set out to find food, and if he had, he would have found no living thing in sight.

The weaker members of the tribe began to sicken and die, and the little ones were so hungry they cried all day and night for the food that none had to give them.

At last the Chief called his wise men together and for long they talked, trying to think of some plan by which the people might be saved. Far into the night the Sha-Men danced and sang their songs, leaping about the great fires, until tired out they fell beside the burning logs, but none could think of any way in which to find food. At last the Chief had a great meeting and spoke to his people.

"It is no use staying here," he said. "We must take our blankets and go down the river to where the great water lies, for there upon the shore we shall find no snow, and, when the water is far out, we can dig clams for our food. The snow is deep and we are starving, but it is better to leave our homes and try to save our lives, than to sit in our houses and die of hunger."

So they set out; the men taking the blankets and the women carrying the babies and leading the smaller ones by the hand.

In this way they walked for many days, for they could go but slowly, they were so weak, and many died as they struggled along and were left lying on the snow as they fell.

One night, just as darkness was coming the men in front gave a great shout, they could see the water! How those starving people hurried on, stumbling and falling in their eagerness to reach the place where their Chief had promised them food was to be found.

At last they came to the shore, only to find that the water was high up and they would have to wait until it went out again before they could have food.

On they walked to the very edge of the shore, and there, where the snow ended, and the water washed softly, they found great piles of dead star fish and devil-fish, left there by the waves. How those starving people fell upon the fish, sitting there amongst them, feasting until they could eat no more, not stopping to make a fire, but eating the food as it was, like hungry animals.

Now, amongst the people was one woman who tried to eat the fish but could not, for it sickened her, and, as she sat watching her people feast upon the rotten fish, she heard them, one after another, give loud cries and hold themselves as though in pain; and it was not long before the whole tribe was shouting and rolling amongst the fish in their agony, for the rotten fish had poisoned them, every one!

From one to another the woman went, only to find that everyone was dead, and, of all that band who had walked so bravely, the long hard miles to find food, she alone was left.

Leaving her people lying there on the shore, she walked on for many miles until she came to a river and, finding a log, she sat on it and paddled across to the other side. By now she was so weak she could scarcely walk, but she kept on, and again she came to a river and once again she found a floating log, and sitting on it, crossed to the other side. Here she struggled along for some time, but at last her strength left her and she fell on the ground unable to go farther.

As she lay among the grasses on the river bank, Crow, who was flying past, heard her crying and stopped to speak to her.

"Why are you crying?" asked Crow. And the woman told him her story. "I alone of all the band am left," she said, "and now I, too, am dying." "Have you strength enough to live a few days longer?" asked Crow. "If you have, I can find a man I know who will be glad to take you for his wife. Lie here and rest and we will come to you before many days have passed."

Crow flew away, and after resting for a while the woman crawled to the edge of the river, drank some water and lay down to wait for Crow's return.

Now, in a little bay on one of the islands at the place that is called Plumper's Pass, there lived a man called Bar-Nacle. He had no people, and had lived alone in his little house at the edge of the water for many years. To this man Crow flew, and found him on the beach gathering mussels for his morning meal.

"Ho, Bar-Nacle!" called Crow, flying down beside the man, "How would you like a fine woman to keep your house for you?"

"You speak foolishly, Crow," said the man. There are no women in this part of the country, as you know well; I must live my life alone here, until I die." And he walked away from Crow, and went on picking the mussels from the rocks.

"It is you who talk foolishly," Crow told him. "For there is a woman not far from here and, if you would like her for your wife, I can take you to her; but we must waste no time for she is dying of hunger, and cannot live many more days."

"You know a woman who would be my wife?" shouted Bar-Nacle. "Quickly! Take me to her! Hurry, for she may die before we reach her!"

"Get your log and paddle," said Crow (for this was long before our people had learned to make canoes, and had to cross from island to island on logs,) "and I will show you the way!"

So they started out on the log, the man paddling and Crow sitting on the end of the log showing him the way. At last they came to the river bank where the woman lay. She was nearly dead, but Bar-Nacle had food with him, and after she had eaten a little he carried her to this log and laid her on it, then, with Crow sitting beside her, he started out for his home.

For many days the man fed and cared for the woman, until her strength had returned and she was able to tell him her story.

"I am alone," said Bar-Nacle, "and as you have no home to go to, I will make you my wife and you will live here in my house and be the mother of my children." So the woman stayed with Bar-Nacle, and their children were the first of the Shtsuw'athun who numbered many hundreds in those long ago days.[388]

Legends of the Swayxwi[389]

The swayxwi is one of the most significant features of Central Coast Salish ceremony and ritual. Ownership of the costume and songs is hereditary. The swayxwi is, first and foremost, a "cleansing instrument," and the ritual purpose of its performance by xwaayxwi (the men who dance the mask) is purifactory.[390] Beryl Cryer undoubtedly received much of her information about the swayxwi masks used in this ceremony from Mary Rice, whose mother, Solowtunaht, with her two sisters, brought the first mask to Kuper Island from Hwmuthkwi'um. Another Puneluxutth' woman, Tsunatunaat, explains how the swayxwi regalia and ceremony came to her family at Puneluxutth' on Kuper Island, and she describes some of the contexts in which it was used. She also tells how the swayxwi came to the people of the Alberni Valley. Although this article appeared in 1936, it is evident from correspondence with William Newcombe that Beryl Cryer had the notes and general information for the piece in hand by October 1933.[391] Beryl Cryer was particularly proud of the fact that the anthropologist Wilson Duff "used my material on the Schwy-Why mask as a Thesis for his M.A. [Master of Arts thesis]."[392]

OF THE MANY LEGENDS ATTACHED TO the ceremonial masks of the Coast Salish Indians, none is more interesting than that of the swayxwi or Squoa-eqoe.[393] This mask is a curious face, painted in black, white and red. It is carved from alder or cedar wood and has extremely prominent eyes, the nose or beak being carved to represent a certain bird or animal, the raven, fish hawk. eagle, snake face, etc. This creature being adopted as the crest of the family using the mask.

The mask came originally from the lower Fraser River where, legend has it, the swayxwi, a mythical being with wide spread wings appeared out of the sky and, after showing his dance, the Sxwnawustun, to Xeel's the Transformer, who came from the Sun to accept it; asked that Xeel's give the dance to the chief most worthy to receive such high honor. Xeel's at once chose Tchear Man Chief of the Hwmuthkwi'um. Through intermarriage, the mask passed to other families throughout the tribe, but even today, the honor of having swayxwi is confined to a comparatively few families.

If, as in the case of the Hwmuthkwi'um, a daughter has swayxwi, in her family, she may, upon her marriage give her husband the right to wear her mask. If widowed, she may use it, provided she has no sons. If she has daughters only, the eldest may use it, or lend it to her husband, but it must never be lent or hired out of the family.

The xwaayxwi wears for his dance, the mask or Sits-Em, with tall feathers standing up from the top—preferably feathers of the wild swan, which in the old days abounded in these parts; the entire mask being surrounded by long sea lion's whiskers, each having a tuft of swansdown at the neck. Fastened to the top of the mask and falling down the back of the dancer is a strip of swuqw'a'lh, or blanket made from the hair of mountain goat, with more sea lion's whiskers and swansdown at the neck. About the tunic are wreaths of white feather, ts'usqun, whilst at the heel are worn clusters of polished deer hoofs, fastened about the ankle with strips of deerhide, kwutsmin. A carved rattle, shulmuhwtsus, of wood or sheep horn from which hang streamers of woven goat hair, s'iluws, is held in the right hand, and on occasions a cluster of scalloped shells strung on a circle of cedar in the left; the rattles being shaken up and down, never back and forth.

Although the first swayxwi mask appears to come from the sky, they are generally believed to live in the sea or in lakes.

Dr. F. Boas tells us, "When a person succeeds in bringing one of them (swayxwi) to the surface of the water, he and his descendants acquire their protection and assume their figure as the crest of the family."[394]

Last week I met Tsonaatun, sister of that old Chief Xalputstun of Hwts'usi', who died a year or so ago. The old woman was laden with sweaters which she had made and was now selling from door to door. When asked whether she could tell me anything of the swayxwi, she nodded vigorously.

"I know more than all the others," she said. "My people had swayxwi before anybody. It was my 'big' grandfather—my grandfather's grandfather who was given the first mask of Xeel's."[395]

She promised to come and tell me all when she had sold her sweaters. Today she arrived, resplendent with a gay purple handkerchief on her head, red, green and black shawl, and a long checked skirt which billowed voluminously about her as she walked.

"I will only tell you a little of our own swayxwi," she said, as she laid aside her shawl. "Our story is too long, but I will tell you how it came to our family and other things that I know about it.

"Well, now, as I told you, my 'big' grandfather brought it to this land. That man had been trading with the Hwmuthkwi'um people and while he was there he saw a young girl, the Chief's daughter, and wanted her for his wife. This girl did not like the young man but her father thought it would be a good thing for a girl from his people to marry a man from another country, so they got ready for the wedding.

"For three days my grandfather sat just inside the Chief's house at Hwmuth-kwi'um, never speaking but just looking over to the corner where the girl sat with her father and mother. No one talked to him and no one gave him food or water, they just looked and laughed and teased him; but he wanted to marry that girl so kept his temper and spoke no word to them.

"On the fourth day the old people called to him to take his mat and sit at their fire, and they gave him food and told him he might have their daughter. Then a great feast was given and all the people from Puneluxutth', where my 'big' grandfather lived, went over to it. Every big canoe was filled with Cowichans, for they had heard that a strange new thing was to be done at the wedding.

"After the feast everybody sat outside the house and the girl was taken away and hidden behind some mats that had been fastened up like curtains. Now a man came out from the house and he was wearing a swayxwi mask—the first time my people had seen such a thing.

"The swayxwi began to dance. Round and round he went shaking his rattle up and down, and singing good luck and happiness to the girl. Now two women who were behind the mats brought out the girl, holding her by the wrists and dragging her along until they got to where the swayxwi was dancing. They gave her to the dancer, and he held her wrist and made her dance with him.

"When the dance was finished, my 'big' grandfather put his mats in the canoe and got in. His wife got in the other end and sat down; they were ready to paddle away when the girl's father shouted:

"'Wait. I have something for you,' and he took a carved box from two men who were standing behind him. Very carefully he put the box in the canoe between his daughter and her husband.

"'Here, my daughter,' he cried, 'here is a present for you, it is a swayxwi mask. The first to leave my family. Take it and give it to your husband to use. Teach him the dance and song—the st'ul'mey'lh'.[396] When you have a son, teach him, and never let there be one of your family who does not learn of the swayxwi and the things that he must do.'

"You see," explained the old woman, "after a man has used swayxwi he must not touch the salt water for four days. He must go to the lake or creek and wash himself two or three times a day, but he must not go near the sea to fish or all the salmon will leave and go down to the bottom to get away the swayxwi. At the end of four days he is clean again and can bathe and fish in the sea."

"And all you who use the mask still keep that custom?" I asked her.

"Ah, yes," she was most emphatic. "If we did not, great trouble would come to us and to our families. All down the years we have done these things and must do them always. You know that I have no son, but I have taught my eldest girl, and when she marries she will tell her husband."

"Well," she continued, "the old father said to those two, 'Because you have the swayxwi, you must keep our name in the family, so remember, call your first son Tschear-Num, and your second Tsxwultun,' and so they promised him and paddled away back to Puneluxutth', and always there have been those two names in our family, for they must never be forgotten and must go with the mask.

"Now, the xwaayxwi does not dance whenever there is a 'good time'; that song and dance is only for important occasions—when a girl is of marriageable age; then the xwaayxwi dances and sings. 'Now make her good and give her a happy life' while two women wash her and dry her with cedar bark. At a wedding where the dancer takes the bride, and, holding her wrist in his left hand, dances with her and hands her to her bridegroom. At a funeral when the dancer carries in his left hand some short branches with which he hits the face of the corpse four times whilst dancing around the bed. He does not sing, but when he has finished dancing he is given a little basket of water. Four times he holds out the basket and then he tips the water on the body and wipes it dry. Now the dead person is ready to go away, the branches have sent all bad thoughts from his mind, and the water has washed him clean. He is good.

"Another time the swayxwi is used is when the first child is born to parents who have swayxwi. The dancer goes into the room where the mother and baby are lying, and there he does his dance, but he does not sing. In one hand he holds his rattle and in the other a string of scallop or cockle shells. Four times he dances to the bed and each time he holds out the rattle and touches the woman and baby with the wool streamers. It takes a lot of money to have a xwaayxwi dance for you," explained Tsonaatun. "All the dance and song takes about twenty minutes, and for that time a xwaayxwi must be paid twenty or thirty dollars, but," she added, "it brings very, very good luck."

Now this is the story of how the first swayxwi mask was given to the people of Alberni.

"Long ago the Chief of that place had no sons, just two daughters, one girl grown up, and one little girl. Every day these two would take their canoe and paddle along the beaches and out to a small rocky island, where they would land and lie in the sun until the water came up, nearly covering the island; then they would paddle for home.

"One day, as they sat out on the rocky island, they saw a little movement in the water and a man's head came up, just as they had so often seen seals lift their heads above water. He wore a strange mask with great eyes which stuck far out and a beak like a raven. For one minute he stayed there, then down out of sight he went.

"Very quietly they waited, hoping that they might see him again, but he did not come, and at last they paddled home. As they were leaving, the eldest girl looked at the sun. 'When the sun is as high as that tomorrow, I will come again,' she thought. 'Don't tell the old people about the man we saw," she said to her sister, "they would laugh at us," and the little girl promised she would say nothing. The next day the eldest girl sat watching the sun get higher and higher in the sky, and at last she got her canoe and started to paddle away. 'Where are you going?' called her mother.

"'Just out to the rocky island,' the girl told her and paddled on her way.

For a long time she waited on the rock, but the man did not come, and at last she had to leave for home. Every day she paddled to the rock, but not once did she see the strange man, 'I will go once more,' she said to herself.

"Why do you go so often to that rock?," asked her mother.

"Oh, just for fun," said the girl; "but I am getting tired of that place; this is the last time I am going there."

The sun shone high above her as she reached the island, and, pulling up her canoe, she hid behind a rock to wait. "If he does not come today I will forget him," she thought.

Suddenly she heard a splash, and, looking out from her hiding place, she saw the man in the mask swimming towards her.

Nearer and nearer he came, and as he swam he lifted himself out of the water and looked about him. Now he saw the canoe, and for a long time he waited, looking at it. Slowly he swam to the island, and climbing up on a rock, walked to where the canoe was pulled out of the water.

He wore a loin cloth of cedar bark and carried a rattle. Now he began to shake his rattle and to dance there beside the canoe. Round and round the canoe he went, and the girl crept out from her hiding place to watch the strange dance. There he saw her watching, and, running to her, caught her by one wrist.

"Come with me," he said. "You need not be afraid. I am called xwaayxwi, and I will bring you good luck," and he led her into the water. Out in the water they walked, deeper and deeper, until the water closed over their heads and they were out of sight.

When night came and the girl had not come home, the old people called the little sister and questioned her. "What does your sister do when she goes out to that rock?" they asked, and the girl told them about the strange man in the mask. "I think my sister went to look for that man every day," said the girl. "Perhaps today she has found him."

Ah, how the old people cried. "She will never come home, she is dead," cried the mother, and she cut off her hair and all day she sat on the beach crying and calling to her daughter to come back to her.

For a long time the girl lived under the water with the xwaayxwi, and in time a baby boy has born to them.

"Now," said her husband, "you must go back and see your mother. I will make two canoes and will fill them with presents, and I will make you a mask to wear."

So now there were two masks, the man's called sts'uluhwus, the girl's Tschul-What.

When everything was ready, they took the canoes up to the top of the water and carried the blankets and put them in, then the xwaayxwi and his wife put on their masks, and, carrying the baby, they got into the canoes.

Now, the poor old Mother had been so unhappy and had cried so long for her daughter that she had gone quite blind. All day long she sat beside the water, listening, listening for the sound of a strange canoe that might bring her girl home again, but more than a year had gone by and she had not come. But at last came a morning when, as she sat beating her cedar bark, then waiting and listening she heard the sounds of a canoe coming, and she knew it was paddled by a stranger.

"Who is it comes in a strange canoe?" she cried to the girl, and the girl, looking out, told her, "I think it must be that man bringing my sister home again. I can see the strange mask that he wore, and the woman with him is wearing one like it."

And now the canoe was beside them, and the woman took off her mask and got out of the canoe, carrying her baby on her back, and after her came the man.

"Mother!" called the woman. "Mother! It is your daughter, have you forgotten me?"

"She is blind," said the man. "She cannot see you, but I will make her well again," and he asked the sister to get him some fresh water in a basket. He took off his mask, and, putting his hands in the water, he washed the old woman's head and face, and, as he washed, her hair grew long and thick again and her sight came back. The girl and her baby made their home with the old people, but the xwaayxwi had to go back to his home in the water, but before he left he taught his wife the song and dance for the mask, and, when her son was old enough, she taught them to him, and, in that way swayxwi started amongst the Tseshaht, the people of Alberni.

Buried Treasure[397]

This account by Joe and Jennie Wyse was probably recorded three years prior to its publication. Although Beryl Cryer has framed the story in the frontier mythology of "lost gold," the narrative by Jennie Wyse is a remarkable record of a specific act of interracial violence, one of many that took place in the wake of the Fraser River gold rush of 1858.

IT SEEMS A FAR CRY FROM THE PLACER diggings of the Cariboo, in the early sixties, to the peaceful little islands which dot our water ways between New Westminster and Nanaimo; yet the Indians tell of many a Cariboo miner being murdered by the Indians of those early times, and their gold hidden on some of these islands, where it undoubtedly remains to this day.

The story I am about to tell you, was told to me by Tl'utasiye', with an occasional word from her old husband Sugnuston, who leaned forward in his chair, a wrinkled old hand on either knee, as he followed the story closely in case his wife should forget the smallest detail.

"Now," commenced Tl'utasiye', picking up her knitting and unrolling yards of white wool from an enormous ball beside her. "The old man this story is about is dead, and all his people are dead, so there can be no harm in telling it to you."

"Well, long ago, when my people were living at Sti'ilup, my mother had a good friend of her own age, who got married to a man called Suppul, and they went to live in his village.

"One day, Suppul and his brother St'ey'xum filled their canoes with deer meat and fish, and paddled off to the place you now call New Westminster, to trade with the white men. They did their trading, and carrying the flour and blankets they had got in exchange for their meat, they walked about looking at the funny things the white people used. By-and-by they went to the beach and there beside their canoe, they found five white men sitting on a log with their boxes and blankets beside them.

"One of the white men held up two blankets and a piece of yellow money, and said something to St'ey'xum, but of course St'ey'xum did not understand him. Then the man pointed to the canoe and out over the water—'Snuneymuxw?' he asked. St'ey'xum nodded his head. 'Good, good!' he said, and he took the money and blankets and put them with his other things. Well, St'ey'xum and Suppul told the five men where to sit in the canoe, and threw their things in beside them.

"Now, amongst their belongings was one box that was very, very heavy. It was quite small, but ah! it was heavy, and it was tied about with lots and lots of rope. One of the men took the box and sat upon it and one of his friends tried to take it from him, but he pushed him away and kept sitting on it and would not move.

"'These men must be very rich!' said St'ey'xum to Suppul. 'They give us gold money and I have seen boxes like that small one before, they come from the house where the money is made. I expect it is full of gold money!' The two talked together in low voices as they got ready to start, and they made their plans, whilst the white men sat listening and wondering what they were talking about. At last all was ready, and away they paddled, with St'ey'xum at one end of the canoe and Suppul at the other.

All that day they paddled, and when it got dark they landed on a little island for the night. After pulling their canoe far up on the beach, they took out the blankets but left everything else in the canoe, but the white men took out the little box and put it with their blankets, and, later, when they all lay beside a big fire of logs, the same man who had sat on the box, lay with his head upon it.

"'I was right,' whispered St'ey'xum. 'That little box has money in it, see how carefully they guard it!'

They were awake and off again early the next morning, the little box, as before, being guarded by one of the men. When the sun got hot, one of the men took a bottle from the blankets and they began drinking, and gave some of their whiskey to the Indians.

"Now they were getting near a pass where the water ran deeply and very quickly between two islands and here St'ey'xum guided the canoe close to shore. 'We will rest here for a time,' he said, and jumping out he pulled the canoe as high on the sand as he could and stood on one side, waiting for the white man to get out.

"No one saw him take his knife from his belt, but, as the first man jumped from the canoe, St'ey'xum drove his knife deep, deep, and the man fell without a sound. With a great shout the next man sprang, but the knife was waiting. It was soon over, for there was St'ey'xum on the beach in front, and behind them was Suppul waiting with his knife ready.

"When all was dead, Suppul began to be afraid. 'What have we done!' he cried. 'See now, we have killed these white men, and soon the white chief will come in his great ship and will take us and kill us!' His brother laughed at him. 'You are no great fighter, Suppul!' he said. 'There is nothing to be afraid of. No one saw us leave with these men, and we need tell no one what we have done. Hurry and help me sink the bodies!'

"They took everything out of the canoe and piled it on the beach, then they emptied the men's pockets and, gathering long pieces of kelp, fastened stones to the bodies and put them in the canoe. Now they paddled out to where the water ran swiftly, put the bodies over and down to the bottom they went.

"They washed out their canoe, cleaned their knives, and were ready to leave. 'First we will divide the things,' said St'ey'xum, and they divided all the white men's things, keeping the little box until the last. Now they cut the ropes and opened it. It was full of gold with a little 'made' money, but not very much. The gold was in pieces like that"—Tl'utasiye' put out one hand and held her other hand across the base of her fingers. "St'ey'xum's wife told me about it when she was an old woman, after my new mother was dead, and she said she often used to look at the funny pieces of yellow gold, and wonder what they could do with it.

"Well, St'ey'xum and Suppul divided the money, but they did not know what to do with the gold, for they did not know how to get it made into money without white men asking questions. Before they reached the village they hid it on a little island and they told their people that they had got all the things they had in the canoe in trade.

"It was not long before the white men's friends began to wonder where they had gone. They were told that the men had taken their gold in a box and had not been seen since, so they guessed that something must have happened to them, and they went to ask the soldiers to help them. Soon a warship was sent to look for the miners, they called in at all the villages and asked questions, but of course, no one had seen the men. At last they went to St'ey'xum's village and the chief was called and questioned, but no one had seen any white man, and at last the warship went away.

"Now St'ey'xum and Suppul had quite a lot of money that they had taken from the box of gold, and some they found in the pockets of the dead men, and they wanted to go and have a good time with it. So, one day, when they thought people would have forgotten about the lost men, these two took their canoe and paddled to Vancouver.

"Well, they had a good time spending their money, but it was not long before they met some white men who gave them whisky, and of course, that meant a fight. All had knives, both white men and Indians, but there were lots of white men and only two Indians, and it was not long before St'ey'xum was killed and his brother had to run for his life. He had no money left and he knew that the white men would be looking for him, so he paddled back alone to the village and told the Chief how St'ey'xum had died.

"Now the box of gold was Suppul's, and no one but he knew about it. Sometimes he would paddle out to the little island where it was hidden and look to see that it was safe, and one day he took his wife out with him and he told her all about it and they opened the box and looked at the gold.

"'Some day,' said his wife, 'Some one will follow you here and will kill you so that they may have the yellow gold. I think you should bring it back to the village and put it where we could watch it; out here anyone could come and steal it and you would never know!'"

"They talked about it for a long time, and at last Suppul saw that his wife was right, so they went home, and that night when all in the house were asleep they dug a little hole behind their big house, put a cedar plank in the bottom and covered the place with old planks and mats, and the next night they paddled to the island and got the box. Very carefully they wrapped it in lots of cedar bark and put it in the hole, then they covered the hole with thick cedar planks and piled rubbish over all.

Tl'utasiye' put down her knitting and looked earnestly into my face. "Long ago," she said, "When I was just a young girl, my old mother told me that Suppul's wife had told her the story, and had shown her the place behind the houses where the box was buried. She said her friend told her that the box was small, but so heavy she could not lift it, and they had to put a rope about it to lower it into the hole. 'Some day,' the woman told my mother, 'We are going to dig it up and hide it in the woods. Suppul is afraid to show it to anyone, and now that there are so many white people about, and no Indians live in the big house, he thinks the box might be found where he has hidden it, and he would be punished.'

"And now," said Tl'utasiye', "this is my part of the story."

"About thirty years ago, my husband and I left our old home and moved to the village of Penelakhut where old Suppul lived. His wife was dead but the old man lived in a little house with one of his daughters. One Summer we all went to the Fraser River getting blueberries, and when I got home I found that I had left nearly all my jam jars at my old home. I left the children with my man, and, taking our small canoe I went to get the jars.

"I stayed one night at my old home with my friends, and started very, very early next morning so that I would catch the right tide through the pass. As I paddled along I saw that the water was a long way out, and I thought it would be nice to stop and get some clams for our dinner. I pulled my canoe right up over the mud in a little bay not far from my village, and taking a thick stick began to dig for clams. It was very hot, and after I had dug quite a lot of clams I sat down under a tree to get cool before getting a few more. As I sat there I saw a canoe coming into the bay, with one man paddling it, and as it got near me I saw that it was Suppul.

"'He has come to get himself some clams,' I thought, but I did not call to him, just sat watching to see what he was going to do.

"He was very old and his eyes were not much good, so he did not see me or my canoe, under the trees. He paddled along to one side of the bay, where there were some rocks, and where the water was always deep; here he stopped and fastened his canoe to a rock. Then he started trying to lift something that was in the end of the canoe. It was very heavy, and he put a rope over his shoulder and slowly, slowly raised himself. Now I saw that the rope was fastened around a small box, but it was so heavy the old man could scarcely move it. At last he got it out of the canoe and sat down on a rock with the box beside him. For a little while he rested and then slowly as before, he went up the rocks and back into the woods, but before he went he put the box down and leaned out from behind a rock, looking every way as though afraid that someone might be watching him.

"Well, I dug some more clams, pushed my canoe in the water and was just getting into it when I heard someone shout, 'Hi, Hi,' and there was the old man, down in his canoe again.

"'What are you doing?' he shouted.

"'Just digging a few clams,' I told him.

"'How long have you been here?' he asked

"'Not long.'

"'Well, did you see me paddle in here?'

"'No,' I said, 'I guess I was too busy getting my clams!'

"'Well,' said the old man, 'Don't you tell anyone you saw me. I don't think I am going to live very much longer, and I am getting everything ready before I die, but you must not tell anyone!'

"'What have you been doing?' I said.

"'Just mending a fence back in there,' he laughed. 'When I am dead I don't want people to say my fences are broken!'

"This sort of talk made me think, and I got out on the sand again and went on digging clams until he had paddled round the point. When he was quite out of sight I paddled over to where he had tied his canoe and went a little into the bush, but the salal was so thick and the rocks were so high I soon lost his trail, but I knew that old Suppul had been telling me lies, when he said he had been mending his fence, for there were no fences on that side of the island, and Suppul's house and land was on the other side, about three miles away.

"Well," continued Tl'utasiye', "For many years I told no one about the hidden box, then, after my husband had died and I was left with all our children to take care of, I began to wonder about that box and I went to see a lady who tells fortunes. This woman lives at Nanaimo—all my people go to her when they want to learn things, she can tell if sick people will get well, or die, and she can find things that are lost. Well, I went to this woman's house and she took me into her room and shut her eyes and went to sleep. Then I said to her, 'Tell me, what was in the little box I saw an old man from my village hide back in the bushes, many years ago?' The woman just lay there sleeping and suddenly she began to speak.

"'There is a small box,' she said. 'It is tied strongly and is, ah, so heavy! Inside that box is lots of big money, not made. I see the box is put in some big rocks and there are some boards over it; but it is big, big money!'

"Pretty soon the woman opened her eyes. 'Did I tell you anything you wanted to know?' she asked, and I told her, 'yes.' 'It is just as I thought,' I told her, 'and thank you!'

"Well, I waited until my eldest boy was quite big and then I told him about the gold, but for a long time he would not look for it.

"'What's the good?' he said. 'If I do find the box and it has gold in it, the Government will take it all!'

"At last I got him to hunt up in the rocks. He spent a long time climbing about looking, and at last he told me he had found the place where he thought it must be buried. 'But,' he said, 'The rocks are too big to move, but it must be the place because I found a broken crab spear standing in the ground with stones piled about it to mark the place!'

"You know," said Tl'utasiye', "we never looked for it again, but long after, before my boy died, we talked about it and he told me he had not meant that he could not move the rocks where the box was hidden, but that there were so many big rocks he could not tell which to look under. Now, I have never told that story to any other person, my husband and I have talked together about it, for after I had married him, I wanted him to look but he said the same as my boy, that he would not be able to use the gold if he found it. So it must still be there, hidden away in some big rock, waiting for someone to find it and carry it home."

Origin of the Thunderbird[398]

Latits'iiya and her daughter visit Beryl Cryer to pass on a story told to them by Mary Rice. The story, well known to W'sanec and Hul'q'umi'num' people, concerns the myth of Sxeeluqun, a young man who receives awesome powers, but abuses them and suffers the consequences.[399] I am uncertain of the article's original publication date, but its style and the setting suggest it was originally recorded and written in the fall of 1932, when Beryl Cryer often visited Latits'iiya and her family.

LATITS'IIYA AND HER DAUGHTER CAME to see me last week, the daughter very smart in a bright blue dress and tiny hat perched on one side of her head, with black curls arranged about it. Latits'iiya, however, will never change her mode of dressing. She still wears a voluminous gathered skirt, with a shawl about her shoulders, and her hair in two plaits tied together at the ends with a scrap of rag.

"I been staying with that old woman Siamtunaat," she announced, as she sat herself on my doorstep. "Ah! she's getting old. So old and so fat; But she talked about you, and she told me a story she said she forgot to tell you, so I finished my washing today and came to give you the story, just like she gave it to me."

She took off her shawl, handed it to her girl to hold, and commenced the story.

"Longer ago than our grandmothers can remember, there lived at Leeyqsun on Valdez Island, a man and his woman and their one little boy, who they called Sxeeluqun.

"Even when this child was a small baby, the mother could not look at his eyes, for they shone like fire, and, as he got older he had to keep his eyes shut, for a strong light came from them like the lightning that comes from the skies in the hot Summer nights.

"For many years this boy was very lonely, for none of the people would talk with him, and no children would play with him, for all were afraid of his bad eyes.

"One day Sxeeluqun went far back in the woods until he came to a lake. Feeling very tired he lay down beside the water and went to sleep. While he slept he dreamed that a great bird flew down beside him. 'Listen, Sxeeluqun,' said the bird, 'search along the edges of this lake until you have found some tall grasses and some smooth rushes and make yourself a hat, like this'—and the bird told him how to weave and bind the grasses about the rushes until a large hat was made. 'My name,' said the bird, 'is Schy-As-Thun, or thunder, and the hat you will make is a Thunder hat. You must keep it on your head, or the thunder will come and shake the world.'

"When Sxeeluqun woke, he set to work looking for the grasses and rushes for his hat, and very soon had enough to work with, Now he wove the grass about the rushes as Schy-As-Thun had told him. and made a fine hat, which he quickly put upon his head. Not thinking, he took It off again, and at once great thunder shook the land, and when he opened his eyes to see what was making the noise, lightning shot from his eyes, up, up, into the skies, so that back at his father's camp people called to each other that surely this was the worst storm they had ever known.

"Suddenly, Sxeeluqun remembered what the Thunder Bird had told him, and quickly he put on his hat. and at once the loud noise in the skies stopped. When Sxeeluqun got back to his home he called to his father. 'Ho, my father! I can no longer live In your house, my eyes are so hot they will burn all that I look upon! Will you make me a house where I may live without doing harm to our people? Make it on the highest place that you can find, so that when I open my eyes I will see only the blue sky above me!'

"So his father and others of the tribe found a high place on Saltspring Island,[400] and there they cleared away the logs and trees, and called to the women to go to the swamps and cut all the Sli-Quis (Bulrushes) they could find.

"For many days and nights all the women worked, cutting the rushes, carrying them into camp and spreading them out in the sun to dry; then, when all were ready, they got their long mat needles, which were rubbed smooth as glass, and threading them with the thin roots from the cedar, they made the rushes into great, long mats.

"At last the house was ready, the rush mats went all around the sides, but there was no roof.

"'See now,' said the father, 'we have built your house in this way so that you may open your eyes, and the burning light, will not hurt anything, but will go up and up into the sky!'

"For some time Sxeeluqun lived alone in his house, high up there on the mountain, but after a time he got lonely and wished that he might have a wife like the other young men of his tribe. So he sent word to the people living in that part of the land that he would bring great storms upon them, such storms as they had never seen. 'The thunder will shake your houses to the ground, and lightning will burn them until only the black ashes are left you!' he said. 'But bring your daughters to me, to be my wives, and I will let you live in peace!' When the people heard his words, they met together to talk it over. All one night the wise men of the tribe talked, but in the morning they had thought of nothing that could be done.

"'We cannot get near Sxeeluqun to kill him,' they said, 'for if he looked at us but once, the brightness from his eyes would blind and kill us. There is but one thing to do: Each family must take their most beautiful girl to Saltspring Mountain and give her to Sxeeluqun , and in that way our homes will be saved!'"

"So now all the young girls were called together, oil and the down from the breasts of birds was put on their heads, and they were taken to the bottom of Saltspring Mountain and told to climb up to the great house of Stthe'qun, where they would find Sxeeluqun waiting for them.

"In this way Sxeeluqun had nearly two hundred young girls living in his home, but still he was not happy. He heard that his uncle, Stqamut, had a very beautiful girl at his home at Saanich, and he felt that if he could have this girl he would want for nothing more; so he paddled to Saanich to get his new wife.

"At first Stqamut was angry, and afraid to let Sxeeluqun see his girl. 'You are not a man!' he said. 'You are filled with such magic that all are afraid of you! What of those other young girls you have in your home? Leave my daughter and go back to those others!'

"Sxeeluqun grew angry. 'Listen to me!' he shouted, 'if you will not give me your girl, I will take off my hat, and I will turn my eyes upon your homes and your people, and then, what will become of you?'

"As he spoke, Sxeeluqun lifted his hat a little way from his head, and at once the thunder sounded all about him, shaking the camp, and all the people came running out from their houses, begging Stqamut to give up his girl and let them live in peace.

"'Take her!' called Stqamut, 'and get back to your house before you bring trouble to my people!' So Sxeeluqun paddled away with the girl.

"Some time later a baby girl was born to them, and Sxeeluqun went to Saanich to tell Stqamut the good news.

"'Come back with me!' he said, 'and see your daughter and your grandchild.' Stqamut went with him.

"Now, as they got into the canoe, Sxeeluqun handed the paddle to his father-in-law.

"'You must do the paddling,' he said, 'and I ,will sit here in the middle of the canoe, where I can look up into the sky!' And he sat with his blanket over his hat and his face turned up to the sky.

"For a time Stqamut paddled along and not one word did they speak, then Stqamut said, 'It is time you paddled a little,' and he dropped his paddle into the water and, leaning forward, held it over Sxeeluqun's head, so that the water dripped on his face.

"'Stop that!' shouted Sxeeluqun But again the paddle dripped on him, and then Stqamut pushed him in the back with the end of the paddle.

"Now, they were paddling between this place that is now called Cherry Point and Saltspring Island, and the water was far, far out. A little rock[401] that is covered when the tide is in was sticking up out of the water, and as they passed near to it Sxeeluqun shook the water from his face and shouted:

"'I will take you no further in my canoe. You must get out on that little rock!' He took the other paddle and paddled to the rock. 'Get out!' he shouted, and pushed Stqamut out onto the rock, and paddled away.

"When Stqamut saw that Sxeeluqun was paddling right away, leaving him there to drown, he laughed out loud and, taking his blanket which Sxeeluqun had thrown out onto the rock, he rolled it tightly, tied it around his body under his arms, then he took his paddle and slipped into the water.

"Sometimes he paddled himself along, and sometimes he swam, until at last he reached the shore.

"Now he hurried until he came to one of the Cowichan's camps. 'Come,' he shouted; 'come with me, for I have had enough of that man Sxeeluqun; he left me out in the middle of the water to drown, and I am going to kill him! Come, help me to catch him, and we will have no more great storms to break our homes and kill our people!'

"Taking some of the strongest men, all carrying clubs made from the horns, of an elk, he hurried up to the house that had been, built for Sxeeluqun. As they left the camp, a hunter passed them carrying a seal which he had speared. 'Let me have that seal!' said Stqamut, and, throwing it over his shoulder, he carried it with him.

"'Make a great fire,' he shouted to the women in the house, 'and roast this seal for your husband, who will be here very soon!'

"Now Stqamut and his friends hid themselves and waited for Sxeeluqun to come home.

"It was not long before Sxeeluqun came walking up the trail and, going into his house, he threw himself down on his bed.

"Ah! that was good luck for Stqamut! He ran into the house, the other men following after him, and, taking a strong forked stick, he speared up the roasting seal and, holding it in front of him, ran at Sxeeluqun.

"In one minute Sxeeluqun was awake. He opened his terrible eyes, and the place was filled with lightening, but still Stqamut went after him, keeping his eyes down. At last he caught Sxeeluqun, and, throwing the burning seal in his face he blinded him, and at once the lightning stopped!

"Now, the men ran with their clubs and quickly beat Sxeeluqun to death, and as the breath went from his body a great bird flew from the house, carrying his spirit away, into the skies. And that is how the thunder and lightning bird first came to our land."

Little Island of Kuper[402]

More than two years after she ceased actively recording interviews with elders, Beryl Cryer submitted the article below, apparently based on another story told to her by Mary Rice. The writing style is much different than the articles published between 1932 and 1935, and appears to have been assembled from old notes. Of interest is the change in the spelling of Mary Rice's "Indian Name," which is rendered "Tzla-Mia," rather than the usual "Tzea-mntenaht" (Siamtunaat), and an unfortunate return to native caricature in the opening paragraph. The story, however, provides a detailed version of a myth familiar to many Coast Salish groups.[403]

SIAMTUNAAT CAME TO MY DOOR TODAY, begging for old clothes. "Anything for mats," she explained. "Any old clothes; I cut them into rags and make them into mats. You give me rags and I sell you a good mat." She was dressed for the part, in her oldest and shabbiest shawl, a faded handkerchief on her head, and a dilapidated pair of men's boots on her feet. I told her that I really did not need any mats, but if she had a story I would like to hear one. "A story." She had "lots of stories." She would tell one at once and get her rags another day. She settled herself at the table, and asked for a cup of tea while she remembered her best story. The tea finished, she was ready.

"This story is about the first people of the Sqwxwa'mush,"[404] she exclaimed, "and how they found the little island we call Kuper. Now, at that time—long before the white people had found this land—there were two Sqwxwa'mush families. The head man of one family was called At-Thult, and the head of the other was Hola-Pult. These people did not build their homes close together, as the Indians did later on, but put one house in one bay and one in another, with a little point of rock between.

"Now, Hola-Pult and his brothers and their families were all great hunters. They were always out in their canoes killing seals, sea lions, duck and fish, and the roof of their great house was always filled with good food drying on the racks. But Ah-Thult and his relations had no luck. Every day they went hunting, but could get but little. Time and time again Ah-Thult would throw his spear, or take aim with his bow and arrows, but his spear would go too far, and his arrows fall short, and with his brothers it was the same, so that many days they paddled home with empty canoes.

"At last Ah-Thult went to see Hola-Pult. 'What do you think is the matter with my family?' he asked. 'How is it that you kill all you want, and yet we can scarcely get enough to eat?'

"Hola-Pult thought for a minute, and then said, 'Maybe you are not clean enough. It may be that the hunting spirit will not come to you because none of you are pure and clean. Perhaps that is the reason.' Ah-Thult agreed and went home for all the rest of that day he sat beside the fire, thinking what he had better do about it.

"Late that night he called his wife to him. 'I am going away,' he said. 'It may be that I and my brothers are not clean and pure to be good hunters, so I will go far away, up into the mountains, and there I will stay until I am clean. Do not cry or feel sorry for me,' he told her. 'I may have to stay for one or two years, but when I am clean I will come back to you, and our children will grow fat with the good food I will kill for them, and our houses will be filled with dried meat hanging above our heads.'

"Early the next morning Ah-Thult started out to find his 'luck.' For many miles he walked along the shore, and after three days and nights he turned into the woods where no man had ever been, and on up into the mountains he made his way. At last he came to a swamp, and, crossing that, found himself on the edge of a big lake. In this place he made his camp.

"Now he began to make himself clean and pure, calling to the spirits to help him. All day long and many times in the night he would run into the water and swim until he had no strength left, then he would lie on the bank, and, taking branches of the hemlock and cedar, he would scrape his skin, rubbing until the red blood ran from the cuts and scratches that the rough branches made upon his body, and as he washed he called and sang to the Spirits. 'Help me, ah Siem,[405] help me to hunt, to kill the seals and sea lions, that my people may grow strong. Make me clean and give me good luck in my hunting.'

"All this time he took no food, only drank the water from the lake, until at last he grew so weak he could not swim, but lay at the edge of the water rubbing the branches about his body. At last he fell asleep.

"No one knows how long he lay sleeping, when suddenly he heard a voice talking to him. The voice told him where to find some medicine to put on his body—medicine that would make him clean, and the voice told him to take a sharp stone and scrape his body again, then, when the blood ran, to mix water with the medicine and rub it in the wounds. For two days he lay asleep, and when he awoke he crawled to where the voice had told he would find the medicine. There it was, good, clean green leaves hanging from a little tree in the swamp.

"Now he found a stone sharp as a knife, and, crawling back to the lake, he cut and scraped his body. He took the green leaves, chewed them, and, putting them into his hands, he put a little water on them and rubbed them round and round until they were soft like a paste. Now he rubbed the cool, green paste all over his body. As the medicine ran into the cuts, it burned like fire, and, shouting from the pain, Ah-Thult rolled on the ground, leapt high in the air, and at last jumped into the lake and began swimming, for the pain had given him strength.

"In his fear he swam right out to the middle of the lake and there his strength left him and he began to sink.

Mary Rice and Beryl Cryer

"Down, down he went to the bottom of the lake, and, as his feet touched the ground at the bottom, it opened and let him through and he found himself in a big house. This house was bigger than any he had ever seen, and in the corners were great piles of bones.

"'Ah,' he thought, 'where am I and what lives here? Something will come and kill me, I know,' and he tried to get up and run away, but found that he could not move his legs.

"For a long time he sat there, waiting for something to come and kill him, but at last grew so tired he fell asleep.

"Suddenly he heard a loud noise and something took him by the shoulder. 'Wake up,' shouted a loud voice, and a big seal shook him from side to side.

"Ah-Thult looked about him and saw that the house was full of seals, sea lions, whales and duck, all walking about and talking like men. A great sea lion came up to him and pulled his mouth open and looked in. 'Ah!' he shouted. 'This man needs cleaning.' 'Leave him alone,' said the seal, who was holding him. 'This is a poor man; he does not know how to wash clean; we must help him.'

"The sea lions all crowded round to look at Ah-Thult. 'All right,' they said, 'we will help this poor man.'

"They got a long rope, made from the intestines of sea lions and they threw this over one of the cedar logs that supported the roof, then they fastened it around Ah-Thult and pulled him high in the air. They got sharp stones and cleaned and rubbed them until they shone; and with these they scraped the poor man until there was very little skin left on his body, and the blood was dripping from him to the ground.

"'Soon you will be so clean you will be able to kill as many of us as you like!' they told him.

"At last they thought he was clean and they let him down and gave him a basket of medicine. 'Take this home with you!' they said, 'and when you go hunting, rub a little of the medicine on your body, then we will not be able to smell you.'

"The biggest sea lion gave him a song. 'When you hunt my people,' he said, 'sing this song as you paddle across the water, the sea lion will only hear the song, and will not see you coming after them!' 'Now sleep,' said the seals, and Ah-Thult lay down in a corner and was soon fast asleep.

"While he lay sleeping, the water came slowly over him, and he floated to the top and, still sleeping, he was washed back to his camp by the waves. As he floated along one of the sea lions swam up to him. 'Listen,' said the sea lion, 'when you get to the land, you must make a wooden sea lion. Take sharp stones and cut the wood till it comes alive, then, when you go to your home take it with you, and you will have good luck!'

"For two days Ah-Thult lay asleep, and when he woke he felt so well and strong he ran and shouted for joy; and he made a song to the spirit that had helped him, saying, 'Thank you, Ah, great Spirit! I am clean and I know that my hunting will be good, that my houses will be filled with meat and that my people will grow strong with much good food to eat!'

"He got busy, finding stones to sharpen so that he could make the wooden sea lion and, when these were ready, he walked about looking at the trees, wondering which would be the best to cut.

"He chose a tree growing close to the water, and cut it down and began cutting and trimming it into the shape of a sea lion. It was very hard wood and it took him a long, long time. Many, many times the moon came out, small and new, and grew big and bright until the night was like day, and Ah-Thult could see to work until early morning, and still the man cut and rubbed his sea lion.

"At last it was finished. Now Ah-Thult sang as he rolled the piece of wood into the water. At last he could go home to his family, his work was finished, he was clean and pure, and now he had his sea lion. He turned the creature round in the water and, putting a hand on either side of it, he gave it three sharp smacks. 'Go!' he shouted. 'Swim and dive to the bottom, but come back to me at once; now go.' One great push he gave it and the sea lion swam out, turned a little, and then, down it went—down, down to the bottom, and there it stayed. The wood was too heavy to float.

"Poor Ah-Thult! He had never felt so sad as when he saw that his sea lion was not coming up again, and he turned to the woods once move to look for another tree from which to make a new sea lion.

"This time he took an oak tree and once again he cut and trimmed it until he had a fine, big sea lion ready to put in the water. Again he rolled it to the lake and started it off, but, just as before, the creature sank to the bottom and was not seen again.

"Ah-Thult did not give up. Again he looked for a tree, and this time he chose a cedar. This wood he found softer and easier to carve, and it was not long before he had a finer and larger sea lion than the others he had made. Before he put it in the water he had found a place where he could dig the red paint that his people put on their faces, and, taking some of the paint he colored the sea lion, and stuck long grass on his face like whiskers and he hollowed out the body. Now it was a real sea lion!

"Early in the morning Ah-Thult took the creature to the water. It was so light he found that he could easily carry it, and, giving it three sharp slaps he pushed it far out to the middle of the lake. Away it swam, diving under the water and coming up again, making a loud, breathing noise as it did so, and, as it swam, Ah-Thult stood on the shore and sang and sang, for his heart was glad to think that at last he could go back to his home and hunt for his people!

Mary Rice and Beryl Cryer

"Now he had to find his way home and carry the sea lion on his back, all those long hard miles down the mountain; but he hurried along, singing to the hunting spirit as he went.

"Ah! how glad his wife and family were to get Ah-Thult home once more! And all had to hear his stories of the house under the lake; and the wooden sea lion was taken to the water and told to swim and dive.

"For two days Ah-Thult rested, but he could not wait longer before trying his 'luck.' The morning of the third day he started off to hunt, and before night he had killed ten fat seals! A great fire was built outside the house and the seals were roasted on the hot coals.

"Now, there was a little wind blowing, and the smell of the roasting meat drifted across the point, to where Hola-Pult sat in front of his house with his wife and brothers.

"Hola-Pult sniffed the air. 'What do I smell?' he said, 'cooking seal meat! That man Ah-Thult must be home again. I will go and see him.' Hola-Pult walked across to Ah-Thult's house, and saw all the seals roasting before the fire.

"'You have found your luck!' he laughed. 'Is that one day's hunting?'

"'Yes,' Ah-Thult told him. 'I am clean and I have been given good medicine to help me catch the seals and sea lions!'

"When Hola-Pult heard that, he thought, 'How can I get that lucky medicine away from Ah-Thult? I will do nothing tonight, but tomorrow, when it is dark, I will steal it from him.'

"Now, Ah-Thult guessed what was in Hola-Pult's mind, and early the next morning he took the sea lion and whispered to it what it must do to help him. Then he carried it to the edge of the water and pushed it in.

"Away swam the sea lion, straight to where Hola-Pult had his house beside the water. Close in to the shore he swam, and, as he want he made a great noise, blowing and splashing so that Hola-Pult heard him, and, looking out, saw the great creature.

"'Ho!' he shouted to his brothers. 'Come quickly. There is a great sea lion swimming past. Come, get the canoes sad we will soon have him.' Five canoes were put into the water, and with five men in each, they set out after the sea lion.

"Now the sea lion remembered the words that had been whispered to him, and he swam slowly, letting the canoes come nearer and nearer, until, one after another, the spears were thrown and all buried their heads in the cedar wood. Now the paddlers took their paddles and tap, tap, tapped on the edges of the canoes, then drove the paddles deep into the water, trying to stop the great creature as it swam out and out to sea.

"On and on they went, and now they tried to sing their hunting song and stop it, then to pray to Sum'shathut, the sun God, but on it went.

"At last they reached Cowichan Gap, and through the Pass they went and across the Channel to Kuper Island. Here the sea lion swam more slowly until it came to the island. Straight to the shore it swam, with a great leap jumped high up the hillside, leaving the canoes at the edge of the water.

"Now Hola-Pult did not know what to do; he had never seen a sea lion jump out of the water before.

"'It may be that this is a magic sea lion' he said. 'We must go carefully, but we will try and get our spears before we leave this place.' Creeping very carefully, they went up the hill, but when they came to the place where the sea lion lay, they found only a log with the spears stuck in it.

"They pulled out their spears, and then, finding that the creature was only made of wood, they laughed aloud and stayed to look about them.

"'This is a better place than our home,' said Hola-Pult. 'Let us paddle back to Sqwxwa'mush and get our wives and children and make our homes in this new land.'

"So the five canoes paddled all the way back, and, after they had packed their blankets, mats and food, they took their families and left for their new home. But when they got to the island and looked for the brown log that had been a sea lion, it was gone, for Ah-Thult had told it to swim back when it had taken Hola-Pult and his people away. And that is the story of how the first Sqwxwa'mush found Kuper Island."

Whatever Happened to Greedy Raven

We end this collection of oral traditions with Tommy Pielle's narration of a well known Hul'q'umi'num' story appended to the September 9, 1934 *Daily Colonist* story "Tales of Sheshuq'um."[406] The style and presentation locate the narrative back at Mary Rice's cabin near the Halhed home on Chemainus Harbour, where so many of the stories that comprise this book were gifted to Beryl Cryer, and which she, through her writing, gifted to us. Huy tseep q'u, ah siem ("Thank you all, oh, respected ones").

FOR SOME TIME TOMMY PIELLE HAD BEEN standing in the doorway, his arms piled high with drift wood, which he now dumped into the wood box with a tremendous clatter.

"If my sister's finished," he remarked, as he sat himself on top of the wood, "I can tell you a good story about the greedy Raven. It won't take long, so you stay a little longer and listen!"

I noticed that he avoided Siamtunaat's eye, as he hurried into his story without a pause.

"Once, long ago, when all the birds and animals were really people and could talk together, a lot of lady birds went berry picking! The birds were the crow, the lark, bluejay, woodpecker and lots more, but I don't remember their names. Then, besides the birds, a snail went, too, and then just as they were starting, Raven asked, might he join the party?

"Well, they got into a big canoe and off they went. When they got to a good berry picking place they landed and got out their baskets, but the Raven said he thought he had better stay in the canoe and take care of it. Now, you know, Raven was a very greedy bird and he was always planning how he could get more food than anybody else. And this time he had thought of a way to get all the berries he could eat without having to go after them himself.

"As soon as the birds were out of sight, Raven went ashore and got a lot of moss. Then he used his spirit power so that when the moss touched water each bundle turned into a war canoe.

"After a time the women came back with their baskets filled with berries.

"'I have taken good care of the canoe,' said Raven, 'and nothing has come near, but I think we had better hurry back now.' So they put their berries into the canoe and started back home again.

"Very soon Raven began to drop his bundles of moss over the side of the canoe and, as they touched the water, they at once turned into a long line of Yukw'ulhta'x war canoes filled with fighting men, chasing after them.

"'Paddle to the shore' called Raven, 'and run and hide in the woods. I will stay and fight!' So as quickly as they could the women paddled back to the shore and, leaving their baskets of berries, they hurried to hide themselves in the woods. Now, snail could not hurry or run, so he crept to the beach and hid himself behind a log.

"Well, Raven stood up in the canoe and shouted to the Yukw'ulhta'x to 'hurry along; he was going to fight them!' and all the time he was calling, he was watching the women hurrying to hide.

"But as soon as all were out of sight, Raven changed the canoes back again into moss and, getting out the biggest baskets of berries, began to eat. He soon finished that basketfull and started on another. He ate and ate until he could eat no more, then he took berries and rubbed the juice all over his feathers and lay down in the bottom of the canoe and began to groan and cry as though he were in great pain.

"Very soon the women came creeping back to see what had happened to Raven. Hearing his cries and seeing no canoes, they hurried to the beach, and there they saw poor Raven rolling about in the bottom of the canoe, with his feathers covered with blood.

"'—Ah!' they cried, 'What have these people done to poor, brave Raven? And see! our berries are gone; only the empty baskets left!' But now snail came crawling into the canoe, and as he came he laughed.

"'Take some water,' he called, 'and wash the blood off that poor Raven, then you will see what is the matter with him, and where your berries have gone!' And he told them how he had watched Raven eating up the berries, and how by magic Raven had turned the war canoes back into moss. The women listened to his story and when he had finished they took hold of Raven and they threw him far out into the water. 'Swim home!' they called to him; 'we will have nothing more to do with you!' and taking up their paddles they left him splashing through the water to the shore."

Tommy Pielle and Beryl Cryer

Notes

1. The word Hwunitum' is derived from hwuni', "arrive; get there; to be there," and conveys the sense of "people who arrived out of nowhere, people who were 'there' and now they're 'here.'"

2. Cowichan Tribes, 2007.

3. As recalled by Ellen White (White and MacDonald, 1992: 153).

4. Cryer to Ireland, July 18, 1967. GR 1738, Box 39, File 15, British Columbia Archives (BCA).

5. In many ways her approach, particularly the preservation of voice and collaborative dialogue, presaged later developments in anthropological theory (see Clifford and Marcus, 1986; particularly Pratt, 1986: 32 on the use of personal narrative to mediate contradictions between personal and scientific authority; Tyler, 1986: 126 on the privileging of "discourse" over "text").

6. Victoria Daily Colonist, January 22, 1933.

7. Littlefield, n.d. Anthropologists of the day often excised political content from their informants' narratives (Robinson and Wickwire, 2005: 28).

8. Mitchell and Franklin, 1984: 27. See Barman 1997–98 for overview of native women and society in late-nineteenth-century British Columbia.

9. Ward, 1981: 590–91; Arnett, 1999. For an introduction to Central Coast Salish culture of this period see: Barnett, 1955; Mitchell, 1990; Suttles, 1987, 1999; Chemainus First Nation Elders, 2000.

10. Quoted in Tennant, 1990: 101.

11. Tennant, 1990: 104.

12. Section 141, Indian Act. Tennant, 1990: 111–13. Manuel and Posluns refer to the legislation as "the darkest hour in the history of the Parliament of Canada" (1974: 95).

13. Victoria Daily Colonist, August 28, 1932.

14. Victoria Daily Colonist, March 5, 1933.

15. Boas, 2002: 41.

16. Marcus and Fischer, 1985: 95, describe "the classic salvage justification for ethnography as a recorder of cultural diversity that was disappearing or being irrevocably altered."

17. Victoria Daily Colonist, November 6, 1932.

18. Archaeologist Donald Mitchell, in 1967, when asked to comment on Beryl Cryer's work was of the opinion that although "faithfully reported ... they would not meet learned standards for anthropological texts or folktales" (Mitchell to Ireland, July 3, 1967. GR 1738, Box 39, File 15, BCA). Anthropologist Loraine Littlefield also suggests that "the journalistic presentation" of the stories is "problematic for anthropology."

19. See for example, Bertrand Lugrin's "The Capture of A-chu-Wun, The Tale of the Big Bad Indian and how he met his nemesis," in Maclean's, January 15, 1936.

20. Tuhiwai-Smith, 1999: 29.

21. The reknowned anthropologist Wilson Duff recognized the value of Beryl

Cryer's research, and included her work in his Master's thesis research and in subsequent publications.

22   Littlefield, 2003: 13.

23   Tennant, 1990: 72.

24   Cryer to Newcombe, November 11, 1933. Newcombe Family Papers (NFP) Add. Mss. 1077, Vol. 11, File 41, BCA.

25   Boas, 2002: 24–25; Crosby, 1907: 53.

26   NFP, Add. Mss. 1077, Vol. 11, file 44, BCA.

27   Basil Halhed, p.c.

28   Ellen White, p.c.

29   Jenness, 1934–35 Homer Barnett, another anthropologist working in the same area generally ignored accounts of Central Coast Salish mythology (Barnett, 1955: 18).

30   Boas, 2002: 153–55. Interestingly, Boas apparently recorded a version of this story in the Snuneymuxw dialect (See Boas, 2002: 39).

31   Atleo, 2004: 4.

32   See Atleo, 2004.

33   Ernie Rice, p.c., 2004.

34   Cryer, 1978.

35   Hwulunitum', "white people"; singular, Hwunitum'.

36   Harris, 1997: 262.

37   Loraine Littlefield, p.c. Information provided by a "favourite niece."

38   Birth Certificate, folio 1174, 1887, Auckland, New Zealand. I would like to thank Beryl Cryer's grand nephew, Basil Halhed, for this and some of the following information regarding his family. See also Cryer, 1978.

39   Cryer, 1979: 229. Maithal Gertrude Ross, née Halhed (1890–1977). Her first name was likely of East Indian origin, in recognition of the family's East India Company connections (Basil Halhed, p.c.).

40   See Olsen 1963, Chemainus Valley Historical Society, 1978 for general histories of the Chemainus Valley. Also Anketel-Jones, 1978: 194, Beauchamp, 1978: 301.

41   Chemainus Valley Historical Society, 1978: 290–91, Cryer, 1978, Robinson, 1978a: 171–72, Campbell, 1978: 253, Anketel-Jones, 1978: 196, for Halhed social life. Olsen, 1963, 106–107 for some references to Richmond Halhed's police career.

42   Cryer, 1978: 230.

43   Photocopies of two photographs with the caption "RBH" accompany the original Cryer manuscript in the British Columbia Archives: "Indian Legends," BCA F82/C88.1. As a police officer, Halhed may have played some role in enforcing the ban on potlatch celebrations. Although technically illegal since 1884, enforcement of the law was limited on Vancouver Island until the 1920s. The narratives Cryer recorded give no indication that local prosecution was taking place.

44   See Ginn, 1978 for a brief history of this mission, and Mutter, 1978, for Roberts family history.

45   Johnson, 1961.

46   Strong-Boag and Gerson, 2000: 171.

47   The appearance of poverty was, of course, relative and based on European perceptions.

48   Lack of accurate documentation makes it difficult to establish Mary Rice's exact birthdate. Littlefield puts her birthdate at 1855 (2003: 10–11). Beryl Cryer estimated 1861 (note in NFP, Add. Mss. 1077, Vol. 44, Folder 12/3, BCA). Family information states 1865 (Bob Rice, p.c.).

49 Ellen White, p.c.

50 Marriage Certificate 1879.09.092569, Roll B 11380 British Columbia Archives. Paris Teeters/Mary Selman (probably a mis-transcription of the name Solomon; her father's English name was Solomon Pielle. The certificate gives her age as sixteen, which would put the year of her birth at 1863. Walter, 1943: 15.

51 Walter, 1945: 15. The Shaws arrived on Galiano Island in 1877 (Steward, 1994: 132).

52 Walter, 1945: 15.

53 Ernie Rice, Ellen White, p.c., Walter, 1945: 15. Although they were close in many ways, Beryl Cryer did not appear to have a clear idea of Mary Rice's marital history. She wrote (1978: 239) that Mary Rice's first husband "was killed in a fight with the Haidas," and that she "was left with four small children. She later married a white man, who lived only a short time longer, being drowned when fishing." This information conflicts with that of the present-day family members who assert that while Paris Teeters may have been killed in such a fight, the father of Mary Rice's four children was George Rice.

54 Xe'xtl'uqun, "crossways" [island]. The name describes the way the island looks "crossing the middle of the water" looking east from the Puneluxutth' village (Rozen, 1985: 111). The island was purchased with money given to George Rice by his father as well as "a pouch of gold" belonging to Mary Rice (Ellen White, p.c.). The family continued to live on the island into the 1940s.

55 Littlefield, 2003: 10. Ellen White, p.c.

56 Cryer, 1978: 239. This would have been prior to 1906, when Donkele retired as principal (Chemainus Valley Historical Society, 1978: 67).

57 Chemainus Valley Historical Society, 1978: 227; Littlefield, 2003: 11. Her grandson, Bob Rice, states that she charged "10 cents an hour at first, and later up to 25 cents an hour." ("Familiar face graces wall in Chemainus," undated article, Newsaper file, Chemainus Valley Archives, Chemainus).

58 Note accompanying photograph in "Legends" manuscript, F82/C88.1, BCA.

59 Ellen White, p.c.

60 Davies, 1984: 249–64.

61 Ellen White, p.c.

62 Beryl Halhed was engaged to another man prior to this marriage. The following notice appeared in the Times (London), June 24, 1912: "Lieutenant A.E.D. Moore and Miss B.M. Halhed. A marriage has been arranged, and will shortly take place, between Lieutenant Aubrey E.D. Moore, R.N., of H.M.C.S. Rainbow, eldest son of the Archdeacon of Oakham and Mrs. E.M. Moore, and Miss Beryl M. Halhed, eldest daughter of Mr. and Mrs. R.B. Halhed, of Chemainus, Vancouver Island, British Columbia." There is no evidence that this marriage ever took place. Thanks to Basil Halhed for this information.

63 Ross to Newcombe, September 13, 1929, NFP, Add. Mss. 1077, vol. 11, file 31, BCA.

64 The Cowichan Leader published the following articles by CRYOSS: "The Coming of Winter," December 15, 1927; "The First of the Cowichans," December 22, 1927; "How the Blue Jay Came," December 29, 1927; "The First Canoe," February 2, 1928; "The Moon

Maidens," February 9, 1928; "The Cedar Sea Lion," April 12, 1928; "The Two Brothers," May 17, 1928; "The Woodpecker People," May 31, 1928; "The First Butterball Duck," June 14, 1928; "The Land of Shadows," June 1, 1928; "How Spaal' Lost His Children," July 26, 1928; "The Story of Schichella," August 23, 1928; "The End of the Wolf Men," October 4, 1928; "Tzouhytatz" November 1, 1928; "How Barnacle Got His Wife," November 29, 1928; "Cowichan Indian Legends (Khullkhullestan)," September 5, 1929.

65 "The Coming of Winter", December 15, 1927, *Cowichan Leader*.

66 Cryer to Newcombe, September 5, 1928, NFP, Add. Mss. 1077, vol. 11, file 41, BCA.

67 Ross to Newcombe, September 13, 1928, NFP, Add. Mss. 1077, vol.11, file 41, BCA.

68 Ibid. She was referring, of course, to the artist Emily Carr whom the "shy and retiring" William A. Newcombe knew very well. Carr called him "Willy" (the Halhed sisters addressed him as "Billy"). He helped the Victoria artist around her home as a handyman, and crated her paintings for exhibition (See Tippett, 1979 index). Upon her death in 1945 he became trustee of her estate and left his own collection of her work to the Province of British Columbia when he died.

69 Ibid.

70 Ross to Newcombe, October 4, 1928, NFP, Add. Mss. 1077, vol. 11, file 41, BCA. The photograph was probably BCA 5269.

71 Cryer to Newcombe, October 27, 1928. NFP, Add. Mss. 1077, vol.11, file 41, BCA.

72 Cryer to Newcombe, November 25, 1928. NFP, Add. Mss. 1077, vol.11, file 41, BCA. "Tceah" was their rendering of the Hul'q'umi'num' word skwitth'uts, "blue jay."

73 *Victoria Daily Colonist*, December 17, 1933.

74 Cryer to Ireland, March 27, 1967. GR 1738, Box 39, File No. 15.

75 *Cowichan Leader*, September 5, 1929.

76 *Vancouver Province*, June 18, 1929.

77 Cryer to Newcombe, October 21, 1929. NFP, Add. Mss. 1077, vol. 11, file 41, BCA.

78 Ross to Newcombe, January 6, 1930. NFP. Add. Mss. 1077, vol.11, file 41, BCA.

79 Cryer to Newcombe, January 16, 1932. NFP, Add. Mss. 1077, vol.11, file 41, BCA. "Mrs. Irving," the woman who replaced Cryer as the Chemainus social columnist for the *Daily Colonist*, told her that she was given the job through the influence of her sister-in-law, "as she was a friend of McKelvie's both having been on the staff of the 'Province' [a Vancouver newspaper]." Ibid.

80 Ibid.

81 Ibid. The columns mentioned were regular features in the *Sunday Magazine* edition throughout the 1930s.

82 Ibid.

83 Cryer to Newcombe, February 15, 1932, NFP, Add. Mss. 1077, vol.11, file 41, BCA.

84 Bierwert, 1999: 87. Bierwert's book is an excellent analysis of the manipulation of voice surrounding the literary and poltical agendas of other British Columbia women writers in the presentation of indigenous stories.

85 Ibid.

86 Ibid.

87 Cryer to Newcombe, "Friday 19th" 1932, NFP, Add. Mss. 1077, vol. 11, file 41, BCA.

88 Cryer to Newcombe, April 2, 1932, NFP, Add. Mss. 1077, vol. 11, file 41, BCA.

89 NFP. Add. Mass. 1077, vol. 44, Folder 12/3, BCA.

90 Cryer to Newcombe, May 10, 1932. NFP Add. Mss. 1077, vol. 11, file 41, BCA.

91 Ibid.

92 Tommy Pielle, Quyupule'ynuxw. (1865–1945). In her original work Cryer used the name "Tommy Pierre." Family members use Pielle, and I have followed suit.

93 Cryer to Newcombe, November 17, 1932. NFP. Add. Mss. 1077, vol. 11, file 41, BCA.

94 Ibid.

95 Cryer to Ireland, March 27, 1967. GR 1738, Box 39, File 15, BCA.

96 Cryer to Newcombe, November 14, 1932. NFP, Add. Mss. 1077, vol. 11, file 41, BCA.

97 Ibid. The Boas publication was *Kutenai Tales*, published by the Bureau of American Ethnology, 1918, and Teit's 1898 *Traditions of the Thompson River Indians of British Columbia*, published by the American Folklore Society, New York.

98 Cryer to Newcombe, December 7, 1932. NFP, Add. Mss. 1077, vol. 11, file 41, BCA.

99 Ibid.

100 Ibid.

101 Cryer to Newcombe, February 26, 1933, NFP, Add. Mss. 1077, vol. 11, file 41, BCA.

102 Ellen White, p.c.

103 Ibid. John Peter, Saytchletsu (1833–1945) a former sea lion hunter, was an uncle of Mary Rice. In 1943 he was regarded as "one, if not the oldest native among the Gulf Islands" (Walter, 1945: 14). See also Robinson, 1978: 175.

104 *Victoria Daily Colonist*, March 5, 1933.

105 Cryer to Newcombe, September 12, 1933, NFP, Add. Mss. 1077, vol. 11, file 41, BCA.

106 Ibid.

107 Cryer to Newcombe, "Wed." month unknown, 1933, NFP, Add. Mss. 1077, Vol. 11, File 41, BCA.

108 Cryer to Newcombe, October 22, 1933, NFP, Add. Mss. 1077, Vol. 11, File 41, BCA.

109 Jonaitus, 1988: 88–92.

110 Cryer to Newcombe, October 22, 1933, NFP, Add. Mss. 1077, Vol. 11, File 41, BCA.

111 Ibid. A note on the back of these photographs states that they were "carved by a whiteman."

112 Cryer to Newcombe, November 11, 1933. NFP, Add. Mss. 1077, Vol. 11, File 41, BCA.

113 Ibid. The man was Chief Edward Hulbertsun of Hwts'usi'.

114 Ibid.

115 Ibid.

116 Cryer to Newcombe, December 6, 1933, NFP, Add. Mss. 1077, Vol. 11, File 41, BCA. The Boas publication was his 1889 "Notes on the Snanaimuq," published in *American Anthropologist* 2(4): 321–28.

117 Ibid.

118 Ibid.

119 Cryer to Newcombe, January 31, 1934. NFP, Add. Mss. 1077, Vol. 11, File 41, BCA.

120 Ibid.

121 Ibid.

122 Today, recording equipment of any kind is not permitted in longhouse gatherings associated with the smilhu and other ceremonies for fear of harming the participants (see discussion in Amoss, 1978: ix; and Bierwert, 1999: 12–126).

123 Cryer to Newcombe, August 10, 1936, NFP, Add Mss 1077, vol. 11, folder 41, BCA.

124 *The Flying Canoe: Legends of the Cowichans* (Victoria: J. Parker Buckle Printing, 1949).

125 Two of these were versions of stories included in this volume, by Joe Wyse (page 250) and Tommy Pielle (page 324). The other two were published in the *Daily Colonist* after 1937 and, based on their style, were part of the original "Legends of the Cowichans" series.

126 Cryer, 1949.

127 "Tzlah-Mia" appears to be another rendition of Mary Rice's honorific name, Siamtunaat.

128 Cryer, 1949.

129 Cryer to Ireland, March 27, 1967. GR 1738, Box 39, File 15, BCA.

130 Ireland to Cryer, April 4, 1967. GR 1738, Box 39, File 15, BCA.

131 Mitchell to Ireland, July 3, 1967. GR 1738, Box 39, File 15, BCA.

132 Ibid.

133 Ireland to Cryer, July 7, 1967. GR 1738, Box 39, File 15, BCA.

134 Cryer to Ireland, July 18, 1967. GR 1738, Box 39, File 15, BCA.

135 Ireland to Cryer, August 1, 1967. GR 1738, box 39, File 15, BCA.

136 Rozen, 1985.

137 Chemainus Valley Historical Society, 1978: xviii.

138 Cryer, 1978: 238.

139 Cryer, 1978: 240.

140 Originally published February 17, 1932, *Victoria Daily Colonist*. Mary Rice's paternal grandfather bore the name Xulqalustun (c. 1790–1886), and was the headman of a house at Puneluxutth' on Kuper Island. He was a warrior, and, it appears, an early convert to Christianity when he was given the name "Pielle." He was the lead signatory on the land sale agreement arranged between the "North Saanich" and the Hudson's Bay Company at Victoria on February 11, 1852, one of fourteen such land purchases made on Vancouver between 1850 and 1854 and commonly referred to as the Douglas Treaties, after the Governor, James Douglas (Tennant, 1990: 17–25; Arnett, 1999: 30–39). Mary Rice was born in his house at Puneluxutth' and spent her early life within the extended family. Here, she would become very familiar with the oral histories of this particular grandfather. The first two articles in the series are a reworking of the 1929 piece entitled "Cowichan Indian Legends (As narrated by Mary Rice, granddaughter of Chief Khullkhullestan)," by CRYOSS, which appeared on September 5, 1929 in the *Cowichan Leader*. Written in slightly different styles, there are interesting additions and omissions between the two versions. The sequence of events, however, is identical.

141 In the 1930s, it was common for English speakers to refer to all people south of Nanaimo and north of Duncan

as "Cowichan," without recognizing the significant cultural diversity in the area (Rozen, 1985). Initially, Cryer does this as well, but soon recognizes the local distinctions.

142 Either Beryl Cryer or Mary Rice has exaggerated here; Rice's descendants today remember her "always telling stories." One of her granddaughters, Ellen White, is a well known elder, educator, storyteller and author. (White, 1981, 1994, 2006).

143 The name Siamtunaat, or "Tzea-mntenaht," as Beryl Cryer transcribed it, came from Mary Rice's aunt who was from Burrard Inlet (Ellen White, p.c.).

144 Q'ulits', "sheltered area, protected," is the Hul'q'umi'num' name for Kulleet Bay on Vancouver Island. Speakers of the "Chemainus" dialect say Sqwul'eets (Chemainus First Nation Elders, 2000: 25). English speakers named it Chemainus Bay after the ancient village of Shts'um'inus, which occupies part of the shoreline. Early in the twentieth century, the English name was changed to "Kulleet" to avoid confusion with the town and harbour of Chemainus further south.

145 One of the three classes of "medicine people," siowa had the ability to see future events. They never healed the sick. See accounts by Mr. and Mrs. Bob of Westholme, and others, for roles and training of siowa (Jenness 1934–35: 210–15; Duff, 1952: 150; Amoss, 1978: 15–16). Visions and premonitions about the coming of non-natives were widespread on the Northwest Coast and in the Interior of British Columbia and Washington (Spier, 1935; Matthews, 1955: 198).

146 Hwlhitsum refers to Canoe Pass, in the vicinity of Steveston.

147 A number of first-contact stories mention the strange food of the newcomers, and misunderstandings over its use. Compare with the Sqwxwa'mush account given by August Jack Khahtsalano: "Everywhere white man go, China, other place, he always change food where he goes. At first Indians not know what whiteman's food look like. When first whiteman come up Howe Sound, up near Squamish, he give Indian biscuits, big round biscuits. Indian not know what they are. He shoot at them and break them up [with arrows in a game]: he not know they are good to eat" (Matthews, 1955: 13).

148 Originally published Thursday, March 3, 1932, *Victoria Daily Colonist*.

149 Hwlumelhtsu, "lookout place," was a village situated in a southeast facing bay on the south end of Kuper Island. Its population in 1863 was approximately 100 people, living in eight large shed houses. After the failure of the first treaty process (the Douglas Treaties), increasing encroachment and unauthorized occupation of native lands led to deadly assaults, beginning around 1858, on isolated groups of Hwunitum' travellers. While some leaders negotiated their own agreements with Hwunitum', other leaders emerged who were opposed to any Hwunitum' settlement on traditional lands. This unstable situation culminated in the April 1863 homicides on Saturna and Pender Islands. People who lived at Hwlumelhtsu on Kuper Island were blamed for the killings, and the village was attacked on April 20, 1863 by Her Majesty's gunboat *Forward*. The attack was repulsed with casualties and James Douglas' colonial government ordered a large naval expedition of 500 sailors, marines and colonial militia to what was now the "Seat of War." The leaders and

families of Hwlumclhtsu were pursued throughout the Gulf Islands and on Vancouver Island, some were killed and many were taken into custody. Some native allies volunteered but others, such as Mary's grandfather Xulqalustun, may have been coerced into assisting the British. In any event, as Mary Rice describes, his assistance was key to the capture of an important Hwlumelhtsu leader, who happened to be a member of Xulqalustun's family, a man named 'Uxchewun, at Montague Harbour, Galiano Island on June 2, 1863. It is interesting how in both this version of the story, and the version that appeared on September 5, 1929 in the *Cowichan Leader*, the oral tradition by Mary Rice draws a continuity between the ship seen at first contact in the late 1700s and the independent traders of the 1860s, as if they were the same people. Of course, as "white people," in sailing ships full of valuable trading goods, they were. The course of events between late 1862 and July 1863, are also collapsed, events are left out, and there is no mention of the battle at Hwlumelhtsu. The village of Hwlumelhtsu was burned to the ground on May 2 of that year by British forces. Many of the people living there were taken prisoner, and four were executed on July 4, 1863 in Victoria. Following the "war," James Douglas forbade anyone to occupy the site. In time, the site of the village and an adjacent 100 acres were pre-empted by Hwnitum' settlers with the help of native wives. Some native families had also moved near the old site by 1882 (see Arnett, 1999).

150 These stories are not uncommon in the oral traditions heard in native communities today (2006). Few accounts have been written down. The stories may be variations of a single

important event, or several that occurred over time, but the basic theme remains the same: a social gathering takes place, liquor is introduced, when the liquor is gone escalating anger leads to the killing of white men, and the looting and burning of their boats. Ultimately the bodies of the slain are loaded with rocks, and sunk in deep water (see Arnett, 1999: 84–85: 9). In some versions, the Royal Navy arrives and people are hanged.

151 (Arnett, 1999: 86–87, 263). In the 1929 version of the story, the implication is that Xulqalustun did not go willingly. "But Khullkhullestan, the chief, they took with them upon their boat, having also other chiefs of other tribes; and these they held until such time as Qhatchewan, chief of the Lamalchas, should be found" (*Cowichan Leader*, September 5, 1929).

152 Sihwoletse' (c.1830–c.1910), also known as George O'Shea. His father, Ashutstun, was killed by 'Uxchewun in 1858 on Valdez Island. Sihwoletse' joined the British expedition because "it gave him a chance to take revenge at this tribe" (Eddy Edwards quoted in Arnett, 1999: 357, n.55).

153 Montague Harbour. An older name used by English speakers was "Stockade Bay", possibly in reference to native fortifications. The Hul'q'umi'num' name for the bay is Sun'nuw', "entering place," and it has a long history of occupation and use by native peoples (Mitchell, 1971). When the area was first mapped in 1858, Admiralty surveyors noted "several Indian lodges … built on the shore of the bay" (Richards quoted in Arnett, 1999: 332, n.97).

154 According to several Hwnitum' accounts, 'Uxchewun gave stiffer

resistance to his capture (Arnett, 1999: 247).

155 July 4, 1863, in Bastion Square, Victoria (Arnett, 1999: 303–05).

156 Originally published Friday, March 11, 1932, *Victoria Daily Colonist*.

157 Originally published circa March 23, 1932, *Victoria Daily Colonist*.

158 Cryer to Newcombe, February 4, 1932, NFP, Add. Mss. 1077, vol. 11, File 44, BCA.

159 Modeste Demers (1809–1871). Consecrated the Bishop of Vancouver Island in 1847, he was instrumental in the introduction of Catholicism to the Central Coast Salish (Arnett, 1999: 63–67,160–62).

160 Loxa (1824–1899), headman of household at the village of Qw'umiyiqun' on the delta of the Cowichan River. See his daughter's account, page 162.

161 Reverend Father Gustave Donkele, a priest of the Victoria Diocese, was the second principal of the school from 1890 to 1906. The school, which closed in 1970, does not have a good reputation among many of its survivors. Several of the school's brick buildings were demolished over the years, and part of the rubble used to shore up Penelakut Spit.

162 There was an "Indian Police" administered by Police Magistrate W.H. Franklyn from 1864 to 1867 (Olsen, 1963: 46–49).

163 In a letter to William Newcombe regarding these photos, Beryl Cryer writes: "I think all are dead—but one, I know, used to work with my father" (Cryer to Newcombe, Feb.15, 1932. NFP, Add. Mss. 1077, vol.11, File 44, BCA).

164 Dixon (1978) describes a visit to these burial structures in 1922, and provides a short account of the reburial. The structures were standing in 1924 when they were photographed by Eloise Street Harises, which suggests the reburial took place sometime after that. (Vancouver Museum: PN 20, 21, 24).

165 Originally published Tuesday, March 29, 1932, *Victoria Daily Colonist*.

166 Charles Rice (c.1885–1937).

167 Pierre Rondeault (1824–1900), an Oblate priest, arrived on Vancouver Island in 1858, and established the Mission of St. Ann's at Qw'umiyiqun' that same year.

168 Fraser River Stolo people used knotted strings to record days and other kinds of information (see Bob Joe's account in Wells, 1987: 56). Further up the river at Spuzzum, Nlakapamux people placed long knotted strings that recorded family information into coffins of the deceased (York, Daly, and Arnett, 1993: 86–87).

169 Originally published May 22, 1932, *Victoria Daily Colonist, Sunday Magazine*.

170 Kwatakwata, "fire-drill" (Jenness, 1934–35: 34).

171 Probably Comox Lake.

172 Originally published May 29, 1932, *Victoria Daily Colonist, Sunday Magazine*.

173 Hilda Rice (1901–1979).

174 Camas, or speenhw, (*Camassia quamash*) harvesting was part of a well-established system of semi-cultivation among the Central Coast Salish (see Turner, 2005). The Hul'q'umi'num' name for camus is speenhw, but when using English they often refer to it as "Ly-camas," or "Lacamas" a word possibly derived from Chinook trade jargon.

175 Mary Rice's father Solomon Pielle (also called Joe Simon) carried the name Xulqalustun. He died in the 1860s, when Mary Rice was young. Her mother, Solowtunaht, was also known as "Maggie" (Marriage Record 1879.09.092569, Roll B, and Bob Rice, p.c.).

176 Originally published June 5, 1932, *Victoria Daily Colonist, Sunday Magazine.*

177 The "white man" was George Rice, whose mother was Squinomish. His father, George Rice Sr., was from Ireland (Ernie Rice, Ellen White, p.c.).

178 Beryl Cryer used editorial licence, or confused Mary Rice's first husband, Paris Teeters, with George Rice. Both men were from the United States, however. Mary Rice only had children with George Rice, who had a heart attack and drowned in 1895, and must be the husband who died "thirty-five years ago" from the date of this 1932 story.

179 Originally published June 12, 1932, *Victoria Daily Colonist, Sunday Magazine.* In the original publication, Beryl Cryer uses different English names for the bride and groom. The original title of the story was "The Wedding of Mary and Johnny Jim."

180 Littlefield, n.d.: 6. See also Suttles, 1987a: 17.

181 For comparative material on Central Coast Salish marriage ceremonies, see Barnett, 1955: 186–93; Matthews, 1955: 197; and Suttles, 1987a: 17, 1990: 465.

182 A comical English cartoon character of an older man with a large white handlebar moustache.

183 Originally published July 17, 1932, *Victoria Daily Colonist, Sunday Magazine.* This article, and the two that follow it,

do not appear in the order they were first published in the *Daily Colonist*. Because Beryl Cryer often submitted more than one story at a time, some stories were occasionally published out of sequence.

184 The comparative literature on Central Coast Salish shamanism is extensive. See Barnett, 1955: 147–51, 209–16; Jenness, 1934–35; Jenness, 1955; Kew and Kew, 1981; and Jilek, 1982.

185 Tsilamunthut (Charlie Wilson) was living at Hwlumelhtsu by February 1882 (see Robert Roberts' Diary, Kuper Island, February 4, 14, June 9,18 entries, CM/A198, BCA).

186 Probably Q'ut'q'it (Mary Anne Pielle, 1866–1959), who lived at Ts'usnu'um (Beaver Point).

187 Originally published July 24, 1932, *Victoria Daily Colonist, Sunday Magazine.*

188 slhuxun', "medicine" (Hukari and Peter, 1995: 78).

189 The count used in this story is not recognizable as everyday Hul'q'umi'num'. For example, the word for "one" is nuts'a.

190 Again, the word is not recognizeable Hul'q'umi'num'. "Two" is yuse'lu.

191 Originally published July 31, 1932, *Victoria Daily Colonist, Sunday Magazine.*

192 Amoss, 1978: 25–26.

193 Quyupule'ynuxw (c.1790–c.1870). See Matthews, 1955: 216B.

194 There were earlier attempts to kill Tsilamunthut (Charlie Wilson) at his home at Hwlumelhtsu. On February 14, 1882, the missionary Robert Roberts reported hearing three shots and "soon afterward Indian Johnnie came up and told me that some persons had shot at Charlie Wilson's" while he

195 sat down to dinner (Roberts Diary, 1882, CM/A198, BCA).

195 Originally published June 19, 1932. *Victoria Daily Colonist, Sunday Magazine*.

196 Jenness, 1934–35: 273; Suttles, 1987b: 106–09, Fig. 2.

197 Florence James, p.c. 2001; Hukari and Peter, 1995: 90. See also the account by Jennie Wyse, pages 227–28.

198 Barnett, 1955: 151–53.

199 The "crude" appearance of the rattle is immaterial. As Jenness learned from his informants, its use was restricted to "only a few noble families" (Jenness, 1934–35: 273).

200 Ritualists use the rattle in various curing rites (Suttles, 1987b: 107). Mary Rice's response to Cryer's questioning demonstrates that she was not willing to share all information with her white colleague.

201 Originally published June 26, 1932, *Victoria Daily Colonist, Sunday Magazine*.

202 Charlie Rice's first wife was Louisa Smith.

203 Hilda Rice (1901–1979).

204 Originally published July 10, 1932, *Victoria Daily Colonist, Sunday Magazine*.

205 Ellen White, p.c. She also states that "it is not a word you can use everyday ... It's almost like you're in a spiritual [state]."

206 Xextl'uqun, later known as Rice Island, and now called Norway Island, lies just offshore of the village of Puneluxutth' at the north end of Kuper Island.

207 See Barnett, 1955: 102–03, Plate VIII, for comparison.

208 "Wild Carrot" (*Perideridia gairdneri*). See Turner, 1982: 108–10.

209 Originally published August 7, 1932, *Victoria Daily Colonist, Sunday Magazine*.

210 The line-by-line documentation of the key events in the story are the only known notes for any of Cryer's published stories. In the accompanying letter, she asks Newcombe if he would not mind "looking up my story in the archives?" The story concerned a native man on "death row" in Nanaimo, who was wrongly accused of murders, and who eventually escapes with the help of his wife. She writes, " ... Mary is usually pretty accurate I find—but in this case I want to be certain that the man Cly-aack [Qleysuluq] was not caught for 13 years ... " More than anything, this letter demonstrates Beryl Cryer's commitment to accuracy. NFP, Add. Mss 1077, Vol. 44, Folder 12/3, BCA; Cryer to Newcombe, May 10, 1932, NFP, Add. Mss. 1077, Vol. 11, file 41, BCA.

211 Compare this account with one by Brown in 1864, in which he describes the "Comiaken" Chief Locha (Loxa) and his use of a similar strategy to destroy a warparty of 150 "Stickeens" (Brown, 1989: 43–44). This took place around 1850, and may be related to the account by Mary Rice.

212 Cryer's notes state that the pursuers were sighted at East Point, Saturna Island, and the party went ashore nearby.

213 Cryer's notes are more specific: Tom Collin's landing, an old name for Miner's Bay, Mayne Island.

214 In the notes given to Newcombe, Cryer writes, "In telling the story she [Mary Rice] says she was a small girl at the time of the murder, and had been married about two years when Cly-aack was tried, which seems to place date of murder about year 1863–64, as she was 18 when married" (NFP, Add. Mss. 1077, Vol. 44, Folder 12/3, BCA).

There is some confusion here. Mary Rice got the story second-hand from her Aunt. Police information suggests the killings took place "on or about the 12th day of July, 1877" (Register of depositions, Attorney General document series, GR 419, Box 25, File 32a, 1883, BCA).

215 In Cryer's notes, their names are "Peter Yuclaas" and "Skookum Tom" (NFP, Add. Mss. 1077, Vol.44, Folder 12/3, BCA).

216 There is an extensive file on this event in the register of Depositions, Attorney General Document Series, GR 419, Box 15, File 2, Box 25, File 32a, BCA. Qleysuluq and his son were arrested and committed for trial on January 3, 1883, and " broke Gaol 8th January, 1884." Skookum Tom ("Skookum Jim" in the story) was living at Hwlumelhtsu in February 1882, and is mentioned a few times in Robert Roberts' diaries. Roberts noted that "Skukum Tom or Tom Cluekias ... did not seem to be a bad fellow although he is accused of being a murderer of Bella Bella Indians or Haidas" (Mission Diary, Kuper Island, Feb.13, 1882, CM/A198, BCA). A few days later, on February 16, he notes a visit by a policeman Stewart "who called to speak to me about Skukum Tom or Clakia an Indian lately returned to Lamalchi Bay and accused of being concerned with others in the murder of some Hyder Indians near East Point a few years ago."

217 Originally published August 14, 1932, *Victoria Daily Colonist, Sunday Magazine.*

218 The Hul'q'umi'num' word for "cat" is pous, and, evidently, could be mistaken by untrained ears for the English word "fish."

219 Originally published August 21, 1932, *Victoria Daily Colonist, Sunday Magazine.*

220 Domestic cherries are best in early July, which suggests that this article was written at least a month before its publication date.

221 See Xulqalustun, Part III, page 61.

222 Originally published August 28, 1932, *Victoria Daily Colonist, Sunday Magazine.*

223 Puneluxutth'. The name refers to the condition of being partly buried. In this story, Mary Rice uses the term in reference to the cedar logs that lay on the beach when the first people appeared. Others relate the name to the great longhouses that once stood along Penelakut Spit, "half-buried" in clamshells and sand (Rozen, 1985: 101–102). The name is derived from punut "bury," spepin "many buried" and uxutth, which refers to the side of a house, or a cedar limb, or whatever is partly covered (Arvid Charlie p.c.).

224 Yuxwula'us "place of eagles" on present-day Telegraph Harbour, Kuper Island.

225 Originally published September 4, 1932. *Victoria Daily Colonist, Sunday Magazine.*

226 Xulel-thw, "marked houses," "painted houses." The original village of Xulel-thw stood on the south bank of the lower Cowichan River, in Duncan, where the Island Highway crosses the river. After flooding in the nineteenth century, the people moved to Willy Island taking the name with them. Then, in the 1920s, they were encouraged by Government administrators to move to the present-day reserve at Westholme, which now bears the name Xulel-thw, or "Halalt" (Rozen, 1985: 126).

227 Photographs of these gravehouses were included in Beryl Cryer's manuscript "Indian Legends" F82/C88.1, BCA.

228 Mary Rice is explaining how the name Xulel-thw is derived from xulxulul's, the Hul'q'umi'num' word for "writing" (Hukari and Peter, 1995: 29).

229 Hwslhuw'lhnenum, "hunter, provider of food" (Hukari and Peter, 195: 21). An "ironic" term.

230 Sunuwnets, "go inside to bottom end," "entering back of the bay," "fresh water behind houses," descriptive term for this part of Chemainus Harbour. The ancient village site was purchased by Cryer's father, Richmond Halhed, and was the site of Mary Rice's cabin and the location of this particular account.

231 She is referring to a settlement that stood on the site of the present town of Chemainus, not to the Shts'um'inus (Chemainus) village at Kulleet Bay.

232 Originally published September 11, 1932. *Victoria Daily Colonist, Sunday Magazine.*

233 Lane, 1951.

234 Margaret Walters (1945: 55) described him as "an intelligent and dignified Indian whom Mrs. Griffiths [a late-nineteenth century settler on Salt Spring Island] especially employed from time to time. His hair was white, an unusual thing in a native ... In his younger days he had acted as a guide to the earliest pioneers in the country and considered himself honoured by their approval. When he passed away on the Griffiths' place [Fernwood Farm] its mistress had him buried in the usual way, but his wife not approving, she later had him removed to be placed near by, according to native custom."

235 "Dog-eating dances" were associated with secret societies and special performances, and practiced over a wide area of the Northwest Coast (MacFie, 1865: 433; Suttles and Jonaitus, 1990: 84). One of the cultural teachings in these dramatic performances was the notion of the depth of depravity humans are capable of reaching if things go out of balance. They were teachings about the nature of reality (Richard Atleo, p.c.).

236 British Naval forces searched the village of Puneluxutth' for native fugitives during May and June 1863, in January 1869, and probably on other occasions as well (Arnett, 1999: 208–54, Colonial Correspondence, File 1169–70, Morley, Microfilm B1342, BCA). Uncertainty over the date of Mary Rice's birth (anywhere between 1855 and 1865) makes it difficult to pinpoint the exact date of the incident she describes.

237 Originally published September 18, 1932 *Victoria Daily Colonist, Sunday Magazine.*

238 See Maranda, 1984 for detailed accounts of Coast Salish gambling.

239 Old village site on Chemainus Harbour.

240 Known in English as Tent Island.

241 Xeel's, the Transformer, a supernatural being who roamed the area in ancient times, creating order and biodiversity. See Bierwert, 1999: 72–112; Atleo, 2004: 59–69 for discussion and references.

242 See Matthews (1955: 392–93) for references to Transformer rocks at the mouth of the North Arm of the Fraser River.

243 Originally published September 25, 1932, *Victoria Daily Colonist, Sunday Magazine.*

244 Hwtl'upnets, "deep water behind [or on bottom of] bay," Maple Bay (Rozen, 1985: 130).

245 Ts'uwxilem (c.1810–1849).

246 For comparative material regarding this famous battle, see Thomas James' account, published in 1907, in Maud (1978: 160–62). See also Jenness, 1934–35: 171; Rozen 1985: 130; and Galois 1994: 70, n. 87.

247 Originally published October 2, 1932, *Victoria Daily Colonist, Sunday Magazine.*

248 Originally published October 16, 1932, *Victoria Daily Colonist, Sunday Magazine.*

249 See Jenness, 1934–35: 278. See Heaton's 1860 census of Hul'q'umi'num' villages (Heaton, 1860), which counted seven slaves out of a total population of 2,104. Slaves were by-products of war, often wounded individuals that survived being killed outright. The Hul'q'umi'num' word skw'uyuth means both "prisoner of war" and "slave," and is derived from the word skw'nuts, "limp from a permanent injury." The economic value of slaves was limited, and slavery among the Central Coast Salish bears little resemblance to the massive racial and economic slavery practiced by "civilized" European, Arab or Asian societies throughout history.

250 Originally published October 30, 1932, *Victoria Daily Colonist, Sunday Magazine.*

251 Pierre Rondeault (1824–1900).

252 Louis Gaboieti, of Italian origin, was in the Cowichan delta by June 1860 (Heaton Census, 1860).

253 Tomanawas, a Chinook trade jargon term for the smilhu "winter spirit dance."

254 Originally published November 6, 1932, *Victoria Daily Colonist, Sunday Magazine.*

255 Cryer to Newcombe, November 14, 17, NFP, Add. Mss. 1077, vol. 11, file 41, BCA.

256 Originally published November 13, 1932, *Victoria Daily Colonist, Sunday Magazine.*

257 Tyee is Chinook trade jargon for "leader."

258 In 1856, Tathlasut, a S-amuna' (Somenos) leader, shot and wounded a former Hudson's Bay Company employee named Thomas Williams, in a dispute over a woman. In response, James Douglas, the Governor of the Colony of Vancouver Island, led a military expedition to the Cowichan Valley. See Arnett, 1999: 54–62 for a description of the events of August–September 1856.

259 "Klootchmen" is Chinook trade jargon for "Indian women."

260 Originally published November 20, 1932, *Victoria Daily Colonist, Sunday Magazine.*

261 This would be the "Squoniston" who signed the Douglas Treaty at Nanaimo, in 1854 (*Papers Associated with the Indian Land Question, 1850–1875*, 1987: 11).

262 Originally published December 4, 1932, *Victoria Daily Colonist, Sunday Magazine.*

263 Probably a reference to the events of 1863. See page 58.

264 From Chinook trade jargon. Mowich could mean "food" or "deer."

265 Low water levels in the Cowichan River the previous fall prompted increasing harassment of the owners of traditional fish weir sites by federal fisheries officers. See Harris, 2001: 127–85 for a detailed account of the campaign to prohibit fish weirs on the Cowichan River. They remained in use until 1936.

266 A photograph of this pole, taken by William Newcombe, appears in Barnett, 1955, Plate VIII. The Hul'q'umi'num' name for the duck-net poles is xwul'xwul'u (Hukari and Peter, 1995: 179).

267 This place is well known to Hul'qumi'num people (Rozen, 1985: 133).

268 Originally published December 11, 1932, *Victoria Daily Colonist, Sunday Magazine*.

269 For comparative ethnography on Xeel's, see Jenness, 1934–35: 6–13; Lerman and Keller, 1976: 40–42; Teachings of the Elders, 1983; Bierwert, 1999: 72–111; Marshall, 1999: 43–46; Boas, 2002: 135–38; White, 2006.

270 See Rozen, 1985: 113.

271 Originally published December 25, 1932, *Victoria Daily Colonist, Sunday Magazine*.

272 Originally published January 22, 1933, *Victoria Daily Colonist, Sunday Magazine*.

273 Littlefield, n.d.: 8

274 Ankuty is Chinook trade jargon for "old."

275 sweem, "horseclam" (Hukari and Peter, 1995: 89).

276 Now collectively called Nuu-chah-nulth.

277 Originally published March 5, 1933, *Victoria Daily Colonist, Sunday Magazine*. I have again departed from the published chronology by switching this story with the February 12, 1933 story, which will follow, to keep the order Cryer originally intended.

278 Suttles, 1987a: 18.

279 Xwsol'exwel, "place of the Solexwel." The original settlement was located in what is now downtown Nanaimo, at what became the site of the No. 1 shaft of the coal mine. Following the 1854 treaty, the people moved further west to their present location on Nanaimo Harbour.

280 Enwines, "village in the centre."

281 A place in Victoria, "possibly near Johnson Street Bridge, or the present-day Parliament buildings" (Hukari and Peter, 1995: 86).

282 Probably Joseph William McKay (1829–1900). An officer for the Hudson's Bay Company, McKay apparently played some role in the "discovery" of coal in Nanaimo (Walbran, 1971: 329). McKay was also a signatory to many of the Douglas Treaties, but not the 1854 agreement (Duff, 1969).

283 Originally published February 12, 1933, *Victoria Daily Colonist, Sunday Magazine*.

284 Originally published March 12, 1933, *Victoria Daily Colonist, Sunday Magazine*.

285 For comparative ethnography, see Albert Wesley's account recorded by Diamond Jenness (Jenness, 1934–35: 5). In this version, the name of the shne'um is "Thochwam."

286 It is estimated that close to ninety percent of Snuneymuxw people are descended from Joe and Jennie Wyse (Littlefield, n.d.: 3, 2003: 11).

287 See Hill and Hill, 1974: 93–95.

288 'uya'thqsun, "sharp-pointed."

289 Rolf Knight writes: "The relief allocation [for native people during the Depression] constituted some five dollars per capita per year for each status Indian in B.C. In practice, few Indian families received any relief and only the indisputably incapacitated and infirm received minimal amounts" (Knight, 1996: 322).

290 False Narrows, on Gabriola Island.

291 Beryl Cryer is mistaken here. The place-name Tl'eeltxw refers to Gabriola Island, not Newcastle Island.

292 Originally published March 26, 1933, *Victoria Daily Colonist, Sunday Magazine*.

293 Hwsaluxul, "place of the saluxul."

294 Today (2006) elders assert that you can determine which village someone is from by the way they talk.

295 naan'um', "talking, having a discussion" (Hukari and Peter, 1995: 50).

296 slhumuhw, "rain." Jenness, in his field notes, states that the first Snuneymuxw man was named "rain" (Rozen, 1985: 46).

297 thq'ulhxw or thq'ulhxe'um, "kneel" (Hukari and Peter, 1995: 219).

298 Originally published, April 9, 1933, *Victoria Daily Colonist, Sunday Magazine*.

299 The site of Tl'eeltxw is in the vicinity of False Narrows.

300 Possibly referring to the Yukw'ulhta'x village at Cape Mudge, Quadra Island.

301 Here, Tl'utasiye' refers to the unnamed warrior who was in charge of this particular expedition.

302 Originally published April 30, 1933, *Victoria Daily Colonist, Sunday Magazine*.

303 Boas, 2002: 153–55.

304 smuqw'a', "Blue Heron."

305 Originally published May 28, 1935, *Victoria Daily Colonist, Sunday Magazine*.

306 spulqwitthe'alx, "dead person's spirit" (Jenness, 1934–35: 291).

307 q'ey'xulhp, "Cascara."

308 Originally published June 11, 1933, *Victoria Daily Colonist, Sunday Magazine*.

309 Olsen, 1963: 52.

310 "Potlatch" is from Chinook trade jargon. The word originated from the Nuu-chah-nulth word pachitle, "to give" (Atleo, 2004: 3).

311 Chief Constable William Stewart. Police records indicate that Stewart had other reasons to visit Thuq'min' on April 2, 1878, specifically to arrest and charge Qapuluq with the killing of six "Bella Bella" people near Saturna Island on July 12, 1877. Qapuluq later served as a witness in the trials of others accused of the same killings. (Register of depositions, Attorney General document Series, 1852–1966, GR 419, Box 25, File 32a, 1883, BCA. See Mary Rice's account of these events recorded by Beryl Cryer (page 112), which leaves out Qapuluq's role.

312 The "race" was a special "washing rite" and public display only used by certain families (see Barnett, 1955: 162).

313 si'win', "wordpower" (Hukari and Peter, 1995: 336).

314 xwaayxwi' is the name given to someone who dances the swayxwi mask (Cowichan Tribes, 2007: 24).

315 Originally published June 25, 1933, *Victoria Daily Colonist, Sunday Magazine*.

316 Originally published July 16, 1933, *Victoria Daily Colonist, Sunday Magazine*.

317 She has the same honorific name as Mary Rice. Cryer renders it "Tse-Um-Tenard."

318 Archaeological evidence demonstrates that the earliest people on the coast subsisted primarily upon sea-mammal hunting (Matson, 1996: 118).

319 Originally published July 30, 1933, *Victoria Daily Colonist, Sunday Magazine*.

320 Ni' 'untsu nu khuk … ?

321 Originally published September 24, 1933, *Victoria Daily Colonist, Sunday Magazine*.

322 As a child, Ernie Rice remembers listening to his grandmother tell stories as she made mats (Ernie Rice p.c.).

323 Originally published October 15, 1933, *Victoria Daily Colonist, Sunday Magazine*.

324 Another version of this story, by Mary Rice, appears in Cryer, 1949: 44–48). In Rice's version the phrase "Q'et'um s'haqw" is also used as a place-name for "a high rock" where Mink first encountered the paddlers.

325 Originally published November 5, 1933, *Victoria Daily Colonist, Sunday Magazine.*

326 An important Puneluxutth' leader at Hwts'usi', and "land claims" activist, Edward Hulbertsun testified at the 1913 Royal Commission on Indian Affairs (Arnett, 1999: 317).

327 Ts'uwxilem. The Hul'q'umi'num' name for Mount Tzouhalem is Shquw'utsun "[the frog] warms its back."

328 John Peter (1833–1949). He was a reknowned hunter of "Steller's sea lions" (shes) and took part in the last traditional hunts, which continued into the 1910s. Wayne Suttles, who interviewed Peter in the 1940s, described him as "one of the last Penelekuts harpooners" (Suttles, 1987d: 237). He was Mary Rice's uncle. For further biographical information, see Walter, 1945; Robinson, 1978a: 175.

329 Originally published December 17, 1933, *Victoria Daily Colonist, Sunday Magazine.*

330 Cryer to Newcombe, February 6, 1932, "Sunday 1st." "Wed" (n.d.), and September 12, 1933, NFP, Add. Mss.1077, vol.11, file 41, BCA.

331 Jenness, 1934–35: 108–20. See also Claxton, 1993.

332 Mim'ne', "February" (Hukari and Peter, 1995: 48).

333 P'uq'ulenuhw, "September" ("Months," photocopy held in Penelakut Band Office, Kuper Island).

334 Hwisulenuhw, "October" ("Months," photocopy held in Penelakut Band Office, Kuper Island).

335 Pune'q, "January" (Hukari and Peter, 1995: 216). Word refers to geoduck clams taken at this time.

336 Shts'ul'we'sum, "December" ("Months," photocopy held in Penelakut Band Office, Kuper Island.)

337 Punhwemun, "May" (Hukari and Peter, 1995: 53).

338 A Salish religious movement that combines elements of Christianity and indigenous teachings (Amoss, 1990: 633–39).

339 Qwi'lus, "June" ("Months," photocopy held in Penelekut Band Office, Kuper Island)

340 Suyum, "December" (Hukari and Peter, 1995: 89).

341 Wilkes James' mother. "Tse-Um-Tenard," in Cryer's orthography.

342 Tth'ul'xwumutsun, "January" (Hukari and Peter, 1995: 216).

343 Tum'qwi'lis, "July" (Hukari and Peter, 1995: 99).

344 Stul'at'luw. The moon covers the period August–September. In her September 12, 1933 letter to Newcombe, Cryer wrote, "I have the 13 Salish months— got them all from old John Peter [Sitxalatsa] at Cowichan Gap [Porlier Pass, Galiano Island]" (NFP, Add.Mss.1077, vol.11, file 41, BCA).

345 Originally published March 18, 1934, *Victoria Daily Colonist, Sunday Magazine.*

346 The archaeological record demonstrates that including tools, food and other items in graves of the deceased was a long-established burial practice among the Central Coast Salish.

347 Mary Rice is referring to the Nuu-chah-nulth who live on the west coast of

Vancouver Island. See Arima, 1983: 93–94, for Nuu-chah-nulth burial practices.

348 See Barnett, 1955: 216–17 for comparative ethnography.

349 Originally published April 22, 1934, *Victoria Daily Colonist, Sunday Magazine*.

350 See page 167.

351 Nanoose Bay.

352 See the account by Mary Rice page 167.

353 Originally published July 1, 1934, *Victoria Daily Colonist, Sunday Magazine*.

354 Johnny and Rosalie Seletze had only recently moved to Kwa'mutsun, having lived most of their lives at Xinupsum.

355 Xinupsum.

356 The Bevan family, which arrived in 1926 (see Turner, 1992: 8).

357 Hwunitum' named the mountain "Tzouhalem" after the famous warrior, Ts'uwxilem. The Hul'q'umi'num' name for the mountain is Shquw'utsun, out of which "Cowichan" is derived.

358 In fact she ties the genitals back between the legs to make them less visible, hence Q'ise'q, "tied genitals" (Rozen, 1985: 172).

359 Ts'e'witun, "clam shell place," "dish," "basin," about five kilometres upstream from the junction of Cowichan River Main Channel and Middle Arm (Rozen, 1985: 164–65). "Large dish" (Hukari and Peter, 1995: 105).

360 "Jaynes" Creek is an old name for Kwa'mutsun Creek. The Hul'q'umi'num' name is Hwkw'sutsum, "trout creek" (Rozen, 1985: 174; Hukari and Peter, 1995: 216).

361 Originally published September 9, 1934, *Victoria Daily Colonist, Sunday Magazine*.

362 Shts'um'inus village at Kulleet Bay.

363 "Lamalchi Bay," winter village site at the south end of Kuper Island.

364 Agnes Thorne, in her version of the story, locates three rocks: one at the Georgia Strait entrance to Active Pass, one at Ladysmith and the other at the south point of Maple Bay, "Paddy Mile Stone" (Turner, 1993:101–02; Marshall, 1999:39).

365 Originally published January, 20, 1935, *Victoria Daily Colonist, Sunday Magazine*.

366 Haweis, 1918; McKelvie, 1949: 36–39.

367 Jenness, 1934–35: 156–58; Maud, 1978: 158–60.

368 In her July 1, 1934 article with the Seletzes, Cryer refers to him as "Johnny Ts-Lai-Tser."

369 This brief account of the flood differs in some details from another longer version Dorothy Bevan recorded from Rosalie Seletze (Turner 1993: 21–27), particularly in regard to where the raft came to rest.

370 Ts'uwxilem's canoe, it is said, "had the shape of a Haida canoe" (Jenness, 1934–35: 157).

371 See Arnett, 1999: 27–28 for references to this event. Not all elders considered Ts'uwxilem to be cowed by the Hwunitum'. A 1930s W'sanec account by David Latess asserts that Ts'uwxilem "attacked the Fort at Victoria, made Sir James Douglas and all the Fort employees cringe before him, and give him powder, bullets, etc., as much as he could carry" (Jenness, 1934–35: 158).

372 S'hwlumelhtsu, "people of the lookout place." According to Hudson's Bay Company information, Tsu'uwxilem was killed some time prior to December 1849 (*Cowichan Leader*, February 25, 1932).

373 Originally published March 3, 1935, *Victoria Daily Colonist, Sunday Magazine*.

374 Cryer to Newcombe, December 7, 1932. NFP, Add. Mss. 1077, vol. 11, file 41, BCA.

375 See Marshall, 1999: 12–13 for discussion of these points.

376 See the excellent discussion in Bierwert, 1999: 113–35. In 1923, a white woman, Mollie Robinson, attended a smilhu at the same location, known to locals as the Westholme Indian Hall. In her recollection of the evening she writes, "I had my paper and pencil to take notes, but I was told NO, I could not do so, so I had to remember" (Robinson, 1978b: 324).

377 Franz Boas made the same observation in 1886. For ethnographic accounts of the smilhu, see Macfie, 1865: 432; Jenness, 1934–35; 183–99; Suttles, 1987c: 199.

378 The "Westholme Indians" would be the people of Xulel-thw (Halalt).

379 Due to increasing colonial persecution of it in the early-twentieth century, the stl'un'uq, or "potlatch," began to be incorporated into the smilhu, until the two institutions were effectively combined. Although Wayne Suttles has suggested that this integration was complete by 1920 (Suttles, 1987c: 199), Cryer's article documents a smilhu that had no "potlatch" component. Evidently, the original smilhu institution was still intact in the Chemainus Valley in 1935.

380 Tamanous, from Chinook trade jargon. Derived from the Chinook word for "guardian spirit."

381 Cryer exaggerates, reflecting western ignorance of the cultural context. Theatrical displays of "dog-eating," "corpse eating" etc. do not necessarily reflect ancient cannibalistic practices. As already noted, the "dog-eating dance" was part of a specialized performance, by specially-trained men, the primary purpose of which was to reinforce the nature of reality—in this case by visually demonstrating the depravity and destruction that can befall those who do not pursue positive, creative endeavours for the benefit of all.

382 Originally published May 12, 1935, *Victoria Daily Colonist, Sunday Magazine*.

383 Jenness, 1934–35: 16–18. Boas recorded another fragment of this story in 1886 (Boas, 2002: 136). See also White, 2006: 67–98.

384 This is an observation some elders still make today (2006). See also York, Daly and Arnett, 1993: 270, n.22.

385 Originally published October 18, 1936, *Victoria Daily Colonist, Sunday Magazine*.

386 The Shtsuw'athun today would not consider themselves to be "Cowichan," which was a general term used in the nineteenth century to refer to people on both sides of Georgia Strait.

387 "Plumper's Pass" was an earlier English name for Active Pass, between Galiano Island and Mayne Island.

388 See Appleby, 1961: 49–50, for another Snuneymuxw account of the first Shtsuw'uthun, told by Wilkes James, whose wife was from Shtsuw'uthun.

389 Originally published December 6, 1936, *Victoria Daily Colonist, Sunday Magazine*.

390 Suttles, 1987b: 201.

391 Cryer to Newcombe, October 22, 1932, NFP, Add. Mss. 1077, vol. 11, file 41, BCA.

392 Cryer to Ireland, March 27, 1967, GR 1738, Box 39, File 15, BCA. See also Duff, 1952: 123.

393 Beryl transcribed the word as "Schwy-why." For ethnographic references to swayxwi, see Jenness, 1934–35: 223; Duff, 1952: 123–26; Suttles, 1987b: 109,117; Lévi-Strauss, 1979.

394 The citation is from Boas, 1894. In early November 1933, George T. Emmons, a famous collector for the American Museum of Natural History, visited Cryer, seeking information and possible specimens of the swayxwi mask. Impressed with her knowledge, he sent her two pages of questions and "2 pages torn from a book—a report by Dr. Franz Boas 'Indian tribes of the Lower Fraser,' with a description of the Sqoa-eqoe [swayxwi]" (Cryer to Newcombe, October 22, November 11,1933 NFP, Add. Mss. 1077, vol. 11, file 41, BCA).

395 One of Jenness' informants told him that "swaiswai masks were given to the Indians by Xe.ls at Sooke, where there is one today [carved] on a rock" (Jenness, 1934–35: 223).

396 An important song, "the form of presenting the energy that goes into the healing powers of that particular work that you're doing" (Ellen White, p.c.).

397 Originally published April 4, 1937, *Victoria Daily Colonist, Sunday Magazine.*

398 Original publication date unknown, *Victoria Daily Colonist, Sunday Magazine.*

399 For comparative ethnographic accounts of Sxeeluqun, see Harris, [1901](2002: 45–51); Jenness, 1934–35: 36–37; Boas, 2002: 144–45; Hayman, 1989: 185; Maud, 1978: 142–469.

400 Ts'uween, "Mount Tuam" on Salt Spring Island.

401 Snuts'a'lo'shun, "big toe," known to English-speakers as "Patey Rock."

402 Originally published May 23, 1937, *Victoria Daily Colonist, Sunday Magazine.*

403 This myth is "The Magic Sea-Lion." See Teachings of the Elders, 1993; Suttles,1987d: 238; Wells, 1987: 169–70.

404 The Squamish people of Squamish River, Howe Sound and Burrard Inlet.

405 Siem, "my dear respected one."

406 In her rough manuscript, upon which this book is based, Cryer omitted the "Greedy Raven" story.

Bibliography

Amoss, Pamela T. *Coast Salish Spirit Dancing: The Survival of an Ancestral Religion*. Seattle: University of Washington Press, 1978.

Anketel-Jones, Rosamund. "The Donald Family: Remembrances of Old Chemainus." In *Memories of the Chemainus Valley: A History of People*, edited by Gordon Elliott, compiled by Lillian Gustafson. Chemainus: Chemainus Valley Historical Society, 1978.

Appleby, Geraldine McGeer. *Tsawwassen Legends: Collected and Printed by the Optimist, Ladner*. Ladner: Dunning Press Ltd., 1961.

Arnett, Chris. *The Terror of the Coast: Land Alienation and Colonial War on Vancouver Island and the Gulf Islands, 1849–1863*. Vancouver: Talonbooks, 1999.

Atleo, E. Richard. *Tsawalk: A Nuu-chah-nulth Worldview*. Vancouver: University of British Columbia Press, 2004.

Barman, Jean. "Taming Aboriginal Sexuality: Gender, Power, and Race in British Columbia, 1850–1900." *BC Studies* 115–116, (Fall–Winter 1997–98): 237–266.

Barnett, Homer G. *The Coast Salish of British Columbia*. University of Oregon Monographs, Studies in Anthropology, no. 4. Eugene: University of Oregon Press, 1955.

Bierwert, Crisca. *Brushed by Cedar, Living by the River: Coast Salish Figures of Power*. Tucson: University of Arizona Press, 1999.

Boas, Franz. *Indian Myths and Legends From the North Pacific Coast of America*, translated by Dietrich Bertz, edited and annotated by Randy Bouchard and Dorothy Kennedy. Vancouver: Talonbooks, 2002. Originally published as *Indianische Sagen von der Nord-Pacifischen Küste Amerikas* (Berlin: Verlag von A. Asher & Co., 1895).

British Columbia. *Papers Associated with the Indian Land Question, 1850–1875*. 1875. Reprint, Victoria: Queen's Printer, 1987.

Brown, Robert. *Robert Brown and the Vancouver Island Exploring Expedition*, edited by John Hayman. Vancouver: University of British Columbia Press, 1989.

Chemainus First Nation Elders. *Eagle Power: A Legend as told by the Chemainus First Nation Elders*. Ladysmith: Coast Peoples Press, 2000.

Chemainus Valley Historical Society. *Memories of the Chemainus Valley: A History of People*, edited by Gordon Elliott, compiled by Lillian Gustafson. Chemainus: Chemainus Valley Historical Society, 1978.

Clifford, James and George E. Marcus, ed. *Writing Culture: The Poetics and Politics of Ethnography*. Berkeley: University of California Press, 1986.

Cowichan Tribes. *Quw'utsun Hul'q'umi'num' Category Dictionary*. Duncan: Quw-utsun Syuw'eenst Lelum, 2007.

Crosby, Thomas. *Among the An-ko-me-nums or Flathead Tribes of Indians of the Pacific Coast, by Rev. Thomas Crosby, Missionary to the Indians of British Columbia*. Toronto: William Briggs, 1907.

Cryer, Beryl M. *The Flying Canoe: Legends of the Cowichans*. Victoria: J. Parker Buckle Printing, 1949.

————. "The Halhed Family." In *Memories of the Chemainus Valley: A History of People*, edited by Gordon Elliott, compiled by Lillian Gustafson. Chemainus: Chemainus Valley Historical Society, 1978.

Davies, Megan. "Services Rendered, Rearing Children for the State: Mother's Pensions in British Columbia, 1919–1931." In *Not Just Pin Money: Selected Essays on the History of Women's Work in British Columbia*, edited by Barbara K. Latham and Roberta J. Pazdro. Victoria: Camosun College, 1984.

Dixon, Ruth V. "Tragedy Swept Penelakut Spit." In *Memories of the Chemainus Valley: A History of People*, edited by Gordon Elliott, compiled by Lillian Gustafson. Chemainus: Chemainus Valley Historical Society, 1978.

Duff, Wilson. *The Upper Stalo Indians of the Fraser Valley, British Columbia*. Anthropology in British Columbia Memoir, 1. Victoria: Provincial Museum of British Columbia, 1952.

————. "The Fort Victoria Treaties." *BC Studies* 3 (Fall 1969).

Galois, Robert. *Kwakwak'wakw Settlements, 1775–1920: A Geographical Analysis and Gazetteer*. Vancouver: University of British Columbia Press, 1994.

Ginn, Audrey. "The Mission at Kuper Island." In *Memories of the Chemainus Valley: A History of People*, edited by Gordon Elliott, compiled by Lillian Gustafson. Chemainus: Chemainus Valley Historical Society, 1978.

Harris, Douglas C. *Fish, Law, and Colonialism: The Legal Capture of Salmon in British Columbia*. Toronto: University of Toronto Press, 2001.

Harris, Martha Douglas. *History and Folklore of the Cowichan Indians*. 1901. Edited by Paul Lindholt. Reprint, Spokane: Marquette Books, 2004.

Haweis, Lionel. *Tsoqalem, A Weird Indian Tale of the Cowichan Monster, a ballad*. Vancouver: Citizen Printing & Publishing Co., 1918.

Hill, Beth, and Ray Hill. *Indian Petroglyphs of the Pacific Northwest*. Vancouver: Hancock House Publishers, 1989.

Hill-Tout, Charles. *The Salish People*, vol. 4: *The Sechelt and the South-Eastern Tribes of Vancouver Island*, edited by Ralph Maud. Vancouver: Talonbooks, 1978.

Hukari, Thomas, and Ruby Peter. *The Cowichan Dictionary of the Hul'qumi'num Dialect of the Coast Salish People*. Duncan: Cowichan Tribes, 1995.

Jenness, Diamond. "Coast Salish Mythology." Ladysmith, Hul'qumi'num Treaty Group. Copy.

————. *The Faith of a Coast Salish Indian*. Anthropology in British Columbia Memoir, 3. Victoria: Provincial Museum of British Columbia, 1955.

Jilek, Wolfgang G. *Indian Healing: Shamanic Ceremonialism in the Pacific Northwest Today*. Surrey: Hancock House Publishers, 1982.

Joanitus, Aldona. *From the Land of the Totem Poles: The Northwest Coast Indian Art Collection at the Museum of Natural History*. New York: Museum of Natural History, 1988.

Johnson, E. Pauline. *Legends of Vancouver*. Toronto: McClelland and Stewart, 1961.

Kew, J.E., and Della Kew. "People Need Friends, It Makes Their Minds Strong." In *The World is as Sharp as a Knife: An Anthology in Honour of Wilson Duff*, edited by Donald Abbott. Victoria: British Columbia Provincial Museum, 1981.

Knight, Rolf. *Indians at Work: An Informal History of Native Indian Labour in British Columbia, 1858–1930*. Vancouver: New Star Books, 1996.

Lane, Barbara. "The Cowichan Knitting Industry." *Anthropology in British Columbia* 2: 14–27.

Lerman, Norman. *Legends of the River People*, edited by Betty Keller. Vancouver: November House, 1976.

Lévi-Strauss, Claude. *The Way of the Masks*, translated by Sylvia Modelski. Seattle: University of Washington Press, 1982. Originally published as *La Voie des Masques* (Geneva: A. Skira, 1975).

Littlefield, Loraine. "Beryl Cryer." Paper presented at the American Historical Association Conference, August 17, 2001.

————. "Beryl Cryer and the Stories She Collected." *Shale: Journal of the Gabriola Historical and Museum Society* 6: 9–16.

Macfie, Matthew. *Vancouver Island and British Columbia: Their History, Resources and Prospects*. London: Longman, Green, Longman, Roberts, & Green, 1865.

Manuel, George, and Michael Posluns. *The Fourth World: an Indian Reality*. Don Mills: Collier Macmillan Canada, Ltd, 1974.

Maranda, Lynn. *Coast Salish Gambling Games*. National Museum of Man Mercury Series: Ethnology Service Paper 93. Ottawa: National Museums of Canada, 1984.

Marcus, George E., and Michael M.J. Fischer. *Anthropology as Cultural Critique: an Experimental Movement in the Human Sciences*. Chicago: University of Chicago Press, 1986.

Marshall, Daniel P. *Those Who Fell From The Sky: a History of the Cowichan Peoples*. Duncan: Cowichan Tribes, 1999.

Matson, R.G. "The Old Cordilleran Component at the Glenrose Cannery Site." In *Early Human Occupation in British Columbia*, edited by Roy L. Carlson and Luke Dalla Bona. Vancouver: University of British Columbia Press, 1996.

Matthews, Major J.S. *Conversations with Khahtsalano, 1932–1954*. Vancouver: City of Vancouver Archives, 1955.

McKelvie, B.A. "Finlayson's Strategy." In *Tales of Conflict*, 36–39. Vancouver: *Vancouver Daily Province*, 1949.

Mitchell, Donald. "Archaeology of the Gulf of Georgia, A Natural Region and Its Cultural Types." *Syesis*, vol.4, Supplement 1. Victoria: British Columbia Provincial Museum, 1971.

Mitchell, Majorie, and Anna Franklin. "When You Don't Know the Language, Listen to the Silence: A Historical Overview of Native Indian Women in BC." In *Not Just Pin Money: Selected Essays on the History of Women's Work in British Columbia*, edited by Barbara K. Latham and Roberta J. Pazdro. Victoria: Camosun College, 1984.

Mutter, Joy. "The Roberts Family: Lamalchi Bay, Kuper Island." In *Memories of the Chemainus Valley: A History of People*, edited by Gordon Elliott, compiled by Lillian Gustafson. Chemainus: Chemainus Valley Historical Society, 1978.

Olsen, W.H. *Water Over the Wheel*. Chemainus: Chemainus Valley Historical Society, 1963.

Pratt, Mary Louise. "Fieldwork in Common Places." In *Writing Culture: The Poetics and Politics of Ethnography*, edited by James Clifford and George E. Marcus. Berkeley: University of California Press, 1986.

Robinson, Harry, and Wendy Wickwire. *Living by Stories: A Journey of Landscape and Memory*. Vancouver: Talonbooks, 2005.

Robinson, Mollie. "Indian Dances." In *Memories of the Chemainus Valley: A History of People*, edited by Gordon Elliott, compiled by Lillian Gustafson. Chemainus: Chemainus Valley Historical Society, 1978.

———. [Newspaper Article]. In *Memories of the Chemainus Valley: A History of People*, edited by Gordon Elliott, compiled by Lillian Gustafson. Chemainus: Chemainus Valley Historical Society, 1978.

Rozen, David L. "Place-names of the Island Halkomelem." Master's thesis, University of British Columbia, 1985.

Smith, Linda Tuhiwai. *Decolonizing Methodologies: Research and Indigenous Peoples*. Dunedin: University of Otago Press, 1989.

Steward, Elizabeth. *Galiano Houses and People Looking Back to 1930*. Galiano Island: Elizabeth Steward, 1994.

Strong-Boag, Veronica, and Carole Gerson. *Paddling Her Own Canoe: The Times and Texts of E. Pauline Johnson*. Toronto: University of Toronto Press, 2000.

Suttles, Wayne. "Private Knowledge, Morality, and Social Classes among the Coast Salish." In *Coast Salish Essays*. Vancouver: Talonbooks, 1987.

———. "Productivity and its Constraints—A Coast Salish Case." In *Coast Salish Essays*. Vancouver: Talonbooks, 1987.

———. "Spirit Dancing and the Persistence of Native Culture among the Coast Salish." In *Coast Salish Essays*. Vancouver: Talonbooks, 1987.

———. "Notes on Coast Salish Sea-Mammal Hunting." In *Coast Salish Essays*. Vancouver: Talonbooks, 1987.

————. "Central Coast Salish." In *Northwest Coast*, vol. 7, *Handbook of North American Indians*, edited by Wayne Suttles and William Sturtevant. Washington: Smithsonian Institution, 1990.

Suttles, Wayne, and Aldona Jonaitus. "History of Research in Ethnology." In *Northwest Coast*, vol. 7, *Handbook of North American Indians*, edited by Wayne Suttles and William Sturtevant. Washington: Smithsonian Institution, 1990.

The Teachings of the Elders. Stories 1–6, Ladysmith: Chemainus Tribal Council, 1993.

Tennant, Paul. *Aboriginal Peoples and Politics: The Indian Land Question in British Columbia, 1849–1989*. Vancouver: University of British Columbia Press, 1990.

Thom, Brian. "Senses of Place and Contemporary Coast Salish Land Claims." In *Recherches amérindiennes au Quebec* 34 (3): 59–74.

Tippett, Maria. *Emily Carr: A Biography*. Toronto: Oxford University Press, 1979.

Turner, Dolby Bevan. *When the Rains Came: And Other Legends of the Salish People*. Victoria: Orca Book Publishers, 1992.

Turner, Nancy. *Plants in British Columbia Indian Technology*. Handbook (British Columbia Provincial Museum), no. 38. Victoria: British Columbia Provincial Museum, 1980.

————. *Food Plants of British Columbia Indians. Part 1: Coastal Peoples*. Handbook (British Columbia Provincial Museum), no. 34. Victoria: British Columbia Provincial Museum, 1975.

Tyler, Stephen. "Post-Modern Ethnography: From Document of the Occult to Occult Document." In *Writing Culture: The Poetics and Politics of Ethnography*, edited by James Clifford and George E. Marcus. Berkeley: University of California Press, 1986.

Walbran, John T. *British Columbia Coast Names: 1592–1906*. Ottawa: Government Printing Bureau, 1909.

Walters, Margaret. *Early Days Among the Gulf Islands of British Columbia*. Victoria: Hebden Printing Co. Ltd., 1945.

Ward, W. Peter. "Class and Race in the Social Structure of British Columbia." In *British Columbia: Historical Readings*, edited by W. Peter Ward and Robert A. J. McDonald. Vancouver: Douglas & McIntyre, 1981.

Wells, Oliver. *The Chilliwacks and their Neighbors*, edited by Ralph Maud, Brent Galloway, and Marie Weeden. Vancouver: Talonbooks, 1987.

White, Ellen. *Kwulasulwut: Stories from the Coast Salish*. Nanaimo: Theytus Books, 1981.

————. *Kwulasulwut II: Salish Creation Stories*. Nanaimo: Theytus Books, 1994.

————. *Legends and Teachings of Xeel's, the Creator*. Vancouver: Pacific Educational Press, 2006.

York, Annie, Richard Daly, and Chris Arnett. *They Write Their Dreams on the Rock Forever: Rock Writings in the Stein River Valley of British Columbia*. Vancouver: Talonbooks, 1993.